SUSAN GLASPELL

Susan Glaspell

A CRITICAL BIOGRAPHY

Barbara Ozieblo

THE UNIVERSITY OF NORTH CAROLINA PRESS

CHAPEL HILL AND LONDON

Manufactured in the United States of America

Designed by April Leidig-Higgins

Set in Monotype Garamond by Keystone Typesetting, Inc.

The paper in this book meets the guidelines for
permanence and durability of the Committee on Production
Guidelines for Book Longevity of the Council
on Library Resources.

Library of Congress Cataloging-in-Publication Data

Ozieblo Rajkowska, Bárbara.

Susan Glaspell: a critical biography | Barbara Ozieblo.

p. cm. Includes bibliographical references and index.

ISBN 0-8078-2560-3 (alk. paper)

ISBN 0-8078-4868-9 (pbk.: alk. paper)

1. Glaspell, Susan, 1876–1948. 2. Authors, American—
20th century—Biography. 3. Feminists—United States—
Biography. 4. Social problems in literature. 5. Feminism
in literature. I. Title.

PS3513.L35 Z78 2000   813'.52—dc21 [B] 00-021108

04 03 02 01 00   5 4 3 2 1

Frontispiece: Susan Glaspell, portrait by William
L'Engle. Glaspell provided a photograph of this portrait for the "Heterodoxy to Marie" album in 1920,
signing it: "I am Susan Glaspell. I am from the painting by William L'Engle—a friend. That is why I look
so nice and refined. I didn't know, when being
painted, that I was going into Marie Howe's album.
Otherwise I am sure I would have looked happier—
she is a woman in whose album I like to be. Greet-
ings!" (Courtesy of the Schlesinger Library, Radcliffe
College, and Daniel L'Engle Davis)

A list of permissions follows the index.

For Renia and Rob

Contents

Illustrations

Acknowledgments

I am very grateful to the many institutions that provided me with the funds and time to work on this book. My research trips to the United States were sponsored by various travel grants from the University of Málaga, the Junta de Andalucía, and the Comisión Conjunto Hispano-Norteamericano. The Spanish Ministry of Education awarded me a Visiting Professorship at the University of Sheffield, which allowed me to take off a year of teaching, work in various British libraries, and visit the United States to continue research. A Visiting Fellowship from the Beinecke Rare Book and Manuscript Library at Yale University gave me the opportunity to examine the library's Susan Glaspell holdings and other related materials, and a travel award from the Author's Foundation of the British Society of Authors helped me finance a research trip to Davenport, Iowa, and the National Archives in Washington, D.C. The United States Information Agency International Visitors Program made it possible for me to meet Robert Károly Sarlós, author of *Jig Cook and the Provincetown Players*, then at the University of California at Davis.

My research took me to many libraries, and both the personal contact and the lengthy correspondence with librarians were always a pleasure. I am particularly grateful to the late Lola Szladits, curator of the Berg Collection of English and American Literature at New York Public Library at the time when I was rummaging through the Susan Glaspell Papers there; other librarians at the collection generously gave me their time and experience, especially Brian McInerney, Patrick Lawlor, and, more recently, Philip Milito. Patricia Willis, curator of American manuscripts at the Beinecke Rare Book and Manuscript Library, deserves special thanks for her patience and support, as do all of the Beinecke staff, particularly Maureen D. Heher. I also wish to thank Donald Gallup for his many useful hints and Ralph W. Franklin, director of the library.

Elizabeth Falsey of the Houghton Library, Harvard University, disinterestedly proffered help and advice on more than one occasion.

I wish to thank other librarians whose help was invaluable in gathering material: K. Haybron Adams, Harold B. Lee Library, Brigham Young University; Julia Bigham, Theatre Museum, London; Raymond Boryczka, Walter P. Reuther Library, Wayne State University; Kathryn L. Bream, University of Michigan Library; M. N. Brown, Brown University Library; Sylvia J. Bugbee and Connell B. Gallagher, University of Vermont Library; Emily Clark, Chicago Historical Society; Philip N. Cronenwett, Dartmouth College Library; Gene DeGruson, Leonard H. Axe Library, Pittsburg State University; Vicki Denby, Houghton Library, Harvard University; Donald Fowle and Jeremy Megraw, Billy Rose Theatre Collection, New York Public Library for the Performing Arts; Marie-Heléne Gold, Schlesinger Library, Radcliffe College; Andrew S. Hannah, University of Chicago; Diane Haskell, Cynthia Wall, Richard L. Popp, and Robert W. Karrow, Newberry Library, Chicago; Cathy Henderson, Harry Ransom Humanities Research Center, University of Texas at Austin; Mary R. Herr, Davenport Public Library, Davenport, Iowa; Rosemary L. Hogg and Barbara Haase, Fenwick Library, and Sara Nell Davis and Lorraine Brown, Institute of the Federal Theatre Project, George Mason University; Carol Hunt, Putnam Museum, Davenport, Iowa; Gregory A. Johnson, Alderman Library, University of Virginia; Mary Kent, Connecticut College Library; John Lancaster, Amherst College Library; Karen J. Laughlin, State Historical Society of Iowa; Elizabeth K. Lockwood, Kenneth Heger, Don Jackanicz, and James Rush, National Archives; Karen McAdams, Stanford University Library; Robert A. McCown and Mark Strumme, Special Collections and Manuscripts Library, University of Iowa; Nancy S. Mackechnie, Vassar College Library; Kathryn Mets, Theater Collection, Museum of the City of New York; Timothy D. Murray, University of Delaware Library; N. Frederick Nash, University of Illinois at Urbana Library; Joyce Onnen and Robert C. Scheetz, Cowles Library, Drake University; Richard Palumbo, Wagner College Library; Michael Peters, University of Chicago Alumni Association; John Skarstad, University Library, University of California at Davis; Saundra Taylor, Lilly Library, Indiana University; Geoffrey Wexler, University of California at San Diego Library; Thomas M. Whitehead, Temple University Library; and Georgianna Ziegler, Van Pelt Library, University of Pennsylvania.

Among others who have offered guidance, advice, and material,

C. W. E. Bigsby, Arnold Goldman, Elizabeth Loizeaux, Marcia Noe, and Robert Károly Sarlós were particularly helpful. I also thank Rachel White at Town Hall in Provincetown, Jackie Freitas of *Provincetown Magazine*, and Livia Gollancz of Victor Gollancz Ltd., who generously gave me access to the Gollancz Archives.

Sirius and Valentina Cook patiently allowed me to interview them, as did Reggie Cabral, Miriam Hapgood DeWitt, Leona Egan, Livia Gollancz, Ana Matson Hamburger, Francelina White Hubbard, Madeleine L'Engle, Charles A. Mayo, Joel O'Brien, Eva Sikelianós, William Tager, Fanis Tchakalós, George Tchakalós, and Marguerite L. Young.

The lengthy letters of Joanne Bentley, Beatrice Hapgood Faust, Luke Faust, Dee Garrison, Betty K. Gorshe, William Hannan, Carl Harms, Kay Ewing Hocking, Scott Koeneman of the *Des Moines Register*, Thomas McDermott, Norm Ross, and Arnold Sundgaard in response to my queries on matters related to Susan Glaspell were immensely helpful.

Among the many people who provided support and encouragement along the way, I would like to thank, in first place, J. C. R. Haffenden. María Angeles Conejo, Marion Edwards, Judith Long, María Teresa López, Townsend Ludington, Juan Antonio Perles, Victoria Rosado, Lidia Taillefer, and Philip Terrie all, in one way or another, helped me see this project through to the end. To all, I am very grateful. I also wish to thank Paula Wald at the University of North Carolina Press for her rigorous and perceptive editing. I dedicate this book to my children, Renia and Rob, and thank them for their patience and interest.

SUSAN GLASPELL

Claire: Only with life that waits have I kept faith.

(with effort raising her eyes to the man)

And only you have ever threatened me.

—Susan Glaspell, *The Verge*, act 3

Introduction

For over ten years, Susan Glaspell (1876–1948) has accompanied me through most of my waking hours; I have read her plays, novels, and letters again and again, trying to understand why the rebel in her chose so often to acquiesce to convention. Sigmund Freud—whose theories of the unconscious supplied Glaspell with the topic of her first play—unguardedly affirmed in his brief biography of Leonardo da Vinci that "biographers are fixated on their heroes in a quite special way."[1] I admit that I have been fixated, but I hope I have successfully avoided the trap that Harold Nicholson, Leon Edel, and André Maurois, among other great biographers, have warned against by refusing to write a thinly disguised autobiography. But I have not shied away from cultivating what Kathleen Barry, biographer of Susan B. Anthony, has termed a "dialectical relationship," whereby a dialogical interaction is established between the subject and her biographer; in this way, I have been able to acknowledge Glaspell's voice without losing my own, while avoiding "the objectification of the other."[2]

The history of American drama has tended to relegate Susan Glaspell, when it has deigned to acknowledge her at all, to the status of wife of George Cram Cook, founder of the Provincetown Players, the amateur theatrical group that discovered Eugene O'Neill. Only recently have academics and theater lovers begun to recognize her name and anthologies found space for her play *Trifles* (later rewritten as the short story "A Jury of Her Peers"). But Glaspell is the author of more than one play: she wrote five short plays and five full-length dramas and cowrote two short plays with her husband and one full-length piece with her lover, Norman Matson. By the time she married Cook in 1913, she was an acclaimed short story writer and had published two novels. After Cook's death in 1924, she turned back to the novel, vying, on different occasions, with

Richard Wright, Sinclair Lewis, John Steinbeck, and Ernest Hemingway for the top position on the best-seller list. She was awarded the Pulitzer Prize for her play *Alison's House* in 1931.

But Glaspell's roster of achievements does not end there. As I have tried to show in this book and in the introduction to the 1994 collection of Provincetown plays I edited, Glaspell's part in the success of the Provincetown Players should not be seen as limited to her wifely duties. The Players could always rely on her for a new play when they needed one; in fact, as she was leaving for Greece in 1922, she handed over *Chains of Dew*, a play she had written with an eye on Broadway that was not wholly suitable for the little theater on Macdougal Street. Her play *Trifles* was the Players' first success, although it was never performed in their New York theater. Staged on the Provincetown Wharf in the summer of 1916, it was bought out by the Washington Square Players, who then claimed the honor of introducing Glaspell to New York theatergoers. Although theatrical history has rightly credited the Provincetown Players with the discovery of Eugene O'Neill, it has preferred to gloss over Glaspell's vital intervention: it was she who convinced the Players— after O'Neill had already succeeded in antagonizing them—to give him another chance and sit through a reading of *Bound East for Cardiff*. Once she had maneuvered him into her magic circle of amateur thespians, she continued to support and encourage him, as she did other young writers whom she took under her wing.

Susan Glaspell was largely responsible for introducing the American theater to British audiences: *The Verge* was performed by Edith Craig's Pioneer Players at the Regent Theatre, starring Sybil Thorndike as Claire. It had received mixed reviews in New York, but the British critic James Agate placed it on a par with Henrik Ibsen's *The Master Builder*, recognizing, moreover, that "the American writer made her case more difficult by applying it to the whole human race, whereas the Norwegian confined it to the individual."[3] Glaspell's other plays were staged by prestigious avant-garde institutions such as the Cambridge Festival Theatre, the Liverpool Repertory Company, and the Gate Theatre. Ellis Roberts of the *Guardian* declared Glaspell "the greatest playwright we have had writing in English since Mr. Shaw began," and *Time and Tide* compared her role in the development of the American theater to that of Lady Isabella Augusta Gregory's in the Irish theater.[4]

On her return from Greece after Cook's death, Glaspell hoped to continue working for the Provincetown Players to keep alive the memory of her husband. She found, however, that Cook was a genius and a saint only in her eyes and that her part in the launching of the Players and O'Neill's career had been quietly suppressed. But not everyone had forgotten her, and in the late 1930s, the Federal Theatre laid claim to Glaspell's enthusiasm and vision, placing her in charge of the Midwest Play Bureau.

But in spite of living an extraordinary life for a woman of her time and her undoubted triumphs and popularity as a playwright and novelist, Glaspell constantly ceded center stage to the men she loved, making it extremely difficult to reconstruct either her life or her personality. Joining the ranks of many famous writers, Glaspell destroyed her personal letters; her extant diaries, held by the Berg Collection of English and American Literature at the New York Public Library, are mostly empty, a few pages half-filled with cryptic sentences to remind her of ideas for plays or stories. The biographer must rely on the traces of her life that she could not destroy, such as her plays and novels, and the letters and autobiographies of friends, in which she is but a minor character in the drama of their lives. And then there is Glaspell's *The Road to the Temple*, the biography she wrote of her husband, in which she transformed herself into his handmaiden, erasing herself altogether.

But a biographer's task, as Virginia Woolf insisted, is precisely to capture the personality of her subject; Susan Glaspell existed and, post-modernisms notwithstanding, she had an identity and played a part in the development of the American theater. So, taking Woolf's lessons to heart, I struggled never to lose sight of the integrity of facts and to manipulate them only "in order that the light of personality shine through" as I worked to weld what Woolf audaciously considered the "granite-like solidity" of facts to the "rainbow-like intangibility" of personality.[5]

Some of the facts of Susan Glaspell's life are documented in various sources, and *The Road to the Temple* does not belie them. Eventually, though, the plodding detective work of gathering facts had to give way to the impossible, quite devilish task of interpretation. With no help from Glaspell, except the elusive dialogue that I have done my best to establish between us, I approached the more intimate aspects of her life, the personality that Leon Edel enjoins the biographer to penetrate.[6] I scoured "the evidence in the reverse of the tapestry" and concluded that the key characters in the drama of her life included a possessive mother who soothed her own frustrated ambitions with her daughter's triumphs, an ineffectual though deeply loving father, an exalted husband ever intent on transforming the world, and a callous lover who abandoned her. In different ways, these people leavened her ambition to transcend the patriarchal limitations imposed on women. Inspired by Friedrich Nietzsche's Zarathustra, Glaspell inched toward perfection, always aware of and frequently questioning the pain involved in "overcoming man."[7]

"The Rules of the Institution" (1914), a story Glaspell wrote after she defied society by taking Cook from his second wife, examines the dilemma any sensitive, intelligent, middle-class woman of the period confronted when she left insouciant girlhood behind. She could slip into the place society had prepared for her and acquiesce to tea parties, charity work, and marriage, or if she had tremendous willpower and drive, she could create a life of her own. Glaspell shows just how difficult it was for women to rebel: "One settled down into the feeling that one couldn't do any differently and wrested a certain mournful satisfaction from the sadness of surrender."[8] The protagonist of "The Rules of the Institution," a college graduate, slowly sinks into the apathy of small-town life, thus creating a prototype for Sinclair Lewis's *Main Street*; when she does rebel, it is the society matrons who protest most vociferously. The patriarchal coat of mail imprisoning women is so subtly riveted that they no longer know they are trapped, and moreover, with blind complacency, they consider it their duty to ensure that the fine links enmesh their daughters as tightly, and as quickly, as possible.

All of her life, Glaspell struggled against this self-perpetuating order "that held life in chains"; her sensitive nature opened her to an acute awareness that the links were often forged with "affection and obligation," but, urged on by a tenacious optimism, she never stopped grappling with them.[9] Her fiction is full of young women who inflict sorrow on those who love them in order to grasp what they understand as the fullness of life. In "The Rules of the Institution," the goal is unspecified; in other works, it is education, experience, or professional success, but frequently the Glaspellian woman, still not quite free of patriarchy's dictates, sacrifices the peace of mind of others—and her own self—to an illusory love.

Glaspell's friend Lawrence Langner (who had refused to cast Cook in the first Washington Square Players production and thus spurred him to found the rival Provincetown Players) captured the effects of her internal struggle to reconcile duty and the need for self-fulfillment in *The Magic Curtain*, his autobiography. Describing the Greenwich Village and Provincetown bohemians of 1915, he wrote: "Then there was Susan Glaspell, a delicate woman with sad eyes and a sweet smile who seemed as fragile as old lace, until you talked with her and glimpsed the steel lining beneath the tender surface."[10] The dichotomy of duty and desire, Victorian submission and modern self-assertion, molded Glaspell's features as much as her person and characterized her writing, lending it the ambivalence Langner detected that can prove both unsatisfactory and disconcerting for today's readers. Like so many professional women, particularly those brought up in strict religious families toward the end of the nineteenth century, Glaspell attempted to combine a career with filial duty and love for a man. Unfortunately, the men she chose were not as talented as she was, but her maternal, self-sacrificing instincts, sharpened by her Victorian upbringing, drove her to raise their accomplishments above her own.

Although Glaspell insisted that her life and achievements were uninteresting compared with those of her husband, I have taken the liberty of representing her as the primary and sustaining member of their partnership. Our ongoing dialogue led me to exchanges that heightened my understanding of her position, and so I present the reader with my version of one of the "six or seven thousand selves"—posited by Virginia Woolf in every human being—awaiting us in Susan Glaspell.[11]

CHAPTER ONE

The Duties of a Daughter

A portrait of Susan Glaspell painted by William L'Engle captures her
determination, but by depicting her looking down, not meeting the observer's gaze, the artist represented the deference that was impressed on
her as she was growing up in a highly religious impoverished family in a
midwestern town where the literary success to which she aspired belonged to the social elite.[1] Her great-grandfather had arrived in Davenport, Iowa, with the Christian Church, but earlier forebears were of more
illustrious lineage. In fact, Provincetown, as Glaspell would later be delighted to discover, played a prominent part in the lives of her most
notable ancestors; both John Carver and William Bradford, the first two
governors of Plymouth Colony, figured indirectly—as grandfathers of
spouses—in her father's family tree. They took their first steps in the
New World on the sands at the tip of Cape Cod, a mile or so from the site
of the clapboard cottage that would become Glaspell's home in 1914.
The "lusty young man" in Bradford's *Of Plymouth Plantation* who was
thrown into the sea during a storm "but . . . caught hold of the topsail
halyards which hung overboard . . . and his life [was] saved" also married
into Glaspell's family.[2] Others were not quite so distinguished: Glaspell's
great-grandfather, Rufus Ricker (born in 1791), traced his ancestry to
Maturin Ricker, whose brother had arrived in America as an indentured
servant in 1670 and sent for Maturin after paying off his debt.[3] They
all inherited the pioneering spirit of adventure that Susan Glaspell displayed: a certainty that perfection, a veritable Garden of Eden, was attainable. Rufus Ricker moved his family westward a number of times,
until in the 1830s, he settled in Davenport, Iowa, where he was judge of
the Probate Court and then clerk of the Circuit Court.

Davenport was built on the site of Oshkosh, a Native American village on the banks of the Mississippi River, opposite Rock Island. The Removal Act of 1830 allowed the government to forcibly eject Native American tribes from their lands—in many cases, lands to which they had been compelled to move by earlier white settlers busily mastering the West and the North. Chief Black Hawk (who would figure in Glaspell's play *Inheritors*) led the displaced Sauks and Foxes in their avenging attack on white settlements. The uprising was quelled by a drunken state militia, and trans-Mississippi lands, previously ceded to the Native Americans, were now "bought" from them at nine cents an acre. The Sauks and Foxes were expelled to territory even farther west, and their village of Oshkosh was claimed as the site of a new white town.[4] But not all settlers resorted to violence upon seeing a Native American. Glaspell, brought up on family stories of pioneer days, reenacted one such episode in *Inheritors* (1921). Grandmother Morton, alone on the homestead, refuses to be cowed by the presence of a Native American: "One time I saw an Indian watching me from a bush. Right out there. I was never afraid of Indians when you could see the whole of 'em—but when you could see nothin' but their bright eyes—movin' through leaves—I declare they made me nervous. After he'd been there an hour I couldn't seem to put my mind on my work. So I thought, Red or White, a man's a man—I'll take him some cookies. . . . Those leaves had eyes next day. But he brought me a fish to trade. He was a nice boy."[5]

In May 1836, Major Gordon surveyed the area, and in one day—sustained by firewater—he platted the town of Davenport with geometric precision, managing, in spite of the quirky meandering of the Mississippi at the site, to form the neat gridiron of blocks that settlers traditionally imposed on their towns.[6] A log house at the corner of Front and Ripley Streets held the first store and post office, and the tavern keeper, blacksmith, shoemaker, doctor, and lawyer, Ebenezer Cook, set up shop nearby. The store prospered, and its owner, Mr. Eldridge, soon built a brick house on the northeast corner of Third and Main Streets, where, in 1839, the First Christian Church of Davenport was organized.

The Christian Church, also known as the Disciples of Christ, was made up of dissatisfied Methodists, Baptists, and Presbyterians who had seceded from their original churches in 1793. It flourished in Tennessee, Kentucky, and Ohio. In their zeal to evangelize, church members moved farther and farther west, professing a firm conviction in individual—and congregational—independence and an equally firm dislike of the rigidity of Calvinism. In accordance with the plan of the New Testament Church, the recently formed Davenport congregation held elections, and James Glaspell was chosen as an elder.[7]

James Glaspell came from Covington, Kentucky, to Davenport in 1838; recognition of his evangelistic spirit preceded him, but he was drawn as much by the fact that other members of his denomination had settled there as by the lure of the new frontier. At forty-nine, with eight children—and three dowries to furnish—he needed much land. One hundred and twenty acres on the gentle slopes to the west of the burgeoning town appeared promising, and as soon as school was out in the old town of Covington—for he was also a teacher—James bundled his family into a covered wagon and brought them over the plains of Illinois and across the Mississippi. He came with his mother Susan, his wife Jane, and their eight children: Silas, Enos, Isaac, James, Barton, Elizabeth, Ruth, and Mary.

Schooling on the frontier had to bend to the more vital concerns of making a living, and children attended only after their farm chores were done. This accommodating schedule permitted James to "conduct in his Davenport home one of the early village schools" and thus continue the work that gave him the most satisfaction.[8] During the long winter evenings, he compiled "The Glaspell Speller," which became one of the first school texts used in Scott County. The Glaspell family, large and active, did not limit itself to church, school, and farm: Isaac, the practical one, persuaded his father to open a store in town to market their farm produce. They set up a frame building on the north side of Second Street, and in 1840, Isaac established himself as a merchant; he would later bequeath a prosperous business to his son James Milton, who introduced watermelons to Davenport.

The idealist in James Glaspell came to the fore in his eldest son. Silas, Susan Glaspell's grandfather, was "an esteemed townsman," an "honorable, upright man in his dealings with his fellow men, and one of the most devoted men in the world to his home and family."[9] Twenty-three when he arrived in Davenport, Silas had converted to the Christian Church in Kentucky and was tormented by a great desire to understand God. He lacked the business sense that made Isaac successful in the outside world. Never content simply to let things be, he devoted his passionate energy to experimenting on the plants and trees that provided his livelihood. He was the first to cultivate strawberries in Davenport, and according to his obituary, "he delighted to experiment in the improvement of fruits and made successful experiments which were quite profitable as well as pleasing."[10] However, the harsh extremes of climate ruined many of his delicious pears and peaches, and Silas was forced to admit that "grapes, berries, cherries, and other small fruits and apples" were most likely to prosper.[11] His costly experiments ate away at his land; he had inherited forty acres of the homestead farm after his father's death in 1847, but he would bequeath to his sons only the old farmhouse surrounded by an orchard and vineyard.

Susan Glaspell commemorated her grandfather's experimental, inquiring spirit in her writing, particularly in two plays, *Inheritors* and *The Verge* (1921). In both cases, the search for knowledge and power over nature leads to madness. Although Silas Glaspell's obituary does not indicate that he suffered from mental illness, it reports that he had endured bad health for a number of years and that "this last nervous attack" had proved too much even for his stubborn spirit.[12] He may well have entertained his five-year-old granddaughter with stories of his experiments and with fantasies of men fertilizing plants to make them grow according to their will, and these childhood memories would later surface in her plays.

Silas married Susan Ricker—who with her parents, Rufus and Lidia, had come to Davenport in 1836—and with his own hands, he built a new family home on his father's farm. Of five children, only two boys survived, Charles and Elmer. Charles moved to Trenton, Missouri, and worked as a conductor on the Chicago, Rock Island, and Pacific Railroad, but Elmer stayed in Davenport. He married Alice S. Keating, who had come to the Midwest in girlhood from Dublin, Ireland. A few letters written in a small, neat hand to Elmer before their marriage hint at a very proper churchgoing young lady, and his replies betray a youth in whom sincere devotion and thirst for knowledge did not quite quench a gamesome spirit. On one occasion, some incident that had led to gossip must have made Alice think it best to absent herself from Davenport; her mother wrote: "I think you are wise not to have Elmer go meet you, all things considered, it would not be best. Don't give Ellen any room to talk. . . . I know she hates him."[13]

Davenport was a small community in which church activities dominated the lives of most residents, and busybodies found much bounty in the affairs of others. But Elmer and Alice paid no heed to the chinwaggers; Elmer's idealism—even though he was but the son of an impoverished farmer—convinced the Irish romantic in Alice that he was the man for her, and they were married in the Christian Church where his grandfather had served as the first elder. They settled at 502 Cedar Street in a house on land that had previously belonged to the Glaspells in the shadow of Silas's remaining twenty-six acres of orchards and the old farmhouse on Telegraph Street.

This was no longer a desirable part of town since the new railroad had split Davenport in the 1850s, creating a fork that enclosed the Glaspell lands and attracted the most recent, poorer German immigrants, but it was all that Elmer could offer his bride. Alice bore three children to term: Charles Raymond in 1875, Susan Keating on 1 July 1876, and Frank on 16 January 1878.[14] The city directory of 1876 identifies Elmer Glaspell as a farmer, but the needs of a growing family must have forced him to try his hand at more lucrative employment, for later directories list him as "teamster," "contractor," "hay dealer," "hay buyer," and, in 1910, "capitalist and sewer contractor." Most nineteenth-century towns left waste disposal and sewage "to the mercy of God" with, predictably, no discernible response, but by 1880, Davenport had developed plans for a comprehensive sewage system.[15] However, it was not until the early years of the twentieth century that the city administration invested tax dollars in ridding the streets of open surface gutters and porous cesspools, thus providing Elmer with work.[16] Susan Glaspell's description of a family's descent into poverty and a father's idealistic business ventures in her novel *Fugitive's Return* (1929) may well have been inspired by memories of Elmer attempting to make ends meet: " 'Too bad we didn't hold on to more [of the land],' her mother would be saying, and Father would turn to figuring in his little book, trying to decide just how low a bid he could make on that street work and get enough to pay for himself and his horses."[17]

The year 1881 was difficult for the Glaspells. Maria, Elmer's cousin, wrote to her Aunt Susan in January: "I am sorry Elmer's family have so much trouble. O that they may cast their care on Jesus!"[18] Elmer was trying to support his family as a teamster, and apparently the first flush of romantic love had faded, for by October 1882, Alice was in Grinnell with relatives; Susie and Frank were with her, and Ray, the eldest, remained with his father in Davenport. A contrite vein underscores the formality of Elmer's appeal in a letter to his wife: he promises that whenever she is ready to return, "everybody will welcome you back joyfully" and "we will try and make it as pleasant for each other as possible."[19] We can only surmise the reason for Alice's temporary absence from her husband's home. Had she found fulfilling her motherly and wifely duties too burdensome? Perhaps a miscarriage—not unusual in those times, and three children was a small brood in the Midwest in the 1880s—had tipped the balance. Elmer's letter does not reveal what was troubling the couple, but it does give a glimpse of him as a father: "I tried to get Ray to sing me a song but the rascal would not do it—I suppose Susie will sing one for Papa when she comes home." His daughter had a good voice and may even have dreamed of pursuing a singing career; among her later Davenport conquests was acceptance in both the Ladies Harmonie Society and the Etude Club, organizations that provided entertainment for local music aficionados. On one occasion, Susan sang Mozart's Sonata in A Major.[20]

Susie not only complied with her affectionate father's requests for songs but, jealous of his love, resorted to quite unladylike strategies to attract his attention. Elmer recalled that she would incite the dogs to fight in order to get him to come and separate them and then put her to bed—with perhaps a story and a cuddle.[21] They shared a love of animals and plants, rejoicing together when the crab apple tree in front of the house was heavy with luxurious blossoms. In 1892, Elmer was at last able to move his family, including Grandma Susan, to 317 East Twelfth Street, a much better part of town where the American-born, affluent, professional men of Davenport lived. Here, he shared the pleasures of planting a garden with sixteen-year-old Susie; by 1918, when America was stepping up involvement in World War I, he reminisced about a "little tree" they had planted that had done so well that "if Hoover finds out about it he will commandeer it for a shipmast."[22]

His daughter was closest to Elmer's heart, and it was to her that he wrote of his loneliness after all three children left home. Susan was just beginning to adapt to the life of a coed, independent at last, when she received a despairing letter from her father: "Dear Daughter. A Father without children, a Home without children, a Piano without a Musician. Homes we have plenty. Rooms we have plenty but they are all empty, and our own hearts, empty of comfort, empty for the want of our children. . . . In the morning in peace there is no one to quarrel with, no one to scold because they don't get up. I look into the rooms as I go downstairs and they are always empty—and then when Mamma and I sit down to the table it seems like a mockery. Mamma asks me what I said, and I say I didn't say anything."

He would have preferred to keep her at home, but he had given in to her stubbornness, had even helped obtain the necessary support from his church to gain her admittance. He now exclaimed: "What a valuable thing an education is! What does it cost? A year of your life and a year of the comfort and company of our daughter taken away from us." He expected her to provide moral support for his sons. In the same letter, he wrote: "I trust you will write to Ray. Also I trust you will write a letter of good religious tone and high moral bearing as well also as a kind and sisterly letter. Bear in mind that he is among strangers and undoubtedly exposed to temptations that you have no idea of. Don't forget this. Consider it both your duty and right and if you are pushed for time I greatly prefer you to neglect me, rather than him."[23]

Elmer was not ashamed to admit how much he relied on his children for company and love. In acknowledging his daughter's superior moral fiber, he revealed not only his adherence to the double standard upheld by society but also his recognition of her quiet strength and resolve. He could not, of course, foresee the temptations that a young woman might be exposed to—or the disappointments and heartache she would cause him in the future.

Once he accepted that his daughter was not going to conform to established social patterns, Elmer drew comfort from the moral teaching he managed to wring out of her stories. On 15 January 1920, transforming her bitter attack on small-town society in her story "The Escape," which appeared in *Harper's Monthly Magazine* in December 1919, into something quite different, he wrote: "Think yours in Harper's very good. What a pity our pride causes us to cover our heart's best impulses as Margaret did."[24] This comment reveals more about Elmer than about "The Escape." Margaret Powers, the protagonist, buries her bruised feelings in a "crust she had built up over things she didn't want to know were there."[25] Whereas indifferent Hemingway heroes, cowering behind a macho facade, are readily recognized as awesome male prototypes, Glaspell's woman is condemned as the village oddball who alienates the community with her quirky behavior. Glaspell attempts in this story to expose the callousness of a society that cheerfully sends young men to be killed and mutilated while allowing the cozy evenings of bandage making that Margaret scorned to pass for deprivation on the home front. In the days of the Espionage and Sedition Acts (1917 and 1918), such observations could not be published with impunity, let alone earn money, unless they could generally be misinterpreted as moralistic tales.

Religion ruled all aspects of life for the Glaspells; the parents missed no opportunity to remind their wayward daughter of God and His sacred Word. In an undated letter written shortly after Christmas 1918 (one of the few Christmases Susan could not get back to Davenport), Elmer counseled her to read chapter 12 of Revelation, aptly chosen to explain war as foreseen and foreordained by God—and, incidentally, as caused by woman.[26] The Christian Church, once it was firmly established in the Midwest, continued its evangelizing further afield. As early as 1874, the women of the Christian Church of Davenport had formed a missionary society that Harry E. Downer, author of the *History of Davenport and Scott County*, claims was "the unknown to fame but real mother of the great International Christian Women's Board of Missions."[27]

Susan did not see missionary work as a means to self-fulfillment, but the Davenport Christian Church endeavor to save souls—her mother's one refuge from household chores—furnished her with sufficient knowledge of the subject to incorporate it into *Brook Evans* (1928), ironically, the only novel Alice Glaspell disapproved of. Young Susan struggled to balance her need to please her parents with her urge for independence and her vocation to write; her success was signaled to one and all when she gave up her job as a reporter for the *Des Moines Daily News* and returned home in 1902 to write; her father proudly registered her as "journalist"—no longer as mere "daughter"—in the Davenport city directory of that year.

Alice was happy to have her daughter living at home again; any neighbor who snidely asked about wedding preparations would have been promptly rebuffed with a publication date. Such prestigious magazines as *Harper's*, *Munsey's*, and *Booklovers* were publishing her Susie's stories, and the editors of the moralizing *Youth's Companion* were clamoring for more.[28] Alice's frustrated ambitions were fulfilled in her daughter's career, and Susan's first novel brought her mother sublime joy and undisguised pride. Susan was in Paris when *The Glory of the Conquered* (1909) was published, and her mother's congratulatory letter reveals her total identification with her daughter. Alice wrote: "I think it must have been over a minute before I opened it—and thought of all it meant to me. This book born and growing amid great physical pain and labor as a mother suffers at childbirth, so you my dear one many times suffered while bringing this book to life and none knows this better than your mother but now the time of travail is over and we will enjoy the fruit. . . . Susie dear—I think it is a wonderful book and I don't think this is just because it is mine, the product of my girl's brain."[29] It is not unusual for a writer to compare literary production to childbirth; the analogy is significant here because it is the author's mother who makes it, thus disclosing her vicarious participation and her rapture. Glaspell's reply suggests that at the time she did not resent her mother's appropriation of her brainchild: "I was very happy over your letter about the book. It was a beautiful letter, and meant much to me. I wanted you to take pleasure in the book, and I am sure from your letter that you are going to. Yes, you know how hard I worked, and all that has gone into it. I never could have done it without you I know that. You have always been wonderfully good to me about my work, made every sacrifice that I might have opportunity for working, and have always sympathized and helped as no one but you could. So you are entitled to a large part of any success the book receives, and I hope, for all our sakes, that it will have at least a fair measure of success."[30]

In a later letter, Glaspell echoed these feelings: "You have always been wonderful in that, taking pleasure in the thing that was good for me, even when it was most hard for you. Don't think I have not appreciated that."[31] Susan was remorsefully aware of her parents' loneliness after she and her brothers left home; she intuited that the older generation relied on the younger—as much as on the church—to give meaning to their meager lives. She feared disappointing them but knew that they would always understand and support her, as did the parents she created in "The Return of Rhoda." Published in the *Youth's Companion* in 1905, this story tells of parents' heartache when their daughter goes to the city to study music. The mother consoles herself by "thinking it's all for the best," a fact the father never disputes despite complaining that "it seems a little lonely at times."[32] The couple is delighted when Rhoda returns; her failure as a singer is forgotten in the joy of the reunion.

Alice Glaspell must have created just such an atmosphere of security for her daughter, firmly believing that it was all for the best, even reluctantly coming to terms with Susie's dalliance with and eventual marriage to George Cram Cook, a twice-divorced eccentric. But after Cook's death, when Glaspell took a younger lover, she told her mother that she had remarried and never brought Norman Matson home to Davenport. Although on the surface, mother and daughter were friends, on a deeper level, Glaspell resented her mother's acquiescence to the role of dutiful wife and consequent need to live through her child. Alice Glaspell could not provide her ambitious daughter with an acceptable role model, and although she was always a good daughter, Susan could never confide in her mother. She kept her informed about the trivialities of life, her apartment hunting, heating problems, search for domestic help, but she could not share the deeper worries that George Cram Cook caused her. But Alice never relinquished the possessive pride she felt for her daughter. On the back of an envelope in which Glaspell had sent her money in 1924 to buy "a few things for yourself," she noted: "Susie's play *The Verge* in London. 100 pounds (received). Sent me check $25. *My girl.*"[33] The emphatic underlining of "my girl" highlights her proprietary feelings toward her daughter and her maternal satisfaction.

Susan Glaspell was in Greece when her father died; leaving her husband alone in Athens, she sailed home at the first opportunity, anxious to comfort her mother. But when George Cram Cook died in January 1924, she did not turn to her mother for solace; she sought consolation and understanding among friends first and then traveled to Davenport for the rest of the winter. By May, she was back in Provincetown, accompanied by Lucy (Lulu) Huffaker, a college friend.

In the years that followed, until Alice Glaspell died in February 1929, Susan visited Davenport frequently, as did her brothers. Of the three siblings, she alone attained a measure of success, justifying her father's faith in her. Frank had moved to Texas and in 1920 was still hoping to make huge profits on real estate deals. There is no evidence that these ever materialized, and by 1923, he was apparently back in Davenport with his wife, Hazel, for Susan responded joyfully to the news that he had "fixed up" and sold some houses their father had built on the old Glaspell property to let out to immigrant workers. She understood her father well enough to realize that "even though some of the property is sold, it would be such a gratification to him that it was at its best."[34]

Ray, Glaspell's older brother, did not do well either, although by 1929 he was settled in Chicago on 1055 West Monroe Street, owner of the King Fire Corporation, which sold furnaces. According to his mother's letters, his business suffered after the coal strikes of the late 1920s and then the Depression.[35] Even when he wrote to his sister about their mother's funeral, Ray pleaded for money, promising to repay old debts in the future.[36] As the eldest, he organized the funeral, although Florence (Flossie), his wife, assured Susan that everything was being done as she would have liked.[37] Later, when her work for the Federal Theatre took her to Chicago, Glaspell would become closer to Flossie and Ray, at times staying with them. She had taken her father's injunction to look out for her brothers to heart, for in 1942 her tax returns listed Ray Glaspell as a dependent with a physical disability, and she claimed a $350 credit on his account. He died in 1945, just three years before his sister.

Although Susan Glaspell lacked the advantages a private, eastern education could have given her, Davenport was considered by some to be "one of the best possible towns" in which to serve a writing apprenticeship. It was quite different from most midwestern towns, and according to Floyd Dell, an aspiring novelist Glaspell befriended, it had "a quality of its own." This was "partly due . . . to the pioneers from New England, who brought with them ideals and a respect for learning; but it is more due . . . to the Germans, who left home because they loved liberty, and brought with them a taste for music, discussion and good beer."[38] The "robust mirthfulness" of this German element came to characterize Davenport and manifested itself most notably in the brass bands that marched through the streets on the slightest excuse. Although more refined musical entertainment was also available—even Ignacy Paderewski gave a concert at the Burtis Opera House—Davenporters organized themselves into clubs and choruses and provided their own music. What they most loved was a concert followed by all-night dancing.

Elmer Glaspell, mindful of his New England Puritan ancestors, would not hear of his children participating in such frivolities. His daughter also shunned the plebeian immigrant distractions; she aspired to membership in the more elite clubs, literary, musical, and social, which preferred to meet in people's homes rather than in Davenport's popular Turner Hall. However, to join such clubs, it was essential to belong to the right set of people—and Susan Glaspell did not. Some of her cousins lived this other life, and when she went to the uptown high school with them, she admired their stylish ways and yearned to be one of them. The move to East Twelfth Street brought her closer, but only as an observer whose sharp mind and penetrating criticism merited a tolerant respect, the most an outsider could hope for.

After graduation, when her cousins and friends left for college or joined the social circuit, Glaspell felt even more out of place; her parents could not send her to college, so she had no choice but to remain at home. She bridled against this life: helping her mother with the chores, participating in church activities, joining the missionary society. A photograph of eighteen-year-old Susan shows her in a short-sleeved, embroidered shirtwaist, willowy and pretty, with unruly hair framing her face and drawing attention away from her long, straight nose; she looks directly at the camera with large, serious eyes, quite convinced that she has a right to all that life has to offer. Scoffing at the ease with which other girls slipped into a society life prepared for them by wealthy parents, she still wished she were one of them. Even if she never allowed herself to articulate her fears, Glaspell was determined not to be trapped, as her mother had been, by the illusion of romance. She questioned the values Davenport society took for granted, believed education alone could save a woman from a stifling marriage, and desperately dreamed of having a writing career.

Davenport did not totally fail the young Susan Glaspell; it offered her a role model who was acceptable to her parents. In October 1878, Davenport resident Alice French published a short story in one of the era's most important magazines, *Lippincott's*. "Communists and Capitalists: A Sketch from Life" is an account of a philosophical dispute between a worker and a countess amid the backdrop of the Chicago Haymarket riots.[39] From that moment on, French, who published under the name of Octave Thanet, represented Davenport in the world of literature. She wrote countless stories for the best magazines and seven novels; between 1896 and 1900, she was probably the highest paid purveyor of short fiction in the country. Her stories were set either in Fairport—a barely disguised Davenport—or on the Arkansas plantation where she spent her winters with her lifelong friend Jane Allen Crawford. The French family enjoyed a senior position in the Davenport oligarchy; her father had been mayor of the town, was treasurer of the school board, and owned several lumber mills. His daughter, naturally enough, believed in the Victorian order of privilege for those with money and education and in the superior spiritual qualities of women, as long as they confined themselves to the sphere assigned them by God and patriarchy. Although the rebellious Susan Glaspell was not cut from the same pattern as Alice French, the older woman's prestige proved that writing was an honorable profession; even Elmer Glaspell was forced to admit that there was no inherent wickedness in such a career. He joyfully reported to his daughter, who at twenty-one was already an accredited newspaperwoman, that "Miss French said you were the smartest the [*sic*] brightest girl in the city."[40] But French was not in the habit of helping or supporting budding Davenport writers, especially young women, who she thought ought to

Susan Glaspell, circa 1894
(Courtesy of the University Libraries, The University of Iowa)

be cooking and caring for their families, not writing; she preferred to spend her time traveling with the entourage of Andrew Carnegie (whom she convinced to donate a library to the town) or entertaining notable guests such as Theodore Roosevelt. In 1910, her Arkansas novel, *By Inheritance*, was a great success, but it was soon forgotten when her patrician stance no longer appealed to readers in a world beleaguered by socialist revolution and headed toward a Great War.

The daughter of a humble farmer, Glaspell could not afford to imitate French's "gentle-woman writer" career; she had to earn a living, but more important, she wanted to prove herself. Few opportunities for employment were open to young women at the turn of the century;

newspaper work was one possibility, but even that was not quite reputable. According to Floyd Dell's *Moon-Calf*, a reporter was expected to "loaf on the job," to hang around in the hope that something newsworthy would happen nearby; he would spend hours at the train station collecting fascinating tidbits about who left town and who arrived.[41] A woman high school graduate from a churchgoing family could hardly be expected to devote her days to such an unbecoming occupation.

Nevertheless, Glaspell managed to convince Charles Eugene Banks, a local poet who was editor of the *Davenport Morning Republican*, to employ her. She was restricted at first to office work such as typing and proofreading, but she soon won Banks's approval and in July 1896 he appointed her as society editor of his new magazine, the *Weekly Outlook*. Banks served as general editor, and his wife occupied the post of associate editor, her presence probably lending an air of respectability to the venture. The *Outlook* was "devoted to social, musical, literary, and dramatic interests" and promised subscribers that its columns and advertising would be "clean" and eminently suitable for reading aloud "in the home circle."[42] The columns were not signed, but evidence strongly suggests that Glaspell, somewhat constrained by the paper's virtuous policies, wrote the "Social Life" and "Socialettes" sections.[43] She began by simply reporting the activities of Davenport's elite; a discreet notice in small type gave the *Outlook*'s telephone number, stating: "We are pleased to receive items of news at any time." With the help of Banks's wife, Glaspell must have avoided dreary days of reviewing the comings and goings at the train station.

Glaspell was too ambitious to be content for long with the mere chronicling of events, however, and she soon started writing sprightly commentaries on any aspect of Davenport morals and mores that caught her fancy, followed by the usual information on social activities. These essays, although less mature and not so well written, are in the vein of Margaret Fuller's *Woman in the Nineteenth Century*. Fuller, one of Ralph Waldo Emerson's circle of Transcendentalists, criticized the minimal opportunities available to women in her time and advocated a wider education that would open up all the professions to women. Like Fuller, Glaspell tended to be moralistic and anecdotal and based her articles on her own experience. She provides a picture of the cultural and social life of a midwestern town in the last years of the nineteenth century, with pithy criticism of the most ridiculous habits. Glaspell spares no one, and no aspect of the life of well-to-do women goes unnoticed. Perhaps because she did not have a natural place in Davenport society, she delighted in subtle revenge, such as when she puzzled over how easily puffed sleeves had fallen out of favor. "Why is it," she asked, "that the thing in vogue invariably looks so eminently consistent, is so pleasing to everyone, is becoming, pretty and graceful, and appears absolutely above criticism, but let it go out of style, be superseded by something else, and straightway in the twinkling of an eye it becomes, and is pronounced, inartistic, frightful, ridiculous?"[44]

Like Elizabeth Cady Stanton before her, Glaspell railed against the skirts in which patriarchy dressed women: "The men object to bloomers, I am told. Dear me! and haven't they objected to everything a woman has adopted looking toward a freer use of her limbs and body ever since the flood?" Whimsically, she described the ideal costume for "wheeling," an activity in which the customary petticoats were dangerous: "But if two or three representative society girls were to come out in bloomer costumes of some soft gray flannel for the trousers and india silk for the shirt-waist, hose and low shoes to match, I venture to predict that any number of us would fall in line at once."[45] The wink and nod that convey the wry tone of the piece imply a dig at all who aspire only to follow the herd and disguised the barbs directed at staid Davenport matrons who might have turned away in umbrage had Glaspell taken up the challenge herself.

Although Glaspell never openly argues for suffrage or any other candescent woman's issue, the freeing of women from society's ludicrous chains is a theme that pervades all of her essays for the *Weekly Outlook*. Tongue in cheek, she praises the "well-meaning congress of Mothers," a reactionary organization devoted to "perpetuating the dignity of the home," and then rejoices that "women are coming to the front in Kentucky this year" by occupying numerous posts as superintendents of schools; she also reports at length on a meeting of the Daughters of the Revolution, at which Mary Newberry Adams of Dubuque spoke on the part women have played in history. Glaspell concludes that "despite the fact that histories have mostly been written by men, who slighted or ignored [women] altogether, [women] were well worthy a place in the foremost ranks of the world's patriots, philosophers and statesmen. . . . Truly we owe more to woman than we seem inclined to put in our school books and if the Daughters of the Revolution succeed in making familiar the facts that prove these things their organization will have accomplished great good."[46]

The *Outlook* demanded that Glaspell devote space to fashion and social gatherings, so she faithfully reported meetings of the Tuesday Club, the Ladies Harmonie Society, and the Etude Club, as well as gatherings at the homes of worthy ladies that involved literary games or competitions of some kind. She also covered the performances of opera and theater companies and frequently published the programs in advance, as well as gossip on the stars. She clearly enjoyed writing these essays, and once she had mastered the technique, there was no stopping her; distancing herself by adopting the persona of a cynical observer, at times she assumed the guise of an older woman and recounted a conversation with an unidentified young man or woman, ending on a note of moral concern or advice, such as when she told her readers that we must be "true to ourselves, listen to no scandal, and look upon the world with trustful eyes."[47]

Her topics were varied, and her wide reading and grasp of contemporary affairs glimmered through the socialites' concerns. She wrote with a wry humor that inevitably turned against the established ideal of the angel on a "pedestal . . . fed on sugar-plums and roses."[48] But the self-righteous matron who failed to comprehend this humor would not be offended because Glaspell's inbred ambivalence allowed the reader to interpret her comments as a condemnation of the new woman.

Thus positioned on the outer rim of Davenport's social life, Glaspell, the alien observer, wrote her essays for the *Weekly Outlook*, all the while dreaming of attending college. After a year of saving, scrimping, and softening up Elmer Glaspell, her college dream came true: the August 1897 *Weekly Outlook* advised its readers that "Miss Susie Glaspell will enter Drake University at Des Moines when it opens in September. Miss Glaspell will keep in touch with journalism by doing special correspondence for the *Outlook*."[49]

Skipping the freshman and sophomore years, Glaspell was admitted as a junior to Drake in September 1897 in preparation for a degree in philosophy.[50] Her courses included philosophy, Greek, French, English, history, and biblical studies. Elders of the Church of Christ had founded the university in 1881 in order to provide young people with a liberal education in science and the arts, and they had determined from the beginning to "offer all the advantages in all departments to both sexes," regardless of "race, color, or creed."[51] But in spite of such noble principles and the admission of a few students from missionary schools in

China and Japan, most students were from local, rural families, thus lending a "quite provincial" air to the classrooms.[52] The campus, initially a "wilderness of thick brush and second growth timber" crisscrossed by cow paths, had grown to occupy the area between Twenty-fifth and Twenty-eighth Streets along University Avenue.[53] This had originally been the northwestern boundary of Des Moines, but by the time Glaspell enrolled, water pipes had been laid, the electric streetcar passed by more or less regularly, and stately homes graced the adjacent streets. The original three faculties—literature and art, law, and medicine—had, by the end of the century, grown into ten colleges or schools, the College of Letters and Science offering four degrees: classical, philosophical, belles lettres, and scientific. By the turn of the century, thanks to generous donations, new buildings had been erected to house the library, administration, and classrooms for the thousand or so students registered, but as yet, there were no residence halls or dormitories.[54] Students boarded in local homes; "lady students" were advised to "room only where there is a reception room for the use of callers."[55] Glaspell, comfortably ensconced in a rooming house on Twenty-eighth Street, identified immediately with the highly idealistic ethic of the university founders and toughened her resolve to become "a helper in the onward progress of society" through her writing.[56]

Although slightly older and more mature than most of her fellow students, Glaspell was "a frolicky young woman" who loved "a good scrap."[57] She soon gained admittance to the highest-ranking clubs and won respect as the mover and shaker of the "group that felt themselves the social and literary leaders."[58] The girls in her rooming house considered her a superior being; late into the night, enveloped in an ample white nightgown, she would enthrall them with her theories of "life and love."[59] The previous year, six women students had founded a club with the high-minded purpose of "emphasiz[ing] the value of personality through intellectual and social development on a high level of responsibility." They chose Margaret Fuller as the "symbol of their intent and ideals" and established a "highly selective membership policy." Glaspell delighted at her prompt election to the Margaret Fuller Club and vivaciously took the lead in all of the club members' discussions.[60] For the first time in her life, she was drawn into the magic circle and did not have to resign herself to hovering on the edge.

In spite of such resounding social success, her first year did not end well; Glaspell was seriously ill throughout the spring and summer, spending some time in the hospital. The nature of her illness is unknown, but the university literary magazine, *The Delphic*, reported in October 1898, when it published her piece, "The Philosophy of War," that she had made a complete recovery.[61] The Spanish-American War, which redeemed Cuba from Spanish tyranny and regaled the Philippines, Puerto Rico, and Guam with American rule, had ended earlier that year; during the conflict, American volunteers (Glaspell's future husband, George Cram Cook, among them) had served in insalubrious military camps where many succumbed to yellow fever and malaria. Military intervention in Cuba had sparked the debate on whether America should adopt England's imperialistic policies, and in her story, Glaspell presents both sides of the argument in the form of a dialogue between a pedantic philosopher and a brokenhearted father whose son had died in the camps. The philosopher, echoing the worst pulpit style Glaspell must have endured at morning chapel, declares that "it has been a war for humanity, and a good thing generally."[62] The bereaved father then tells the story of his son, who, "brimming with national pride," fell victim to political ambitions and inefficient organization. The story presents the concern with the conflict between the personal and the public good that would reverberate throughout all of Glaspell's writing; the issue would frequently be presented as the question of a woman's right to personal fulfillment, but Glaspell was never indifferent to the human problem on the larger public stage.

The Philomathian, the university's most prestigious literary society, welcomed Glaspell into its ranks; her experience as a journalist in Davenport compelled respect, especially among younger students and those from rural areas. Every year, the Philomathian offered faculty and students an evening of musical and literary entertainment. The honor of giving the last performance in the March 1898 proceedings went to Glaspell. According to *The Delphic*, she more than fulfilled all expectations:

> The closing number, a story by Miss Glaspell, was no surprise to those who have observed her literary work throughout the year. "In a Factory Town" was a finely written story dealing with the labor problem. In delicacy of touch, aptness of allusion, and epigrammatic quality, her work far surpassed the standards of the amateur. Especially was this true however in that the *finale*, the very essence of the story, was not lacking. Her production was not a sketch, a description, a reverie, but a story, with unity and design, faithful in

detail to the life it essayed to portray and fit to move the sympathies in behalf of a suffering people. Miss Glaspell has pointed the picture as it is—darkened and forbidding.[63]

Unfortunately, *The Delphic* did not print the story, but we can surmise that it was influenced by Alice French's "Communists and Capitalists: A Sketch from Life," although Glaspell would surely have been more understanding of the worker than the bosses.

By her second year, Glaspell's prestige as a writer and orator at Drake was confirmed by her election to the post of vice president of the Debating Society. Debates were held regularly with students from Monmouth College in Monmouth, Illinois, and Glaspell exercised her rhetorical powers with great relish. She put the same skills to use in the oratorical contest that was held in December of each year at which a Drake representative was chosen for the state and—with luck—interstate competitions. Along with other ambitious students, Glaspell yearned for the honor of representing the university; she also aspired to being the first Drake woman to compete for the state prize. In 1898, she chose Otto von Bismarck as her subject; his recent death inspired her to write a somewhat naive eulogy in which she argued that, where greatness is concerned, the ends justify the means. The unification of Germany, not the oppression of a people or the curtailment of democratic liberties, was her theme.[64] Allowing the "longer periods" to fall "with the force of blows," Glaspell dazed her audience and won the contest.[65] The Philomathian Society celebrated her victory at the home of one of its members, Nelle Burton, and "an uproarious good time" was had by all. Not to be outdone, the Margaret Fuller Club surprised Glaspell with an informal reception a few days later.[66]

But the euphoria of her resounding success was shattered at the start of the new term when Glaspell learned that the local authorities, confusing the regulations of the state and interstate contests, had sent the wrong number of signed copies of her speech to the judges of the state society. Drake University was banned from participating, and the organizers refused to change their minds. Nonetheless, a Drake contingent, including Glaspell, traveled to Mount Vernon for the contest; once the official proceedings were over, the audience demanded that Glaspell be allowed to recite her piece. Knowing she had nothing to lose and determined to put the other contestants to shame, Glaspell stepped boldly onto the platform and "delivered her oration with such power as to arouse the wearied audience and command from it the closest attention." *The Delphic* assured its readers that Glaspell would have won the contest for Drake and quoted the *Cedar Rapids Republican*, which affirmed that "it was easily the best oration that came from the platform, from every standpoint."[67]

The Delphic, a rich source of student gossip that unabashedly proclaimed in its masthead that "literature is the highest of arts," published a number of Glaspell's pieces during her Drake career. Competing with Lulu Huffaker, who would become her closest friend in years to come, in 1898 Glaspell ran for the office of *Delphic* editor, a position of inordinate prestige among the students; this election was "one of the stirring events of the college year."[68] But Glaspell was to be disappointed; she was not chosen, and to her secret chagrin, Lulu was appointed associate editor.

Although her college days were peppered with the usual minor frustrations, including the occasional low grade, such as a humiliating 40 for work on Victor Hugo in her French class, Glaspell ended on a high note.[69] Graduation celebrations included an evening of entertainment at which she read a story, "Old College Friends." The *Delphic* reporter considered it "from the standpoint of literary finish . . . the finest effort of the day."[70] According to a 1931 history of Drake, Glaspell left her mark on her alma mater and, as "a famous novelist," ranked "among the immortal" of the university's graduates.[71]

Elated by her success, Glaspell proudly accepted a position on the *Des Moines Daily News* but was appalled to learn that she had been assigned to the statehouse and legislative beat.[72] Ignorant of local politics, she was at first overwhelmed by the grandiose gold-domed Iowa statehouse and would ascend its grand stairway of imported marble almost on tiptoe. But her élan carried her through, and she soon lost all of her small-town awe for ornate reception rooms and imposing Supreme Court chambers. Glaspell's clear, judicious mind and her pluck endeared her to delegates and legislators alike; some were friendly, others paternalistic, but she was sufficiently wily to gather "enough news to keep [her] from being disgracefully scooped."[73]

But run-of-the-mill reporting did not satisfy Glaspell for long; she idealistically conceived of herself as a reformer whose mission was to show humanity the way to greater achievement through her writing. She persuaded the editors to entrust her with a column on current affairs, in which she reclaimed the detached wry tone she had developed for the *Weekly Outlook*, fabricating a highly critical "News Girl." From this van-

Susan Glaspell, graduate of Drake University, 1899
(Courtesy of the University Libraries, The University of Iowa)

tage point, she plied her readers with ironic commentary and advice, taking her cue from local events or her reading. When several articles that appeared in the *Ladies Home Journal* particularly incensed her, she devoted an entire column to attacking the author's outdated convictions. The *Ladies Home Journal*—which in later years would publish some of Glaspell's stories—had first appeared in 1883 and by the end of the century had become the most widely read and influential women's magazine.[74] Traditional in many respects, it had no truck with the growing suffrage movement, but its pages rejected the frail, ethereal lady, promoting instead the self-disciplined, hardworking woman who knew how to run her home. Glaspell objected to the articles in question because they accused the young college-educated American woman of "buy[ing] indecent books and haunt[ing] the theater for indecent plays." Her "News Girl" assured readers that Des Moines college girls, far from acquiring immoral habits, had "learned how to think and formed a desire to be of use in the world."[75] On another occasion, she bitingly criticized the preening delegates in "satin and gush" who had succeeded in transforming the Congress of Mothers into a paltry social event and would "never in a thousand years revolutionize the world."[76] With equal vigor, the "News Girl" turned on Iowa politicians who assembled at the state capital only "because they need an annual or semi-annual square meal at the Savery or Kirkwood."[77]

The most dramatic case Glaspell covered for the *Des Moines Daily News* was the Hossack murder, which impressed her so greatly that, sixteen years later, she used it as the basis for *Trifles*, the play that made her name. Glaspell first reported on the case on 3 December 1900 and covered it until the jury's decision was announced on 10 April 1901. Her initially hostile, fully orthodox attitude toward Mrs. Hossack, accused of bludgeoning her husband with an axe as he slept, became more sympathetic after she visited the Hossack home. There, taking in trifling clues that together formed a picture of Mrs. Hossack's life, Glaspell talked to members of the family and neighbors. In spite of the varied experiences that she had gained in over a year of reporting, she was horrified to learn that Mr. Hossack had beaten his wife regularly. This revelation of the grimier side of the institution of marriage opened her eyes to the fact that women can be trapped with no hope whatever of escape or help from society; possibly, she even found herself understanding her mother's position more clearly. Too late, Glaspell tried to sway public opinion with sympathetic reporting and headlines such as "Mrs. Hossack May Yet Be Proven Innocent."[78] But in spite of her efforts, Mrs. Hossack was found guilty and sentenced to life imprisonment with hard labor; two years later, however, unconvinced by the evidence, a second jury ordered her release. This case lay heavily on Glaspell's mind; she may have tried unsuccessfully to mold it into a magazine story. It was not until 1916, when she was more experienced with the wrongs inflicted on women, that she found the appropriate angle. In *Trifles* (1916)—and the short story "A Jury of Her Peers" (1917)—Glaspell transformed the case, giving the women who had been silenced at the trial voices of their own; she focused on the motive of the crime—totally incomprehensible to a jury of men—and thus attempted to clear Mrs. Hossack's name and make amends for her tardy understanding and her inability to help at the time.[79]

Weary of newspaper work, and humbled by the Hossack case, Glaspell returned to Davenport. Her parents, in whose dreams she took over Alice French's role as Davenport's respectable doyenne of arts and letters, urged her to come home, offering a space of her own and financial peace of mind. Nevertheless, in 1942 Glaspell would write, "I boldly gave up my job and went home to Davenport to give all my time to my own writing. I say boldly, because I had to earn my living."[80] Almost two years of reporting had given her a lot of material; "I was always running into things I saw as short stories," she later confessed.[81]

Although she wrote copiously, fluently transforming her experiences as a reporter into short stories, the works she submitted for publication had an unpleasant way of returning from magazine editors accompanied by polite notes of rejection. Her mother fluttered around her, and Davenport, for all of its social and cultural vitality, seemed to hem her in. Encouraged by Lulu Huffaker, who spent long periods with her aunt in Chicago, Glaspell registered for two courses at the University of Chicago Graduate School in the summer of 1902. She did not finish the course in American literature, and "The Essay in English Literature" course earned her only half a credit.[82] But Glaspell probably had other things on her mind at this time; she was attractive and intelligent, and the lack of documentary evidence as to youthful pangs of love does not mean she led a celibate life. The radicals of Davenport who welcomed her into their circle on her return from Chicago tried unsuccessfully to shock her with their discussions of free love and came to the conclusion that she was clinging to "an ideal of fidelity" inspired by a cataclysmic love affair— an experience, if true, that she would eventually make good use of in her first novel, *The Glory of the Conquered* (1909).[83] Glaspell acknowledged that she "put herself" into her novels, and indeed many parallels exist between her experiences and the lives of her protagonists; thus, it is very tempting to posit that at some point in her twenties or early thirties she had an abortion, as does Ruth, the heroine of *Fidelity* (1915). In this novel, which she based largely on her relationship with George Cram Cook, Glaspell deals very discreetly with such a traumatic experience.

The idealist in Glaspell had hoped to be offered a place at the University of Chicago Settlement, which, modeled on Jane Addams's Hull House, described itself as "a body of educated people living in a neighborhood for the purpose of co-operation in social work and for learning the concrete facts of life at first hand."[84] But Glaspell found that "there were a great many girls who wanted to do settlement work," and her Chicago stint was productive only in that a resulting short story, "The Girl from Down-Town," was accepted by the *Youth's Companion* for its April 1903 issue.[85] She had published only one other story since she had left Drake ("On the Second Down," *Author's Magazine*, November 1902), but her luck was about to change. Her onetime employer, the *Des Moines Daily News*, jubilantly reported that the *Youth's Companion* "said her stories were so well received by their readers that they wished at all times to have one or more on hand."[86]

But Glaspell clearly did not enjoy writing exemplary tales for young people; she preferred to risk rejections from the less conventional *Harper's, Leslie's, Munsey's, The Speaker, The American, Booklovers Magazine*, and *The Black Cat*. All of these periodicals published at least one of her stories between 1904 and 1912, but it was *The Black Cat* that gave her the measure of recognition she craved by awarding her first prize in the magazine's 1904 short story contest. "For Love of the Hills" appeared in the October 1905 issue, and Glaspell exultantly received the $500 prize. The story deals with a homesick young woman in Chicago who helps an older woman who is losing her sight return to the Colorado mountains. Perhaps more revealing, the protagonist, young and female, is making her way on her own in a masculine world. All she asks of Chicago is "a chance to do the work for which she was trained in order that she might go to the art classes at night."[87] The Christmas story "At the Turn of the Road" that Glaspell published a few years later in *The Speaker* is a variation on the same theme, but this time it is the aspiring artist who is given a chance to go home for Christmas by an older man who has sacrificed friendship in order to acquire wealth; he assures her that "the human heart was not made to feed upon gratified ambition."[88]

Many of the stories Glaspell wrote between 1902 and 1912 are based on the experiences she gained during her dalliance on the statehouse beat; after the success of *The Glory of the Conquered*, she collected them in one volume, entitled *Lifted Masks* (1912). The majority are straightforward tales that disclose the good instincts that dirty politics smother in men of state.

During this time, Glaspell learned to adapt her writing to the needs of different audiences; she also forced herself to acquire the trick of conforming to a blueprint, thus assuring the acceptance of her work. Some years later, complaining of the stereotypical Broadway play, she would write: "Plays, like magazine stories, were patterned. They might be pretty good within themselves, seldom did they open out to—where it surprised or thrilled your spirit to follow."[89] A piece in which Glaspell did strike out on her own was "For Tomorrow: The Story of an Easter Sermon" (1905), which was published in the more thought-provoking *Booklovers Magazine*. Here, her Emersonian idealism dominates the plot. Mary, molded as much by her father's dedication to the "spirit of truth" as by a university degree and travel in Europe, fights to persuade her clergyman brother to keep faith with his inner convictions, even at the risk of shattering his parishioners' complacency—and sinking his career. Glaspell's belief in the oneness of humankind's experience and the vital importance of the spirit of truth is propounded by her youthful heroine, who unquestioningly accepts her father's dire message: "The institutions and forms of today must pass, the spirit of truth ever remains. . . . The spirit of truth never has proved, and never can prove, an idle destroyer."[90] But the story is marred by the lack of any tangible "truth"; the characters deal only with its "spirit," leaving us in the dark as to the precise nature of the clergyman's religious crisis. The story "His America" (1912) takes us slightly closer to this spirit by putting the argument in terms of political parties that represent the dreamers who idealize America and the realists who get things done. In both of these stories, as in "At Twilight" (a 1912 reworking of "The Tragedy of a Mind" printed in *The Delphic* in 1898), Glaspell reveals the importance she attaches to the individual in her scheme of "oneness." In "At Twilight," an ingenuous, though well meaning, student consoles an aging professor who is about to be replaced by a younger man: "Don't you see? He's there waiting to take your place because you *got* him ready. Why, you made that younger man! Your whole life has been a getting ready for him. He can do his work because you first did yours. Of course he can go farther than you can! Wouldn't it be a sorry commentary on you if he couldn't?"[91] Of all of these stories, "For Tomorrow," although it tends to be wordy, is the best written, offering a discerning account of a moral dilemma and how a brother and sister surmount it. Glaspell articulated these same convictions for the stage during her Provincetown years, with one crucial difference: she moved away from the patriarchal statehouse world that governed her early writing and turned the spotlight on womankind.

After 1912, Glaspell published most frequently in the *Ladies' Home Journal* and *Harper's Monthly Magazine*. The type of stories these two journals accepted differed markedly. For the antifeminist *Journal*, Glaspell wrote of love and matrimony, subtly changing themes she had used earlier.[92] In "Whom Mince Pie Hath Joined Together" (1913), the homesick woman artist is now stranded in Paris, where she is courted by a childhood friend; eventually she agrees to marry him but only after she has established her potential economic independence. Bowing to *Ladies' Home Journal* conventions, this talented artist acknowledges that even if her art does not pay, her culinary skills will; she can always sell the mince pies she learned to make back home.

To the more literary *Harper's*, Glaspell submitted stories of a quite different caliber.[93] She focused less on the story line and more on transmitting her views on the individual in society. The oneness of creation, the fact that we must all enter into the stream of life and thus cannot afford to bury ourselves in learning, art, moneymaking, and so on, is at the heart of these stories. The protagonist, man or woman, learns that life is not complete without such participation—and most frequently, as in "The Nervous Pig" (1919), this participation is achieved through love of another. But it is not a swooning, romantic love; it is a love in which the protagonist is prepared to sacrifice individuality rather than face isolation. Exceptions are "The Rules of the Institution" (1914), in which Judith decides she has a right to ignore society's conventions, and "Beloved Husband" (1918), in which Amos Owens, unable to change his hardworking ways and adapt to the easier life he has provided for his family, decides to shoot himself. The best written of these stories is "Pollen" (1919); more concise than the others, it sets out its lesson in clear language. Ira Mead eventually has to admit that his corn, the best in the state thanks to his knowing and loving care, will be tainted by inferior seed carried on the wind unless he shares it with his neighbors. Thus he offers it to people he has always shunned, and Glaspell hints that his personal life will now be fuller and happier. Sacrificing his superiority as a farmer, he ensures that his corn will have "those things which would let it realize its possibilities to the utmost."[94]

When Glaspell concentrates on a moral dilemma, she eschews action, reducing the plot to the spiritual development of a character, although on occasion, as in "Beloved Husband," she stuns the reader with a sudden dramatic twist at the end of the story. Unfortunately, in most of her fiction, as Glaspell allows an idea to take over from the plot, the prose tends to become convoluted, and the pleasing simplicity of the earlier stories is lost in an attempt at stylistic sophistication. With a gracious nod at Alice French's Fairport, Glaspell sets some stories in a fictional mid-western town, Freeport—a replica of Davenport, with its provincial mores and cultural pretensions. The most successful of these stories is "Finality in Freeport" (1916), a nearly factual account of the library crisis she precipitated with her Monist Society friends, George Cram Cook and Floyd Dell, over the library's refusal to purchase a copy of *The Finality of the Christian Religion* solely because of the ambiguous title of the book. But this episode belongs to the following chapter.

CHAPTER TWO

Escaping Main Street

———•◦⟨∞⟩◦•———

Ever since she could remember, Glaspell had been weaving fantasies around the Cook family, generally casting the younger son George (1873–1924), whom she observed from a safe distance, as the hero. With the advantages that only money could bring in the pioneering Midwest of the 1830s, John P. Cook had studied law, run successfully for the state senate, was elected to the House of Representatives for the Thirty-third Congress, and, with his brother Ebenezer, opened a bank. Thus, the Cook Memorial Library, Cook Home for the Old, and Cook Memorial Church stonily provoked Glaspell into a futile search for buildings named after her ancestors. (There was a Glaspell Street in Davenport in the area where her great-grandfather's farm used to be.) By the turn of the century, the Cook law firm was a fixture in Davenport, and Ellen Dodge Cook, mother of George and Ruel, was allowed to be as eccentric as she desired. In 1881, she had the old log cabin her grandparents had built moved to a site along the river, where, "freshly chinked, the massive white-oak logs, squared and silvery, have a place of honor under oaks and hickories" and she could look out "across the gleaming Mississippi to willowed islands and the opulent peaceful hills of Illinois."[1] Eyebrows were perhaps raised at such extravagance, but those who dared to visit Ma-Mie (as her boys called her) valued her understanding of the wide world. The aging Hungarian refugees of 1848 particularly appreciated her love of ideas, and through them, the cabin acquired an aura of past civilizations that the children of settlers could only imagine. Piqued, Glaspell dreamed of "the novel that could be written about the Cabin, the drama of taking Plato or Ruskin from shelves beside the wide fireplace in the pioneer house."[2]

When Glaspell returned from Des Moines after resigning from the *Daily News*, a friend arranged an invitation to the cabin for her. Small, energetic Ma-Mie, who disguised shyness with brusque self-assertiveness, appeared "inaccessible" to Glaspell, who would acknowledge much later that "this was because she was as timid as I was."[3] Ma-Mie called on "Jiggie," her husky, thirty-odd-year-old younger son, to help the conversation along, but George Cram Cook, twisting his "one prematurely grey lock," was royally contemptuous of all farmer's daughters who aspired to literature and quite indifferent to this "strikingly handsome young lady" his mother insisted he entertain.[4] He quickly quashed a naive conversational gambit that Glaspell dared venture, leaving her feeling foolish— and vastly inferior.

By 1903, Cook had given up a promising university career in order to write. His impressive list of publications had earned him an instructorship at the new Stanford University in San Francisco the previous year—most certainly a step up from the drudgery of teaching future farmers the rudiments of composition at the University of Iowa, where he had been employed for three years.[5] The publication of his first novel, *Roderick Taliaferro* (1903), although not wildly successful, crested his curriculum vitae and aroused in him visions of a sturdy, sensitive American Tolstoy turning the soil at dawn and penning midwestern *Anna Kareninas* at dusk. Unfortunately, his wife of two years, Sara Swain, did not share his inclination for roughing it in a pioneer's cabin somewhere outside of Davenport, however romantic the setting, and life with her turned into a hellish nightmare.[6] In 1905, Sara finally left him, and Cook, realizing that the exigencies of truck farming did not leave much time or energy for writing—and that he was, in fact, financially dependent on his father— gave in to drink and depression.

Cook's extreme mood swings had always been encouraged by Ma-Mie, who interpreted them as a sign of genius; she would love her third daughter-in-law best because Glaspell instinctively imitated her maternal indulgence. In her biography of Cook, *The Road to the Temple* (1927), Glaspell avoids hypotheses of neurological, or, for that matter, pathological, disorders; unquestioningly, she accepts his account of having what must have been a nervous breakdown after Sara left him, although she writes: "He himself had different names for it—melancholia, intellectual insanity, hyperesthesia of the emotions, but those were only things used, a medium. His experience was religious. He had done it—what Jesus did, what the great mystics have done, had cast off self utterly and walked with God."[7] His closest friend, Floyd Dell, was more realistic about Cook's uneven temper: "When George was happy he was, not only to my adoring young gaze, but to that of others, a figure of gigantic creative energy, superhuman, with a Promethean fire shining in his face. And when he lapsed into sadness, there was something lumberingly, lumpishly, hugely Saturnian about him."[8] According to Dell, it was in these brooding moods that he twisted his lock of gray hair, a gesture that the future Provincetown Players would always associate with their founder.

Floyd Dell (1887–1969), "an infant of nineteen" with "a mind of the first order" when he first met Cook, was a precocious poet and journalist; Cook described him as "slight, [with] a cough, and in passion and gift of expression [he] is like Shelley."[9] His family had moved to Davenport when he was sixteen, and he had promptly unearthed and been disappointed by the socialist local. Thus, in 1907 when he received an invitation to a meeting of a "new free-thought society," Dell was hugely flattered and attended in the hope that he would at last meet the town's other rebellious souls.

At the first meeting of the society, "a dozen assorted free-thinkers sat around the large dinner-table" at the home of one of their number.[10] The egocentric Dell remembered the meeting because he had the wit to suggest a name for Davenport's oddballs that "pleased" George Cram Cook. They would call themselves the Monist Society, based on a term Dell borrowed from the Darwinian zoologist, Ernst Haeckel, who believed in the essential unity of mind and matter. Dell had been introduced to Cook previously but had been studiously ignored; he envied Cook's position as the town's most eccentric intellectual and childishly wanted the older man to acknowledge him as a fellow genius. This time, the man and the youngster hit it off, and although the Monist Society continued to meet and its membership grew, Dell did not care whether it "lived or died." Cook had recognized his potential, and "they could talk to each other better without the accompanying presence of the fifty or so members of the Monist Society."[11]

But for Susan Glaspell, who, it was rumored, was resolutely faithful to the memory of a lost love, the Monist Society proved to be a development of seismic proportions, for, as she would later write, "it was there I began to know Jig."[12] The *Black Cat* prize had established her reputation as an author in Davenport; younger writers now looked up to her, and the ladies' literary society, the revered Tuesday Club that Alice French presided over, had admitted her into its sanctum. Although Glaspell still remembered how much she had coveted the honor of membership when she was writing for the *Weekly Outlook*, she now recognized the conservative complacency of Davenport's literary matrons. Her progressive, liberal ideas shocked these ladies, and she found herself debating whether it was better to disturb their settled existence with new ideas or simply let them be. She was finishing her first novel, *The Glory of the Conquered*, at the time of the founding of the Monist Society and ached for intellectual talk and stimulus. She knew nobody in Davenport with whom she could satisfactorily discuss the concept that governed her novel, the evolutionary idealism that she insisted on applying to women as well as men: perfection is attainable, but it must be fought for. Even her father failed her; he stuck to his religious and social convictions, smugly maintaining that a woman should marry and obey her husband because Eve had sinned. Although she loved and respected her father, Glaspell's experiences in Des Moines and Chicago had led her to Darwin and Nietzsche, away from the Christian Church in which she had been raised. Therefore, the Monist Society offered a welcome outlet for her frustrations and ideas and provided new friends. As Glaspell explained, it "attracted . . . all of us who were out of sorts with what we were supposed to believe."[13] She now felt supported in her refusal to accompany her parents to church and relished the thrill of forbidden Monist meetings on Sunday afternoons, for in spite of its more liberal German inhabitants, Davenport literally closed down on Sundays.

When the freethinkers, following Dell's lead, asserted that "the universe isn't two things. . . . It's one thing. . . . Monism!," Glaspell knew she had found people who would understand her.[14] She freely expressed her own belief, articulated earlier in stories such as "For Tomorrow," in the need for oneness and the transcendence of humankind's limitations, which could only be achieved in a struggle that would not be "woundless" but would bring those few individuals sufficiently courageous to risk pain and failure nearer to perfection.[15] Cook looked again at the slender woman whose serene hazel eyes were lit up by the same Nietzschean idealism that sustained him. He had recently given a paper that had sent a tremor through the staid members of the Contemporary Club, but fearing his father's disapproval, he had not done more than upset the surface. He had spoken of the "heroic history" of evolution, of one-celled plants and animals that had taken the leap and dared become more until some of them "crossed the difficult gap from invertebrate to vertebrate life" and eventually developed a brain. He asked:

May there not be men who are and shall be wild precursors of life's conquest of a new element? . . . Into what new and at first terrible environment do inspired men like Nietzsche, insane with truth, plunge and return gasping? In lonely rooms in the cities of men some souls have entered regions more desolate and unadapted to life than the high arctic—facing there a fate beside which freezing to death is peace. Out there you deal with phases of this fathomless universe you were not made to deal with—you do not inherit powers thereto adapted. The Nietzsches know their dangers perfectly, and yet they go—and perish. Likewise the Selachians went out and perished. Therefore we can breathe.[16]

So Cook drew Dell and Glaspell to him, and soon the three were deep into discussions of evolution, Nietzsche, and socialism. Dell, whom Glaspell described as a "cock-sure young Socialist," worked hard to convert the two idealists away from their belief in a chosen few to total trust in the power of the working classes.[17] Cook was the more fervent pupil, although his conversion did not last long. In 1910, he ran unsuccessfully for Congress as the Socialist Party candidate in Iowa's Second District, and in 1911, he wrote *The Chasm*, which Upton Sinclair acclaimed as an "out-and-out Socialist novel."[18] Also in 1910, he subjected the Contemporary Club audience to a simplistic defense of socialism, in which he reneged on his faith in the superman, declaring that the aim of the movement was to "teach the people so to organize themselves as to control the state"; he affirmed that "a nation does not exist, as friend Nietzsche, the latest great individualist maintains, for the purpose of producing half a dozen great men."[19] But he could not conceal his conviction that the socialist minority—to which he belonged—was privileged to lead the way.

As the monist and postmonist discussions flourished, Cook was impatiently awaiting his divorce from Sara. In the summer of 1906, as Cook was recovering from a breakdown—or mystical experience—Charles Eugene Banks, poet and newspaper editor (with whom he had coauthored the play *In Hampton Roads* in 1897), introduced him to a lively young woman from Chicago named Mollie Price; "she was young and free, and he felt something gallant and brave in her."[20] But Mollie was not to be easily pinned down, and after a few months of passionate trysts, lusting for further adventure, she joined a touring theater company and then went to New York to work on Emma Goldman's anarchistic magazine,

Mother Earth. Cook, overcome with passion, wrote grotesquely extravagant letters to Mollie, declaring that as he thought of her, "a small soft tassel in my corduroy trousers swelled a little" until "there wasn't room for it where it had been," and exclaiming with Whitmanesque fervor, "Oh full and joyous soul, oh wild, mad inundated soul."[21] On other occasions, this "tassel" became "the masculine cotter swollen stiff, its little mouth watering—it and I alike full of firm faith that over there in you was an orifice capable of containing the pink six and a half inch circumference."[22]

Word spread in Davenport that Cook, still undivorced, was pining for a Chicagoan lassie; although his father made his displeasure known, thirty-four-year-old Cook could not curb his ardor for twenty-year-old Mollie. But the dutiful son, not wanting to upset his parents excessively (and no doubt swayed by financial considerations), did not follow Mollie to New York. He insisted that they be legally married before openly living together. Nonetheless, in many respects, he had moved beyond Victorian moralities. The lovers were perfectly frank with each other, openly describing in their letters other sexual experiences they enjoyed during the long waiting period that society and law imposed on them and that Cook, "afraid I might impregnate you," saw as a means of birth control.[23] Cook struggled, not quite successfully, with his gut reaction to Mollie's philandering: "I am at heart monogamous. Unfortunately for my logic my desire that I be monogamous is not so strong as my desire that you should be. Which manifestly won't do in spite of much extant sophistry in support of exactly that position. I do not, at present, desire any woman in the world but you, and this, I suppose, helps strengthen the feeling that it would be righter and nicer if you felt the same way."[24]

On 24 December 1907, Cook railed at Mollie that 321 days had gone by since he had last seen her, but life had offered him some consolation during this time in the form of a rendezvous with Glaspell. Glaspell had been in New York in November to look for a publisher for *The Glory of the Conquered*, and Cook had asked her to bring back news of Mollie. He called on her on her return and was delighted by her person; "The girl herself is charming," he informed his Molliekins.[25] She was so charming that he invited her to supper at the cabin, only to be rebuffed by a last-minute cancellation. Cook, nettled by her refusal, told his betrothed that Glaspell had promised to "explain later. Meaning: the same old thing— the incredible attitude toward a man undivorced that prevails in this provincial place." He then inquired, "So you have given your infinitely dear body to Tom?," and assured her that he was glad, not for himself, but for her.[26]

It is impossible to know why Glaspell canceled the supper; Dell and another friend were also to be present, so it is unlikely that Davenport society would have disapproved, and it is also unlikely that Glaspell would have taken society's opinion into consideration. Perhaps the distance—the cabin was about nine miles out of town—and lack of transportation dissuaded her, for a few days later, she accepted an invitation to dine with Cook in town. Blissfully unaware of what was brewing, Cook posted Mollie: "Susan Glaspell is not taboo. She couldn't come down here to be sure, but last night my mother had her at our house in town—or rather, I did, for Susan and I talked and read most of the evening up in the attic den. I walked home with her, and am to go to see her."[27] Cook's letters to Mollie were now full of Glaspell, who, secure in the knowledge of Cook's engagement, thrilled at meetings that verged on the forbidden; one evening, she read him and Dell part of her novel, and he reported to Mollie: "'Tis great good stuff. Susie terrifies me with her overpowering ideal of life-long constancy to an early and vanished love. . . . Sweet as she is, she inspires such an attitude that to think of my kissing her is as though a devout Catholic should picture himself flirting with the Virgin Mary. Not but what it would be nice."[28]

Cook also wrote to Glaspell; he ended one letter, "You don't know how good it was to me to sit and talk last night with a really truly girl—oh a most wonderfully nice girl too. Weren't we all scared when we found the time? Guilty wretches! I hope Public Opinion in none of its forms will punish any of us, Susie."[29]

Both Dell, who chaperoned the couple, and Cook were awed by Glaspell's sobriety and sense of purpose. It took them some time to detect the humor that underlay it. Cook was dying to kiss her, "to see how she'd take it," he assured Mollie, but was too "terrified." The two men tried to shake up her sense of propriety—Dell by reciting "some super warm sonnets," which disappointingly only provoked a literary discussion on the merits of the form. Then Cook and Dell collaborated on "a sonnet to her on the subject of shoes and socks and their shocking Susan." Glaspell responded by stretching her foot and raising her skirts sufficiently to afford a provocative glimpse of silk stocking, which, she informed Cook, was identical to the stockings she had sent his beloved. She hoped Mollie would one day show him hers. Cook coyly assumed she meant "when they're off," to which Glaspell affirmed slyly with an innocent, "Of course." She followed this up by lending Cook a book Mollie had recommended; Cook reported this to his betrothed: "And here she got square again for that shoes and socks sonnet by saying as she handed it to me, 'I hope you won't be shocked.' "[30] A few days later, he confessed: "I don't know what gave me my untrue idea that she was superhuman. It was unjust to her."[31]

Glaspell and Cook bottled up any illicit feelings they had for each other when, in January 1908, Cook's divorce came through and he was finally free to marry Mollie. He was bewildered by parental and social expectations and a confused desire for both Mollie and Glaspell. Considering the difference in their ages irrelevant, not wishing to acknowledge that Mollie was almost a stranger since in eighteen months they had been together less than a dozen times, and obdurately disregarding the significance of numerous infidelities on both sides during that time, Cook plunged into his second marriage. Wretched, Glaspell wished he had never entered her dreams or her life; true, he had never given her any reason to hope for more, but they were both aware of a mutual yearning, and she longed for him and hated herself for wanting to ruin Mollie's happiness. She would never forget one night when "something outside ourselves brought us together, and there was a new thing between us ever after."[32] Cook wrote chastely of that occasion: "There in the starlit night their fingers exchanged a quick pressure. It sealed something between them—wide as the stars, long as time."[33]

In July, Glaspell left for Paris with Lulu Huffaker, her closest friend from Drake University. She resolved to forget Cook, and as they visited Holland and Belgium and then settled in Paris in a "little flat in the Latin quarter" on a quiet side street where "everything was cosy and homelike," Glaspell gradually accepted the futility of her love. Huffaker immersed her in Parisian bohemia, dragged her along the "quaint old streets," and insisted that she attend a full program of French classes, lectures, concerts, and operas. They spent the afternoons over cups of tea with friends, "many [of whom] had regular receiving days, and one would hear names, and meet people already well known, and many destined to be heard from later." Huffaker wrote stories for New York papers, and Glaspell mulled over a new novel, finding it extremely difficult to "fully throw *The Glory of the Conquered* [and Cook] from my mind."[34] But she did write some short stories, which she left with her "publishers in New York City on [her] way home."[35]

The Glory of the Conquered was published on 12 March 1909 while Glaspell was still in Paris. She was extremely excited at its appearance and almost wished she were back home to share her glory with her mother. She wrote: "I think you will understand from the way you felt in reading the book how much of myself I put into it. I put in it all that I had to give."[36] However complicated the emotions that inspired the novel, the plot is simple and in some ways echoes Elizabeth Stuart Phelps's *The Story of Avis* (1877).[37] Glaspell's Ernestine is a young painter who has reached the verge of greatness and is acknowledged as the "one American woman who was an artist instead of 'a woman who paints,'" but she has the courage to give up her work in order to help her husband, Karl Hubers, a famous scientist who has gone blind.[38] Karl dies, and Ernestine, after a period of mourning, returns to her easel and her brushes to produce a masterpiece that, she is convinced, only her love could have engendered.

In her first novel, Glaspell does not experiment with style or structure; her unaffected voice, occasionally lightened by a beguiling drollery, carefully avoids the maudlin and thus holds the reader's attention—although today's reader would prefer more medical details on Karl's illness and fewer declarations of ideal love. The uncluttered plot, linear in development, leads unswervingly to Glaspell's conclusion that although love can bring great joy to men and women, only work done well, at great emotional cost, will provide the satisfaction of recognizing "the oneness of the world."[39] Although Glaspell does not criticize the hypocritical, moneygrubbing mores of the turn of the century in the style of the realistic, muckraking novel, she subtly repudiates commonly held attitudes that relegated women to the role of mere playthings of men. Although the love between Karl and Ernestine is rapturous and he sincerely wants her to continue painting after their marriage, he reveals that the new twentieth-century values are alien to him when, recognizing the esteem in which the European, male-dominated art world holds her, he muses: "It seems so queer to me that you really do anything. . . . I mean it seems so queer you should really amount to anything."[40] He clearly values work, however, for after he goes blind, in a mood of rare self-pity, he exclaims, "What is a man without a man's work?"[41]

For Karl, literature and art are topics for women's clubs and cannot be compared in importance to science, a man's field. But for Ernestine, literature is a reflection of life, and she perceptively sees just where it fails: "So many things in literature stop short when the people are married. I think that's such an immature point of view—just as if that were the end of the story."[42] Glaspell realized that marriage, in her society, was the end of the story for women—none of her writing would ever deal with the romantic topic of how to ensnare a husband (but curiously, *The Visioning* [1911], her socialist novel, while mocking conventional marriage, is the only one to end with a hint of wedding bells).[43] In *The Glory of the Conquered*, marriage is tolerated as a way out of a frustrating newspaper job for Ernestine's friend Georgia, who nonetheless sees the futility of a girl "slav[ing] through the years she should have been frivolous only to have some man step in at the end and induce her to surrender the things she had gained through sacrifice and toil."[44]

If literature reflects life, in the case of *The Glory of the Conquered* it would be truer to say that the novel looked into its author's future. Ernestine's happiness is blighted by the death of an infant child, as Glaspell's would be by the birth of a stillborn child; protagonist and author care for their respective husbands with "the fierce tenderness of the defending mother" until they are both unexpectedly widowed.[45] In her fiction, Glaspell sees fit to grant an emotion akin to the "sublime joy" of motherhood to Ernestine only after Karl loses his sight and is rendered "in-valid" in the male sphere.[46] Rochester had to be similarly emasculated before Jane Eyre could publicly acknowledge her love and devote her life to him. To Glaspell, such sacrifice, in spite of her Christian upbringing, was not sufficient satisfaction. She viciously turns the screw when she kills Karl; only then can her heroine triumph, in work rather than in love. Ernestine, although a great artist, must, according to the codes of the day, be depicted first and foremost as a "real" woman who has borne a child and loved a man, but Glaspell recognizes that motherhood and love are obstacles to artistic fulfillment and clears Ernestine's path. Thirteen years later, when Cook died, Glaspell's grief charitably veiled the irony of life's sorry imitation of her art.

A woman's right to fulfillment through work instead of through motherhood or wifehood is vindicated in all of Glaspell's later writing, even though she argues at times that love is more important than productive work. Other themes present in *The Glory of the Conquered* that run through all of her works are an Emersonian need to be at one with nature and, even more persistent, the desire to overcome, to perfect, to do that which no one has ever done before and "take a bound ahead."[47] All of the concepts that *The Verge* (1921), her most experimental play, explores are in fact present in *The Glory of the Conquered*. Although Cook did not influence the writing of this novel, he immediately identified with the struggle it portrayed. He wrote Glaspell a long letter on his feelings about it:

I . . once, in a sweeping renunciation of selfishness, in self-abnegation, in giving-up (fatal, non-resistant, Christian word) the thing I most desired, was Christian to the core. (This at the time when I was most outspoken against conventional Christianity.) I most died of it. Self-renunciation is a long step toward spiritual self-annihilation. Christianity (the inmost reality of it, not its forms and husks) was a pit I once fell into, and the experience has left me suspicious of things that look like that pit.

Now you can see that there are some things in your book that must look like that pit to anyone who has had such an experience as mine. . . . I think the real truth about it is that you have fought your way out of the inmost essence of Christianity (the thing that was so nearly fatal to me) but without at the same time throwing off certain externals, certain virtues for instance commonly associated with Christianity, but not essentially Christian. For instance, I suspect in advance the title "The Glory of the Conquered" but Floyd goes to the essence of it and there finds you not Christian, but better than that, human, celebrating in reality the glory of the unconquered. Grim unconquered eyes look out of your book. There is "the right rebellious / Courage never to submit or yield" that Satan has in Hell.

So I see that all I do not covet of your book is the inessential a certain strain of Christian submissiveness which is apparent, not real.

. . . I love it for its throbbing vision of love made more beautiful by the film of tears that floats across the eyes. I feel in it your own heart's knowledge of love—saddened by knowledge that love is less strong than death—and often less strong than life itself—capable of ceasing though life itself goes on—as Karl's life must go on without his eyes.[48]

Cook did not disenchant her; she gathered that he understood the private mood that had made her write *The Glory of the Conquered* and loved him for it. He had also seen beyond the "Christian submissiveness" that served to make Ernestine's strength of purpose acceptable in a man's world, and he admired her—and her author for creating such a heroine.

According to Cook, Dell also lauded *The Glory of the Conquered*, exclaiming: "I make one fell covet of the whole thing. I covet her ability to write a novel."[49] Dell, in his autobiography, remembers that they had admired "the liveliness and humor" of the novel but that Cook had "deplored . . . the lamentable conventionality of the author's views of life."[50] If that was so, he did not tell Glaspell. A few years later, she gave *The Glory of the Conquered* to two of her closest friends in Provincetown, authors Hutchins Hapgood and his wife Neith Boyce. Hapgood was critical in his appraisal, though honest about his motives: "Neith and I, superior as we thought in our realistic experience, set this book down as a good example of the pre-Dreiser period of soft fiction. Perhaps we were somewhat influenced by the fact that the book was a good seller."[51]

The Glory of the Conquered certainly fits recent definitions of the much-maligned subgenre of the sentimental novel in that Glaspell's protagonist overcomes difficult circumstances and triumphs in a man's world; it offers "a blueprint for survival," even victory.[52] However, it differs from the nineteenth-century sentimental novel by not identifying success with marriage. In fact, the novel argues that only through her work can Ernestine achieve satisfaction and a feeling of oneness with herself and the world. *The Glory of the Conquered* is, of course, a sentimental novel according to the most basic definition: it is about a tragic love. But although overtly it conveys the message that love is the most important aspect of life for men and women, when read on a deeper level, it shows that only satisfactory, joy-bringing work can fulfill a human being of either sex.

Although, as Glaspell would discover, Davenport's self-righteous matrons disapproved of Ernestine's hard-won independence, critics welcomed *The Glory of the Conquered*. One reviewer stated: "This book may well become the model for the novelist of tomorrow. It is reactionary in that it tells a simple story quite simply, but it takes the nobler qualities of man and gives them full play."[53]

Glaspell returned from Paris in time to give her annual lecture for the ladies of Davenport's Tuesday Club. On 8 June 1909, she delivered an address entitled "Present Tendencies in Fiction," which denounced the commercialization of literature.[54] More than ever, she realized the disparity between her ideals and those of society at large, especially society as represented by the Tuesday Club matrons; most of these women, while flattered to have a published author in their midst, looked askance at the young woman who preferred a career to marriage. As a young girl, Glaspell had ached to join them, but she had moved so far beyond this circle of respectable Davenport ladies that she was irredeemable. Her frequent visits to the Cook cabin were also viewed with suspicion, although the ladies could only speculate about what drew her there.

Mollie Price Cook had just weaned her six-month-old daughter, Nilla, whom Glaspell adored; she would always be fond of the girl, frequently standing in as mother for her, fretting over late hours and first kisses. She also liked Mollie, whom she had come to know well in New York; she admired the younger woman's free spirit and her seemingly insouciant flouting of Davenport conventions. But Mollie was finding it extremely difficult to settle down to motherhood, and she hated Davenport and the priggish, gossiping society ladies who objected to her "going around in overalls and bare feet"—an act of rebellion Glaspell did not dare imitate.[55] Mollie wrote to Dell, who had fallen more than a little in love with her the previous summer: "Some of these days I have been so tired and glum that my very soul ached. . . . And they are talking terribly about me. . . . Susan has had it pretty hard, too, since her book came out."[56] Not expecting an adverse reaction to *The Glory of the Conquered* from the Davenport establishment, Glaspell turned to Mollie and Nilla for solace, as well as to Jig, with whom she could discuss her new novel, *The Visioning*.

The parallels between Cook's *The Chasm* and Glaspell's *The Visioning*, both—thanks to Glaspell's efforts—published by Stokes in 1911, are easy to spot. The two novels seek to convince the reader that an ideal world, like that of Edward Bellamy's *Looking Backward*, is indeed possible. The authors draw the ideology they claim will transform the unjust, war-torn, and hungry world from Dell's socialist convictions, tempered by a purely American idealism garnered from an amalgam of Emerson's transcendentalism, Nietzsche's overcoming, and Haeckel's oneness. Cook's novel is more disquisitional and certainly more ambitious; he naively attempts to portray the Russian Revolution of 1905 with no firsthand knowledge to sustain him and stretches the plot to ensure that Marion can fall into Bradfield's arms at just the right moment. Glaspell, on the other hand, begins her novel with a barely plausible episode that is laden with suspense and drama; she is then faithful to the bounds of possibility within the improbable situation she has created as she magisterially charts the psychological development of Katie Jones and her brother, Wayne. Katie and Wayne slowly turn from total acquiescence to the old system and the unthinking discipline demanded by their army lives and learn to adopt a more generous spirit that is prepared to question the existing order and meditate on its significance.

The Chasm and *The Visioning* not only recognize that the wealthy and privileged are responsible for the miserable conditions suffered by the working classes but also expose how society stifles the woman of the middle and upper classes, leaving her no means of valid self-expression. Marion, Cook's protagonist, realizes that her options are limited: she can preen herself as an "ornament," or she can dedicate herself to spurious charity work, as does a minor character in *The Visioning*.[57] Another possibility, devotion to preserving "those beautiful old things which the generations have left us," all the while smiling sweetly into a husband's eyes, constitutes the future that Katie boldly rejects.[58] Glaspell's protagonist, echoing the convictions expressed by Mary in "For Tomorrow," learns to question the old values and decides that "nothing's too precious to be touched—if touching it can make things better."[59] Her transformation from a "bully Army girl" to a thinking person is completed when she realizes that her happiness lies with Alan Mann, not only a common soldier but a deserter to boot. Thus, rejecting class divisions in her acceptance of the equality of all human beings, Katie transcends the institutional prejudices she has absorbed since childhood and acknowledges the power of progress and oneness.

Cook's attitude toward women was, in many ways, highly enlightened. Ma-Mie had shown him what a woman could aspire to even when her horizons were bound by marriage. She wrote to her son, then at Harvard and desperately counting on spending a year in Greece, for which the family did not have sufficient funds: "I also have always longed for the art of the world, and wondered sometimes why I was held here, but that fact has forced my spirit to find its own beauty."[60] She directed him to the artistic spirit of Greece and taught him that a woman, as much as a man, is an independent creature, but she also infused in him a belief in his ability to attain genius, which placed an intolerable burden on him. Ma-Mie had deposited all of her love and faith in Jig, so that as an adult, he sought the same sort of confirmation in women, hoping they would become an avenue to genius for him. He wrote to Mollie while they were still courting: "It is immortality that a man seeks in the body of a woman—yes and he is seeking to give it as well as to attain it!"[61] Years later, unable to accept the fact that Glaspell, a mere woman, was the better playwright, he jotted down an idea for a play: "Play of Madame Curie and her husband—she discovering radium through the guidance of his superior sources of knowledge, he having sunk back into the unconscious."[62] Glaspell quotes this in her biography of Cook but fails to comment on the light it sheds on his need to prove his superiority. He never wrote a play on Marie Curie, but he did create a hero who influences the mind of his beloved in *The Spring* (1921).

As a bachelor, Cook had given much thought to matrimony and sex. In a diary entry on 14 January 1900, he set out his creed: "I believe it is impossible to live aright under present laws and usages—either married or unmarried. . . . The woman must not be owned by the man. She should be financially independent, and like animals should have intercourse only for the sake of children. . . . The father of her children she should be absolutely free to determine. . . . The best solution under present conditions is probably marriage with very strong self-restraint, and a mutual pre-agreement to separate at the wish of either."[63]

Cook had never worked out where such freedom would take him. He spent the summer of 1909 delighting in his daughter Nilla and falling deeper and deeper in love with Susan Glaspell. By November, Glaspell was feeling distinctly uncomfortable in Davenport and left to stay with a friend who had joined the Forest Service in Colorado, where "possibilities [were] wrought in the proportions of the mountains—wide, lonely, naked, austere, but calling upon human achievement to grow great."[64] Cook wrote an enigmatic "S." beside November 1909 in a chronology of his life that he devised to help him construct his never-written autobiography. Beside December, he recorded the cryptic words "to Colorado." But for all of its promise, Colorado was devoid of love, and Glaspell returned to Davenport early in 1910. Cook had done more than mope while she was away; Mollie was expecting their second child. Harl would be born in August.

The normally dreary month of February was brightened for intellectual Davenporters by the controversy raised by the publication of University of Chicago professor Foster's *The Finality of the Christian Religion*. Glaspell inquired why the library had not acquired a copy of the book and accused the library board of unwarranted censorship, asking why "the religion of the future must be investigated at private expense?"[65] The president of the library board thought it best to shield himself with the law, which he interpreted as not allowing "religion, past, present or future, to be investigated or taught, or discussed at public expense."[66] A veritable battle ensued, with the *Davenport Democrat* printing letters for and against a book that no one had read but that zealous guardians of religion assumed—hastily misconstruing the title—advocated the demise of religion. According to Glaspell's description of the hostilities, "the tempest" was brewed "in the very largest teacup."[67] The candidate for mayor that year sagely aligned himself with the protesters, and their votes won him the election. Eventually, the library board was persuaded to buy the book, but as Glaspell snidely explained in "Finality in Freeport," a story she published some years later, "the three thousand citizens who had been ready to fight and die for the book managed to restrain their impatience and, doubtless on the theory that they could not all read it at once, politely waited their turn—so politely that there were many days when the book rested peacefully upon the shelves."[68]

After Glaspell instigated this struggle for religious liberty in Davenport, Cook came to her aid with great alacrity and, at the peak of his militant socialist fervor, insisted on pointing out that the library building had been subsidized by Andrew Carnegie, whose millions came from the "unpaid labor . . . of the steel-workers of Homestead."[69] The episode brought the two writers closer together, and as Mollie awaited the birth of her son, Cook and Glaspell spent more and more time allegedly discussing a novel they would coauthor. When Dell, who by this time was married and working on the *Chicago Evening News*, visited the cabin in the summer, he and his wife "heard the two sides of the same upsetting story. George . . . had come to realize that he had been in love with Susan all along, without knowing it."[70] Davenport society relished the scandal, siding with Mollie and making life impossible for the lovers. Glaspell went to New York, and Cook left for Chicago, where he worked on a dictionary project until Dell managed to get him a job writing for the *Friday Literary Supplement* of the *Chicago Evening News*.

The need to justify a love that hurt others so much would always haunt Glaspell. In *The Road to the Temple*, in which she obliterates herself, she articulates her feelings as impersonally as possible: "Love may be strong as death. Death you will face easily for love, for that somehow does itself. Even more than disgrace you will face for love. You will risk hurt and shame to those you love. You will violate your own sense of fairness and right. In a world that is falling around you love dwells as sure, as proud, as if life had come into being that this might be."[71] In almost everything she wrote from this time on, particularly *Fidelity* (1915) and *Alison's House* (1930), Glaspell tried to resolve the contradictions that her love for Cook had generated. She had always been aware of the conflict between the individual's needs and the social good, and much of her writing questions whether individuals should sacrifice themselves to the good of others, to the imperatives of society, art, literature, politics, and convention.

Sustained by her mother's pride and appreciation, Glaspell had managed to stare down Davenport's accusatorial gaze after the publication of *The Glory of the Conquered*, but she received very little encouragement from home for *The Visioning*. Davenporters recognized the resemblance between the army garrison in the novel and the garrison on Rock Island, and tempers flared at the suggestion that townspeople had served as models for the minor characters; censorship of the army and commendation of a woman rebelling against a stifling marriage set even more tongues wagging, especially once Glaspell's romance with Cook became public. So Glaspell could imagine how *Fidelity* would be received in Davenport and was glad she would not be there when it came out. Emotionally, it was the most taxing novel she had ever written, but she did not shrink from the task, perhaps seeking a cathartic release from her feelings of guilt. Cook supported her in this autoanalysis, in which she made his youthful thoughts on love her own and set out the terms of their marriage: namely, that they would never sully their love by clinging to its fading shadow.

For the plot of *Fidelity*, Glaspell elaborated on her own experience, a technique she used in most of her fiction. Here, Ruth Holland falls in love with a married man, Stuart Williams, whose wife refuses to grant him a divorce. Ruth and Stuart leave Freeport, but news of their illegal union follows them from town to town, and they are ostracized in all communities. After eleven years, Stuart's wife realizes that she is ruining her own life by indulging in hatred for Ruth and Stuart, and, at long last, she instigates divorce proceedings. But Ruth, recognizing that love has waned, decides to leave Stuart. She says to her brother, "It isn't unfaithful to turn from a person you have nothing more to offer, for whom you no longer make life a living thing. It's more faithful to go."[72]

This seemingly straightforward tale is carefully constructed around moments of suspense and disclosure, moving fluidly between the past and the present and between the main plot and various subplots that parallel it. Ruth Holland's story is introduced from the standpoint of Deane Franklin, an admirer from her school days whose marriage to Amy collapses because of his sympathy for Ruth's impossible predicament. Nevertheless, it "occurred to him that if it had not been for [Ruth] he might have fallen into accepting many things more or less as the rest of the town did. It seemed now that as well as having caused him much pain she had brought rich gain; for those questionings of life, that refusal placidly to accept, had certainly brought keener satisfaction than he could have had through a closer companionship with facile acceptors."[73]

The novel is a meditation on the transience of love and on its effects not only on the lovers but also on everyone connected with them. Glaspell scathingly attacks small-town society, its refusal to progress to new modes of living or to countenance those who do not conform. She is particularly scornful of women who, like Amy, Deane Franklin's wife, fail to cast off the mold in which society has formed them. Amy believes that "woman . . . [is] the guardian of society" and accepts wholeheartedly that "society is nothing more than life as we have arranged it. It is an institution. One who defies it—deceives it—must be shut out from it."[74] Such convictions echo those expressed by minor characters in *The Visioning*, and it is perfectly clear that Glaspell's sympathies lie with women who dare to step outside the bounds of convention, as does Ruth Holland. But she generously recognizes the forces that hold other women back: fear of losing their "privileged" status in patriarchal society leads them to adopt a conservative stance, but even more compelling is a profound maternal instinct that prompts them, "no matter how daring for themselves, [to be] cautious for others."[75] In *Fidelity*, Glaspell is content to merely hint at the dilemma of the society wife; in later writing, the play *Chains of Dew* (1922) and the novel *Ambrose Holt and Family* (1931), she focuses on how difficult it is for a society wife to escape.

The other type of woman that Glaspell introduces into her cast in *Fidelity* is the wife who does not allow a dour marriage to stifle her love of life. Annie, a school friend who was not of Ruth's "set" socially but who does not shun her when she returns to Freeport after her father's death, is realistic and brave; she recognizes that the romantic love she had for her husband did not last, that it did not "open up . . . to companionship," and that therefore she either has to "give up—go under—or get through myself what I wasn't going to get through anyone else."[76] Annie was "keenly alive," yearning for a life outside the round of daily chores, but "valiant" and quite "unconquerable." Her baby draws Ruth to her, satisfying for a while Ruth's longing for children, denied by the circumstances of her relationship with Stuart.

Before *Fidelity* could be written from the relatively peaceful vantage point of conjugal bliss, Cook had to obtain his second divorce. The obligatory waiting period was hard on both Cook and Glaspell; they could not meet in Davenport, and Chicago, full of acquaintances, was not a safe haven. Mollie, too vital and intelligent to stay quietly in Davenport, had taken the children to California, where, for a time, she ran Prince Hopkins's school for boys, Boyland. Although Maria Montessori highly approved of the school's liberal teaching methods, which were similar to hers, the local police, suspecting pro-German activities, did not. After firmly declaring herself a pacifist before a Los Angeles court, Mollie decided to return to Chicago to be closer to the children's grandparents, who were anxious to oversee their education.[77] After Cook's death, she would marry William Rapp, a young man who reminded her of her first husband. Rapp was one of the last people to see Cook in Greece before his illness and death. On his return to Chicago, he delivered photographs and news to Mollie and, in spite of her determination never to remarry, wooed her and won her hand in the twinkling of an eye. According to Nilla Cook, Bill and Mollie were "ridiculously happy."[78]

While Cook was in Chicago, Glaspell—with the faithful Lulu Huffaker—conquered the bohemians of New York's Greenwich Village, paving the way for Jig. She reveled in the easy atmosphere of Washington Square, where nobody raised their eyebrows at free love, divorce, or remarriage, where rents were low, and where, according to the reporter of revolutions Jack Reed,

> We dare to think as Uptown wouldn't dare,
> Blazing our nights with arguments uproarious;
> What care we for a dull old world censorious
> When each is sure he'll fashion something glorious?[79]

The Liberal Club, where Dell was busy entertaining bohemia with his short plays, was one of Glaspell's favorite haunts; here she met the people who would take part, in one way or another, in the drama of the years to come: the sisters Anna and Rose Strunsky; William English Walling, who married Anna; Ida Rauh and Max Eastman; Neith Boyce and Hutchins Hapgood; Mary Heaton Vorse; Edna Kenton; Jack Reed; and Harry Kemp, among others.

Novelist and journalist Mary Heaton Vorse, eager to escape New York's clammy heat, had happened upon Provincetown, an ideal spot in which to sequester herself and her children during the summer. Others of the bohemian crowd followed her to the sleepy fishing village at the tip of Cape Cod's crooked finger, which beckoned the writer or artist, promising a sort of summer extension of Washington Square. Cook and Glaspell spent the summer of 1912 there in a whitewashed clapboard cottage so close to the sea that the tide, rejoiced Glaspell, was always trying to "climb in my window."[80]

After what seemed like an interminable waiting period, Cook's divorce came through, and on 14 April 1913, Susan Glaspell, then thirty-seven years old, and George Cram Cook were married in Weehawken, New Jersey. As was customary among Greenwich Village bohemians, she kept her maiden name. There were no jovial wedding announcements or celebrations; for her parents' sake, Glaspell would have enjoyed a church wedding in Davenport, with all of the attendant ritual, but for herself, the religious aspects of matrimony played no part in her feelings. As for Cook, he had come to hate the solemnity and pomp of such occasions, having been there twice before. So they were married very quietly by the mayor in the home of Mrs. Frederick, an ex-Davenporter; dinner with Huffaker at the Brevoort marked the official beginning of a new life for Glaspell and Cook.[81] They withdrew to the rented cottage in Province-town for their honeymoon, planning to spend at least a year in what Cook assured Dell would be "a bully atmosphere for work."[82]

The year was marked by two cruxes in Glaspell's life: she conceived a child, and she lost it. In *The Road to the Temple*, Glaspell surrenders but one page to her frustrated motherhood, giving no dates and thus refusing to satisfy our curiosity as to premarital intimacies (and there are no letters comparable to those Cook sent Mollie to supply us with vicarious thrills). All Glaspell tells us is that "the doctor was not jovial that day in the fall. The other doctor is out of town no one to give the anaesthetic; the nurse has not come from Boston. Jig helps the doctor. I was turned the other way, but saw his face in the glass, as he was carrying things away."[83] Cook helped Glaspell recover emotionally from the stillbirth of their child, and early in 1915, she had a fibroid tumor removed; they both wanted children, but sadly "there were other disappointments."[84] Although Glaspell was prepared to admit that the absence of children gave a greater intensity to their love, she refused to accept that her work could ever take the place of a baby. For her, even the suggestion that she did not place motherhood above all else was offensive, although in her writing she rarely depicts her heroines as mothers. Many of them have children, but in almost all cases, motherhood is secondary in their lives; the one exception is Irma Lee in the novel *Fugitive's Return* (1929).

In the spring of 1914, the house at 564 Commercial Street opposite their cottage came up for sale, and Cook and Glaspell, deftly burying socialist prejudice against acquiring property, bought it. It was a similar clapboard cottage but with a half story added under the sloping roof, numerous small rooms, a dark staircase, and hateful partitions down-

Susan Glaspell
(Courtesy of the University Libraries, The University of Iowa)

stairs, which Jig demolished with exuberant swings of the axe accompanied by raving cries of "Let there be light."[85] He transformed the ground floor into a sitting room, dining room, and kitchen and made the upstairs into two small rooms and one large room at the front. Glaspell took particular delight in the view from this upstairs front room of the ancient willows and elms along Commercial Street and the indefatigable waves that beat and burst on the pilings of the old wharf to the left of the cottage they had rented.

The spacious, airy room was to be her bedroom/study, but, as Glaspell wrote in *The Road to the Temple*, "that was the summer misfortune befell my heart, and the doctor said I could go up no stairs."[86] This unspecified "heart lesion" contributed to the aura of delicacy that, while characterizing her manner and appearance, effectively disguised her inner strength.[87] But Jig would not allow a weak heart to ruin her enjoyment of the best room in their little house; he enjoined her and Ma-Mie, who had come to help them settle in, bringing "energy and shrewd amusement" with her, to wait a while before converting the sitting room into his wife's bedroom.[88] He then cut a hole in the kitchen ceiling and from an odd assortment of pipes, planks, and rope constructed "the marvel of the village"—an elevator. It was "painted bright blue," Glaspell proudly reported in *The Road to the Temple*, "and the pipes that balance my weight are silver, and look like organ pipes."[89]

As always, Cook gave himself totally to the task at hand, playing at bricklayer, plumber, or carpenter as the need arose. Glaspell, as much as Ma-Mie, beamed with maternal pride at his craftsmanship; ecstatic, she watched as her husband made a dining table from boards of North Carolina pine that he sawed, "burned with gasoline paint torch," and waxed to bring out the grain of the wood. Identifying a "perfect musical staff" in the pattern of one board, he etched into the wood the notes of an old Dutch song, to which, at the height of his socialist enthusiasm, he had written "The Song of the Worker." Friends who sat around the table talking, drinking, and rubbing the wood energetically to give it a "richer and more luminous" luster every evening would, "at certain moments of conviviality . . . bend over the notes . . . and sing":

> The song that we sing is the death of your day!
> The sledge that we swing is the smash of your sway—
> Blow after blow till your chains let go,
> And the hold of your gold gives way.[90]

The Provincetown natives were fascinated by the house—as well as the eccentric goings-on of the arty bohemians from New York—and called it "The Gay House." Jig painted the window frames red and, following the advice of artist Charles Demuth, daubed the inside walls with orange and yellow paint. Ma-Mie demanded a purple door to her room, but her son's door had to be "the deepest blue of the sky, blue of eternity."[91] In this house, Glaspell lived her romance with Cook and then her idyll with Norman Matson; she kept it as her home until her death.

Cook and Glaspell were so absorbed in their little cottage that even the outbreak of the European war in August 1914 could not ruin their enthusiasm. But talk around the "musical table" or rowdy midnight bonfires on the beach turned inevitably to the war; the "spirit of gentle hilarity" that a bottle of good whiskey brought from New York generally provoked was transmuted into a violent mood of guilt and uncertainty.[92] The older Provincetown bohemians were forced to recognize that their liberal idealism had not prevented war and sank into a soul-searching, apathetic gloom, whereas their younger, wilder comrades naively clung to a belief in their power to influence emperors, tsars, and kaisers. Recruiting Ma-Mie to help with the wording, these innocents drafted a resolution calculated to convert the world's rulers to the principles of socialism and thus end all wars.[93]

Not all of the summering bohemians were so solipsistic in their reflections on the war; Glaspell and Cook at last found an opportunity to marry Nietzsche and socialism in an optimistic appraisal of events. Jack Reed, although horrified by America's commercial attitude toward the war, voiced their lucubrations in *The Masses*: "We, who are Socialists, must hope . . . that out of this horror of destruction will come far-reaching social changes." He then distanced Provincetown and the United States from the conflagration, asserting: "This is not Our War."[94] The Provincetowners adopted pacifism and nonintervention as their creed and preached a glorious role for their country: the United States' contribution to the progress of humanity would reside in "keeping alive in the world the light of reason."[95] When the United States eventually entered the war, Cook would echo such rhetoric in his justification of the work of the Provincetown Players, the only little theater that survived conscription and voluntary enlistment. He was not alone in his disapproval of President Woodrow Wilson's decision to come to the aid of European democracy; women who were denied the vote found themselves in jail for pointing out that true democracy should begin at home, and *The Masses*, edited by Max Eastman and Floyd Dell, was accused of conspiracy against the government and obstruction of enlistment in 1917. Two trials were held in *The Masses* case, but each time, the jury disagreed and in October 1918 the matter was dropped.[96]

The clapboard cottage on Commercial Street was shaken by cataclysms of a more personal nature than those that tore through Europe. Glaspell was learning about life with Cook. She learned to live with his moods, to glide over the days of depression and dejection and to rejoice with him in

George Cram Cook
(Courtesy of the University Libraries, The University of Iowa)

moments of unbounded enthusiasm. At this time, when not immersed in carpentry and plumbing, Cook was intent on starting a "literary-political weekly of the English type" to promote American writers.[97] For inspiration, he imported kegs of wine from Brooklyn, which he christened after his Greek heroes, Sappho, Aeschylus, Sophocles, and Euripides, and he continued to believe in free love and seek out women who would heal his soul.[98] Glaspell, following Ma-Mie's example, cajoled and mothered him, giving those who were not too close the impression of a bond of "exceptional congeniality"; the chains of love fettered her own ambitions and impressed her into his game of Big Bear and Little Bear.[99] But there were moments when she could not stand his surly cafards and escaped to

Davenport to visit her parents. Cook wrote groveling letters begging her to return and was overjoyed when "the L.B. has figured out (rightly!) that maybe the B.B. does love her after all."[100] Glaspell always returned to Cook, but inevitably his mood swings affected her sense of stability. She was acutely conscious of her generally frail health and took great care of her heart. And now dental problems added to her worries; perhaps as an excuse to get away from Cook, she insisted on treatment in Chicago.

When Cook was not drunk or depressed, he turned for company to Hutchins Hapgood, an extrovert journalist and writer who shared his ideal of free love. They would pace "up-along" and "down-along" Provincetown's one street "interminably talking about the universe," frightening away lesser idealists who did not understand that "they could find so much of it to talk about" and who hurried off as soon as they saw the pair.[101] When not talking about the universe, Jig and Hutch played chess while their wives tended the Hapgood children and chatted. Neith Boyce and Glaspell were roughly the same age and had similar backgrounds; Boyce had come to New York from Indiana and was a journalist and novelist by the time Hutch met and wooed her. An independent young woman, like most Greenwich Villagers, she kept her maiden name and continued to write after marriage, but she found Hapgood's extramarital affairs difficult to tolerate, especially when he was overcome by jealousy at her attempts to follow his example. Glaspell frequently turned to Boyce for solace and advice, and she would always find an understanding friend in Hapgood.

One night, Jig's overwhelming interest in kings, queens, and pawns made Glaspell feel neglected and she retired, leaving the two men at their chessboard. According to Hapgood, she always felt threatened by the "self-sufficiency of Jig and me in the game." Some hours went by, until Glaspell, resentment magnified by sleeplessness, rushed back to Hapgood's home "with blood in her eye." Jig, bemused by his wife's unaccustomed wrath, abandoned the game and allowed himself to be led home. But now Hapgood, the moves of queens dispelling all possibility of sleep, walked "up-along" Commercial Street pondering the moon; as he passed by the Cook house, his musings were disturbed by Glaspell's ecstatic cries of "darling, don't bite." Years later, when Hapgood demurely reminded her of this incident, Glaspell responded with a "laugh and blush."[102]

The Greenwich Villagers who withdrew to Provincetown for the summer did not wholly succumb to the holiday spirit; they brought with them work habits that kept them at desks or easels all morning. And even talk on the beach could be classed as work when it helped a young novelist overcome serious problems of structure or plot. Sinclair Lewis was writing his first novel at the time, and Glaspell, always drawn to younger, boyish novices, spent many hours discussing his work and the topic that so interested her—the fate of the young woman trapped in a midwestern town. When *Our Mr. Wrenn* was published, Lewis inscribed a copy to his mentor, "To Susan Glaspell, but for whose encouragement and understanding this book would never have been finished, and to George Cram Cook—prince—from the author."[103]

Winters in Provincetown were miserably cold, and although Glaspell and Cook had intended to stay year-round, they often escaped to New York, friends, and well-heated apartments. Cook needed the stimulus of civilization to write the "New York Letters" he still sent regularly to the *Chicago Evening News*, and Glaspell was glad to be among friends. They delighted in long evenings of talk at the Liberal Club and quickly spent any check they received for the publication of a short story at the Brevoort, a restaurant favored by Villagers at times of relative opulence. Otherwise, they ate at Polly's, officially the Greenwich Village Inn, where Cook could be sure of abuse from Hippolyte Havel, Emma Goldman's onetime lover. The rotund Bohemian spat "bourgeois pigs" at all of the Villagers but then indulged in heated discussions on anarchy and culture. Mabel Dodge's multifarious "salon" on Fifth Avenue, just above Washington Square, appealed to neither Glaspell nor Cook. She seemed too frivolous to them, and Cook could not tolerate the spotlight shining on someone else for long. Dodge's public passion for Jack Reed, and then Maurice Sterne, grated on the remnants of their Victorian sensibilities.

Every other Saturday in New York, Glaspell left her husband to his own devices and joined the "unorthodox women" at their Heterodoxy luncheons at the Liberal Club.[104] Marie Jenney Howe, "a rare person who did a great deal for the liberation of women," started these luncheons in 1912 in an effort to free women, even if only for a few hours, from the burden of their daily obligations.[105] Her sharp intelligence and affectionate nature inspired them to cathartic self-expression; they defied taboos and forbidden topics and discussed men, women, suffrage, and even birth control, then a criminal offense. Glaspell's friends were Heterodoxy women, including Mary Heaton Vorse and the literary critic Edna Kenton, Cook and Glaspell's most stalwart aide during later crises. Crystal Eastman, a lawyer whose brother, Max, was editor of *The Masses*, was also a member, as was his wife, Ida Rauh, who would star in the productions of the Provincetown Players. Other members included writer and feminist theorist Charlotte Perkins Gilman, playwright Zona Gale, socialist and labor organizer Elizabeth Gurley Flynn, and the feminist actresses Helen Westley and Fola La Follette.[106]

In February 1914, Howe organized two feminist mass meetings at the People's Institute of the Cooper Union under the joint title "What Is Feminism?" Male Greenwich Villagers, among them Floyd Dell, Max Eastman, and George Middleton, La Follette's husband, were included among the speakers invited to offer short papers on what feminism meant to them. Although Cook did not contribute a paper, he undoubtedly considered himself a feminist in his espousal of free love for both men and women, and he agreed with his young friend Dell that "the women's movement of today is but another example of that readiness of women to adapt themselves to a masculine demand."[107] He also must have discussed the matter when putting the universe to rights with Hapgood, applauding his conviction "that when women work efficiently and intimately in the larger society . . . there will be a new charm to men's work . . . and something of the color and appeal and romance of the sex will be introduced into the work-a-day world."[108] Glaspell found such attitudes shallow and cheap, but although she envied the women in certain states who had the right to vote, she was never militant in the suffrage movement, preferring to expend her "limited strength" on expressing her convictions in plays and novels.[109]

CHAPTER THREE

A Sense of Mission

Cook's regular column, the "New York Letter," in the *Chicago Evening News* paid for their winter lodgings and afforded what both Cook and Glaspell considered an invaluable "perk"—theater tickets. At the Jewish Neighborhood Playhouse, their favorite, they were fortified by that "strong inherited religious feeling" they regarded as essential to the mystery of a national drama.[1] But the evenings they spent at Broadway theaters left them deeply dissatisfied, their imaginations unchallenged by the prosaic old "patterns" of box-office successes.

They were not the only midwesterners aching for authentic dramatic experience. According to legend, the Greenwich Villagers were initiated into the dramatic arts by an impromptu production of Lord Dunsany's *The Glittering Gate*, the Irish Abbey Theatre success, on the premises of the Washington Square Bookshop.[2] Although the acting was atrocious, a thespian nerve was so stimulated that the Liberal Club, egged on by Floyd Dell, set up a "dramatic branch." Dell offered a short play about "a Spanish grandee and his gypsy sweetheart" for the debut of this company and looked about for actors. Dismissing Cook, whose silver locks and Anglo-Saxon features belied any ancestral Spanish blood, Dell turned to Lawrence Langner, an English-born patent lawyer who sported a black mustache. Langner, though a little dubious, accepted the part only to discover at the first rehearsal in Theodore Dreiser's apartment that his gypsy sweetheart was to be played by a young woman from Chicago whose dark eyes were her sole qualification for the part. But Langner's precise British enunciation set Dell's teeth on edge; he could not envision a Spanish grandee whose accent did not betray midwestern origins, and accordingly, preempting Langner's resignation, he thanked him and donned the Spaniard's costume himself.

Although Liberal Club members who had not been slighted by author or actors applauded wholeheartedly, the miffed minority hatched plans for a theater of their own. Langner led this faction, along with Ida Rauh, who had done some acting before she married Max Eastman; now that her marriage was tottering, she resolved to revive her histrionic skills. They gathered a group of theatrically inclined mavericks, including Robert Edmond Jones and Sam Eliot (who were already known for their scenic designs), Helen Westley, Edward Goodman, Philip Moeller, and Josephine A. Meyer from the Socialist Press Club. Cook, Glaspell, and Lulu Huffaker, who shared Langner's enthusiasm for Maurice Browne's Chicago Little Theatre, were also invited. Glaspell was in Davenport visiting her parents for Christmas, but Cook kept her posted on the activities of the newly named Washington Square Players. He wrote scathingly of the efforts to entice two millionairesses to donate their fortunes to the new theater, but by 26 January 1915, he had become more personally involved, confiding his aspirations—which would not be satisfied by the Washington Square Players—to his wife: "You know I Harbor a Belief that maybe I can act."[3]

The Washington Square Players finally found a little theater that suited their purposes: the Bandbox Theatre at 57th Street and Third Avenue, which seated 300 people. Langner, business manager for the novice thespians, consulted with Edward Goodman, their chosen director (whom Huffaker would later marry), and rented the theater for performances on Fridays and Saturdays. The first bill was made up of three short plays by Langner, Goodman, and Maurice Maeterlinck and closed with a divertissement that was "heartily applauded." This opening program reflected the aims of the Players—as well as their future development—as set out in their manifesto: "Preference will be given to American plays, but we shall also include in our repertory the works of well-known European authors which have been ignored by commercial managers."[4]

The first night, 19 February 1915, was marred by a "quaking in a dozen pairs of shoes" as the Washington Square Players prepared to raise the curtain on a full house.[5] Backstage, time flew by as hitch after hitch was overcome, but in the auditorium, it crawled: would the curtain ever go up? The murmuring of the restless audience rose and fell as tempers frayed and patience gave out. Glaspell did her best to appease Cook, entreating him to wait just a little longer. But finally Cook could stand it no more and offered a formidable early example of audience participation. " 'I've had enough of this,' he cried . . . and went into a violent outbreak about it being a quarter of nine, and the curtain not yet up."[6] But the professional critics, who had received invitations from Huffaker, press agent for the Washington Square Players, were not put off by the late start; they gave their blessing to the novices, claiming they had made a "Big Hit" and that "if they keep up their present pace they will make the Bandbox an institution."[7]

Cook was irked that the Washington Square Players had chosen to ignore his newly discovered acting skills and perhaps even peeved that they had not named him their director. But he was fascinated by this new American theater and advocated the rejection of European masters in favor of new American playwrights. Thus, when Glaspell suggested they write a play themselves, Cook pounced on the idea; psychoanalysis, a fad that had absorbed Greenwich Villagers for some time, would provide the material for his renewed storming of the Washington Square Players.

After the summer of 1914, their ideals shattered by the outbreak of war in Europe, Greenwich Villagers had turned inward for release from tensions that previously had found an escape route in vinous political discussions or elegant highbrow mixing with dangerous radicals such as Big Bill Heywood or Emma Goldman. Psychoanalysis, which was initially "thought to be just as queer as all the other attempts people were making to achieve some kind of social adaptation," had been elbowing itself into their sphere for some time. Mabel Dodge had held an unsuccessful "Psychoanalytic Evening" during her winter of fame in New York; of the two famous practitioners of psychoanalysis at the time, Ernest Sachs had refused to come, and A. A. Brill offended many guests with his "assertions about unconscious behavior and its give-aways."[8] But the new fad gradually threatened to take over as those who could afford it sought the help of ever more expensive analysts who would show them how to free their libidos. Sigmund Freud's work on the subconscious was Americanized into a "new science of the soul" that taught that all repression was pernicious.[9]

Rumblings of Freud's theories had reached the United States well before his only visit in 1909. The unconscious had fascinated nineteenth-century intellectuals, and by the beginning of the twentieth, sufficient adventurous spirits had succumbed to the spell of hypnosis and the theory of associations to assure Freud a feverishly excited audience when he lectured at the Clark University twentieth-anniversary celebrations. According to Ernest Jones, his biographer, Freud composed "each lecture in half an hour's walk beforehand" and in his five lectures managed to survey the whole field of psychoanalysis, offering an optimistic and relatively simple version—"condensed almost to the point of caricature"—of the theories he had worked out in *The Interpretation of Dreams*, *Three Contributions to a Theory of Sex*, *The Psychology of Everyday Life*, and *Studies in Hysteria*.[10] Reactions to the published lectures were not all favorable: "An ordinary reader would gather that Freud advocates free love, removal of all restraints, and a relapse into savagery," was a common objection to his teaching.[11] American proselytizers, among them Max Eastman, found sufficient evidence in Freud's Clark lectures to affirm joyously that "we have but to name these nervous diseases with their true name, it seems, and they dissolve like the charms in a fairy story."[12] Others were more discerning: Hapgood would later admit that the 1910s and 1920s had seen a gross "misinterpreting and misapplying [of] the general ideas underlying analysis"; as late as 1927, Sandor Ferenczi, who in 1909 had accompanied Freud to America, wrote that psychoanalysis in the United States was still "somewhat superficial and that the deeper side [was] somewhat neglected."[13]

Hapgood was older than many of the Greenwich Village set, and his private struggle against bourgeois values had armed him with a skeptical detachment that frequently made him a better judge than most. He scorned the newest fad, believing that "there is something in the human soul which is beyond analysis, and that is the woe caused by the realization of the infinite."[14] Others of the group, however, saw their salvation in Freud's teaching. Eastman and Dell, converted at Dodge's "Psychoanalytic Evening," were the earliest apostles of Freud in the American intellectual world. Troubled by writer's block, various symptomatic ailments, and the dilemma of reconciling willful sexual inclinations with their wives' standards of fidelity, they were dazzled by the promise of psychoanalysis and blinded to its incompatibilities with the socialist teaching of *The Masses*, which they edited.[15] They reduced Freudianism to the discovery of the "importance of sex in human life" and believed that it "suggested an intelligent reappraisal of social and moral restrictions"; self-appointed apostles of the new cure, they wrote for popular magazines about dreams, repression, and the unconscious.[16]

Eastman and Dell carried their enthusiasm into the Liberal Club, where they oversaw the anxious and at times cynical Greenwich Villagers' ruminations on the tenets of psychoanalysis and worked hard to convince them to be "psyched" and thereby cured of all writer's blocks, marital infelicities, depressions, and irritabilities. Preferring not to pay the vast sums that professionals such as Brill and Smith Ely Jelliffe demanded, the Villagers easily shed their inhibitions—those being pre-Prohibition days—and recounted their dreams to one another in the hope of getting to the bottom of their problems. It was a time when intimate thoughts could be kept secret only with great difficulty. Glaspell protested that "you could not go out to buy a bun without hearing of some one's complex," and Sherwood Anderson (the obsession with psychoanalysis having quickly spread to Chicago) discovered that "it was a time when it was well for a man to be somewhat guarded in the remarks he made, what he did with his hands."[17]

The ferment surrounding Freudianism struck Cook and Glaspell as excellent matter for a facetious play. Prompted by Cook's earlier "mystical experiences," they were intrigued by the insight into the unconscious that psychoanalysis promised, although they were somewhat dubious about the claims made by popularized accounts. The prevailing belief that insanity could be fended off or hysterical symptoms cured by a couple of confessional sessions with a "priestly analyst" struck them as an unwarranted simplification of the problems of humankind.[18] So did their fellow Villagers' blithe declarations that dreams were the manifestations of sexual desires stifled by American puritanical society, desires that if repressed could lead to unhappiness or even the lunatic asylum. Exploring various dream analysis scenarios convinced them that this latest nostrum, if taken to extremes, could have disastrous consequences, but it also revealed an inherent capacity for histrionics that offered enormous promise for the theater, which inspired them to create a play that would be more intellectually stimulating than what they saw on Broadway. In their apartment on Milligan Place, Cook and Glaspell "tossed the lines back and forth at one another, and wondered if any one else would ever have as much fun with it as we were having."[19] Much to their chagrin, however, the finished play, *Suppressed Desires*, was rejected by the recently formed Washington Square Players as "too special."[20]

Glaspell delighted in the writing of the play; it gave her the opportunity to work with her husband—thus keeping him away from the libations at the Liberal Club and the Brevoort—and after her intimate struggle with *Fidelity*, it seemed like pure relaxation. She could not know that *Suppressed Desires* would initiate a new way of life for both of them; as she jotted down Cook's ripostes to her arguments for psychoanalysis, she indulged in the freedom provided by "comedy (not of character) but of ideas, or, rather, of the confusion or falseness or absurdity of ideas."[21]

In *Suppressed Desires*, Henrietta Brewster is addicted to the new fad and worships her analyst, the infallible Dr. Russell. In preparing a paper on psychoanalysis to give at the Liberal Club, she litters her husband's work-table with literature on the subject, including copies of the *Psycho-Analytic Review* (to which Eastman directed readers of *The Masses* who wished to "understand the daring ideas of Sigmund Freud").[22] Her husband, Stephen, has had enough of Henrietta's nonsense: she is poisoning his life with her search for complexes and, following the example set by physicians at the Phipps Clinic in Baltimore, wakes him every night to discuss and analyze his dreams.[23] Mabel, Henrietta's unsophisticated sister, who thinks that psychoanalysis is "something about the war," is visiting from Chicago; Henrietta is convinced that Mabel "needs more from life than she is getting" and pounces on her first "Freudian slip" to carry her off to Dr. Russell's office.[24] Meanwhile, Stephen decides to call on "that priest of this new religion" in the hope that he will be sufficiently honest to "tell Henrietta there's nothing the matter with my unconscious mind" and so free him from his wife's nagging about undiscovered complexes.[25]

Dr. Russell, clearly not hampered by the reticence Freud had encountered in his patients or by any symptoms of transference, arrives at his interpretation in record time. He sees no need to delve too deeply into hidden memories, for the suppressed desires he discovers have nothing to do with childhood traumas. In a mere two weeks, he is prepared to affirm that Stephen's dream about the walls of his room "receding and leaving me alone in a forest" has nothing to do with his work as an architect but is conclusive proof that he wishes to be free of his wife.[26] Mabel's slightly more complicated dream that she is a hen told to "step lively!" is quickly unraveled to show that she wishes she were her sister—HEN-rietta—because she loves Stephen—STEP-HEN B-ROOSTER.[27] Henrietta is indignant that her mentor has betrayed her in this way and promises to burn her books on psychoanalysis. Stephen is quite happy to ignore the analyst's dictum and remain with his wife, and the couple tell Mabel to "keep right on suppressing" her desire for Stephen and high-handedly persuade her that "psychoanalysis doesn't say you have to *gratify* every suppressed desire."[28]

The play is a spoof of then current unprofessional opinions on psychoanalysis and owes a great deal to a skeptical article by Edwin Tenney Brewster published a couple of years earlier in the popular *McClure's Magazine*.[29] Brewster urges readers to judge Freud's ideas for themselves, although he ends with the suggestion that perhaps "the whole thing is only a crazy dream of Dr. Sigmund Freud." He introduces his topic by comparing the mind to "a tidy little apartment" with unknown "cellars and galleries and caverns" where the primitive, uncouth impulses are exiled and range freely.[30] An earlier Greenwich Villager had used similar analogies: Edgar Allan Poe's "The Fall of the House of Usher" clarifies the terrifying implications of Stephen Brewster's exclamation: "I've got the roof in the cellar!"[31] Edwin Tenney Brewster examines a number of examples of dream analyses from Ernest Jones's accounts of psychoanalytic cures, almost all of them concerned with unhappy marriages and suppressed desires for another man or woman. One dream interpretation depends on a pun involving the name of a hated doctor who had mistreated the dreamer in childhood and could well have inspired the punning that *Suppressed Desires* exploits.

Brewster's article makes one error that Glaspell and Cook perpetuate: he does not distinguish between suppressed and repressed desires, writing: "Every dream, in the Freudian formula, is the more or less disguised fulfillment of a *suppressed* wish. . . . The worst of it is that these same *repressed* wishes that appear in dreams affect also, most inconveniently, our waking lives."[32] According to W. David Sievers, Freud's translator, A. A. Brill, "distinguished between *repression*, which is an unconscious process, and *suppression*, which is a conscious disciplining of one's impulses as required by civilization." Sievers points out that "Susan Glaspell's satire should rightly have been called *Repressed Desires*."[33] However, strictly speaking, it should have been *Repressed and Suppressed Desires*: Mabel is told to *suppress*—for the good of the Brewsters—desires that are no longer *repressed* since the analyst has brought them to the fore by explaining them. (Glaspell and Cook do not seem to have been aware of the distinction since they use "suppressed" throughout.) The confusion is quite understandable in that, as we have seen, Edwin Tenney Brewster uses the two terms indiscriminately (as does Nathan G. Hale Jr. as late as 1971) and Hugo Munsterberg, the Harvard professor of psychology whose work the Cooks would have known, uses "suppressed" throughout his 1907 article in *McClure's*.[34] A more serious misinterpretation of Freud lies in Henrietta's selfish dismissal of Mabel's putative suppressed desire for Stephen. Henrietta assures her sister that the lunatic asylum no longer looms since her desire has been named: "Dr. Russell has brought it into your consciousness—with a vengeance. That's all that's necessary to break up a complex."[35] This facile solution echoes Eastman's optimistic fairy-tale presentation of psychoanalysis and Freud's own second lecture at Clark, in which he attempted to simplify his already simple examples of psychoanalytic cures achieved by a return to the pathogenic memory by stating: "We decide to lift the repression, and peace and quiet are restored."[36]

The disappointment caused by the Washington Square Players' rejection of *Suppressed Desires* was tempered by the arrival of the first copy of Glaspell's novel *Fidelity*, as well as by a slight improvement in the weather, which allowed for early removal to Provincetown. Once there, Glaspell hired a local woman to help spruce up the clapboard cottage and impatiently awaited the arrival of Ma-Mie, who would bring Nilla and Harl, Cook's children, as soon as school ended. The novel had sapped her emotional resources, and she rejoiced in the prospect of spending a quiet summer surrounded by family and friends; she hoped for lazy afternoons on the beach followed by fish dinners at Polly's, who, as during previous summers, cooked for the displaced Greenwich Villagers. The Cooks fell back into the routine of enjoying convivial evenings with the Hapgoods, and it looked as if Jig and Hutch, although more disillusioned than before, would continue putting the world to rights over their chessboard, while Boyce sewed and chatted with Glaspell. It may well have been on one of these evenings that Glaspell alluded to her disappointment at the Washington Square Players' unfeeling rebuttal and discovered that Boyce had also sketched out a short play that could easily be put into shape for production. Jig, overhearing this, launched into his favorite theme: the necessity, particularly now that the culture of Europe was being threatened, of creating a true American literature. Why not start off with drama? Why not in Provincetown? Why not with plays written by them? Hapgood looked on quizzically, ever the cynical, detached observer, but as the other three grew more excited, he eventually intervened. He had not been aware that Boyce had written a play. Boyce, slightly discomfited, raised her steady green eyes to him and, as she always did, immediately won his approval.

She had good reason to feel hesitant, however: her sketch betrayed the confidence of a friend. The passionate love between Jack Reed and Mabel Dodge had been no secret in Greenwich Village, and in the summer of 1913, Provincetown had delighted in the silken tent on the dunes to which the lovers habitually withdrew at nightfall. Now, in 1915, Dodge was unhappily attempting to forget one lover by captivating another. She had arrived in Provincetown with an exotic entourage, an unsuccessful ruse to disguise her infatuation with Maurice Sterne, a Latvian-born artist, who, like Reed before him, was finding it extremely difficult to snatch a peaceful moment away from Dodge to devote to his work. Edna Kenton, a Chicago friend, who heard of the entertainment from a not too sympathetic Jig Cook, described the scene to Carl Van Vechten:

Inciting tales breathe from Provincetown. Mabel D's latest passion is one Sterne—do you know him?—Russian Jew—artist—has lived many years in India. Bayard B[oyesen], Bobbie Jones [Robert Edmond Jones], and Mary Foote are staying with her—the whole village is again aware she is IN LOVE. She is wearing East Indian robes this season, turbans et al; is taking up the Vedantist ways of escape, and sits by the hour communing with God or her yogi—my terms are vague, not having dipped lately into the incarnation of Krishna Mulvaney. Sterne, however, wishing to work, fixed up a studio for himself and quiet hours somewhere, but what's the use! Mabel is a dear, devoted thing. Bobbie Jones wears golden shoon and silver-embroidered scarlet coats anywhere, and winds scarves round and round and round himself, and the mandarin-coated and the Indian-turbanned, and the scarlet-coated and lettered meet and mingle with the natives of the town upon the narrow path they call their main artery of trade.[37]

Thus Boyce felt that, the Reed affair being over, at least as far as Dodge was concerned, she was not being indiscreet by divulging Dodge's earlier cavils on the subject of fidelity. Dodge had once written to her, in confidence, expressing her fear that Hutch would make her predicament into a "thesis to discuss in Greenwich Village":

Reed and I love each other as much as any people can—that's why we torment each other so—but one of us has to give in on this. . . . Yet if I didn't *feel this* and feel this important it would be because I would have him as I would a whore—indifferent to what he did so long as he doesn't deprive me of himself. It *can't* be meant to be that way! . . . To him the sexual gesture has no importance, but infringing on his right to act freely has the first importance. Are we both right and both wrong—and how do such things end? Either way it kills love—it seems to me. This is so fundamental—is it what feminism is all about? . . . I know all women go thro this—but *must* they go on going thro it? Are we supposed to "make" men do things? Are men to change? Is monogamy better than polygamy?[38]

Boyce, of course, was deeply touched by her friend's dilemma: the wife of Hutchins Hapgood, that "warmest, most sympathetic hound," was constantly tormented by his ideological need for friendships with other women.[39] But her way of dealing with the situation was different from Dodge's. Boyce had four children to bring up, a house and husband to run, and frequently an insufficient income that had to be supplemented through her writing, but she was selflessly devoted to Hutch, whom, according to Dodge, she safely held on a leash, smiling "a secret smile."[40] Dodge had no such domestic duties; undogged by financial worries, she could surrender her days to love or "ennui" and seemed to make a habit of marrying the least suitable candidate. Moreover, although undoubtedly a New Woman in the liberties she took with older codes of behavior, her attitude to womanhood was undeniably Victorian: "The fact is, like most real women, all my life I had needed and longed for the strong man who would take responsibility for me and my decisions. I wanted to lie back and float on the dominating decisive current of an all-knowing, all-understanding man. I had never known any such man. . . . So that need in me for a man who would act like a man had remained as strong as ever it had been in my childhood."[41]

Boyce had toyed with the idea of putting the tale of Dodge's amours into an Arabian Nights setting, with prince and princess surrounded by beautiful serving maidens, presumably hoping to shield her friend—and possibly herself—from being identified with the protagonist, but she was not happy with the effect.[42] Now Cook confirmed that such contemporary dilemmas should not be shrouded in Arabian veils: America needed a drama based on its own experience, set out in its own idiom, that would stir the imagination of its people. Boyce produced a typescript of a realistic version entitled *Constancy* within a few days, and the two couples enjoyed the reading, occasionally tightening dialogue, cutting repetitive affirmations of love, and allowing Hutch his way with the censoring of antimale jokes, such as the following:

Rex: It's always the woman that *does* give the apple!

Moira: And since Adam not one of you has been able to resist! You poor things! I believe it wasn't Adam's rib that was taken to make Eve but his backbone!

Rex: Hang Adam and Eve! . . . I wish, though, that God had put into her a touch of imagination, while he was about it! You don't hear that he gave her any of Adam's brain!

Moira: Perhaps Adam had none to spare.[43]

The two lovers, Rex and Moira, discuss the meaning of fidelity. For Rex, episodic sexual encounters with other women are irrelevant. He needs freedom to come and go, to immerse himself in other activities; all he can promise a woman is that he will always return. Moira envisages love as complete surrender to the loved one; she is prepared to devote herself entirely to her lover, to spend every minute in his presence, to live through him in fact, and she expects the same from him. For her, fidelity is not in the return but in the constant presence. The ending of the play is inconclusive: it presents no resolution to such absolutely opposed points of view. In fact, its weakness lies in the impossibility of creating drama in such total opposites: Moira and Rex have no common ground in which a dramatic encounter and denouement can occur. Moira is too reasonable in her demands, whereas Rex is an utter cad, the unreformed man who will never accept that a woman has any rights unless they happen to be to his advantage. He is the Anatol of Arthur Schnitzler's series of plays of that name—which, ironically, Reed was to mock in his comedy *The Eternal Quadrangle* (1916).[44]

Their enthusiasm grew as the two couples discussed their plays, *Suppressed Desires* and *Constancy*. Ma-Mie gave advice as to costumes and sets, and Nilla and Harl clamored to be allowed to watch. Hapgood saw no reason why the plays should not be performed in their long front room, and it was unanimously decided that *Constancy* should be played on the verandah—thus Rex could make his entrance by scrambling over the wooden railing, realistically expressing his fear that Moira would not let him in the door.

Fearing Dodge's wrath when she realized that her dilemma was being used for purposes of entertainment, Boyce paid her a long visit and came away not only with her blessing but also with the promise that Robert Edmond Jones would help with the scenery. Bobby, ever an advocate of the theatrical ideal of "the simple, the smashing, the posterish," had recently returned from a year's study with stage designer Max Reinhardt in Germany and was happy to put his innovative ideas to use.[45] Unfortunately, neither the plays nor the acting space gave him much scope, but his collaboration would achieve legendary proportions.

The casting of the plays proved to be no problem. Cook and Glaspell took the parts of Stephen and Henrietta, and Lulu Huffaker was roped in to play Mabel, Henrietta's befuddled sister. Hutch refused to play Rex to Boyce's Moira, so Joe O'Brien, Mary Heaton Vorse's husband, seemingly fully recovered from an operation he had undergone the previous autumn for stomach cancer, was enlisted. None of the players had any professional acting experience, but the parts and the setting were so real to them that they could be themselves. Bobby Jones arranged the Hapgoods' reading lamps for maximum effect, threw cushions in artistic arrangements on the verandah couch, and supplemented insufficient lighting with candles, and on 15 July 1915, playwrights and actors anxiously awaited their audience.[46]

Jig was inordinately nervous. Glaspell finally removed him from the makeshift theater by cajoling him into taking a walk on the beach: "We held each other's cold hands and said, 'Never mind, it will be over soon.'"[47] She alone understood what the evening meant to him. It was not merely an amateur performance of a play he had cowritten but a new beginning; it was the expression of a community, the creation of a native theater that would draw the nation together in a mystical, all-comprehensive "I." In his vision of this new community, Cook included all of the participants—playwrights, actors, backstage technicians, and audience— through whom he hoped to "reshape at least one small part of a society nearer to the heart's desire," for he believed "that in the freeing of creative forces a life together might come into being which would itself be a creation, and greater than any one of us."[48] He also hoped for psychological relief from the war-storm in Europe, which, contrary to initial predictions, was still raging, and he was among the few who maintained that a city—and a nation—could, if governed "by scientific wisdom, [be] by enlightenment lifted into beauty."[49]

The evening began with the performance of *Constancy*, which was an unqualified success. The Hapgoods' sitting room was crowded with sympathetic, though critical, friends who took the play as a cue for yet another discussion on the New Woman's ambitions. Opinions were divided: Dell sided with Hapgood and argued that liberty must prevail in any relationship, whereas Ida Rauh, Glaspell, and Boyce believed in constancy, though they rejected a devotion so absolute that it annulled either partner's potential. Dodge, shielded by Maurice Sterne, maintained her customary aloofness and refused to comment. Eventually, Hutch and Bobby, plagued by requests for drinks—which would not be offered until after the second performance—engaged the audience in the transformation of the acting space. Chairs were shuffled around and moved back onto the verandah, so that the auditorium now occupied what had been the stage for *Constancy*. *Suppressed Desires* was acted in the sitting room, with the audience looking in from the outside.

Jig and Glaspell made a plausible couple arguing over psychoanalysis. Her tenacity and natural gravity made Henrietta's subjugation to the new fad fully convincing, and Jig's carefully controlled, fiery exuberance created a credibly henpecked, frustrated husband.

The audience loved both plays, and as word of the happening spread, many in Provincetown felt slighted at not having been among the chosen. They urged the Cooks and the Hapgoods to repeat the evening, but although the actors were not averse to further histrionics, it was clear that a larger venue was needed. Vorse was so thrilled at her husband's recovery from cancer and delighted by his rendering of Rex that when he suggested they convert the larger of the fish-houses on their wharf into a theater, only a smidgen of Jig's charm and cajolery was required before she succumbed. Margaret Steele, who had been using the shed as a studio, graciously agreed to move her canvasses into one of the smaller buildings; everyone lent a hand to move the boats, tackle, and rubbish accumulated over years of disuse to clear an acting space. Excited by the theatricals and forgetting for a while her worries over the war in Europe and the Women's Peace Conference she had recently attended, Vorse rummaged through her past and came up with a stage curtain from her childhood days in Amherst, when plays in the attic had been a regular form of entertainment. The lighting of the fish-house presented certain difficulties because of the hazard of fire. Bobby Jones placed four people with lamps in the wings and arranged lanterns with tin reflectors in front of the stage; "four people stood beside the lamp bearers with shovels and sand in case of fire, and with these lights the fish-house took on depth and mystery."[50] The problem of seating was not even considered. "Let each bring his own!," bellowed Cook.

Torrential rain threatened to ruin the first performance at the Wharf Theatre; water poured through the long-unrepaired roof into strategically placed pans, and the actors and organizers feared they would be playing to an empty auditorium. But the audience, armed with umbrellas and chairs, overcame the elements and claimed their right to participate in the new drama. Vorse would never forget how the umbrellas, placed against the wooden roof supports, "stirred, then slowly slid down an enormous knothole to the sand thirty feet below." Other umbrellas followed "with the stealth of eels."[51]

The thespians soon settled happily back into the summer routine: mornings for writing, painting, and sculpting, afternoons for lying in the sun, and evenings for sparkling gatherings either in someone's home or around a driftwood fire on the beach. Glaspell resolutely returned to the short stories she was working on, but her husband now found it impossible to tackle anything that was not directly concerned with the theater. In search of someone who would listen—and not daring to barge into writers' studies—he made the rounds of the artists who, setting up their easels outdoors, proved vulnerable targets for his preachments on a hypothetical, essentially American style. Scuffing self-absorbedly along the narrow high-tide beach, he would stop with delight at Charles Hawthorne's easel and observe the founder of the Cape Cod school of art conducting a class. A pretty model sitting elegantly under a parasol was the focus of the semicircle of young ladies who were intent on imitating Hawthorne's technique of brushing in the dazzling Provincetown light. Cook provoked embarrassed blushes with his comments on models, nudes, and the need for an American subjectivity. Hawthorne paid little attention to him; he had recently lost numerous students to the avant-garde Summer School of Painting inaugurated by Ambrose Webster and was aware of Cook's radical tendencies. Ever since the 1913 Armory Show—which had "perfectly fascinated" Cook—had brought modern European art to New York, the traditional depiction of landscapes and figures was losing out to fauvist, cubist, futurist, and postimpressionist methods of portraying reality.[52] Provincetown now resembled a veritable battlefield on which traditionalists and modernists fought for a tenuous livelihood, as well as recognition. Cook was tickled by the insults they hurled at each other. The academicians accused the experimenters of "deliberately violating every canon of sane art—apparently for the perverse pleasure of violation." The modernists saw Hawthorne as an "old mummy" who turned out the "deadest salon stuff."[53] Desperate to repeat the wharf happening and conscious of the cathartic value of theatrical experience, Cook decided to transpose the artists' argument onto the stage and wrote *Change Your Style*, mocking both factions.

The play gave the two embittered contestants equal say, and to please the lay members of the audience, Cook included two other Provincetown characters in the cast: the kindly John A. Francis, landlord and general store owner, was barely disguised as Mr. Josephs, landlord and store owner, and Mabel Dodge appeared as Myrtle Dart, "Lover of the Buddhistic," aptly dressed in "East Indian robe and turban."[54] Fittingly, artists Charles Demuth and Bror Nordfeldt played the rebel apprentice and the head of a "Post-Impressionist Art-School." But not even Cook could approach Hawthorne with the offer of a part, so Max Eastman, coerced by Ida Rauh, who wanted to play Myrtle Dart, became, if only for one night, the head of an "Academic Art-School."

Once again the fish-house was turned into a theater. On 9 September 1915, an eager audience trooped "up-along" Commercial Street to the tottering Lewis Wharf. The program was made up of Cook's skit on the Provincetown artists and Wilbur Daniel Steele's *Contemporaries*. In spite of its banal theme, *Change Your Style* appealed to everyone. The Provincetown summer people identified both the characters and the clichés on art that were currently being bandied about by one and all and happily turned a blind eye to the shortcomings of plot and structure.

Contemporaries was quite different; a serious commentary on political events of the previous winter, it demanded more of both actors and audience. In the winter of 1913–14, unemployment had risen drastically in New York, and hunger was exacerbated by the extreme temperatures of that January. A group of young rebels lead by "a bright East Side Jew," Frank Tannenbaum, who had been befriended by Emma Goldman, attempted to force religious establishments to feed and shelter the unemployed.[55] They led ragged, hungry men into churches, disrupting evening services and shaming ministers and congregations into organizing help. On 4 March 1914, they elbowed their way into Saint Alphonsus Catholic Church, where the priest, seeing this plea for charity as political agitation, sent for the police. Tannenbaum was arrested and, charged with inciting to riot, sentenced to a year at Blackwell's Island. Vorse, among other Greenwich Villagers, had been involved in the efforts to obtain his release and the escalating unemployment protests that followed. She urged Cook to accept the play Steele had written shortly after the church raids.[56] *Contemporaries* transfers the unrest of the poor of New York to Jerusalem, thus establishing an identification of all rebels with Jesus Christ that only becomes clear at the end of the play, when dawn breaks and the stage, hitherto submerged in darkness, reveals the secret setting. The candlelit wharf stage—with prudential buckets of sand and water in the wings—dimmed Steele's imperfectly worked-out analogies but whipped up anew the feelings of audience members, most of whom had participated in the protests.[57]

The performance marked the end of the summer, and most Greenwich Villagers, for whom the wharf signified nothing but a summer sport, straggled back to their winter abodes. But the Cooks stayed on, the old fish-house holding more than memories: for Jig, it embodied the challenge of the future; for Glaspell, it represented a burden she would have to nurse. In her words, Jig's absorption with the offspring he had sired in Provincetown was absolute: "The summer people had gone. Jig would go out on the old wharf and 'step' the fish-house. Weren't there two feet more than he had thought? He would open the sliding-door that was the back wall, through which fish, nets, oars, anchors, boats, used to be dragged, and stand looking across the harbor to the Truro hills, hearing the waves lap the piles below him. He would walk back slowly, head a little bent, twisting his forelock."[58]

She was now on her own with Jig and his plans; there was no outlet for him and few drinking companions who would listen to grandiose schemes for a theater that would grow until it solved the problems of the whole nation. Glaspell appeased and reassured him, even conspiring about the distant future, as long as he agreed not to dash off to New York to rent a theater for that winter. She missed the summer people who had bustled around Jig, carrying out his instructions, laughing, swearing, drinking, and talking, giving her moments of respite from the responsibility of sustaining his frenzied projects. Throughout the summer, Joe O'Brien's affectionate attention had provided her with more than momentary solace; knowledge of near-death had endowed him with a perceptive sympathy soothing to her strained nerves. Shared interests had brought them closer, and she listened keenly as he spoke of "the [Industrial Workers of the World] and the damned magazines and the Germans," loving his gaiety and his passion and the hard realism that contrasted so strongly with Cook's untempered idealism. But in October, O'Brien was rushed to the hospital; Boyce accompanied Vorse, and later in the month, she wrote her husband of O'Brien's sudden death.[59] Glaspell commiserated with Vorse, a widow for the second time in five years, but her grief was painfully personal, for she had lost a companion who had, more than once, given her "a keen grave look of understanding."[60] She wrote a eulogy for him, entitled simply "Joe," which *The Masses* published, thus honoring a comrade.

By December, Vorse was back on the Cape; she had been immobilized by grief, Veronal, and morphine but had rallied to meet the demands made on her by her children. Glaspell was impressed by her resilience and wrote to her mother that Vorse "is a wonderful person, and has got hold of herself and is going on in a simple brave manner that is very beautiful." In spite of the disappointment she knew the decision would cause her parents, Glaspell opted to stay with husband and friends over Christmas. Her mother sent a basket of mouthwatering delicacies, "olives and lovely cherries and spiced peaches," which she served with cold turkey and salad for Christmas supper. Dinner was eaten at the Hapgoods' home, and Christmas Eve was spent with Vorse around a tree that the three families had decorated for the children. The rest of the holiday, the weather "sunny and just cold enough to feel good," Jig exulted in his new toy, a "kodack—just a little brownie, but he had been wanting one to take some things here," which Father Christmas, disguised as Glaspell, had left in his stocking.[61]

Throughout the winter, Cook continued to spin dreams of a theater. His persistent questions inevitably came just as Glaspell was slipping a new sheet of paper into the typewriter, thus breaking her concentration. "Why not write our own plays, and put them on ourselves, giving writer, actor, designer, a chance to work together without the commercial thing imposed from without?," he blasted at her, and without waiting for an answer, he proceeded to outline how "unsuspected talents" would blossom at the first flutter of applause from a discerning audience.[62] Although easily carried away by dream visions, Cook had just enough practicality to recognize that he could do nothing without a stage, however primitive. Back in New York, he suggested—"half-jokingly," he later claimed—that Jack Reed's apartment at 43 Washington Square be converted into a theater.[63] Reed's indignation was too forthright to ignore, so Cook had to content himself with productions of *Suppressed Desires* at the

Liberal Club and Ira Remsen's Macdougal Street studio.[64] But he still mulled over the wharf fish-house, converting it in his mind's eye into the home of a new American theater.

By June 1916, Cook and Glaspell were back in Provincetown, where Glaspell immediately established an inviolable work routine—she wanted her mornings free to write. Cook, realizing his wife's health could not withstand physical labor, gave in without a murmur and withdrew to the wharf fish-house. He would make his demands on her later, but the creation of a valid acting space now consumed his days. With Vorse's blessing and the aid of other Provincetowners who were willing to turn their artistic skills to carpentry, decoration, and electrical installation, he converted the fish-house into an ideal theatrical space.[65] Four movable sections created a ten-by-twelve-foot stage, and the possibility of arranging the sections on different levels and enlarging the acting area by pushing the sections outside of the sliding back wall more than compensated for the lack of space.[66] The ability to open the back wall offered a realistic backdrop that had never been surpassed by David Belasco, the blue Truro hills dissolving into ocean and sky in an uncircumscribed horizon.

Cook, ahead of his time, dreamed of a flexible space for his theater: "Nothing there but infinity and the stage, and the stage broken up into big plastic elements with which you may compose. The four sections combine into one deep stage; they separate into main and inner stages, to be used in swift succession of changing scenes—so restoring to drama its Elizabethan power of story-telling."[67] In 1920, he would realize part of this dream: in the small Macdougal Street theater, he constructed a plaster likeness of infinity in the grottolike backdrop for Eugene O'Neill's *The Emperor Jones*, his dome, the first authentic Kuppelhorizont on an American stage. But his complete vision of a magically variable theater that would bring audience, actors, and playwrights together in a cathartic release of the spirit was not to be fulfilled in his time.

In 1916, such concerns had to give way to the practical details of running a summer theater. Following the example of Maurice Browne and the Chicago Little Theatre, Cook solved immediate financial difficulties—and assured his players an audience—by selling subscriptions for the whole season at $2.50 for two seats at six performances, which would feature new plays by as yet undiscovered American playwrights, including another play by Glaspell. He charmed enough holiday-makers to bring in $217.50, sufficient to refurbish the fish-house, and with artists and writers to aid him, he hammered wooden benches into place, wired the shed, and hung up a curtain of sorts to suggest an illusion of theatrical mystery.[68]

The first bill was relatively easy to put together: Boyce contributed *Winter's Night*, Reed offered *Freedom*, and *Suppressed Desires* completed the night's entertainment. On the first night—Thursday, 13 July 1916—Glaspell finally convinced Cook to come home and relax for a couple of hours before the curtain went up. She also thought it would be a good idea for them to run through their lines since at the one rehearsal, he had ad-libbed so freely that it was all she could do to keep the dialogue going in the right direction. But Cook was overcome by nerves and worry: the high of preparation had given way to a plummeting uncertainty and depression. Was he capable of creating a truly American theater? Would this season vindicate his lost years as a university instructor, farmer, and critic? As always at such moments, Glaspell put her husband first and dismissed her own first-night tremors. She was by now adept at bringing him out of such moods. This time, however, her skills were not needed; cries of "Fire!" broke the afternoon quiet and routed Cook's depression. Blood racing, he blindly dashed out of the house, across Commercial Street, and onto the wharf; thin wisps of smoke were trailing disconsolately over the fish-house. Within minutes, all of the East Enders were on the scene, and Cook's raging orders, desperately bellowed out over the hubbub, directed operations. His hoary head towered over all others as he heaved buckets, threw sand, and poured water to save American drama from the consequences of a smoldering cigarette butt carelessly tossed by an unthinking landsman into a wide crack full of dried seaweed.[69] Later, the Players surveyed their theater. The damage was not excessive: two walls were charred and some benches would have to be replaced, but there was still time to make repairs before the curtain went up. Nordfeldt got hold of a can of black paint, and with the help of Cook and actor Edward Ballantine, all four walls soon resembled canvasses that could well have been entitled "After a Fire."

The excitement had dispelled Cook's misery. He acted superbly that night, following Glaspell's lead and never once straying from the text of the play. Glaspell merged into the audience for the remaining two plays but took little in. She was worried about the other promised bills—of as yet unwritten plays—and wondered how she could provide the piece that

Cook had demanded of her. Horrified, she had protested that she did not even know how to write a play, let alone produce one to order. Cook's answer, proof of his faith in his wife's talent, was indicative of his conviction that the only thing American playwrights needed to prove themselves was some sort of performing space. "Nonsense. You've got a stage, haven't you?," he growled at her.[70]

Glaspell still considered the novel and short story her medium and felt that she knew nothing of the theater. *Suppressed Desires*, a joint effort, had been great fun to write, but she had never taken it seriously and had been amazed at its success. She knew that she could not let her husband down—she was always afraid of losing him, just as Mollie and Sara had lost him—and that both Greenwich Village and Provincetown, full of handsome young women who believed in sexual freedom, held many temptations. Cook had to be satisfied, his faith in her justified. When the wharf was empty, she would sit on the stage, close her eyes, listen to the waves breaking underneath, the gulls calling overhead, and allow her ideas to crystallize into images. The crude wooden boards of the stage-blocks took her back to her days as a reporter on the *Des Moines Daily News* when she had visited the kitchen of Margaret Hossack, who had been accused of murdering her husband.[71] She remembered the horror that kitchen had inspired. For the first time, she had clearly understood what marriage could mean, especially a childless marriage: the loneliness, the frustration, the utter dependency on a man engrossed in his work and oblivious to the wife as a person. Her own situation may well have triggered the memory: she had now accepted that she would not have children, and for the last year or so, all Cook could focus on was the theater. He saw her as a playwright, and she recognized that she would have to conform to his vision if she wanted to retain a sense of dignity and equality in this marriage that she had desired so intently and sacrificed so much to achieve. So the picture that was growing in her mind was weirdly pertinent to her own situation. At the time, in 1900, she had considered writing a short story about the case but had been unable to give it the right focus. Now, understanding the implications of what she had seen in that midwestern kitchen, she returned to her desk and wrote the first scene of *Trifles* (1916). The arrogant sheriff, the zealous county attorney, and Mr. Hale, a neighbor, stride into the gloomy kitchen followed by two women: the sheriff's wife and Mrs. Hale. As the men preempt the women at the stove—a space traditionally reserved for the weaker sex—while the women hover near the door, ceding their customary sphere of influence in a self-abnegating, habitual response to the men's complaints about the bitter cold, Glaspell heard their words as the stage claimed her story "for its own."[72]

In *Trifles*, Minnie Wright, who never appears onstage, has been charged with strangling her husband. While the sheriff and his men search the house for clues of a motive, the wives gather a few items of clothing for the prisoner. Mrs. Peters and Mrs. Hale are only nodding acquaintances, and the deferential, cowed sheriff's wife irritates the more defiant Mrs. Hale, a robust farmer's wife who will take no nonsense from woman or man. But as they uncover hints of domestic unhappiness that unequivocally point to the motive the law needs to convict Minnie, an understanding grows between them until finally "their eyes meet for an instant," sealing an unspoken bond. They find a strangled canary in Minnie Wright's sewing box and fear that although the men have been unable to interpret the clues provided by the unsifted flour and dirty towels they find in the house, they will not be blind to the connections between the canary and the rope around Mr. Wright's neck. Mrs. Peters rushes forward to hide the evidence but is too agitated to touch the lifeless bird; Mrs. Hale drops it deftly into her large coat pocket just before the men return to the kitchen.

The play focuses on the two women as they stumble upon the truth: they see the prison house that patriarchy has constructed of marriage. Although distressed by the murder, they exonerate Minnie for her crime; looking around the kitchen, they can identify with the burdens of her harsh existence and accept their responsibility for what happened. "Oh, I *wish* I'd come over here once in a while! That was a crime! That was a crime! . . . We live close together and we live far apart. We all go through the same things—it's all just a different kind of the same thing."[73] In *Trifles*, Glaspell voices her concern with the dilemmas of womanhood; she openly condones the breaking of patriarchal codes of behavior that strangle women and deny them self-fulfillment.

Even though the play is set in the Midwest, the women of Greenwich Village—many of whom had escaped the boredom of small-town life in their flight to New York—could identify with Minnie's frustration. They recognized the horror of being caged in a stultifying relationship, denied all means of gratifying self-expression. As suffragists and feminists, they also approved of the bonding between Mrs. Peters and Mrs. Hale and their defiant stand against the justice of the sheriff and his men.

The husbands and partners of these New Women also supported the play, but for their own peculiar reasons; outwardly they endorsed women's suffrage, but like Hutchins Hapgood, many were inwardly terrified of where feminism might lead. In *Trifles*, although the women rebel against traditional mores, they are all effectively silenced. Minnie, having murdered her husband (who undoubtedly deserved his fate), is safely locked away in prison. Her two neighbors dare to protect her by hiding the evidence their shared experiences lead them to uncover, but they are clearly not going to oppose man's justice by actively speaking out for Minnie. Accordingly, although Glaspell condones the breaking of codes of behavior that strangle women, she does not alienate the men who make them up. *Trifles* represents an awakening to the dilemmas of womanhood, but it offers no solutions. It is the only early Provincetown play that is continually reprinted in collections of short plays and, recently, in anthologies of women's writing and American literature, a distinction it deserves because it is handsomely crafted around the missing woman, the silenced Minnie Wright. The sparse dialogue rings true, and not one word or emotion is wasted, creating an effect of aching misery, which the rude boards of the wharf fish-house must have reinforced. The harmony of the theatrical experience that Gordon Craig, the British scenery designer and theorist, advocated was fulfilled in this short play, which has become a classic of its genre.

The Players urgently needed more plays in hand, however, before Glaspell could possibly finish *Trifles*. They were to meet at Cook and Glaspell's cottage to read new offerings for the second bill, but the only hope of enlivening the evening seemed to lie in the punch, for which the thespians had agreed to provide the necessary ingredients. No one expected much from the young, handsomely morose man who was going to read yet another of his plays—no one, that is, except Glaspell, who, intuiting hidden depths behind Eugene O'Neill's façade of nonchalance, had engineered this reading. He had appeared in Provincetown with the anarchist philosopher Terry Carlin, Hapgood's protégé, and they had taken rooms over John Francis's store. While Carlin philosophized with Hapgood, O'Neill made futile attempts to join the theater people.[74] He had presented his credentials as a playwright: his father was the famous actor James O'Neill, he had spent a year at Harvard in George Pierce Baker's English 47 playwriting class, and he had published a volume of five plays. His achievements did not impress the Greenwich Villagers; they saw him as a "half-baked youngster who persisted in believing in his genius despite an equipment pitiably scant of education and general culture" and who had resorted to "the usual stunt of people without ability" by publishing his own plays.[75] O'Neill's aloofness did not endear him to the outgoing Villagers, many of whom were almost old enough to be his parents. He made matters worse by trying to impress Jack Reed—who was about the same age—by reading a play that was "frightfully bad, trite and full of the most preposterous hokum" about Mexican generals.[76]

But Glaspell was taken with his distant manner, which she interpreted as a sign of insecurity, and with his large, burning brown eyes. On the beach, he would sit slightly apart from the group, staring through them into the horizon, and she admired him as he streaked through the water, swimming strongly, easily outdistancing even Jig. She alone knew how to draw him out and found his talk of the sea and the theater exhilarating. They discussed the implications of the death of Greek tragedy, how to structure the plot of a play around a character, thus eliminating the trivial sexual misadventures Broadway relied on, and how to bring death and destiny onto the stage. So she had sought out Carlin and asked him to tell O'Neill to bring the play about the sailor dying at sea that he had outlined for her. She did not want the others—just that one.

O'Neill had been hesitant about offering this play, which had been turned down by the Washington Square Players and, albeit in an earlier form, summarily dismissed as "not really a play" by George Pierce Baker.[77] When Carlin passed on the invitation from the slender lady who had befriended him, O'Neill was racked with doubt; he was afraid of another snub from this snooty bunch of aspiring amateurs but desperate to get his plays produced and to see their effect on an audience. He knew that the fish-house was the ideal theater for *Bound East for Cardiff* (1916) and felt deeply grateful for what he saw as his last chance with Cook and his group. Like all of the other plays he carried around in a biscuit box— no less than eleven short pieces—this was a brief study of a specific mood, and like many of his plays that the Provincetown Players later staged, it forcefully evoked the power of the sea, bringing home the inevitable destiny of humankind. O'Neill re-created the atmosphere of a seaman's forecastle magnificently. Cocky, Driscoll, Olson, and Smithy take on distinct personalities with their first utterances; they would reappear in *The Long Voyage Home* (1917) and *The Moon of the Caribbees* (1918), just as Yank would resurface in *The Hairy Ape* (1922) and his soul brother Matt Burke in *Anna Christie* (1920). As in *Anna Christie*, in *Bound East for Cardiff* the fog separates the sea from life on land, creating a microworld of passions and unattainable desires. There is no plot, only the sailors' talk and Yank's death. Standing on the wharf, hearing the sea break against its wooden pillars and conscious of the salty spray on his skin, O'Neill understood that he would have to take the risk and offer *Bound East for Cardiff* to the gentle, self-assured woman whose bobbed hair belied her Victorian manner. But he was nervous. Carlin's word that he had nothing to lose was meaningless; he was handing over his play to an unknown future.

The meeting was in full swing when O'Neill arrived, still wondering whether he could go through the ordeal of reading yet another play to these intellectuals playing at theater. Glaspell gently took the manuscript from him and, pressing a glass into his hand, told him to sit down in the dining room, where the musical table was graced with a huge bowl brimming over with a wicked concoction.[78]

Urged by his hostess's ingratiating smile, Frederick Burt, the only professional actor present, offered to read the play. As Glaspell listened, she was flooded with relief and joy. Her intuition had not betrayed her: here was a playwright worthy of Jig's dream of uncovering American talent and creating a truly American theater. More than any success of her own, that evening converted her to her husband's vision and convinced her of her obligation to help him in his self-appointed task. Recapturing the general mood, she later wrote: "Then we knew what we were for."[79] Her report of the first performance of the play recalls much of that uncanny evening in words that are redolent of the ancient spirit of the people portrayed by J. M. Synge, the Irish dramatist whom the Players revered:

> I may see it through memories too emotional, but it seems to me I have never sat before a more moving production than our "Bound East for Cardiff," when Eugene O'Neill was produced for the first time on any stage. Jig was Yank. As he lay in his bunk dying, he talked of life as one who knew he must leave it.
>
> The sea has been good to Eugene O'Neill. There was a fog, just as the script demanded, fog bell in the harbour. The tide was in, and it washed under us and around, spraying through the holes in the floor, giving us the rhythm and the flavor of the sea while the big dying sailor talked to his friend Drisc of the life he had always

wanted deep in the land, where you'd never see a ship or smell the sea. It is not merely figurative language to say the old wharf shook with applause.[80]

But that evening was not all sobriety. Glaspell may have written of it "through memories too emotional," but the hobo poet Harry Kemp remembered the performance for the part he had played. Slightly put out that the parts of Driscoll and Yank had fallen to others, he had nevertheless accepted the role of the seaman Davis. Even though his character only had half a dozen or so lines, Kemp caused consternation by skipping "two whole pages of script" and thereby rousting Yank from "the imminence of death." As Kemp remembered it, Cook sat up to whisper hoarsely: "Damn your soul, Harry Kemp!" The actors resisted the impulse to "burst out into guffaws," and the audience, held by the spell of death, apparently never noticed Yank's momentary revival.[81]

A decade later, when Glaspell wrote of those days in *The Road to the Temple*, she expunged O'Neill's initial failure to electrify the Players and minimized her own part in his discovery, building instead on the myth that Edna Kenton had already established.[82] In 1922 Kenton, the unofficial press agent for the Players, published a potted history of the Provincetowners in *Billboard*. But Kenton was not in Provincetown in 1915 or 1916. Relying on hearsay and the memories of others, she artfully dramatized her story of "the smiling Muse of drama" busily "tying threads" on the sand dunes. Accordingly, in her account, when Carlin arrives in Provincetown, he is immediately accosted by Glaspell, who is scouring the town for plays. He tells her that " 'a young fellow came in on the boat today with a trunkful.' 'Bring him down to Mary Vorse's tonight,' said Miss Glaspell, 'and tell him to bring ONE play!' "[83] This story, with minor variations, has been repeated in all of the accounts of how O'Neill was discovered by the Players, and it was not until 1930 that Kemp put things straight—as far as he remembered them—in his "Out of Provincetown: A Memoir of Eugene O'Neill."

The other legend that grew up around the Players was perhaps not quite as harmless. Glaspell herself contributed to it when she wrote that life throughout the summer of 1916 was "all of a piece, work not separated from play."[84] Indeed, it became almost a slogan of the group that they were "playing." They were not seriously confronting the established drama, not in competition with Broadway or other little theaters; their success was achieved "in the spirit of play."[85] In *Time and the Town: A Provincetown Chronicle* (1942), Mary Heaton Vorse began the chapter on the Players with the following words: "No group of people ever had less sense of having a mission than did the Provincetown Players." But in all truth, George Cram Cook was obsessed by a vision of a community theater, as even Vorse herself acknowledged in the same memoir: "The plays touched off a fire in him since for years he had been thinking of the theater as a community expression—the old dream of people working together and creating together." The only chronicler of the achievements of the Players to do so, Vorse recognized Glaspell's contribution when she declared: "Not enough has been said about Susan Glaspell. . . . Nor without her would George Cram Cook's intensive work in the theater have been possible. Her constant encouragement and her humor as well as her irony were the things which nourished him and made his never-ending tasks possible."[86]

But the very idea of the Players was cast with a definite sense of mission, belittled perhaps by everyone except Cook himself, the Zarathustra who was never shy of voicing his aspirations. Neith Boyce wrote to her father after the 1915 performance of *Constancy* and *Suppressed Desires*: "Nothing happens. . . . I have been stirring up the people here to write and act some short plays. . . . I wish I had more interesting things to tell you—but as I said, nothing happens here."[87] But it was Boyce who helped Cook express his mystical ambition; after a long evening with her, "as an affirmation of faith," he wrote: "One man cannot produce drama. True drama is born only of one feeling animating all the members of a clan—a spirit shared by all and expressed by the few for the all. If there is nothing to take the place of the common religious purpose and passion of the primitive groups, out of which the Dionysian dance was born, no new vital drama can arise in any people."[88]

By June 1916, Cook's determination had matured, and the summer people were unwittingly trapped by his purpose. "He was going to take whom he wanted and use them for the creation of his Beloved Community," wrote Glaspell.[89] With egotistical prescience, he appointed himself creator of the great American drama that would heal the nation and feared only that circumstances would conspire against him and he would miss his chance: "Suppose the nascence depends not on blind evolutionary forces, involving the whole nation, but on whether or not the hundred artists who have in them potential power arrange or do not arrange to place themselves in vital stimulating relationship with each other, in order to bring out, co-ordinate and direct their power. Suppose the stage of economic, political and social evolution is such that a great creative movement can either appear or not appear in the second decade of twentieth century America, according to the deeds or omissions of a hundred poets, painters, novelists, critics, scholars, thinkers."[90]

Thus, when the summer drew to a close, Cook announced that he would continue his work in New York. Glaspell was "appalled," she later said, and "afraid for him." Of all the neophyte actors, playwrights, and technicians, only she understood how much of himself he had put into that season. "He was the center; for the most part, he made the others want to do it, as well as persuaded them it could be done. I felt the energy must go into keeping that fire of enthusiasm, or belief, from which all drew."[91] Although she did not admit it, she supplied the energy that kept Cook aflame, and her resources were ebbing after those strenuous, albeit satisfying, months. The demands on her had been excessive; she felt drained by the peremptory cries for sympathy and adulation with which her husband and the Players accosted her, setting her up as intermediary for their hopes and desires, as buffer in moments of conflict. O'Neill, who was becoming more and more absorbed in an affair with Louise Bryant, Jack Reed's wife, was no substitute for Joe O'Brien, whose quiet understanding had sustained her the previous summer; like Cook, he exacted her total engagement whenever he turned to her.

O'Neill had achieved his primary artistic ambition: thanks to Glaspell's discernment and Cook's determination, he was a produced playwright. The Wharf Theatre audiences loved *Bound East for Cardiff* and *Thirst*, another sea play, but a number of untouched manuscripts still lay in his box, and Cook's faith in his talent was a flattering spur. Although he despised the Broadway melodramas that his father starred in, he had no doubts about his goal: critical acclaim in New York. The example of European little theaters inspired him to hope that Cook's amateurs would conquer the critics of New York just as the Théâtre Libre had conquered Paris, and the Intimate Theater, Stockholm. Thus, he goaded Cook to look to Manhattan; these players would be his laboratory and the stepping stone to professional recognition.

Cook's other committed supporter was Jack Reed, who had witnessed the value of the theater as a vehicle for community expression in Mexico and had proved it by staging the Paterson Pageant at Madison

Square Garden in aid of the Paterson, New Jersey, silk strike in 1913. The three men emptied many bowls of wine at the musical table while Susan tempered their ambitions or, exasperated, escaped upstairs to her typewriter.[92]

Eventually they called a meeting for Monday, 4 September 1916, at eight o'clock in the Wharf Theatre. Robert Emmons Rogers took the chair, and the other twenty-eight summer players arranged themselves on the planks that had been made into benches at the beginning of the season. The sense of purpose was clear: they were going to found a theater. At that first official meeting, they named themselves the Provincetown Players. They elected Cook president and formed a committee (Burt, Reed, Eastman, and Cook) to draw up their constitution.

The following evening, the Provincetown Players met again and ratified a constitution declaring that their "purpose shall be the production of plays written by active members, or by others in whose work the active members may be interested."[93] Then Reed presented his resolutions, which were adopted "in lieu of by-laws" and set the Provincetown Players apart from all of the other little theaters then busy in America. Reed began by stating unequivocally: "*Be it resolved:* That it is the primary object of the Provincetown Players to encourage the writing of American plays of real artistic, literary and dramatic—as opposed to Broadway merit. That such plays be considered without reference to their commercial value, since this theater is not to be run for pecuniary profit."[94] The resolutions then went on to ensure the preeminence of the playwright by specifying that all authors must produce and direct their own plays. A demanding schedule of a new bill (made up of three short plays) every two weeks throughout the winter was lightly accepted. Margaret Nordfeldt was elected secretary, and until March 1916, when she was ousted by Dave Carb, she impartially and meticulously kept the minutes of the Players' meetings. The immediate financial problems were solved by exacting a contribution from the wealthiest members and adding it to the proceeds from the final bill of that summer.[95] Last but far from least, a good home had to be found. Thus, with her mythologizing prowess, Kenton has Cook heading off for New York with a simple brief: "to lease anything old enough and shabby enough—drab home or stable—to be taken over for next to nothing by experimenters without an exchequer."[96]

CHAPTER FOUR

The Luck of Children and Fools

The "Fire from Heaven" that energized Cook, giving him the ardor to challenge Broadway, did not touch his wife, who felt utterly depleted by the brouhaha of the summer's theatricals. Glaspell was staggered by Jig's dreams of a New York theater but knew her husband well enough to understand the futility of protest. He would never surrender a vision until it consumed him, needing her in the meantime to boost his self-confidence and protect him from the mockery of lesser spirits. Thus, her duties with the Players went beyond playwriting and rehearsing: throughout the summer, it had been up to her to stoke Jig's "fire of enthusiasm, or belief, from which all drew."[1] The round of meetings that gave birth to the Provincetown Players had consumed her remaining resources; she did not feel up to a winter of facing similar demands on her strength and sympathy, receiving nothing, not even appreciation, in return.

Glaspell knew that the aggravations of the last few months had to be allayed before she could continue as her husband's unacknowledged keeper, but Cook, as always when absorbed in breathing life into his conceptions, behaved as if she were an unwanted alien. It was impossible to write in these circumstances, and the summer brought its stack of bills without supplying the cash to pay them. When Glaspell stated that she was going to Vermont, Cook nodded abstractedly and joked that he would love to see her frisking with the calves on her friends' farm. He absented himself from his dreams long enough to take her to the Boston boat, Nilla tagging along in the vain hope that they would stop at the candy store. The driving wind and rain of a sudden September storm precluded any lingering good-byes or last-minute reconciliations, even if Cook had been sensitive to Glaspell's pain. Possibly, as the boat slipped from its moorings, he remembered that Glaspell had proved herself as a playwright: oblivious of stares and sniggers among the passengers, who may well have recognized him as Yank, he might have imperiously raised his voice above the wind and hurled a last demand at the fragile figure of his wife: "Write—another—play!"

Glaspell smarted at this appropriation of her time and energy, but love's memory transformed the scene into a romantic farewell in *The Road to the Temple*: "Two hundred and forty-five dollars in his pocket, in the glow of vision, energetic with belief, Jig boarded the train to look for a place for the Provincetown Players in New York. He stood alone on the back platform, waving to me. 'Don't worry!' he called, as the train was starting. Then something I couldn't hear, and I went running after him. He cupped his mouth with his hands to call back: 'Write another play!' "[2] Cook's letters, however, indicate that Glaspell was away when he departed on his New York mission, so the legendary words must have been uttered at some other time, possibly as envisioned above. One thing is certain: at the end of the summer of 1916, Glaspell felt rejected and exploited; if the theater was all Jig cared for, he could keep it. She doubted she would return to Provincetown before he left for New York and toyed with the idea of going straight from Vermont to Davenport—at least her parents wanted her with them. She worked herself up into believing that Cook had abandoned her for the theater. His daily letters prove his total dissociation from her feelings; he was unaware that anything could exist outside his task of creating a theater in New York. Comments by fellow Players that his *Change Your Style* was too local for production outside Provincetown were more on his mind than Glaspell's despondency. Likewise, he was more distressed by his inability to unearth the manuscript of *Suppressed Desires* that Dave Carb wanted for a St. Louis production than by her silence; the manuscript, after it was eventually found and despatched, brought performance royalties, he would later boast, equal to those paid to Broadway playwright Zoe Aikens. Also figuring prominently in his letters were reports on the whiskey supply, the parties held to celebrate the future of the Provincetown Players, and the inevitable hangovers.

These self-absorbed letters to his "Little Bear" made no impression on Glaspell. Even Cook's nostalgic account of the ceremonial taking down of the curtain at the Wharf Theatre could hardly move her, she was so jaded. But the news of a possible home for the Playwrights' Theatre must have roused her, and she decided to return straight to Provincetown from Vermont. Cook wrote that he would leave for New York immediately. Floyd Dell had found suitable premises but, fearing to tread on the elected president's toes, had refused to take the responsibility for making the final decision. Ignoring Nilla's tantrums at having to cut short the rehearsals for a children's play, Jig set out for Boston, where his children and Ma-Mie boarded a westbound train, and he, narrowly missing Glaspell, headed for New York. She could only construe his haste as further evidence of indifference but resignedly settled down in the now peaceful cottage to fulfill his injunction to write another play.

Cook's postscript to his next letter was jubilant: "139 Macdougal Street leased by Provincetown Players! Hurray! Paid $50.00 first months rent from Oct. 1st. So that much is settled."[3] He did not explain how he convinced Jennie Belardi to rent the parlor floor of her 1840 brownstone just off Washington Square to the Players, but he had clearly captivated the Italian widow. She became a subscribing member, taking the Players under her motherly wing and ensuring the approval and patronage of Greenwich Village Italians.

On 20 September 1916, Cook announced that he had found an apartment. He had been staying with Jack Reed at 43 Washington Square South (an area known as the "Genius Side"), but Glaspell's conviction that he did not want her to live with him grew until it reverberated so strongly in her letters that he sacrificed a morning to search for adequate quarters. He rented 1 Milligan Place, just around the corner from the theater, for $21 a month. It had "two tiny hall-bedrooms" and was virtually unfurnished; Cook planned to "improvise some furniture from boxes."[4]

Glaspell must have arrived in New York at the beginning of October full of hope that Cook had managed to turn their new apartment into a winter home, but she wrote nothing of Milligan Place in *The Road to the Temple*. The conversion of 139 Macdougal Street into the Playwrights' Theatre took center stage: "When I arrived in New York . . . my first glimpse of Jig was standing among shavings, lumber and bags of cement explaining the Provincetown Players to a policeman and an impersonal-looking person from the building department."[5]

We can only trust that Cook met her train. Dinner at the Liberal Club or Polly's, where the whole crowd would have gathered to welcome her, was followed by a wine-warmed first impression of the cold, unwelcoming rooms at Milligan Place, her arrival celebrated by an unmade bed in an otherwise empty apartment. When Glaspell awoke in the morning, she was alone; Cook had preferred 139 Macdougal Street to dalliance with his wife. A lack of breakfast utensils drove her out in search of hot coffee; most of the Provincetowners made Greenwich Village their winter quarters, and Glaspell was welcome everywhere. So it was not until mid-morning that she finally crossed Washington Square and faced her rival. It was an unprepossessing four-story brownstone, the first house south of the southwest corner of the square. A fusty old building that defied her imagination, it had been built not to house dubious histrionic activities but as the dwelling place of a Puritan family. But the voices emanating from the shuttered house left no room for Puritan gravity. Glaspell, recognizing her wifely obligation, strode in right on cue. Jig faced his interlocutors: " 'Now here is Susan Glaspell,' he said, as if I had entered just for this. 'She is writing plays. And there is a young Irishman, O'Neill'—turning to the Irish policeman. We all went downstairs to have a drink and talk it over."[6]

What Glaspell saw must have destroyed any remaining illusions of a peaceful winter. The ground floor of a somber dwelling had been gutted without respect for the spirit of its onetime occupants. The characteristic brownstone two-parlor-and-dining-room structure had rightly struck Dell as full of theatrical promise: the dining room was being converted into a stage, and the two parlors would become the auditorium. Cook, relying on the professional help of Donald Corley, who worked as an architect whenever his theatrical duties did not wholly absorb him, was intent on working miracles. They had satisfactorily removed the double doors between the dining room and the second parlor, thus creating what could be taken for a traditional proscenium arch, but they were not yet content with the auditorium. The previous evening, joyful at having his "Little Bear" with him again, Cook had not been able to resist unfolding his plans. Now Glaspell understood what, half asleep, she had not been able to grasp the night before. Corley, convinced by Cook's enthusiasm that the laws of gravity could be defied, had totally removed the dividing wall. But the otherwise approving Mrs. Belardi had intervened: building regulations specified that a steel girder was required to hold up the sagging ceiling, and she insisted that if her property was to be tampered with, there should at least be no danger of floors falling through. This, Glaspell learned from a temporarily disheartened Jig, would cost $200, leaving the Players with only $45.[7] The building inspectors were not appeased by the offer of drinks; the Players had knowingly violated the law. "The work was done quietly on a Sunday and the debris surreptitiously carted away by the Players in the dead of night," according to one account. They were hauled to court and would never forget Ida Rauh's defense; she had "studied law before her discovery of the drama, [and] argued the case with some of the histrionics that later brought her fame on Macdougal Street."[8]

While Cook and Corley debated how to create an adequate space for the audience, other members of the Players were absorbed in converting the space into a chromatic dream. Under the direction of Charles Demuth, Bror Nordfeldt, William Zorach, and Joseph Lewis Weyrich, the Players transformed into painters and released their repressions in a blaze of color. They decorated the proscenium arch in "vermillion and gold, violet and blue," thus affording a spectacle that would compete with the play for the audience's attention and would, they may have hoped, distract from the intense discomfort of the circuslike benches that other Players were constructing.[9] After further consideration, so as to draw all eyes to the stage, they painted the walls a somber "smokiest of deep warm greys."[10]

Glaspell avoided the theater while all of this was going on. She set up a study for herself in one of the hall bedrooms at Milligan Place, and while Cook melodramatized steel girders and building inspectors, she mulled over their depleting bank account. Frank Shay had agreed to publish *Trifles* and *Suppressed Desires*, and although it was now clear that even amateur productions of these plays would bring in considerable royalties—in 1920, Cook would jubilantly claim that *Suppressed Desires* "averaged forty dollars a week" after its publication in *Representative One-Act Plays*—Glaspell believed that a well-placed short story would be of more immediate value.[11] She also considered writing a novel based on *Trifles* but found that the story could not be expanded without losing the effect that compactness had offered. It did translate readily into a short story, "A Jury of Her Peers," however, published in *Everyweek* in March of the following year. Glaspell managed to retain the dramatic intensity, while the narrative form allowed her to develop the feelings of Mrs. Hale and Mrs. Peters, which in the play had to be conveyed by the acting. She also wrote "The Hearing Ear" and rejoiced at the letter of acceptance from *Harper's*.[12]

Meanwhile, work raged on at 139 Macdougal Street. With Cook thrusting himself here, there, and everywhere, the architects and painters raised the floor level of the stage and inclined the auditorium, while the remaining thespians discussed the first bill. Reed's resolutions had specified that the Players as a community would be responsible for selecting the programs. *Trifles* and *Bound East for Cardiff* were strong favorites for the opening bill, but the Washington Square Players had already purchased performing rights for Glaspell's play. This may well have caused bad feeling among the Provincetowners, but Cook argued that they needed the money and that Glaspell had already written another play for them anyway. Although the Players rejected the commercial theater on principle, Cook and Glaspell were clearly not immune to the power of financial reward and professional acclaim. O'Neill's piece about the dying sailor was an obvious choice for the first bill; no one doubted that even without the backdrop of the sea *Bound East for Cardiff* would captivate a New York audience. The Players also agreed on Louise Bryant's *The Game* for the opening bill, and the third choice was Dell's *King Arthur's Socks*. Cook had enthused in one of his September letters to Glaspell about Dell's new play, informing her that she had been cast as Guinevere, but Glaspell had ignored this further demand on her time. Although she had acted in her own plays in Provincetown and enjoyed the greasepaint, she was sufficiently self-critical to acknowledge her inexperience on the stage. Once she read Dell's play, a skit on free love in the context of the ancient legend, she must have firmly refused to have anything to do with it. Although she insisted that the reason for her refusal was her lack of acting ability, Dell felt slighted.

Rehearsals finally got under way, but in spite of Dell's previous experience with amateur theatricals, he could not handle directing a cast of friends in his own play. Teddy Ballantine took over. This failure marked the beginning of Dell's gradual withdrawal from the Players. It also demonstrated that the original Provincetown resolutions could not always be observed: already in the first bill, a play was being directed by someone other than its author.

The next task was to ensure that the actors had an audience to captivate. As a private company, the Players could not sell tickets but had to rely on "invitations" to fill the auditorium. The subscription system Cook had operated so successfully in Provincetown (thanks to which most little theaters survived) was threatening to let him down. Staking his all on the theater he had conceived, he dreamed of disappointed Broadway audiences flocking to Macdougal Street for plays of real artistic merit. He devoted a number of evenings—with active members, a reasonable supply of wine, and Glaspell's steadying influence at hand—to composing the first circular inviting New Yorkers to subscribe. He asked them for $4 in exchange for an associate membership, which covered "initiation fees and dues" and a seat for the season's performances. The response was extremely slow. The Players gloomily foresaw empty houses, but Cook was sanguine, if a little vague as to when the season would begin. The circular announced that "on or about the third of November" the Players would "open their first New York season." The idea that New York might fail to provide the little he asked of it—an audience—did not cross his mind: his circular, the Players' first artistic manifesto, stated the history and objectives of the Provincetown Players and testified to his naive faith in the venture:

> The present organization is the outcome of a group of people interested in the theater, who gathered spontaneously during two summers at Provincetown, Massachusetts, for the purpose of writing, producing and acting their own plays. The impelling desire of the group was to establish a stage where playwrights of sincere, poetic, literary and dramatic purpose could see their plays in action, and superintend their production without submitting to the commercial manager's interpretation of public taste. Equally, it was to afford an opportunity for actors, producers, scenic and costume-designers to experiment with a stage of extremely simple resources—it being the idea of THE PLAYERS that elaborate settings are unnecessary to bring out the essential qualities of a good play.[13]

The emphasis was on the stage and its workers, but Cook was to learn that without an audience, his Players were doomed, so in later announcements he was careful to flatter, cajole, and bully those whose presence was essential to his project.

A thousand circulars were sent out, and the Players anxiously waited for the post to bring back subscriptions. Three hundred checks trickled through the letterbox, prolonging the Players' despondency. But, unexpectedly, "faith and courage soared free from worry into a paradise of pure fun" when Jack Reed brought in 400 new subscriptions.[14] Gambling on Emily Hapgood's admiration of Robert Edmond Jones's scenic designs, he had coaxed her, as president of the New York Stage Society, to buy the Sunday and Tuesday performances of each bill for $1,600, thus assuring the Players full houses while replenishing the empty treasury.[15] The urbane audience that duly filled the Playwrights' Theatre on those nights was at first a cause of "terror and embarrassment" for the Players; however, members of the Stage Society soon recognized that the bare benches of the theater were not designed for socializing and, thrilled by the New York premiere of *Bound East for Cardiff*, learned indulgence for the experiments of the neophyte thespians.[16]

Help was also forthcoming from the Liberal Club, many of whose members were Provincetowners. Having dabbled in theater in the past, the club had collected costumes, lighting, and props, which it now offered the Players at half price on the condition that it could occasionally rent the theater for $5. Thus, the Players, "intellectually mature people, recruited from every profession and caste, and committed to no single cause or cult," found in their own Greenwich Village sufficient support to give them the start they needed.[17]

The Players' various backgrounds and busy professional lives were not always beneficial to the group. Their constitution, drawn up at the close of a Provincetown summer, had not taken into account the rigors of the working week. During this first October and early November, the Players met twice a week to read submissions and cast their votes, thus meeting Reed's stipulation that plays would be selected democratically. The process proved time-consuming and burdensome. Glaspell resented the frequent meetings that took up so much of her writing time, and although she was aware that Cook needed her tact, she felt that he demanded too much of her. She suffered when plays submitted by her friends were not well received. Neith Boyce had reworked *Constancy* into the fairy-tale mold she had initially favored, but the new version, *The Faithful Lover*, was rejected by a vote of eight to three. Happily, at that same meeting, her play *The Two Sons* was accepted (by a vote of ten to two), so Boyce's disappointment was mitigated.[18] The next meeting was even more disturbing. C. Guy Heguemborg had been invited on the strength of a dubious recommendation to read his comedy *Wanted*. The Players listened politely—all but Ida Rauh, who fidgeted, yawned relentlessly, and eventually, "with true Jewish freshness, got up in the middle of it and got something to eat, making as much noise as possible."[19] Once poor Heguemborg had departed, the play was "unanimously rejected" and the Players sniffily voted that "persons [who] are not members do not have the privilege of appearing before the Provincetown Players to read their plays."[20] The self-righteous members then settled down to listen to Mary Vorse read *Tomorrow*. When she finished, there was a "sickening silence" that threatened to last forever.[21] Jig stared hopelessly at Glaspell, silently begging her to save Vorse from the further embarrassment of a vote. But Vorse, suddenly overcome by guilt at having abandoned her sick son for the evening, was already trilling good-byes.

These meetings, painful to both authors and listeners, gradually became less frequent, and the ideal of democratic selection was relinquished. In time, a play-reading committee was formed. Edna Kenton would later claim that "Susan Glaspell and I were the only members of the group who really read every play that came into us during those six years."[22]

On 17 November 1916, Glaspell awoke with a hollow feeling she well remembered from her speech-making days at Drake: that night she was to make her acting debut before a New York audience. Cook had proposed a bill of revivals, and a dearth of new plays, coupled with memories of earlier successes, had convinced the Players of the expediency of this idea. *Suppressed Desires*, the Hapgoods' *Enemies*, and Reed's *Freedom* were chosen for the second bill. Glaspell had refused to play Guinevere in Dell's skit, and now, her natural reticence compounded by the fear of offending Dell, she earnestly insisted that as playwright, playreader, and Cook's mainstay, she had her hands full. She hoped that Rauh, whose acting she was honest enough to admire in spite of a nagging wifely apprehension, would play Henrietta, and since Margaret Nordfeldt had been cast as Mabel, she considered herself free to write. But after Rauh dropped out, Cook badgered Glaspell into taking the part. There was nothing for it but to accept that her days would be broken up by rehearsals at a moment's notice whenever Cook, who was playing Stephen, could tear himself away from his carpentry at the theater.

Suppressed Desires, in accordance with the resolutions passed in Provincetown, was directed by its coauthors, which meant that Glaspell took care of the practical details while Cook theorized on the dubious value of psychoanalysis, maintaining that the Viennese doctor divulged what he himself had discovered years earlier in the cabin: suppression of desire is sublimated in the spirit. The final rehearsals were held in the theater, and Glaspell, who until now had struggled to remain the disinterested observer, succumbed to the musty magic of the transformed parlors where the sobriety of an Apollonian past mingled with the anticipation of Dionysian revels.

But the dress rehearsal was no revel. Glaspell was nervous and devoutly wished she had not agreed to perform. Apart from coping with stage fright, she had to ensure that Cook would appear on time, dragging him away from fussing with lights, props, seating arrangements, or, even worse, yet another inspector who had to be convinced of the legality of their activities. Sitting beside Boyce in the auditorium during *Enemies* while Justus Sheffield and Rauh enacted undisguised scenes from the Hapgood-Boyce home, Glaspell understood Boyce's vulnerability and the sacrifices her marriage demanded. She almost wished the play had not been revived; it offended her sense of the private. Such personal conflicts were out of place in New York, whereas in Provincetown they had appeared as mere fun. *Freedom* (directed by Arthur Hohl of the Washington Square Players because Reed was undergoing a kidney operation), which had tickled her at the Wharf Theatre, had lost its zest. The *New York Herald* reviewer, who had paid for his seat in order to be able to write up the Provincetown Players (the Players did not believe in giving complimentary tickets), felt let down too. "*Freedom*," he fretted, "was rather a disappointment to the members of the Provincetown club, who expected more from John Reed, the author. It seemed that in a prison cell he chose a woefully far fetched setting for light intellectual farce. *Freedom* was a miscalculated mix-up, in spite of its many smart epigrams."[23]

A fraught dress rehearsal traditionally augurs well for the first night, and indeed, the *Herald* notwithstanding, cheers rewarded the Provincetowners. Glaspell drew a sigh of relief but was still terrified of the Sunday performance, when the audience would consist of subscribers from the Stage Society. The Saturday *Herald*, though not thrilled by *Freedom*, was kind to *Suppressed Desires*: it judged the play "the one decidedly amusing novelty" of the bill. The reviewer also reported that Nicholas Satan Inc. had "applied for the tropical rights for this play, for production on the Devil's Hall circuit."[24] If this came off, it would solve the Cooks' financial problems that winter. For the first time, Glaspell felt justified in having sacrificed her writing time to acting.

A tradition that was never broken had been set after the premiere of *Constancy* and *Suppressed Desires* at the Hapgoods' home in 1915: the Players-to-be had laid in a supply of liquor to celebrate the inauguration of their theater. Now, with a stage of their own, Cook believed that after a first night the Provincetown Players should drink together to rid themselves of tensions and grievances accumulated during rehearsals. That Friday evening, they gathered at the Liberal Club, where four quarts of three-star Hennessey brandy, two quarts of rum, two quarts of peach brandy, two quarts of lemon juice, and ten pounds of sugar, all indispensable for their exhilarating "Fish House Punch," mingled with a melting block of ice.[25] The expense of these "Wind-up Parties"—$78.01 (recorded as petty cash in the minutes) for the first—certainly suggest such an almighty punch rather than the more modest imbibing that Glaspell's account of their parties implies: "We were very poor at times, but never so poor we couldn't have wine for these parties. It was important we drink together, for thus were wounds healed, and we became one. . . . We had said hard things to one another in the drive of the last rehearsals, the strain of opening night. Now I might see Jig's arm around a neck he had threatened to wring. 'Jig, you are getting drunk,' someone would say. 'It is for the good of the Provincetown Players,' he would explain. 'I am always ready to sacrifice myself to a cause.' When the wine began to show the bottom of the bowl, 'Give it all to me,' Jig would propose, 'and I guarantee to intoxicate all the rest of you.' He glowed at these parties."[26] Such parties continued until dawn, and more than once, Glaspell, who was not a heavy drinker, would retire early, leaving Jig in thrall to Dionysus.[27] He held his liquor well and would come home in the early hours apparently totally in control. He would then reenact for her what had been said— and not said—after she had gone, expecting her to share his amazement at human folly as well as his joy in the rare discovery of a kindred spirit. Eventually, exhausted, he would fall asleep. Saturday would go by quietly, all of the Provincetowners needing to piece themselves together for that evening's performance.

—————••❮❀❯••—————

Although Glaspell was completely worn out after the final performance on Tuesday evening, for the rest of the week, she attended rehearsals for the third bill. She had promised to help Boyce and O'Neill with their new plays, *The Two Sons* and *Before Breakfast*, but she found that O'Neill had an august, experienced director to help him. James O'Neill had seen *Bound East for Cardiff* and had been disappointed that the melodramatic qualities of the play had not been brought out by the actors, so he had offered to help prevent his son's future plays from being mangled by what he considered amateurish incompetence. Eugene O'Neill wrote *Before Breakfast*, the monologue of a disgruntled wife, to test an audience's endurance when subjected to the prolonged presence of a single actor on the stage—a trial run for *The Emperor Jones* (1920).[28] The husband commits suicide offstage as his wife, played by the red-haired Mary Pyne, rants on; the audience sees only "his sensitive hand with slender fingers" as he reaches out for the bowl of hot water she hands him.[29] The text certainly lends itself to melodramatic exaggeration, and O'Neill paced the short aisle of the Playwrights' Theatre as his father taught Pyne the art of histrionic acting shunned by the Players.[30] Glaspell marveled that a Broadway-style production guaranteed to satisfy any commercial theater audience could be achieved with a play she herself had accepted for performance in their theater. This was conclusive proof that, however important the text itself might be, the theatrical experience had to be a work of harmony among director, actor, and playwright.

Glaspell had also voted for Boyce's play, *The Two Sons*, which examines the relationship between a mother and her two sons, showing how the mother's treatment of the children has influenced their behavior. Boyce, whose elder son had suffered from polio as a child, was clearly exploring the consequences of overprotectiveness. In her play, the mother is tender toward the artist Paul, whom she had nursed through childhood and whose engagement to Stella she resents. Her older son Karl had left home early to become a sailor and is now on leave. Convinced that his mother hated him and that his brother considered himself superior, Karl had grown up jealous and vindictive. Unable to believe in his mother's love, he is distrustful of women, delighting in meaningless flirtations. Following a pattern established in childhood, when he had avenged himself by taking his brother's toys, he now takes Stella from Paul. But Paul is too good and too devoted to Karl to harbor ill-feelings. If James O'Neill had stayed for the rehearsals, the play could easily have been transformed into a tear-jerking melodrama in spite of Boyce's subdued style, but under the direction of the author, inexperienced as she was, the play came across as a tragedy of misunderstood maternal love.

The play touched Glaspell deeply, and many years later, she would address a similar theme in *The Comic Artist* (1928). Eugene O'Neill may well have lingered in the theater during Boyce's rehearsals, discussing the brothers' love-hate relationship. The tension between the siblings drew him. His love for his own brother, James, was deep but tinged with an ambivalence he could never understand, so Boyce's focus on the mother offered him an insight into his own family drama. He too would explore a similar theme in *Beyond the Horizon* (1920) and examine family relationships in *Ah, Wilderness!* (1933) and *Long Day's Journey into Night* (1956).[31]

The third play on the bill, *Lima Beans: A Conventional Scherzo*, although eventually voted in by the Players, was a bone of contention all along. Alfred Kreymborg, an imagist poet and editor of various poetry magazines, including *Others*, yearned for excitement in the theater comparable to the excitement he had experienced in the world of poetry. Greenwich Village disappointed him until he found the Provincetown Players, having earlier dismissed the Washington Square Players as "effete." On his first visit to the Playwrights' Theatre, he was "thrilled to the hypothesis that at last something was happening in the theatre," although he feared that the Players' "absorption in realism" would blind them to the merits of the play he eagerly submitted.[32] Indeed, the Players did not approve of his "fantastic treatment of commonplace themes set to a stylized rhythm," and not one of them thought they could act in it.[33] But Reed, by threatening to resign, forced them to accept the play and, in accordance with the Provincetown regulations, to allow Kreymborg to direct it.[34] They sandwiched his piece between *Before Breakfast* and *The Two Sons*, thus providing a lighthearted contrast to those almost melodramatic studies of family life.

Lima Beans skips along to its own rhythm, which Kreymborg beat out with a pencil at rehearsals for the actors, fellow poets Mina Loy and William Carlos Williams.[35] But it deals with a theme similar to that of the other plays: the inevitable, frequently painful, sacrifice-demanding twists of human relationships, which Kreymborg cleverly reflected in the pantomimic quality of the movement and speech of the husband and wife. Kreymborg does not probe deeply into the feelings of his characters or explore their motives. The wife's obeisance to the husband may well have piqued the sincere feminists among the actresses, accounting in part for their refusal to perform in it—certainly Mina Loy "sniffed a little at the commonplaceness of the marriage theme"—but the play does not make a transcendent statement about a woman's role in wedlock.[36] It is a whimsical account of the enigma of love (the Italian *scherzo* means "joke"), and the effect of "spontaneous play" delighted even the militant feminist Edna Kenton.[37]

Kreymborg's play represents a type of drama that both Gerhard Bach and Robert Károly Sarlós, critics and historians of the Players, believe lost out among the Players in "the internal war of experimentation between the forces favouring an idealism based on socio-realistic outlook and the forces favouring an idealism completely devoid of contemporary concerns."[38] Bach divides the Provincetowners' development into three well-defined stages: an initial stage in which social realism prevailed, a middle phase in which the war between "the realistic prose play" and the "symbolistic verse play" was waged, and a third stage in which "renewed social realism [was] interspersed with experiments in expressionism."[39] The immediate outcome of the battle in the middle phase (which originated with Marguerite and William Zorach's determinedly unrealistic sets for *The Game* as early as 1916) was a bill offered by the "Other Players" for four days in March 1918. Quite a bit of maneuvering—if we can trust the maneuverers' memories—went into the organization of this recalcitrant group, whose name honored the innovative poetry magazine *Others* as well as the Provincetown Players. Kreymborg, supported by William Zorach, who had confided to him that the Players' success with realism was thwarting his artistic ambitions as a stage designer, ordered a bottle of wine and sat down with Cook to convince him to be more "daring and elastic" in his choice of plays.[40] Although he was a newcomer to the group, Kreymborg (who in his autobiography loyally credited the Provincetown Players with the transformation of the American theater) was very much aware of the nondemocratic power wielded by its leading members. His enthusiasm for the new and untried and his faith in everything American must have spoken to Jig's heart because the Players soon offered the poets use of their theater for a nominal sum. The bill was "an intoxicating success," and the Other Players, to quote Kreymborg, "lost their heads."[41] Peeved by the Provincetown Players' refusal to rearrange their schedule in order to give the poets more time at the Playwrights' Theatre, the Other Players relocated to the charming Bramhall Playhouse, where, in spite of Heywood Broun's enthusiastic review, financial failure soon compelled the group to renounce its independent status.

The program included two plays by Kreymborg, Edna St. Vincent Millay's *Two Slatterns and a King*, and Kathleen Cannell's *Static Dances*. Cannell, by profession a journalist, was a devotee of stylized movement or what she called "static dance." She had appeared with the Provincetowners in *The Game* but was not interested in realistic acting. Under the stage name Rihani, she performed in various Village nightspots, offering what Broun was to call "Cubist" dance.[42] We have no comments by Cook on this bill, but given his faith in the power of music and dance, he surely must have approved such a departure from everyday realism.

Helen Deutsch and Stella Hanau, writing not long after the event and thus representing general opinion, did not believe that Cook's influence was negative: "Kreymborg and the Zorachs soon found themselves heading a faction which wanted to present poetic drama exclusively; the Provincetown, they felt, was too devoted to the kitchen sink. . . . The Provincetown gave its rebellious child the theatre for the production of *Jack's House* and *Two Slatterns and a King*, realizing, probably, that one of the finest things any cause can produce is a noble rebel."[43]

But we must question whether Kreymborg and his rebels against realism in the theater had a valid cause. Cook's theatrical aspirations were contradictory: on the one hand, his desire to create a truly American theater led him toward ritual and thence to poetic expression, and on the other, he recognized the potential of the "kitchen sink" drama to portray the essence of America. As a playwright, he favored the poetic—*The Spring* (1921) was an unsuccessful attempt at blending a poetic past with a realistic present—and Kenton assures us that, in spite of the technical difficulties of creating illusion on the stage, the Provincetown Players preferred "poetic and fantasy plays" to "thrillers and shockers."[44]

The rebellious advocates of poetic drama, according to Bach and Sarlós, were not given free rein until the 1919–20 season, when Cook and Glaspell took a sabbatical from the theater. Indeed, that year, more poetic plays were produced than ever before. Djuna Barnes, Alfred Kreymborg, Wallace Stevens, and Edna St. Vincent Millay were largely responsible for making the season a success, although Millay's *Aria da Capo* (1919) was the only big hit. Edmund Wilson, who, like so many young men, ached to marry Millay, would recall in *Shores of Light* that he had felt "thrilled and troubled by this little play." He wrote: "*Aria da Capo* was an eclogue, highly charged and deeply disturbing, like all her best work of that time; but the characters—as was suitable—were pure abstractions."[45] Millay herself was delighted with her piece and wrote to her mother: "I have actually written the *Aria da Capo* play and finished it, you know the one, Pierrot & Columbine & the shepherds & the spirit of Tragedy.— Well, it's a peach,—one of the best things I've ever done."[46]

After graduating from Vassar, Millay had cherished ambitions of becoming an actress. She joined the Players in 1917, captivating Dell with her reading of the ingenue in his *The Angel Intrudes*, and was soon known as "the beautiful young actress at the Provincetown."[47] She was also known as the author of "Renascence," the poem that had *not* won *Lyric Year*'s poetry prize but had nonetheless brought her critical and popular acclaim. The Provincetown Players staged her *The Princess Marries the Page* in the first bill of the 1918–19 season, together with O'Neill's *Where the Cross Is Made*. The fairy-tale lightness of Millay's divertissement made a startling contrast with the young Irishman's tragedy of obsession and insanity. Broun, for one, was not impressed by O'Neill's gauche attempt to put realistic ghosts on the stage, praising Millay's play as "being visually the finest piece of the evening."[48]

Aria da Capo, in spite of its magical air, "perfectly expressed," to quote Joan Dash, Millay's biographer, "the sense of bitterness and loss, the cynicism, the belief that nothing will ever be any better because history is a treadmill."[49] The play begins with Pierrot and Columbine enacting the eternal harlequinade of apparently frivolous nonsense in which the alert spectator recognizes the tragedy of mortality:

> Columbine: I haven't heard the clock tick for an hour.
> Pierrot: It's ticking all the same. If you were a fly,
>   You would be dead by now.[50]

They are interrupted by Cothurnus, the omnipotent stage manager, who has decided that Corydon and Thyrsis should play their scene, thus condemning Pierrot and Columbine to an endless reenactment of first lines. Corydon and Thyrsis, embodying the delights of the shepherd's life, stake out their territories with streamers that mark—in a false echo of *A Midsummer Night's Dream*—a "vile Wall" and embark on games of possession whereby they quickly lose their pastoral innocence.[51] "Yours / mine" acquires deadly significance as they struggle for water rights and wealth, learning distrust along the way. As Corydon strangles his onetime friend with a necklace of jewels, Thyrsis forces him to drink a bowl of poisoned water. Only in the agony of death does Corydon understand that their differences were merely a game they had consciously chosen to play. Cothurnus reappears and, kicking the two bodies under a table, summons Pierrot and Columbine to replay their farce of love.

In *Aria da Capo*, the only play Millay would later consider worth republishing, Millay expressed the absurdity of life and death and the indifference of those in power. The flippant veneer of her terse antiwar statement ensured its passage through the nets of the most zealous guardians of the Sedition Act. Millay created the light mood by abandoning iambic pentameter—the accepted rhythm for verse drama—for a lighter, more popular, four-beat rhythm with a caesura reminiscent of Anglo-Saxon verse. But in spite of this departure from the traditional, her popularity as a poet and playwright in the 1910s and early 1920s waned when T. S. Eliot's admirers spurned her work as too classical in form and subject matter; they forgot that she had disclosed the banality of life and rediscovered the verse play years before Eliot turned to the genre.

The sets for *Aria da Capo*, in keeping with the conventions established by the Provincetowners, were beautifully simple, in line with the trim language and form of the play. Charles Ellis, the abstract painter, placed Craigian screens of differing heights to the right and left of the stage "in such a manner as to give the effect of depth and distance." Following Millay's instructions, he created a stylized design in black and white, thus achieving the "merry" interior she required to set the tone for the futile death and indifferent love of her harlequinade.[52] The ingenious combination of the popular and the pastoral, the swift wit, the metatextuality of the play, and its political insight—foreshadowing developments in the second half of the century—fascinated audience members, who by now had been educated to appreciate departures from the tired realism of the love-or-property plot purveyed by Broadway. Bach asserts that "Edna St. Vincent Millay had as much potential for dramatic symbolism as Susan Glaspell had for realism. It may be conjectured that had the Provincetown Players at this point decided to support experiments in symbolic verse drama, Millay would have evolved as the Provincetown representative. Her verse play, *Aria da Capo* (1918), is the first American play to make explicit use of dramaturgic devices later to be employed by the Theatre of the Absurd. *Aria da Capo*, besides its modestly expressionist setting, is quite likely an early forerunner of the Absurd tradition. Its importance as such, however, has yet to be acknowledged."[53]

The Provincetown Players had come together in what Kenton called a spirit of play, but they also acted in a spirit of rebellion against the established order, a desire to pass beyond that which was known into a territory as yet undiscovered in America. European innovations were inching their way into the commercial theater in spite of the opposition of the old guard, headed by David Belasco, but it was the Provincetown Players who, looking into their own selves for new frontiers, made American theatrical history. They adapted to their resources and needs every promising European dramaturgical strategy, such as Craig's screens, but more important, they adopted his concept of the unity of the stage experience. They were also quite clearly prepared to produce a considerable diversity of plays. The only plays they rejected outright were those not written by Americans and those that simply could not be done on a small stage. Kenton gives as an egregious example a play on the Civil War with forty speaking parts, a scene at Gettysburg, and cannon fire offstage; even Cook balked at the challenge of squeezing forty actors onto a stage that could only accommodate three in comfort.[54] Cook complained so frequently of the dearth of good plays by Americans that he was not likely to refuse a play merely because it did not comply with the canons of realism, and he was always eager for the type of play that would never be accepted for production in a commercial theater. Bach's charge that the Provincetown Players stifled the poetic drama emerging among its members is unfounded. Even the 1919–20 season, directed by the younger Players, boasted only one truly successful poetic play—Millay's *Aria da Capo*. Furthermore, Cook, O'Neill, and Glaspell gradually turned away from realism, and it was Cook who led the way with *The Spring*, although Glaspell had tentatively experimented with stylization as early as 1917 in *The People*. Their ventures in this direction were not always successful, but even in their own work, they were ready to experiment with new forms and styles.

In spite of constant mutual assurances that the war in Europe would soon be over, by the end of 1916, even the most naively optimistic member of the Players did not anticipate a speedy resolution of the conflict. The reelection of President Woodrow Wilson did little to assuage the worries of those who opposed "preparedness" for America's entry into the war. The Players felt the need to make a positive contribution to pacifism, and at a meeting on 10 January 1917, "after considerable discussion it was decided to make the seventh bill a program of war plays." O'Neill contributed *The Sniper*, and the bill was completed with pieces by Michael Gold and Rita Wellman.

The third, fourth, fifth, and sixth bills were not successful. Kenton acknowledged that the plays were not of the best quality because of the pressure of time: it was proving impossible to find and rehearse three new plays every other week.[55] The fifth bill had in fact fallen behind schedule and precipitated a minor crisis that affected Cook deeply: his onetime farmhand and guide to socialism, Floyd Dell, abandoned the Players. Dell had allowed them carte blanche with his play *A Long Time Ago* (1917) and was horrified with the result. Duncan MacDougal, exulting in the revelations he had witnessed with the Irish Players, gave the actors wooden clogs, "so that nothing could be heard except *clump, thump, bump!*"[56] Such elevation of experimental effect over artistic consideration was unacceptable to Dell. Although not totally unexpected since his friendship with Cook had been under the pall of sexual rivalry and disapproval for many years now, this defection grieved Cook. As always, it was up to Glaspell to bring him out of his depression.

The Players had recently acquired a professional director, Nina Moise, who stayed with them until April 1918. A drama major from Stanford, she immediately captivated Cook, the former English instructor at her alma mater, and, horrified by the Provincetowners' antics, tried to cure them of their conviction that "anything one did in life could be done on the stage."[57] Cook did not limit himself to the role of director of the Players; at the time of the Dell crisis, he was also rehearsing Kenneth MacNichol's *Pan*, serving as both director and actor. Glaspell, aware of the strain he was under and that Moise's professional expertise could save the Players from disaster, convinced her to offer Cook "a little help."[58] Cook not only agreed to Moise's suggestions but was greatly relieved; he was beginning to understand that if his dream of a theater in New York was to prosper, the experimenters would have to surrender some of their power to experienced hands. The Players, exhausted by months of group work, elected production and scenic committees, with Moise chairing the first and Donald Corley the second.

In spite of her commitment to the Players and her untold endeavors as Cook's guardian angel, Glaspell still found the time and energy to write. Giving herself entirely to the stage and abandoning the idea of writing another novel, she concentrated on creating a dramatic form suitable to her temperament. During the first two seasons on Macdougal Street, she offered the Players a series of one-act pieces in which she developed her understanding of theater technique, as well as honing her skills. Her protagonists, all rebellious women who would disown society, display her growing angst at the unsatisfactory relationships between men and women. Glaspell's apprenticeship with the Players would culminate in *The Verge* (1921), a drama that transcends the established boundaries of theater as well as society.

The People, which Glaspell wrote in the autumn of 1916 and which was unanimously accepted for production, was about to go into rehearsal, and she was again faced with the dilemma of how to apportion her time and energy between directing and acting.[59] This time, however, the Provincetown resolutions could legitimately be broken by placing the play in Moise's hands. Relieved of that task, Glaspell, who identified closely with the principal female character, the Woman from Idaho, agreed to take it on. Acting was the Achilles heel of the little theaters, and the performance skills of the Players—like those in all of the little theaters in New York—were berated by reviewers. John Corbin of the *New York Times*, while extolling Washington Square's little theaters, could find nothing to commend in the acting, which he thought totally lacking in technical skill and "more notable for its intention than for its achievement."[60] When the renowned Jacques Copeau, avant-garde director of the Vieux Colombier, visited the Playwrights' Theatre in 1917, he sided with other critics in mocking the acting of the Provincetowners: "They do not know how to stand on stage, nor how to enter or go off, and the platform sounds hollow under their badly-calculated steps." Nonetheless, Glaspell earned his exceptional praise for her portrayal of the Woman from Idaho. She "touched me to the core," he said, "by the simplicity of her attitude, the pure quality of her person, the inimitable feeling in a nuance of her intonation." A few days later, in a speech to the Washington Square Players, he could not contain his delight in her acting and, without mentioning her name, held her up as an example of what actors should aim for, insisting that "the actor [must] become a human being again, and all the great changes in the theatre will follow from that."[61] The Provincetown Players had indubitably scored a success over their Washington Square colleagues, and Glaspell's triumph was tipsily toasted.

Glaspell's *The People* was inspired by the financial problems and crises of artistic and literary ethics that periodically overtook *The Masses* and was probably designed as a dig at the growing cynicism of its assistant editor, Floyd Dell. For Glaspell, the play was a statement of the convictions she shared with Cook, which she would express more fully in later writing. In her short stories and *The Glory of the Conquered*, her first novel, she had already stressed that visionary commitment was an essential factor in the progress of both the individual and humankind. *The People* shows that love of an ideal can transcend petty quarrels and trivial financial worries. The Woman from Idaho convinces the editor of *The People* of the significance of his task, quoting Abraham Lincoln: "Let us here highly resolve that these dead shall not have died in vain." With a wide, loving gesture, she pleads: "Let life become what it may become!—so beautiful that everything that is back of us is worth everything it cost."[62]

When the play opens, the poet Oscar Tripp, the associate editor of *The People*; the printer Tom; and an assistant named Sara are awaiting the return of Edward Wills, the editor. He has been on an unsuccessful fund-raising trip and arrives in a foul mood, fully prepared to close down the periodical because of its financial problems. A number of contributors and well-wishers arrive on the scene, allegorical embodiments of different approaches to the publication. The Artist believes that not enough space is given to art, the Poet argues for more poetry (insiders would have recognized that these figures represented John Sloan and John Reed at *The Masses*), the Earnest Approach demands sobriety, the Light Touch promotes gaiety, the Philosopher pushes form, and the Firebrand (evoking Hippolyte Havel, their pet anarchist) damns the bourgeoisie with every utterance. The ensemble is successfully choric, and the repetitive speeches only just miss the rhythmic effect Kreymborg had achieved in *Lima Beans*. Even so, the writing is sufficiently stylized—and competent direction would have brought this out—to create a Strindbergian dream world. After these critical friends explain where the publication has failed, the Boy from Georgia, the Man from the Cape, and the Woman from Idaho, representatives of the simple folk, come to dedicate themselves to its cause. They too are each reduced to one outstanding characteristic: the Boy is "a freshman with a good allowance," naïveté and idealism personified, and the Man, "a mute ponderous figure," has miraculously been awoken from his stupor by *The People* and has come to claim "the rest of it."[63] It is up to the most articulate of the three, the Woman from Idaho, to clarify his taciturn utterance: "We've come because you made us want something we didn't have, made us want it so much we had to move the way we thought was toward it—before the sun goes down."[64] It is she who convinces the editor that he has a responsibility toward his readers; he has adopted a Whitmanesque stance, has called them to follow him into a greater awareness of the beauty of life, and cannot let them slip back into their ignorance. She inspires him with the valor to continue his mission, just as Glaspell frequently roused Cook to shake off the dejection caused by adverse criticism of the Provincetown Players.

Glaspell's later plays would be compared with the work of George Bernard Shaw. British audiences in particular were receptive to her dedicated treatment of an idea, whereas Americans often complained that she was too "talky." The enthusiastic reviewer of a 1923 production of *Inheritors* recognized that Glaspell's "insistent vision of life" would hardly be applauded on Broadway: "One is at once aware that Miss Glaspell has transgressed the sacred formula of the American theater. Her play deals directly with neither property nor sex."[65] Family heirlooms and affairs of the heart do not occupy Glaspell; her subject is the individual's struggle for beauty and perfection and what happens when this instinct is suppressed. In *The People*, she explores how the urge is awakened and shows that it is simple folk, not artists, who keep it alive. But in this one-act play, as in others she wrote for the Provincetown Players during this period, Glaspell also recognized the need to amuse the audience and, according to Deutsch and Hanau, "revealed a gift for comedy."[66] *The People* has its lighter side, of course, but it is a far cry from comedy. Glaspell's conviction that the radical publication has a mission that can save the world prevents her from sufficiently enjoying the situation and personae she has created, and as one critic complained, "the humor becomes too heavily freighted with the suggestion of seriousness, the characters merge into caricature, and the spectator listens to the preachment of some beautiful thoughts that live as words, as ideas, but surely not as drama."[67] Undeterred by such opinions, Glaspell continued to strive for humor, but her real talent lay in serious drama; her short plays of this period are assuredly comedies of manners, but the laughter is subdued by the weight of the knowledge of humankind's duplicity.

The other play Glaspell wrote for the Players that winter explores the consequences of misconceived nonconformism. She had returned to Davenport in December for a short visit and yielded to Ma-Mie's pleas that she make the rounds of Davenport society with her. Her childhood perception of alienation was renewed, although in reverse. The daughter of a poor farmer, she had striven for acceptance and been sorely hurt by unfeeling rejection. Gradually she had gained entrance into certain magic circles: the Tuesday Club had opened its doors to her, and society organizers had accepted her in their midst as a reporter, but she had always felt on the edge of things. Now, as a published writer and playwright and as Cook's wife, the scandal dispersed by Ma-Mie's patronage, her presence in all of the best drawing rooms was eagerly sought, but she was unwilling to mingle with the coterie of small-town highbrows, with their pretensions and pseudo culture. She was aware of the humor of the situation and wrote with splendid wryness to Louise Bryant: "Just today I finished a comedy which I am hoping is funny. It seemed so to me as I read it over, but perhaps I am a prejudiced person."[68] On her return to New York, she read *Family Pride* to the committee and the members enjoyed it, although it was not performed until November 1917, under the title *Close the Book*.[69]

Glaspell had indeed written another bitter comedy of manners. This time, she makes a mockery of prized conventions and concepts of respectability by reducing high ideals of freedom to such trivia as dinner obligations. John Corbin of the *New York Times*, who braved the wooden benches to see each new bill, was delighted by the wit of *Close the Book* and praised Glaspell for "dissecting [the poses of the Villagers] with a scalpel."[70] Jhansi, the young protagonist who casts herself as a gypsy, glories in her self-imposed status of alien. She hopes that Peyton, whom she plans to marry, will eventually throw off his grand family ties and "take to the open road" with her.[71] But Peyton's family, founders of the town and its university, cannot stomach his marriage to an intruder with no pedigree. They dig into the past, where they discover a perfectly respectable family for Jhansi. She is no stray waif—her parents died in a typhoid epidemic and she was adopted by friends. As Jhansi's carefully built structure of rebellion based on alienation collapses, Peyton reads the fine print in *Iowa Descendants of New England Families* and bestows the dubious "respectability" Jhansi values on both families by revealing the misdeeds of their ancestors. Jhansi is placated, Peyton's grandmother insists he close the book and come in to dinner, and the audience suspects the laugh is on them, for Glaspell has subtly raised various issues of social behavior and mocked all fanaticism.

Two elements central to Glaspell's later work appear in *Close the Book*: the stray or unwanted child and the older woman—a grandmother or mother—who shows greater understanding than any other member of her family. The older woman makes her first appearance in this play. Although Glaspell says very little about her mother-in-law in *The Road to the Temple*, their relationship does not seem to have been troubled by any of the classic misunderstandings. (She wrote very little about her own mother.) Her portrayal of the mature woman is always wholly sympathetic, and Ma-Mie was most likely the model for this grandmother, as for later grandmothers in her plays and novels. But the return of the unwanted child is disconcerting (Anne in *The Visioning* escapes from an unhappy home). Although Glaspell mocks the entrenched caste categories of Davenport and shuns Davenporters' advances toward her, she cannot forget her childhood dreams of mistaken parentage and ensuing alienation. Her unwanted children will always find a home and a measure of happiness, but their very existence in her writing points to a deep insecurity and dissatisfaction, which surfaced even more clearly in her next play, *The Outside* (1917).

This time, Glaspell does not strive to amuse her audience. She had always been struck by the resilience of women and of nature, and, inspired by the incessant struggle between the woods and the dunes on the "front-line" of the shore, she links woman's survival to that of nature.[72] Recognizing that her forte lay in realism rather than surrealistic allegory but attracted by expressionist symbolism, she carefully set her piece in a locale she knew well: the old lifesaving station on the outer edge of Cape Cod's crooked finger, where the sea had sculpted a cliff of sand so high that the crew members, no longer able to launch their boats, were forced to surrender, leaving the bare boards of the station to Glaspell's dramatic imagination. (Mabel Dodge had actually refurbished the station and entertained the Provincetown summer folk there, and when she tired of it, Eugene O'Neill took it over as an ideal writer's retreat.) Glaspell peopled the play sparsely: Mrs. Patrick, Allie Mayo, and three lifesavers who are trying to resuscitate a man they found washed up on the sand in front of the old station are her only characters. The men cannot redeem what the ocean has taken, but their struggle inspires the two women, who had rejected all communication with society when their husbands left them, to return to life. First, Allie Mayo, whose husband disappeared in a whaling accident, and then Mrs. Patrick, abandoned for another woman, quicken to that higher force of nature that commands life and in which, as women, they participate. O'Neill's protagonists submit to the destiny the sea imposes on them, but Glaspell's women, though wounded by the insensitivity of men, are close enough to the life force to reassert their voices and claim a victory.

The humiliation of the deserted wife haunted Glaspell. She herself had taken Cook from another woman, and although she had worked out her guilt feelings in *Fidelity*, the fear that history would repeat itself would never leave her. Jig constantly gave her cause for concern, and he did prematurely desert her in death. Glaspell would rework *The Outside* into a short story, "A Rose in the Sand: The Salvation of a Lonely Soul" (1927), in which she dispenses with the lifesavers trying to revive a drowned man and concentrates instead on the metaphor of the battle for survival between the woods and the dunes.[73] The winter winds blow the sand over bushes and shrubs but then "things take root in the sand, and when there's enough growing there they've *got* the sand. It's anchored."[74] The cyclical nature of this battle finds a resonance in Ellen Paxton, the jilted wife who cannot have children. At first, she refuses to acknowledge that the boundary of the outside, the "line of death," is being challenged at all, but when a wild rose, "alone and undismayed, fragile and authoritative," blooms in the sand near the water pump, she acquiesces to the power of life.[75] She marks her victory over death and the laws of man by agreeing to take in an orphaned, illegitimate child. In the novel *Fugitive's Return* (1929), Glaspell will again use the story of a deserted wife who is silenced in humiliation but eventually rediscovers her voice and rebels against the world of men by caring for a young girl exiled by her patriarchal community.

The form of both novel and story favors an elaboration of psychological and narrative detail that is denied by the exigencies of the theater and has to be provided by the dialogue of the lifesavers in *The Outside*. Glaspell explores an idea through words, not actions; the drama is not supplied by the events—there is never any hope of restoring the drowned man—but by the reawakening of the protagonist to her natural gift of life. No hint of comedy lightens the mood of doom inscribed by the sea; it is lifted only when Mrs. Patrick accepts the cycles of life and agrees to partake in the season of growth.

In *Woman's Honor*, produced in the spring of 1918, Glaspell again tried to amuse her audience, but the deep import of her seemingly trivial plot overwhelmed her.[76] The characters are all stock comedy figures and are identified as stereotypes of the different models of survival open to women: "the Motherly one," "the Shielded one," "the Silly one," and so on. This unhappily slight sketch chides women for adopting such man-desired poses—and men for believing in them—by portraying them as worthless projections of the male imagination. A young man wrongly accused of murder will not reveal his alibi for fear of tarnishing his mistress's reputation, but he cannot evade the host of women who claim they have a right to sacrifice their "honor" for his life. But the rudimentary comedy is stifled as soon as the women realize that they are, in the words of the Shielded One, "victims of men's dreadful *need* for nobility."[77] (Time and again, Glaspell worried about the male need for an icon, reworking the theme from different angles in the plays *Bernice* [1919] and *Chains of Dew* [1922] and in the later novel *Ambrose Holt and Family* [1931].)[78] Glaspell's rightful disgust with woman as man-made object does not allow her to work out the humor of the situation; the conflict between her longing to see women breaking out of the shackles of received morality and her "need" (natural or inculcated) to pamper men finally thwarts her wit.

The critic Isaac Goldberg once again lamented the battle between the Dionysian and the Apollonian that consumed Glaspell's imagination, and although he conceded that the play contained "some acute criticism of the masculine mind," he regretted that it "wavers between the farce and the serious play."[79] Others were more favorably disposed. The *New York Evening Globe*, for instance, enthused: "The theme of the play is not only exceedingly amusing, but quite unhackneyed."[80]

The challenge of the full-length play goaded the Players, although it was not until 1924 that O'Neill publicly put the one-act drama behind him.[81] The short play was the staple of little theaters for the obvious reason that its brevity made it easier to handle both for unsalaried players whose days were taken up by working for a living and for inexperienced directors and producers. But Cook was the first to take up the challenge by writing *The Athenian Women*.

The history and culture of ancient Greece had always gripped Cook's imagination, and when America entered the Great War in the summer of 1917, perplexed by the barbarity of armed encounters, he turned to Thucydides and immersed himself in the history of the Peloponnesian conflict. He came to the conclusion that there were multiple parallels between the two wars, attributing to Thucydides "a prophetic foreknowledge that he was writing the story of a war so typical that its outlines and events would recur."[82] The consequences of war tortured Cook; he could not bear to think of the cultural losses it made inevitable, nor did he see any reason why a country should squander its resources on destruction when it could be creating beauty. Fearful that America would not rise again like the phoenix from the ashes after this world conflagration, he endowed the Provincetown Players' continuing dramatic efforts with a sacred purpose: "The social justification which we feel to be valid now for makers and players of plays is that they shall help keep alive in the world the light of the imagination. Without it the wreck of the world that was cannot be cleared away and the new world shaped."[83]

The Peloponnesian War led him back to Aristophanes' peace plays. The salacious *Lysistrata* attracted him most of all, but not for its ribaldry. Cook had always suffered from a tendency to idealize woman, boldly attributing to her—even before his second wife Mollie Price allied herself with Emma Goldman—a soul and an intelligence denied her by most men. By 1917, married to a member of the Heterodoxy and surrounded by women intent on breaking social conventions and entering the public sphere, he shared with Glaspell his pleasure at Lysistrata's refusal to allow the magistrates access to the gold reserves hidden in one of the temples of the Acropolis. Lysistrata argues that, having been "in charge of all your housekeeping finances for years," the women are perfectly capable of controlling public spending.[84] But it is not just money that Lysistrata and her followers refuse the men. They have all sworn not to allow their husbands any sexual congress until peace is declared.

In 411 B.C., when there seemed to be no hope of an honorable end to the war between Athens and Sparta, Aristophanes piquantly turned the political impasse into a divertissement for the Athenians at the Lenaea, the festival of the god Dionysus. By no means a simpleminded pacifist, his love and understanding of Athens were such that he could laugh at the sexual insatiability of her men—and women. Denied sex, the women were about to break their vow, while the men, bent double to hide their swollen "cipher rods," would do anything to mount their wives again.[85] The erotic scenes in which women tease their menfolk only to deny them satisfaction, the bawdy language and constant reference, through both words and signs, to their "giant carrots," must have given the Athenians a good laugh, releasing some of the tension created by the state of war.[86] Aristophanes was not seriously suggesting that peace lay in the hands of women; he was in fact mocking them for wanting their husbands to stay at home. But Cook, idealist and lover of humanity, was earnestly moved by the play when he saw it in New York in 1913. He wrote to Glaspell of this apparently desolating experience: "I cried because that great possible beauty had been slaughtered out of existence. I cried because of the beauty of the mind of the man who saw and said: 'Let our mothers save us!' And they did not save."[87] So now, desperate for peace in his world, he clung to the hope that the Greek dramatist seemed to be offering him. He turned a blind eye to the vulgar comedy and insisted on "some impulse among the Athenian women, or no such play by Aristophanes."[88]

Confident of his interpretation of history and infatuated with his own ideas, Cook went so far as to state in the preface to his new play that it "diverges more from our historical accounts than from the events themselves."[89] The world war appeared to Cook so similar to the Peloponnesian War that he ascribed to political events in Athens a meaning that only the twentieth century could give, although he eventually rejected a modern setting for the play. The result was *The Athenian Women*, a play that transformed the Greek playwright's waggish impudence into a sober attempt to save the world. Casting Aspasia of Miletos as the prototype for Aristophanes' Lysistrata, he credits her with the scheme of a sex strike. Her "feminine genius" convinces Kallia, the wife of Pericles, to use her influence with the Athenian women to persuade them to gather in the temple of Demeter, thus withdrawing from the world of social—and sexual—obligations.[90] The women are joined by Agesistrata from Sparta, and with the help of Lysicles, who is in love with Aspasia, eventually convince the assembly to vote for peace. Pericles arrives in search of Kallia, and we discover that their marriage was not a love match, although Kallia has learned to love her husband. He, however, is now irrevocably drawn to Aspasia. This woman's superior intelligence and enthusiasm, combined with the flattery she deploys to convince him that he will be remembered as the patron of great works of art, conquer his emotions. He cannot, or will not, let her go, and Aspasia succumbs, lamenting the rupture of her bond with Kallia but rejoicing in the feminine influence she will find through Pericles. In the third act, fourteen years later, the people of Athens turn against Aspasia and Pericles, and war is declared against Sparta. This time, Aspasia is helpless. By betraying her sister, she has forfeited her following and can do nothing to turn the tide of events.

Cook was no Aristophanes, and the comedy inherent in the subject is expunged by his serious purpose and idealistic rhetoric, which ultimately fail him. Determined to link two ideas utterly foreign to *Lysistrata*, Cook is intent on demonstrating women's superior sensibility: Aspasia sacrifices her sensual gratification in order to create beauty. But he argues that beauty must prevail over destruction since it is the surest way to harmony—and immortality—for the one who creates it. Aspasia lures Pericles to bow to her demand for peace; his power in Athens now comes from her. But the price she must pay is, for a modern audience, too great: she has betrayed her faithful friend and ally Lysicles and must break her bonds with Kallia. We doubt the public good that can come of private treachery, and even Cook cannot extort a satisfactory ending from history and is forced to allow for the accusation of impiety brought by the people of Athens against Pericles and Aspasia.

To be fair to her (and to Cook), Aspasia does struggle against Pericles' demands on her sexuality. For a while, she insists that Pericles must not reject the love Kallia offers him. But no woman, in Cook's eyes, could possibly refuse a Pericles who cries: "You are what my life has always needed—a woman my equal. . . . You are escape from coldness—the cry of my blood! You are my generosity—you are the wind of the spirit blowing white hot the fire of my forge!"[91]

The scene between Aspasia and Pericles is long and wordy, but Aspasia succumbs, with words any man supposedly longs to hear: "You are the strongest man in the world—and I—will be—to you—the loveliest woman."[92] Quite understandably, Kallia is wounded and refuses to continue her friendship and admiration for the woman from Miletos. Cook, oblivious of the tension he has created in his obsessive defense of beauty, is unaware of the inherent paradox: he is willing for women to bond together to prevent wars and create beauty but assumes that such bonds can be readily sacrificed to keep men happy. He does not realize that he is reducing woman to a commodity, a sexual object whose only source of power is ultimately her body, which she must barter in blackmail. To make this palatable, he espouses the cause of the New Woman, who argued that women enjoy sex as much as men, and so portrays Aspasia melting willingly into Pericles' arms. The irony of this unacknowledged inner drama was lost even on the Women's Peace Party of New York. Interpreting the play as a cry for a peace forged by women, they insisted on a repeat performance at the Bramhall Playhouse in support of their cause. The Players—Cook and Glaspell most guilty of all—somehow forgot their war on the commercial theater and celebrated the move "uptown" wholeheartedly. The Bramhall, though small, was plush in comparison to the Playwrights' Theatre, and East 27th Street was closer to the heart of Broadway than Washington Square.

Glaspell was inordinately proud of Cook's achievement. *The Athenian Women* expressed the idealism that had brought them together, and the writing of this play consecrated their relationship. She identified with Aspasia and understood why friendship and professional advancement had to be sacrificed to the needs of a beloved man. Her quick ear for natural speech patterns helped create dialogue as she read the scenes with Cook, and no doubt it was her sense of justice that shaped the scene in which Aspasia tries to appease Kallia, swearing that their bond cannot be broken by love for Pericles. A misplaced humility, exaggerated by faith in Cook's achievement, convinced her that Ida Rauh should play the role of Aspasia, even though she was jealous whenever Jig rehearsed with the eccentric Jewish actress. Cook, tingling to work with Rauh, who he believed understood his flame, cast himself as Pericles, assuming noble Grecian airs in a short tunic that, although it displayed his muscular figure, "was not able," as one reviewer put it, "to make Pericles seem much more than a very recently commissioned second lieutenant in the reserve corps."[93]

But Cook knew very well that the only person who understood and supported him completely was his wife. As they returned home after the closing night of *The Athenian Women*, he promised, to himself more than to her, that "after a few years we will go to Greece. Maybe I can translate *The Athenian Women* into modern Greek, and produce it in Athens."[94] They did go to Greece a few years later, and Cook did translate his play; it was left to his wife to have it published after his death in both languages in a parallel edition.

Following the success of *The Athenian Women*, Cook turned his attention to the fortunes of what he increasingly saw as "his" theater. He planned to rename his Players and tour the world (and to rent a theater in Washington, D.C., to present a bill of the best plays). He fantasized that Jacques Copeau would allow the rechristened American Players to perform in his theater, the regal Vieux Colombier.[95] More urgent, though, was the need for a new theater at home since 139 Macdougal Street was too cramped and the battle with the building department continued to be vexing. As the *New York Sun* explained to its readers, the presence of a stove in the old building meant that the theater was officially classed as a tenement, and "after a winter's controversy the city wins and art is to be cooked out."[96] Although the Players had rented extra rooms upstairs for their second season (1917–18), which offered a meeting and relaxation area and, more important, dressing rooms of a sort, Cook was increasingly dissatisfied with the premises. He coveted the theater of his imagination where plastic blocks would afford a flexible acting space and a dome or Kuppelhorizont such as that of the Berlin Volksbuhne would ensure an illusion of infinity. He initiated a search for new premises and financial aid; the minutes of a meeting on 6 May 1918 record the opening of "a separate account called the Provincetown Playhouse Fund." In spite of pleas for help to such known benefactors of the arts as Otto Kahn, the fund grew very slowly, and eventually the Players took out a lease on 133 Macdougal Street (which had been a bottle factory and a stable).

Meanwhile, Edna Kenton had found what she thought was the ideal theater—the old French Opera House on Greenwich Avenue. The rent was not much more than the rent for the old stable at 133 Macdougal. But Cook argued that the cost of the restoration of the old Greenwich Avenue building would surpass their means. He also realized that once the Players were installed in the French Opera House, he would have to forego his dream of a custom-made theater. Although Kenton was a long-standing friend who was faithful to the last to Cook's vision of the Players, their relationship was under stress in the spring of 1918. Kenton had published an account of the work of the Provincetown Players in the *Boston Evening Transcript* in which she stressed their experimental and anarchic character but neglected to mention their director, George Cram Cook, by name.[97] Naturally enough, he was hurt that she "valued at zero" his work for the Provincetown Players and, adding insult to injury, attributed their success to lack of organization.[98]

Kenton committed another sin of misjudgment in her text: she claimed that the Provincetown Players had proved that "a theater can exist in New York without a press agent, and without critics."[99] Although critics were always welcome, the Players had steadfastly refused to indulge them by creating a "free list." In fact, as late as 1922, a cartoonist for the *New York Tribune* could mock the Players with a saga of the lost reviewer who "passed place four times but thought it garage—Villager standing in front of theater had never heard of it."[100] But a more sobering consequence of their refusal to comply with the customs of the commercial theater, Kenton's claim notwithstanding, was that they were denied the public recognition they now sought.

The ties between the Provincetowners and the Washington Square Players had been strong since the beginning of the older group. It was, after all, their rejection of *Suppressed Desires* that had provoked Cook to found his own theater in the first place—a theater specifically designed for the American playwright. The Washington Square Players, who mostly turned to European drama for their repertoire, now frequently produced the successes of their scion. Their somewhat bigger, more comfortable Bandbox Theatre, and the royalties they were able to pay, could command the plays of both O'Neill and Glaspell. Now, on the verge of disbanding, they were the recipients of accolades for their promotion of the artistic theater, praise that was not always deserved. John Corbin of the *New York Times* wrote: "The best index of the achievement of the [Washington Square] Players is perhaps to be found in the new artistic personalities to which they have introduced us. Is there any dramatist of the Great White Way who equals Susan Glaspell in subtle feminine intuition, in keen social satire? In her little unconventional tragedy of *Trifles* she disclosed a whole region of poignant feminine suffering. In *Suppressed Desires* she threw a flood of genial ridicule upon Greenwich Village's pose of 'freedom.' Her talent is for genre painting at its most intimate, a talent which, except for the [Washington Square] Players, would never have been known to our theatre."[101] The Provincetown Players were not amused. Maddened, Cook confronted the *Times*, but Corbin replied that the Provincetown Players were private, so they were unable to introduce personalities to the general theatergoing public.[102] A profile of Glaspell entitled "Who Is Susan Glaspell?" did not appease the Provincetowners' hurt pride, especially its effort to flatter Glaspell: "Although she is still a Provincetowner, they could not hold her entirely to themselves."[103]

Clearly, it was high time to change yet another of the original Provincetown bylaws. The third New York season would open in a new theater with a full-time paid secretary, complimentary tickets for critics, and—tellingly—subscription to Romeike's clipping service, which would furnish the Players with copies of all newspaper mentions.

CHAPTER FIVE

Her Husband's Keeper

As soon as the production of *Woman's Honor* ended, Glaspell felt free to return to Provincetown. She wanted to see if the rose bush outside the old lifesaving station had survived the winter, examine the new formations of sand dunes, collect strangely twisted pieces of driftwood, and, moored by the thunder of the ocean's breaking waves, create the voices of her new play. But as she got off the train, the unexpected bustle of the station disconcerted her, and it took longer than usual to find John Francis. He gathered her bags and asked after Jig, his blue eyes twinkling. Business was good, he explained; the Atlantic fleet had based units in the once-quiet fishing village, and the port was closed to civilian traffic. Swaggering sailors lorded it on Commercial Street.

On the tip of Cape Cod, the anxiety over German submarines that had gripped the country exploded into a crackling alarmism. Some residents even began to look on typewriters as possible instruments of communication with the ocean depths. Only the Greenwich Villagers, it seems, remained unruffled when a German submarine just off the Cape Cod shore attacked the steel tug *Perth Amboy* on 21 July 1918. Agnes Boulton, whom Eugene O'Neill had married in April, described the incident: "Then, one morning, there was the sound of gunfire, and after that, panic; for a German submarine was seen in the harbour, or just outside of it, emerging and then disappearing. No one knew where it was going or what it was going to do. There was a panic in the town, a mingled hush and expectancy. Strangely enough, I do not remember our taking it too seriously. Gene did not seem worried or afraid—mainly, it gave him an opportunity to write a long letter to his parents describing the dangers of war."[1] There was no official reaction to this incident. Mary Heaton Vorse recounted that the fleet of submarine chasers and the U.S. Naval Air Station troops kept away from the scene, while local fisherman Captain Kendrick charged "a dollar a round trip to go an' see the German submarine! But I don't promise nawthin'!"[2]

Until May 1918, the war had been strictly a moral issue for Cook and Glaspell; they had not been personally affected. But now that men between the ages of thirty-seven and forty-six were forced to register, Cook, at forty-five, still qualified. He had no desire to repeat his experience of soldiering; his brief stint in 1898 had been more than enough, and he mulled over the possibility of refusing. Glaspell feared "where his intensity might take him, once that fight were begun," and "urged delay, stressing his own idea of keeping burning, to the measure we could, the light of creative imagination." In zealous self-righteousness, he scrawled on a questionnaire, "I will not go into Russia to fight or police Russian working-men."[3] But he did not declare himself a conscientious objector or attempt to dodge the draft. So it was with relief that he wrote to his wife: "Registration was simple. . . . The registrar, Louis Espresso, said I needn't expect to be called—that I'd be about 4th class."[4]

The Provincetown Players were opposed to the war and American participation in it, but by the middle of 1918, seven of their number were in Europe and more were slated to go. They had symbolically protested against the horrors of combat in their program of war plays in February 1917, just before America entered the war, and in March 1918, miraculously escaping the attention of the censors, they produced *The Athenian Women*, in which Cook attempted with characteristic exaltation to bring art to bear on life.[5] Their plea for money for a new theater in the spring of 1918 met with shocked disapprobation from those who believed that all efforts should be concentrated on the war, and Cook's idealistic defense of their work convinced few:

> It is now often said that the theatrical entertainment in general is socially justified in this dark time as a means of relaxing the strain of reality, and thus helping to keep us sane. This may be true, but if more were not true—if we felt no deeper value in dramatic art than entertainment—we would hardly have the heart for it now.
>
> One faculty, we know, is going to be of vast importance to the half-destroyed world—indispensable for its rebuilding—the faculty of creative imagination. That spark of it which has given this group of ours such life and meaning as we have is not so insignificant that

we should now let it die. The social justification which we feel to be valid now for makers and players of plays is that they shall help keep alive in the world the light of imagination. Without it the wreck of the world that was cannot be cleared away and the new world shaped.[6]

The Players had been shocked by the Espionage and Sedition Acts and horrified by the censure imposed on *The Masses* and on Emma Goldman's *Mother Earth*. They had attended the trial of the editors of *The Masses*, who had been charged with obstructing the war effort, and had emerged more convinced than ever that the law was an absurd construct. The issue of free speech ignited Glaspell; her firm belief in individual freedom had been an integral part of her novels and stories, though tempered by acquiescence to what she saw as the essential values of society. Now she found the individual up against a force much more powerful than custom or tradition; politics, patriotism, and a much deeper loyalty were at stake. It would take her some time to work these moral issues into a play, *Inheritors* (1921), which would weave together the historical roots of her community and the dilemma of the present.

———— ··◄⟨∞⟩►·· ————

Professional discipline demanded that the Villagers devote their mornings to writing, and Glaspell adhered to a strict routine. But she looked forward to the moment of release from her typewriter when she would go downstairs and wait on the porch for O'Neill, who was staying in the cottage opposite 564 Commercial Street, to come by. Although he was now married to Boulton, who seemed quite a child to Glaspell, he still felt strongly drawn to the delicate, resolute woman who had shown faith in his work during that first Provincetown summer. Glaspell looked forward to his visits. Cook had arrived from New York. Absorbed in plans for the new season, he was also exploring new outlets for his genius and devoted much time to playing with bits of clay he picked up in the artists' studios; he would, of course, have bombastically refuted charges of neglect, but his wife did miss his company. Moreover, Glaspell loved to hear O'Neill talk and to see the intense concentration build up in his gloomy eyes as he wrestled with her more optimistic view of life.

Such conversations were an integral part of Provincetown days and left their mark on both playwrights. In Glaspell's struggle to bring "life" into the theater, O'Neill recognized the burden of imperative dramatic duty under which he himself worked. Friedrich Nietzsche's Zarathustra boasted that he would "make company with creators, with harvesters, with rejoicers: I will show them the rainbow and the stairway to the Superman."[7] The couple who had made O'Neill's theatrical debut possible saw themselves as creators who hoped to contribute to a better world by channeling the imagination of their audiences. Glaspell, realizing "more intensely than the fishermen, that the tide comes, the tide goes," told O'Neill that with such knowledge, "you cannot leave things just as they were before."[8] He was more indifferent, seeing life as a struggle doomed to failure, avoiding all political and social movements because "life as a whole is changed very little, if at all, as a result of their course."[9] But Glaspell, author of *The Glory of the Conquered*, believed passionately in the value of the struggle, even in the value of defeat. She was not prepared to wait passively on "the birth-cry of the higher men," who, according to O'Neill, would "come at the command of the imagination and the will."[10] She tried to infuse in him, as she did in Cook, the authority to control the imagination of weaker men. Her heroines wield power, even from beyond the grave, as in *Bernice* (1919), the play she would shortly write, in which the protagonist stages her death in such a way as to build up her husband's confidence in himself. Bernice's superiority is sufficiently real for her to transform the man who claims to love her. O'Neill was not capable of depicting a woman whose "diff'rence" from others could elevate her above them. Glaspell was—she confidently transferred Nietzsche's claim from man to woman, knowing that woman was able to "conquer . . . [her] own civilization."[11]

Now the two playwrights also had the future to discuss. In April, O'Neill had granted a six-month option (which would become two years) on *Beyond the Horizon* to the Broadway director John D. Williams. Williams hoped to engage the Barrymore brothers to play Andrew and Robert Mayo. Through O'Neill, Glaspell had access to the professional world of the theater, a world she increasingly wanted to storm, in defiance of Cook's dedication to the amateur and his initial scorn for commercial success. She dreamed of plays that would teach Broadway audiences to enjoy serious theater and hoped she was capable of writing such plays. Meanwhile, she alone knew that Cook had been put out by O'Neill's acceptance of Williams's offer. He had expected his protégé to give the first option on all of his plays to the Playwrights' Theatre, and he was constantly reminding the younger man of his obligation to write a new play for the coming season.

When O'Neill suddenly stopped calling for his noon chats with Glaspell, she blamed her husband for frightening him off with his demands. But it was Boulton who, complaining that O'Neill was neglecting her, had put a stop to his visits. Much younger than Glaspell, shy and uncertain of herself, Boulton had drawn O'Neill with her gray-blue eyes when he first saw her on her arrival in Greenwich Village in October 1917.[12] Even though she realized she was being "foolish and young-wifeish," she could not help feeling left out. She acknowledged that Glaspell was "very attractive" and that men found her conversation "stimulating and helpful." To Boulton, she seemed "an ethereal being, detached and yet passionate. She was so far beyond me in her knowledge and understanding of everything that was going on in the world—economics, the rights of mankind, the theatre, writing, people—and she was able to talk of them when necessary with charm and interest."[13] The following autumn, Boulton, invulnerable in motherhood, would become Glaspell's closest friend and confidante, but in the early months of her marriage, she resented the interest O'Neill showed in any other woman. She felt threatened by Glaspell's "gift of pointed and significant gaiety," which she was at a loss to interpret, and by the older woman's sharp powers of perception, which, at their first meeting, had led Glaspell to point out Boulton's resemblance to Louise Bryant, O'Neill's great amour of the previous season.[14]

Before the summer was properly over, Cook returned to New York to resume the fight with the building department and, if necessary, the search for a new theater. Judging by his handwriting, a scrawl instead of the usual neat, close hand, he also stepped up his drinking. On 11 September 1918, he reported freely on an evening of imbibing and soliloquy, the subject under discussion being not the theater but the war and the draft. He disdained the futile rebellion of the younger men who preferred Levenworth prison to the army since they were counting on a reduction in the twenty-year sentence for refusing the draft. He scoffed at the new laws on exemption that now only covered those involved in "essential industry," forcing men with dependents into active service: "I have a feeling a new tyranny is being born which will not permit us to live on our own terms." In a more sober mood, he added: "I'm wondering if somebody will open this letter to spot that's the atmosphere we live in." Then, wallowing in drink and solitude, he spilled his heart out in an abandoned sob: "Susan dear, can't at all remember the reasons why I love you more than anybody else."[15]

Once he recovered, he plunged into the battle with the city's building department and soon forgot the world's wars—so much so, that even news of his mother's sudden death in Davenport did not move him: "One September day, after riding her bicycle to the village, she returned to her Cabin, was talking in her usual manner with one of her grandsons, when suddenly she said: 'I feel so strange,' slipped down, was dead."[16] The family delayed the funeral but eventually a telegram from Cook informed them not to wait for him. Reluctantly, Alice Keating Glaspell stood in for her daughter and son-in-law: "I did not want to go, was not very well, but some of the family phoned here twice and asked Father and I to go, he said he couldn't—so I went. They sent an auto for me about 2 P.M."[17] The casket, covered with flowers, was laid out in the cabin. That Jig Cook did not drop everything to attend his mother's funeral is a measure of his utter involvement with the theater. Even so, given his profound attachment to his mother, it is difficult to comprehend. His letters to his wife during this time make no mention of Ma-Mie or the loss her death must have been to him. It is possible that Glaspell later destroyed those letters since there is a gap in the correspondence between 20 September and 24 October 1918 and no indication that Glaspell joined him in New York or that he went back to Provincetown. But she did write in *The Road to the Temple* that "Jig wished he might have seen her once more, told her more patiently what it was he felt, showing her, perhaps, that his feeling came from things they had shared."[18] Still, the only sign of grief lies in the drunken mess of some of his letters.

The extension of the draft in the autumn of 1918 swallowed up so many male actors that the Provincetown Players was the only noteworthy New York little theater opening that November. Cook thus wrote his wife: "You see our losses will be made up by accretions from the wrecks of Washington Square and Greenwich Village Players."[19] He finally reported that they would definitely move to 133 Macdougal Street and wrote: "It revives my interest to fit up a new and bigger place."[20] Clearly Glaspell had chided him in her letters on his state of mind and overindulgence in drinking. Provincetown was now very quiet, and she was sticking to her writing schedule, revising *Tickless Time*, which they had drafted together in August, and working on a new play, *Bernice* (1919), that would be her first full-length piece. She had not been pleased to receive Cook's scrawls; she knew that he was more likely to succumb to Dionysus, and other temptations of the flesh, when not with her but had hoped that his obligations with respect to the theater would restrain him. She must have felt like packing her bags and joining him in New York at times, but she held back because of the expense this would have incurred; they had planned not to rent an apartment until November, and while alone, Cook was living in the theater.

On 21 April 1918, the Provincetown Players had agreed "that the office of unpaid secretary be abolished, and that there be established a paid secretaryship."[21] Stella Ballantine, Emma Goldman's niece, introduced "a tall good-looking, red-haired young woman" as a possible candidate for the post.[22] This was M. Eleanor Fitzgerald, or Fitzi, who had often applauded the Provincetown actors and was in need of a job. Even more, she needed an all-absorbing interest that would fill the vacuum her life had become. She was the lover of Alexander Berkman, the anarchist who claimed in his *Prison Memoirs of an Anarchist* to be the first American to be willing to sacrifice his life "in the interests of the people."[23] An infamous strike at Andrew Carnegie's steel plant in Homestead, Pennsylvania, in June 1892 had seemed to Berkman and his companion Emma Goldman an opportunity "to arouse a vital interest in the sufferings of the people" and "bring the teachings of Anarchism before the world."[24] Berkman planned to kill Henry Clay Frick, the manager of the plant, and then commit suicide. But his shot misfired; he did not kill Frick, and the police discovered the nitroglycerin cartridge he had hidden in his mouth before he could use it to blow himself up. Berkman was sentenced to twenty-two years in prison but was released in 1906 thanks to the untiring efforts of Goldman to free him.

By this time, Goldman had set up her magazine *Mother Earth* (where Mollie Price had worked before marrying Cook), and after his release, Berkman helped out in editorial matters. Benjamin Lewis Reitman, Goldman's lover, whom she had met when championing the anarchist cause in Chicago in 1908, introduced Goldman to Eleanor Fitzgerald, a naive young woman from Wisconsin, who took over editorial and secretarial duties. Fitzi's organizational talents and her gentle mothering soothed Berkman's wounds. He eventually left Goldman's household to live with Fitzi, moving to San Francisco in late 1915, where they worked together for the anarchist cause, publishing *The Blast*, a weekly paper. But Goldman and Berkman were fated to come together again; she was in San Francisco on 22 July 1916 when a bomb killed ten and wounded forty in a Preparedness Day Parade. Although five men were charged, only Warren Billings and Tom Mooney were convicted. Rousing the International Workers' Defense League (created in 1912 but recently dormant), the two Russian immigrants, supported by Fitzi, worked to defend the accused. Many years later, Fitzi would write: "Thirty-three years ago I made speeches on behalf of the Mooney-Billings case up and down the West Coast and then the Eastern Coast, going from labor union to labor union. I induced the great lawyer-orator Bourke Cochran (free of charge) to come to San Francisco as lawyer for the defense of four labor men and the wife of Mooney."[25] Before the West Coast authorities, in their zeal to hang all radicals, could clamp down on Berkman and Goldman, the two anarchists returned to New York. An extradition order was issued for Berkman who, by then, had already been imprisoned in the Tombs—the dreaded New York prison—for conspiring to obstruct the draft. Goldman's strenuous efforts kept him safely there until the order was withdrawn in November 1917.[26]

This was not the end of Fitzi's problems, however. Jack Reed had covered Berkman and Goldman's trial for spreading antiwar propaganda in *The Masses* (just before the post office refused to mail the monthly because of its antiwar policy), in which Harry Weinberger had defended the two supposed conspirators, who were then imprisoned briefly, awaiting an appeal to the Supreme Court. But the appeal proved to be merely a delaying tactic for the sentence, which was finally enforced in February 1918: two years' imprisonment followed by possible deportation. Thus, in the autumn of that year, Fitzi was alone, denied not only the company of the man she loved but also the support and resourcefulness of Goldman. With Stella Ballantine, she worked for the Political Prisoners' Amnesty League, fighting to free the two anarchists and those "who refused to take up arms to shoot their fellow-men," but she needed a source of income, for even the *Mother Earth Bulletin* (published for a few months after *Mother Earth* had been banned from the mails in August 1917) had been declared unmailable in May 1918.[27]

Fitzi was therefore relieved to find a job that made use of her organizational capacity and occupied her time and her thoughts. She made herself indispensable to Cook and Glaspell (although they were later to doubt her judgment) and soon became the "business manager, financier, general factotum and everybody's confidante."[28] In October 1919, Berkman was released from jail, and Fitzi's happiness was shared by the Provincetowners. It did not last long; in December, Berkman was taken to Ellis Island for deportation, and his request that his common-law wife be allowed to go with him was denied. It was Goldman who accompanied him into exile on 21 December 1919, leaving Fitzi to the "smaller stage" of the Provincetown Players, where she threw herself into her self-set task to make at least "a few . . . conscious of decency, justice and truth."[29]

———·•·◄◘►·•·———

The new premises at 133 Macdougal Street, rejected by the Washington Square Players as too small in 1915, became Fitzi's "foster child."[30] Larger than number 139, this "pre-Victorian" four-story building offered the Players an elegant upper floor, which Christine Ell converted into the Provincetown meeting place and restaurant. The basement was used as a theatrical storeroom, and Cook and his carpenters partitioned off a corner for the Players' dressing rooms. The ramp that had led into the stable became a minute lobby with a diminutive box office where Fitzi reigned, assuring all that she did not even notice the "faint, pungent aroma of horses and manure" that no amount of cleaning and disinfecting could altogether remove.[31] It was Jack Reed who, during a furlough from his duties as war reporter, availed the Players of the significance of the humble origins of their Playhouse. He infused the stable with the aura of mythical ambition when, forbidding anyone to remove a hitching ring they had discovered embedded in the wall of the auditorium, he inscribed around it the words: "Here Pegasus Was Hitched."[32]

The auditorium was slightly bigger than the auditorium in their old venue, seating a larger audience with a touch more comfort, but the real improvement was the size of the stage, which was almost double that of the old boards.[33] The Players again transformed themselves into painters, carpenters, and electricians and fitted their new theater with a modern switchboard and dimmer, "smoothly running curtain," and sloping auditorium with "deep indigo blue" ceilings and "rich tawny orange" walls. This time, they restrained themselves when painting the proscenium arch and merely left a plain "deep smoke grey" rectangle.[34] While he was overseeing these preparations, Cook camped at the theater, donating the money he saved on rent toward the cost of renewal.

The new theater was far from Cook's dream come true; he wanted domes, light, and space, in which, like Whitman, he could create the myth of America and regenerate his nation. Practical only when it came to details of carpentry or plumbing, Cook soared whenever confronted with the possibility of giving birth to "an American renaissance of the twentieth century."[35] In writing *The Athenian Women*, he had appropriated Nietzsche's aristocratic vision of culture as a unifying force that dissipates conflict, but no matter how he construed the historical data, he could not change the outcome and undo the wars of Athens and Sparta. Even though history refused to mold itself to his dreams, however, he never relinquished the conviction that the well-being of a nation depended on the chosen few "kindling communal intellectual passion" by keeping alive myth and ritual.[36] What Cook failed to understand was that the United States had no common myth to fall back on. In vain, he looked to the example of ancient Athens, believing he could re-create the festival of Dionysus in Greenwich Village and transform myth and ritual into art, thus raising the cultural level of the crowds and evoking "a powerful sense of communal identity."[37] He even had a model closer in time: W. B. Yeats, seeing himself as a poet-priest of Irish nationalism, aspired to heal his people through Celtic legends ritualized into sacred drama. But Yeats was sufficiently anchored in his times to doubt the probability of the ultimate success of his endeavor. He knew that ritual and myth are valid only if relevant to living experience and that tradition and an age-old history are worthless unless harnessed to the present.

Cook, the mystic from Davenport, had taken upon himself a much more difficult task than that of Yeats. His country did not have a "usable past" to work from, "no shadow, no antiquity, no mystery, no picturesque and gloomy wrong, nor anything but a commonplace prosperity, in broad and simple daylight," as Nathaniel Hawthorne had speciously lamented.[38] Cook envied the Jewish Neighborhood Playhouse its tribal traditions and hoped to evoke similar rituals—and thus overcome the major handicap Hawthorne had identified for any American writer—by using Native American material in his own writing. But *The Spring* (1920), a play that postulates a deep underlying unity between the red man and the white, fails to arouse any sense of ritual; nor, unhappily, does Glaspell's *Inheritors* (1921), in which the native is simply a historical presence. Inspired by Cook's probing into the American past, Eugene O'Neill started work in 1921 on his own attempt at the numinous, *The Fountain*, which was not performed until 1925, and also failed to effect any sort of spiritual regeneration.

Cook's encounter with Jacques Copeau had given him another contemporary model. Votaries of Dionysus, the patron god of drama, both men aspired to fill the "immense void" that had arisen when Greek tragedy died. The drama was for them a Bacchic expression of a community whose prosperity depended on the ritualistic reenactment of the primal unity of humankind.[39] What his students, "les Copiaus," would later achieve in Burgundy, where they created artistic performances for local festivities, such as *La Fête de la Vigne et des Vignerons* (1925), presented at the harvest festival in Beaune, is precisely what Cook was aiming for. If he had not died in 1924, he may well have done the same for Delphi in Greece, where he at last found an authentic mythic tradition to uphold him.

The search for roots and authenticity led the Players to write and perform a number of plays in the 1918–19 season that used ethnic or minority material for their plots and characters. Florence Kiper Frank's *Gee-Rusalem* has a Jewish protagonist, Alice Rostetter's *The Widow's Veil* boasts an Irish setting, Mary F. Barber's *The Squealer* portrays Irish miners in Pennsylvania, and Bosworth Crocker's *The Baby Carriage* reflects the ethnic mix of New York. Not surprisingly, none of these plays had the effect of tribal ritual that Cook was searching for, although they did successfully depict different social sectors.

Meanwhile, Cook grew ever more impatient with his failure to embody the putative American spirit on his stage. Increasingly, he understood that he was failing within his smaller community of Players. The hundred that should create the American Renaissance were not responding to his call; the initial fervor he aroused in Provincetown had abated. Helen Deutsch and Stella Hanau, in *The Provincetown: A Story of the Theatre*, remark on the "sense of creative impulse" and the group spirit that directed the "ardent" Players during those first years, when Cook was closest to achieving his coveted "beloved community."[40] But the early productions undoubtedly served a therapeutic end. Although Cook never put his ideas down in any rational form, his convictions on the role of drama in society resemble those of Konstantin Stanislavsky or even the more experimental Jerzy Grotowski. The early Provincetown Players had been a "laboratory of human emotions" where his friends had been able to "get it off their chests" by writing about their personal problems or by acting in plays that reflected their own dilemmas.[41] They tried, as Copeau believed little theaters should, to create "this one small nucleus from which action can radiate and around which the future can form."[42] Cook's message to the public when he begged for continuing support in spite of the war was based on his faith that the theater would be a significant force in the rebuilding of the world once the cataclysm was over.[43]

Although the first Players revered Cook, acknowledging that his "sublime, gallant, crazy theatrical faith kept us operating," none of them shared his intense commitment to creating an American drama. The emphasis for Cook was on "American" rather than "drama," and he understood his mission to be "to cause better American plays to be written."[44] Marguerite and William Zorach, Bror Nordfeldt, and Charles Demuth were absorbed in their sculpture or painting; Mary Heaton Vorse, Jack Reed, and Louise Bryant focused on politics and journalism; and Hutchins Hapgood, Floyd Dell, Wilbur Daniel Steele, and Max Eastman were writers and social reformers first and foremost.[45] The number of active members—twenty-nine in 1916—had fallen to fourteen by March 1918; of the original members, only Cook, Glaspell, O'Neill, and Ida Rauh remained. O'Neill still saw the Players as a showcase for his work, although he had already set his sights on Broadway. Rauh was infatuated with Cook and with the idea of herself as the "Duse of Macdougal Street," and after her split from Eastman, she needed the distraction that the theater offered. The new recruits were younger, more serious-minded, more professional, but, as Edna Kenton saw it, "not quite one hundred per cent pure."[46] She lamented this encroachment of professionals on Cook's dream, while he, impervious to their advance, still insisted on "the right to experiment and to fail of what outsiders call success."[47]

This difference in outlook inevitably led to tensions during the third New York season. Glaspell came to wonder whether it was all worthwhile and searched for plausible ways to get Cook away from the theater without damaging his faith in himself. She understood his search for beauty, his need to feel that he was "freeing creative forces" and "transform[ing] the souls of men."[48] But she saw, better than he did, that his commitment was not appreciated by the younger Players, who complained ever more loudly that Jig was not a businessman. Glaspell, never a materialist, cuttingly assured them that "he can finance for the spirit," but she could not convince them to share his vision or find satisfaction in challenging the Broadway box-office ethic.[49] They aspired to a professional theater and demanded competent organization and leadership, not lofty, liquor-inspired words. Someone like Copeau, who had developed his theories on the theater and the art of acting, could have steered them. Although he had saluted Glaspell's intuitive acting, he was too humble to abandon his theater entirely to intuition. In contrast, Cook dogmatized that "the gifted amateur had possibilities which the professional may have lost."[50] He peremptorily dismissed all notions of training and consistency and affirmed adamantly that the stage of the Playwrights' Theatre would automatically attract American talent. Many of the younger Players concluded that Jig simply did not know what he was doing; they were irritated by his stance of prophet to the playwright god and offended by his explosions when they tried to oppose him.[51]

As always, it was left to Glaspell to smooth things over. Heroically, she defended her husband against all attacks. His euphoric outpourings in the days of their courtship were still fresh in her mind. She particularly cherished a letter from Chicago in which he had written about the ideal relationship between a man and a woman: "It is not outside the possibilities of these two to grow into achievements from which shall radiate hitherto unformulated ideals of art and love. Lovers who make each other better artists! Artists who make each other better lovers!"[52] She understood him so well that she could even quash her misgivings about Rauh's passionate advances, stifling her protests when Jig spent whole nights away from her, intent on putting "some little thing . . . right" in the theater.[53] She recognized his need to immerse himself in details that did not require the presence or even the approval of the whole group. Such work, like the modeling in clay that he had taken up in Provincetown, allowed him to reach down into the spiritual oneness he forever sought. He could perhaps find it in himself, but to bring it out in a disparate body of determined individuals bent on pursuing professional theatrical careers was proving difficult for a man who was at heart an "autocrat" and a visionary bacchant. Glaspell could see that "much as he wanted to leave not one unfree spirit in the theater, he had a peculiarly strong urge to put right a thing that was wrong." And she admitted: "Sometimes, Jig was about as true as a hurricane to the group ideal." But she was always amazed at how quickly his rages worked themselves out and how willing he was to give himself to others as long as he felt appreciated and needed.[54] She knew better than anyone else just how much he needed a sympathetic audience, how "he grew mightily in power" at the slightest

encouragement.[55] Ma-Mie had never tired of showing her son unconditional appreciation. Glaspell had learned a lot from her example; now it
was up to her to bring out the best in the husband she had fought to win.

Pitted against the selfish ambitions of youth, Cook agonized over the
inexorable passage of time. He was nearing fifty and asking himself what
he had done with his life. Hapgood describes him as a man who never
paused, going "from one flashing thought or impulse to the next . . . too
much alive to fix anything, so that . . . [he] left no obvious monuments, or
few."[56] This failure to leave monuments was always on Jig's mind; he had
abandoned a university career for farming; he had tried politics and
journalism; he had written two novels. Now, challenged by his "beloved
community," he inevitably questioned his total commitment to the creation of an American drama. Disheartened, he wondered "why people
undervalued him."[57] The protagonist of O'Neill's *The Fountain* (1925),
Juan Ponce de Leon, echoes Cook when he laments that it is "too late . . .
I am too weary. I have fought small things so long that I am small."[58]

In this spirit, Cook transferred his personal fear of aging into an obsession with the mechanics of timekeeping. Logically, given his passion for
the primeval, he studied ancient methods of measuring time and discovered that modern calculations hurry it along too fast. As always, his
enthusiasm was contagious, and Glaspell knew better than to deny him
the euphoria of sharing his conceits with her. She knew that rather than
pooh-pooh his sudden rejection of clocks in favor of the humble sundial,
she must find a means of channeling his sophistry into more profitable
paths. In this case, her ingenuity was not overtaxed; she revived the
delightful game of lobbing speeches back and forth that had culminated
in *Suppressed Desires*. For a week or so, Cook followed her faithfully, out
on the dunes or down Commercial Street, throwing out predications on
the nature of time, life, death, or love, as the mood took him. They
recovered the carefree spirit of their marriage as they explored the consequences of a return to sun-time and toyed with a scenario replete with
dramatic possibilities. But then, withdrawing from her once again, Cook
enjoined his wife to transcribe their exchanges and create the play he
could only talk of. He had satisfied himself that time was humankind's
miscalculation and now calmly dismissed the prickly process of aging; he
spoke no more of burying all of their timepieces. However, the sundial

apparently continued to torment him, for the next summer he set to work on a dial that would grace the sunniest spot in their garden.

Tickless Time was the play that sprang from Cook's obsession during the summer of 1918. It was performed that Christmas on a bill with Rita C. Smith's *The Rescue* and O'Neill's *The Moon of the Caribbees*. Heywood Broun, impervious to the mood O'Neill masterfully portrays in this short play, judged it "a disappointment," a local victory for Cook over O'Neill, for Broun singled out *Tickless Time* as "easily the best of the three plays" and even praised the acting of James Light and Norma Millay.[59] Such a review would surely have sparked one of the infamous Provincetown "firecracker quarrels," since Rauh was bound to resent attention given to another actress, and O'Neill would not have relished being upstaged as a playwright.[60] As always, it would have been up to Glaspell to step in, placate, cajole, and pet, until all differences were forgotten over a bowl of punch.

Rauh was presently to find consolation in a wholly different kind of notoriety. Norman Jacobsen, who had contributed cartoons to *The Masses*, made the Playwrights' Theatre famous for a day when the *New York Tribune* published his cartoon of the Players at rehearsal. Two of the members, identified as Rauh and O'Neill, are lounging about, very much at their ease, while "waiting their turn." The caption, mocking O'Neill's mania for exhaustingly detailed stage directions, reads:

Ida: You playwrights are nothing if not unreasonable.
Eugene: How so?
Ida: This part calls for a one-armed seaman.
Eugene: Easy! Just keeps his arm inside his . . .
Ida: But the stage directions read: He places both elbows on the
    table in a gesture of despair.[61]

Cook must have enjoyed the joke at his playwright's expense.

The piece that Glaspell was trying to finish—*Bernice*, the only play she ever worked on in New York—had been gestating in her mind for some time. The process of creating the absent protagonist of *Trifles* had keenly impressed on her the fact of woman's irrelevance in the world of man. She had learned that in order to awaken man's interest, woman had to resort to the stratagem of nonpresence; thus, an invisible heroine, like

Minnie Wright, would most successfully present woman's case. The year 1917 had been an important one in the struggle for woman's rights: the New York State referendum on woman suffrage had been won, Jeannette Rankin of Montana had gained a seat in the House of Representatives, and the Woman's Party had begun picketing the White House. After a number of passive demonstrations, the women, angered by President Woodrow Wilson's decision to fight for democracy in Europe, raised banners that roused the mob of male patriots. "Kaiser Wilson" and "Democracy Should Begin at Home" were slogans that led to charges of obstructing sidewalk traffic and the imprisonment of ninety-seven women. Among these were four Heterodoxy members: Alison Turnbull Hopkins, Doris Stevens, Paula Jakobi, and Alice Kimball. All but Kimball served time in the notorious Occoquan workhouse in Virginia. These sentences and the treatment the women received made them "the earliest victims of the abrogation of civil liberties in wartime."[62]

Glaspell was no militant suffragist. In an interview with Alice Rohe in the *New York Morning Telegraph* in 1921, she affirmed: "I am interested in all progressive movements, whether feminist, social or economic . . . but I can take no very active part other than through my writing. One can't work with too many things. . . . When one has limited strength one must use it for the thing one feels most important."[63] She would have endorsed Elizabeth Cady Stanton's explanation that women met at Seneca Falls in 1848 to discuss "our own inalienable rights, our duties, our true sphere" and would have agreed with her declaration: "If God has assigned a sphere to man and one to woman, we claim the right to judge ourselves of his design in reference to us, and we accord to man the same privilege."[64] Glaspell believed in the right of the individual to full self-development, but she recognized the conflict inherent in this right; she was fully aware, from personal experience, that women were powerless in society, and she had learned the cost of opposing convention. She must have doubted the extent to which the vote in itself would help. Indeed, in *The Verge*—performed just before her interview with Rohe and after women had been enfranchised—she shows that a woman is still trapped by society, marriage, and motherhood and that the only way out is to transcend accepted concepts of sanity. Crystal Eastman, when she stated that the enactment of the federal suffrage amendment by the Tennessee legislature was "a day to begin with, not a day to end with," was echoing Glaspell's, and most Heterodoxy members', attitude toward suffrage.[65]

The Heterodoxy lunches were Glaspell's only overt commitment to

Susan Glaspell, etching by Bernard Sanders
(Courtesy of the University Libraries, The University of Iowa)

feminism aside from her writing. She enjoyed these meetings where she could relax, safe from Cook's insistent demands on her energies and the outraged Players' pleas that she intercede when his wrath broke on them. Among the Heterodites, there were no "duties or obligations," and every woman talked or listened as she pleased.[66] This free exchange of experiences generated something like group therapy and gave Glaspell a window on the lives of other women. The absent protagonist of *Bernice* (1919) is the product of deep thought about the role of women and a bitter protest at their age-old silencing. Glaspell would never have admitted that she had been silenced by Cook; she insisted that she gladly gave up her career as a novelist to devote herself to his baby—the Provincetown Players. As she wrote, somewhat defensively, in 1929: "From 1915 to 1922 I gave up practically everything else, though I had an established position as a novelist. I wanted to do this, and I am glad I did."[67]

Nonetheless, she never entirely abandoned the novel or short story during this period and gained in experience and stature as a writer while working for the theater. Cook's desire to go to Greece, which she supported for his sake, eventually led to a severance of her ties with the Provincetown Players and her return to fiction. But during her seven dramatic years (in which her reputation was largely made), her goal was not so much to write plays as to play the helpmate to Cook and reconcile him to his successes and failures. But Glaspell was assuredly a New Woman; she had been the first in Provincetown to bob her hair, and even before that act of rebellion, she had the courage to leave home, head off to college, have affairs, and marry a divorced visionary—all of which placed her quite outside the pale in Iowa in 1900. But once she took a husband, although she kept her own name, she devoted herself to him and expected—and largely gained—satisfaction from the knowledge that she kept him going in the world.

But the residue of this Victorian conviction that a woman should devote herself entirely to her husband without intruding upon his public activities clashed with the feminism of Greenwich Village, where men and women promoted mutual sexual satisfaction and social intimacy as essential to a good relationship. Both parties found it difficult to enact the change from nineteenth- to twentieth-century morals and mores. The men of Greenwich Village made a show of searching for a woman they could both talk to and kiss.[68] Max Eastman was honest enough to admit this in his autobiography, *Enjoyment of Living*. "There is so much egotism usually in men's love that I wonder how women stand it at all," he mused.[69] Certainly, Glaspell was not alone in putting her needs second to those of her husband, and in some ways, she was sadly fortunate: she had no children to distract her from the writing that validated the Provincetown Players.

The story of Neith Boyce's marriage offers a classic example of womanly self-sacrifice that Glaspell must have drawn on for her play *Bernice*. Although Hutchins Hapgood, her husband, professed to believe in free love for both of them, Boyce masked her disapproval with a strategy of detachment. Eventually, though, attracted to another man, she contemplated following her husband's example, only to find Hutch crazy with jealousy. The ensuing struggle and her renunciation of her lover brought on Boyce's nervous breakdown, but she held onto her marriage. As their biographer suggests, "In truth, Hapgood had demanded from Boyce an increased interest in him, not the revelation of her own deep feelings, particularly if such feelings were critical."[70] In an autobiographical novel based on the early years of his marriage, Hapgood complained that his wife "has never accepted my form, my essential self as beautiful." Nevertheless, he could say, "I hated and loved her never-failing egoism, the unconscious completeness with which she remained herself."[71]

Hapgood was in fact unconsciously hypocritical about feminism, absurdly maintaining that

the general situation put the man at a disadvantage. The Woman was in full possession of what the man used to regard as his "rights," and the men, even the most advanced of them, suffered from the woman's full assumption of his old privileges. To be sure, man retained the same "freedom," or what was called freedom, that he had always had, but his "property" had been taken away from him, and no matter what his advanced ideas were, his deeply complex, instinctive and traditional nature often suffered, a suffering the woman was relatively spared. . . . [Woman] has the power and the primitiveness of the earth. Woe to the more artificial male, dependent on the unconsciously remembered past and on wilful desire to maintain the impossible structure of civilization—woe to this delicate spiritual organization if he gets in her way![72]

Although Cook made a show of believing that both men and women are free creatures, with full rights to determine their existence, his Zarathustra complex made it difficult for him to treat any person as an equal. His diaries are ironically revealing on this matter; Glaspell used them extensively in her hagiographical biography *The Road to the Temple*, admiringly glossing his account of an earlier love for a young woman named Vera whom he had wanted to free from her "little fears." Seemingly convinced by what she understands as his spirit of self-sacrifice, Glaspell exclaims: "What were his visions for if not to light a way for her?"[73] Posthumously in thrall to her Iowan superman, she quotes Cook's outpourings, which would be questionable in any age: "He felt in himself some savage power to take possession of her . . . stamp his image on her spirit as a coin is stamped on metal. . . . He held himself back from this. He did not want to be her master."[74]

Glaspell must have suffered from the stressful ambivalence of her position in marriage—and observed the strains in the marriages of her friends—for her plays and novels frequently portray independent women who will not be mastered. In *Bernice*, she coolly examines women's opportunities to turn the tables; it is a theme she also pursues in *Chains of Dew* and expands in *The Verge*. In none of her plays does she "sentimentalize femininity" in exploring relationships between men and women. In 1914, Florence Kiper (author of *Gee-Rusalem*, which the Players staged in 1918) had written on American plays from a "feminist viewpoint," lamenting that male playwrights idealized their female characters, thus "revealing themselves in regard to the woman movement."[75] Glaspell, though not politically active, was very much interested in the "woman question," and in her plays, she "set forth sincerely and honestly, yet with vital passion, those problems in the development and freedom of women that the modern age has termed the problems of feminism," thus fulfilling the role of the woman playwright that Kiper had foreseen.[76]

Glaspell was certainly not interested in plagiarizing the mundane details of the amorous intrigues going on around her. The critic Arthur Pollock correctly perceived that she "does not deal with the common things of life or of the theater, but with the rare. . . . [The] action is a mental action. . . . [It] deals with what [Henry James] calls 'secondary experience.'"[77] It was this "secondary experience" that Glaspell labored over throughout the winter of 1918 in New York—secondary because it pertained to the mind rather than to visible activity and because it was more concerned with the dilemmas of womanhood than with those of the patriarchs. By the middle of March, her first full-length play was in rehearsal. Codirecting with Cook was always apt to become an ordeal, but he had unconsciously picked up ideas from Nina Moise, and this play, set in an ordinary American home, automatically dominated his fantasy. *Bernice*, the Provincetowners' second full-length production, played from 21 to 27 March 1919. It was staged along with Jack Reed's *The Peace That Passeth Understanding*, which the Players thoroughly enjoyed and which blended "German cabaret and Soviet agit-prop techniques" to give the effect of an "animated cartoon."[78] But reviewers did not share their enthusiasm; at least one critic condemned Reed's effort as a "childish skit."[79]

The *New York Herald* acclaimed *Bernice* as a play "of the Ibsen type," though "much more modern than the work of the Norwegian."[80] A penetrating study of the power games people play, it hones in on the intimacies of a married couple who conduct their relationship according to bohemian standards: the titillations of free love are encouraged by, and for, the husband.[81] Glaspell, caught in the trap sprung by an intellectual rejection of Victorian morality, examines how women can best cope with men's need to prove themselves superior. To this end, she returns to the stratagem that had been so successful in *Trifles* and inverts the norm of the detective story: the female protagonist, the possible perpetrator of a criminal act, is absent, and only women possess the knowledge and understanding necessary to uncover the mystery she has molded. But, just as in *Trifles*, all of the women in *Bernice* are eventually silenced; even Margaret, the friend who takes on the role of psychoanalyzing sleuth so as to decipher Bernice's motives, will not disclose her findings to the other sex.

Craig and Bernice represent a typical Village couple. She is an intelligent, self-sufficient woman, and he is a struggling writer of middling talent who, although he professes undying love for his beautiful wife, searches elsewhere for the unconditional admiration vital to his wellbeing. Glaspell had many male models to choose from: Floyd Dell, Max Eastman, Hutchins Hapgood, Harry Kemp, and Eugene O'Neill, not to mention her own husband, whose gaze often strayed. Having set the scene firmly in the Village she knows so well, Glaspell takes control of Bernice and Margaret and turns the tables on the philandering male, using his very tactics, by dramatically silencing Bernice.

Remembered as "loving, and thoughtful, and gay," though often "detached," Bernice has died suddenly of an undiagnosed complaint and is laid out in an adjoining room as the play opens.[82] The closed door is an awesome reminder of her demise. It falls to Bernice's devoted servant Abbie, who alone kept vigil until the end, to convey her last words to her husband, Craig, to whom she reveals that Bernice took her own life. Craig's wild cry—"You thought she didn't love me. You think I didn't matter. But Bernice killed herself because she loved me so!"—betrays his almost comical egotism since Abbie has given absolutely no reason for her mistress's action.[83] But Craig is incapable of seeing Bernice as an individual separate from himself, although he had earlier lamented (echoing Hapgood), "She never seemed to need me. I never felt she—couldn't get along without me."[84]

But Margaret cannot accept that Bernice, who had "loved life so," would kill herself, and she wheedles the truth out of Abbie: Bernice died naturally but first made Abbie promise she would tell Craig she had taken her life. This perplexes Margaret even more; Bernice was no revengeful, power-seeking Hedda Gabler, and she cannot attribute to her friend the hatred she imagines necessary to tell such a lie. Understanding comes only when she realizes that Bernice, fully aware of the social and psychological role required of her as a wife, had foreseen Craig's coxcombry: her death, staged as a lovelorn suicide, will give him the aplomb he needs to succeed in his career. This resolution of Bernice's Freudian logistics is brought about by Craig's confession as much as by Margaret's meditations, both alone and with Abbie, and gives the play its structure and plot.

Throughout act 1, Abbie's agitation grows; her reticence and need for reassurance in the scene with Bernice's father is designed to engage the audience and to hint at mysterious happenings—of which the father will remain completely oblivious. The tension is relieved when Abbie finally fulfills Bernice's last request. The second act culminates in Abbie's second revelation; our curiosity has been skillfully whetted by Margaret's refusal to accept Abbie's initial statement about Bernice's suicide, but this climax, although it provides an instance of peripeteia, fails to satisfy. Guided by Margaret's intuition, we approach the third act. Suspense is alleviated by a return to prosaic everyday matters. Craig's sister fusses over schedules and flowers and Bernice's father seeks ordinary human sympathy, thus distracting us from the mystery at hand. Only Margaret, dominated by the compulsion to clear Bernice's name, misinterprets Craig's grief and fears he will take his life. But Craig, as Bernice had foreseen, has already extricated himself from initial guilt pangs by calling on the self-flattering conviction that he did in fact possess the power he had longed for. In the first act, he had confided to Margaret that "a man's feeling [about a woman] is different."[85] A man, according to Craig, has to feel that he can "destroy" or at least "reshape" the life of a woman. Corroboration of this "manly" rule then comes from the father, who comments that Craig had never "had it in him" to "dominate" Bernice.[86] Cook's wish to master a woman, which had thrilled Glaspell when she was writing *The Road to the Temple*, affected her differently when she encountered it in her daily relationship with him and observed it in the men around her. Craig is childish, if not outright comical, in his dependency on Bernice; he stays Margaret's confession of the truth with an outburst about "having" Bernice and thus unwittingly provokes Margaret's moment of anagnorisis.[87] She can now clear the dead woman's name, both to herself and to Abbie: "Oh—Abbie. Yes, I know now. I want you to know. Only—there are things not for words. Feeling—not for words. As a throbbing thing that flies and sings—not for the hand . . . but, Abbie—there is nothing to hide. There is no shameful thing. What you saw in her eyes as she brooded over life in leaving it—what made you afraid—was her seeing—her seeing into the shadowed places of the life she was leaving. And then—a gift to the spirit. A gift sent back through the dark. Preposterous. Profound. Oh—love her Abbie! She's worth more than love we have power to give!"[88]

Margaret finally reaches the truth: in opening the door to the room where Bernice lies, she transcends the alienation inherent in death as well as in life and comprehends the motives of another human being, thus breaking down the barriers created by everyday modes of communication. Coming from the room of death, she now leaves the door—which until then symbolized the inability to reach out to others and, in its intractability, dominated the set—"wide open behind her" and speaks to Abbie.[89] Language is still a cipher; she hesitates and fumbles for words, resorting to abstract formulations, as do all of the characters throughout the play when they speak of Bernice or of their emotions. As she says, "There are things not for words." But she must share her insight with Abbie in order to return Bernice to the living or at least vindicate her. Glaspell had used withdrawal from communication as a structural and thematic device in *The Outside* and would return to it in her novels, but not before she tried to forge a language that could articulate the inexpressible in *The Verge*.

Margaret's moments of perception are the cruxes that hold the audience. As in Shaw's plays, her intellectual drama provides the plot, thus reducing action to a minimum and hinging all on the tension generated by a family's struggle for self-discovery. The Provincetown audience and the critics took this "talky" play in stride;[90] they had been well prepared by O'Neill's experimental *Moon of the Caribbees*, which relied entirely on mood. In comparison, Glaspell's probing of family relationships must have seemed packed with activity (it also pointed the way toward O'Neill's later themes). *Bernice* skillfully evokes the gloom, guilt, and threatening melodrama that are inevitable at the death of a loved one, but it evades sentimentality. Her characters search for "the unknown hemisphere of the soul" or the "oneness of all men's mind in the human mind," which Cook would explore in *The Spring*.[91] Once Margaret reaches that deeper, quasi-pantheistic understanding, she wins a sense of unity and peace. She knows that she has penetrated the silence of death and overcome the language of the oppressor; she can now formulate Bernice's secret, albeit in fractured sentences, and elucidate the dead woman's last request. Empowering her husband, who has been only a mediocre writer unable to command language, Bernice has effectively established her own power as the other—woman and spirit. The patriarchal ploy of silencing a woman bears unexpected results; whereas William Faulkner in *As I Lay Dying* denies Addie Bundren any real significance in the lives of her husband and children, Bernice, in death, shows herself to be her husband's master. Ironically, of course, she also gives him the one thing he had demanded of her all along: fuel for his sputtering ego.

The straightforward story line allows Glaspell a fair amount of social criticism, underpinned as always in her work by a sly sense of humor. Laura, Craig's sister, is a "type" that appears in all of Glaspell's full-length plays; she is the practical member of the family who can focus on the unpleasant details of a funeral and relish another's last rites. She is the upholder of Victorian morality, the respectable wife who blames Bernice (not Craig) for "not having the power to hold Craig" and who can superciliously say, on the evening of Bernice's death, "I don't think Bernice was a very good wife for a writer."[92] Craig, whose self-absorption lends itself to comedy and in whom so many of the audience would have recognized themselves, is hardly a likable figure. One critic curtly designated him a "conceited cub," whereas John Corbin excused him on the grounds of "masculine vanity," which "all of us know."[93] Bernice's father, although treated sympathetically, also comes in for well-deserved criticism as the representative of an older generation that has opted out of life in a desperate reaction to the war and "a world that won't have visions."[94]

In writing *Bernice*, Glaspell set out to dramatize a conceptual dilemma. Her earlier short plays had successfully ridiculed a specific idea—family pride or woman's honor—but now, more confident of her skills, she goes beyond portrayal or ridicule. She tackles the concept that a generous understanding of others can lead to "oneness" and therefore peace with oneself and others; but she complicates this Nietzschean-Cookian tenet by appropriating a heroine that had fascinated seventeenth-century France. In Racine's version of the story, Bérénice plans suicide but suffers the supreme sacrifice when she agrees to live in order to enhance her husband's public image and career. Glaspell's absent protagonist emulates her namesake when she claims suicide, subjugating the private to the public good, the female to the male. Thus, *Bernice* is a forthright statement about patriarchal society, which Glaspell sees as imposing a two-fold denial of self-definition on women: as a woman in her own right, Bernice is trapped by marriage, and as a woman bound to her husband's love and professional unsuccess, she is trapped by his inadequacy. As in *Trifles*, the only available triumph for the silenced female seems to be through friendship, or bonding, with those of her own sex.

Both contemporary reviewers and today's critics have failed to capitalize on the feminist brief in *Bernice*.

Glaspell was aware of the limitations of the one-act play, and she was convinced that this time her larger canvas required a different shape. Since Cook had proved with *The Athenian Women* that the Province-towners could produce a full-length play, she opted for the three-act format, with no violent action onstage—a particularly well-suited formula given the small space and limited resources she had to work with. Although the Provincetown experiments in stylized productions had excited Glaspell, she intuitively chose realistic representation and a straight Belasco interior. The decor, however, had to do more than simply represent a living room; like the expressionist sets for *The Verge*, the room had to reveal its past occupant. "Everything is Bernice," elegizes her father.[95] The simple order of the beautiful room contrasts with the hesitant abstract speech, laced with lyricism, that Glaspell relied on to purvey the intricacies of the mind.

Although undoubtedly identifying with Bernice, Glaspell agreed to play Abbie, the devoted servant, and offered the more challenging part of Margaret to Rauh. For once, the critics did not damn the acting; the *New York Herald* graciously considered the play to be "well acted for the Provincetowns," and John Corbin of the *Times* must have given Glaspell enormous pleasure when he wrote: "The little play is quite beautifully simple and deft, perfect in each of its several characterizations as in the great central personality of Bernice."[96] The *Boston Evening Transcript* identified Glaspell as "the ablest playwright contributing to [the Provincetown] stage."[97] There is no record of O'Neill's reaction, but we can assume that he shared Glaspell's delight in her success. His wife Agnes Boulton certainly thought highly of *Bernice*. Comparing Glaspell's play to his *Beyond the Horizon*, which she loyally favored, she wrote in a letter to O'Neill: "Its appeal is limited by its subtlety, although it has much of truth and fineness, but your plays are tremendous in their power."[98]

CHAPTER SIX

Toying with Broadway

The Provincetown Players' change in policy with regard to publicity and reviews had been inevitable; Broadway bewitched even the pure of heart on Macdougal Street. Royalties, headlines, and neon lights proved stronger than Cook's vision of an ideal community, a vision that he had implicitly, albeit unwittingly, agreed to betray when Glaspell surrendered *Trifles* to the Washington Square Players in 1916. And Eugene O'Neill, although scorning the cheap tricks of the commercial theater that his father tried to teach him, never turned his back on Broadway; in his dreams, he was the princely dramaturge destined to break the spell that hooked audiences on histrionic reenactments of clichéd plots. Arthur and Barbara Gelb, O'Neill's biographers, hold that he perceived the Provincetown venture as analogous to Stockholm's Intimate Theater—which in 1907 had first produced the plays of August Strindberg—and recognized that the Players provided a "real opportunity to prove himself."[1] He felt no scruples about exploiting the reduced stage and sophisticated audience that the Playwrights' Theatre offered aspiring American playwrights. Edna Kenton shows him "playing" with the audience as no other dramatist had ever done, audaciously building on their "stark laboratory reactions to his own experimentations."[2] In her unpublished history of the Provincetown Players, she comments wryly: "Half the time, we who knew him best did not know what kink lay behind his maddest insistences."[3] In 1922, when it was clear that O'Neill had proved his ability to enthrall Broadway, Kenton wrote: "There is no manner of doubt that O'Neill would have eventually arrived by the direct Broadway route, but there is large room for discussion as to how he would have arrived, whether inspired and original as now or battered and dejected, without the Playwrights' Theater for testing ground from his earliest beginnings. One wonders—and with reason—whether *The Emperor Jones* or *The Hairy Ape* would have been produced, would have been written even, without the untrammeled freedom to experiment for six utterly free years on a stage founded and to be sustained for the production of just such plays as these."[4]

The success of the Provincetown Players has always been attributed to the plays of Eugene O'Neill; Kenton's musings on where his career would have headed without the Players have never been taken up. The importance of the Players for O'Neill, however, was not restricted to their stage and audience; vital to him, though never acknowledged, were the camaraderie and empathy of the founders. Glaspell and Cook offered recognition of his talent and, more important, a passion for endlessly discussing the origins and destiny of humankind. Robert Károly Sarlós, in his study of Cook, acknowledges that "Jig's effect upon the work of O'Neill is both too pervasive and too subtle to be documented point by point," but he has no doubt that Cook had a major formative influence on both *The Emperor Jones* (1920) and *Lazarus Laughed* (1928).[5] Indeed, Nilla Cook would write to Sarlós many years later that *Lazarus Laughed* was "definitely the outcome of the attacks Jig made on Gene for sticking to the conventional, after the *Emperor*, which had opened the way to new forms."[6]

Glaspell's influence on O'Neill has never been fully evaluated, although Eugene Solow recognized it as early as 1930; he was the first critic to claim that "Susan Glaspell and Eugene O'Neill influenced each other in many more ways than one."[7] More recently, Linda Ben-Zvi has detected the impress of the structure and staging devices of *The Verge* on *The Hairy Ape* (1922) and has uncovered Glaspellian traces in *Desire under the Elms* (1924) and *Strange Interlude* (1928). In *Desire under the Elms*, the power of the dead wife and mother is reminiscent of *Trifles* and *Bernice*, and Sam, Ned, and Charles in *Strange Interlude* revolve around the powerful feminine figure, Nina, thus echoing Tom, Dick, and Harry's relationship to Claire in Glaspell's *The Verge*.[8] On the whole, however, critics disregard Cook and Glaspell's effect on O'Neill, thus minimizing the Provincetown Players' formative influence on his development as a dramatist.

But O'Neill's and Glaspell's names were linked by the foremost drama critics of the day, their achievements valued as comparable. Ludwig Lewisohn, writing shortly after Cook's death, declared that "the Provincetown group produced Susan Glaspell and Eugene O'Neill and disappeared."[9] As early as 1922, Isaac Goldberg correctly identified an unusual reversal of gender roles when he explored the differences in character that distinguish their plays: "Between Susan Glaspell and Eugene O'Neill there lies a fundamental artistic difference that may be rooted in the difference of sex as well as of temperament. . . . O'Neill is at bottom the man of feeling, Glaspell is the woman of thought. . . . As O'Neill inclines toward the masterful man, so she leans toward the rebellious woman. . . . Where O'Neill feels his thoughts, Glaspell thinks her feelings."[10]

It would be fascinating to know Glaspell's and O'Neill's views of this analysis, but when Goldberg's study appeared in 1922, Glaspell was in Greece and O'Neill was immersed in writing or producing new full-length plays—*Welded* (1924), *The Fountain* (1925), and *The Hairy Ape*. His relationship with Cook was by then seriously taxed by the older man's growing megalomania, but his admiration for Glaspell and her work grew steadily.

When Glaspell engineered a sabbatical from the theater for the 1919–20 season for herself and her husband in May 1919, she was desperate to get Jig away from the hassle and the temptations of New York. For many months, she had watched him struggling to stick to the spirit of pure amateurism in which he had created his theater. She knew that more and more often he turned to drink, or to Ida Rauh, for consolation when things went wrong, and she trusted that the intimacy of the little house at the far end of Provincetown's main street would give him the break he clearly needed and help repair their marriage. Declaring that she and Cook needed time off to write new plays, Glaspell maneuvered the strings backstage and the Players agreed that James Light and Ida Rauh should take over as directors for 1919–20. Glaspell also looked forward to the refreshing conversations with O'Neill that she promised herself in Provincetown; as things turned out, a birth—and a bereavement—would conspire to bring them together, furthering the assimilation of concepts and ideas that is inevitable between artists.

Agnes Boulton, in her account of the first years of her relationship with Eugene O'Neill, *Part of a Long Story*, tells how pleased O'Neill's parents were that their youngest had married and "more or less settled down." James O'Neill forgot his previous disappointments in his son when he heard that a baby was on the way, showing his approval with a gift calculated to "make [Eugene] happier than anything else"—the abandoned Peaked Hill Bar lifesaving station on the open Atlantic coast of Cape Cod, which had earlier inspired Glaspell's *The Outside*.[11] Boulton shared O'Neill's delight at owning their first home, which was whimsically described in a tax sale as "bounded by lands unknown" to the east, south, and west and by the Atlantic Ocean to the north.[12] It would provide O'Neill with the quiet he needed to write and proximity to the ocean he loved, "the closest thing to living on a ship . . . without actually heaving anchor," and would offer Boulton a release from the unwarranted jealousy she had felt the previous summer when O'Neill had spent hour after hour with Glaspell.[13] But as her confinement drew near, she rejoiced at being able to move closer to her old rival, to "Happy Home," a cottage that "could be kept warm" and had the further advantage that she "could call to [Cook and Glaspell] from the window."[14]

The summer of 1919 passed peacefully for Boulton; she wrote of this period, "Gene was beautiful that summer . . . and I too was full of a physical at-oneness with life and nature."[15] For the Cooks, it was more hectic: they had a collie pup, Nezer, and Jig's two children, Nilla and Harl, for company and no Ma-Mie to keep them in order. Glaspell, her ambition roused by O'Neill's imminent Broadway production, yearned for time to write. (*Beyond the Horizon* would finally go into rehearsal that autumn.) Even more, she ached for the lusty, genial man she had married in 1913, and more and more she hated New York, the theater, and Rauh for taking him away from her. As Boulton observed, loving "Jiggie" Cook gave Glaspell "considerable to think about."[16]

By 1919, Cook was a vexatious man to be with at the best of times, rarely at peace with himself or his surroundings. Instead of soothing him, the hot longueur of a Provincetown summer revived his fear of old age (he was nearing fifty), which had not been put to rest by the writing of *Tickless Time*. He needed to dominate the passage of time, to act out his protagonist's obsession and build his own sundial, erecting it on a worthy pedestal. Through such a work of art, he would gain a measure of immortality. As a student at Harvard, Cook had written: "There is a fascination about a pliable lump of potter's clay. . . . The imagination is quick to take hints and fill the shifting line with noble or ignoble life."[17] This fascination had persisted, and Glaspell tells how he once took a lump of clay from Fred Burt's studio at the Modern Art School: "It was as if his fingers had wanted that clay a long time." He surprised their "artist friends" with his skill and won their praise for his "instinctive sense of form."[18] Modeling provided a challenge for his restless hands and obsessive mind and a release from real-world frustrations. That summer of 1919, it overrode all other interests. Glaspell recounts that, as the winter approached, he was still "modeling the four figures for his sun-dial. Dawn . . . Noon . . . Sunset . . . and the North Star."[19]

When she wrote *The Road to the Temple*, Glaspell placed herself in the shadow of her husband, blurring their relationship with the haze of hagiography and rarely giving a hint of her own feelings and desires. But the casting of the figures for the sundial draws from her a heartfelt—albeit humorous—plea for the abused assistant she played to Cook's maestro:

> It was my business to have more plaster right there, the water at just such a temperature, and to pour at precisely the right tempo at the exact moment or—"God damn it, it's ruined!" At first I was hurt by profanity; had I not been getting the things ready for hours? Had I not done my best? Could angels ask more? Yes, indeed they could, and did. I do not know just what went on in the house of Benvenuto Cellini, but in our locked house you had the feeling death would be done for a slip of the arm. And why not? Was not this the work into which the moods of the days had gone? Were not these the figures to support the sundial, and symbols of our relation to truth beyond our world?[20]

Cook's Herculean frame, trembling with the excitement of creation, his white forelock pushed back with long, plaster-thickened fingers and his nearly delirious eyes blazing at her, would indeed have inspired fear in his apprentice-wife when she innocently but repeatedly ruined the emerging masterpiece. We can be sure Cook did not limit himself to the mild exclamations Glaspell records.

But Glaspell did not delight in mixing plaster and was glad to have the company of Nezer, the sleek, dashing collie who would run after the sticks she threw on their long walks in the winter woods. Cook inevitably refused to accompany them; in his eyes, walking was a tame sport. Nezer, however, did force him on one long expedition after he followed a stranger out of town. The hiker was not able to shake Nezer off, and the Cooks' spreading alarm soon had all of the dog-loving Cape Codders on the trail of the adventurous pup. Cook, once he recovered his friend, growled about the $50 taxi bill the pursuit had occasioned.

"We can't afford [it]," he explained.[21] Nezer, who had only learned to count to four, wagged his tail and no doubt wondered what the fuss was about.

The children had left at the end of the summer. Autumn winds took to shaking "the little house on the sand," blowing straight through the groaning clapboards and leaving behind the dank caress of the ocean.[22] Jig consorted with Dionysus in an effort to keep warm, bellowing his anger at damp firewood, which sputtered and would not light. Glaspell's dream of "togetherness" before a cozy fire in their own home after a day's good writing never materialized. Her husband's restlessness was fueled by missives from Rauh, who reported on the battle for power from the front lines on Macdougal Street. Eventually, the lure of good argument, companionable drinking, and Rauh's warm apartment was too much for Cook. Promising to return as soon as he had solved the Players' disputes, he departed for Greenwich Village. Glaspell was left to "manage the stoves alone" and spend long, lonely evenings tormented by visions of Jig and Rauh and flagons of wine. Cook's letters did not cheer her. Boulton, with whom she shared news from New York, reported to her husband the goings-on at Macdougal Street and railed against Rauh: "Ida is a b—ch, is my opinion. She's just made up her mind to keep [Cook] down there—somehow. She's hit his weak spot." She recorded that Glaspell was "terribly blue and hurt, by Jig's letter."[23]

Dejected, Glaspell could not concentrate on the comedy she had planned to write. Dialogue that had seemed potentially hilarious now exuded tragedy, and her characters insisted on fulfilling their own destinies and disregarding her wishes. Her only relief came from friendship with Boulton, a friendship unexpectedly strengthened by the birth of Shane O'Neill on 30 October 1919. Glaspell delighted in the baby, although once again she was reminded of her own inability to bear children. Faithful to her tenet that failure is essential to ultimate achievement, she came to terms with this reminder of her previous disappointment, finding consolation in the happiness of her younger friend. For Boulton, the baby sealed her love for O'Neill, who acknowledged his son as part of "us" and as the third in "a sort of Holy Trinity."[24] The child was also a vindication of her own creative capacity. Boulton had published stories in pulp magazines before meeting O'Neill, but in their relationship, she unquestioningly cast herself as the inferior writer, allowing him to take over her ideas, as in the case of her novelette "The Captain's Walk." O'Neill, excited by the story, had rewritten it as *Where the*

Cross Is Made (1918) and later used the same plot in the full-length play *Gold* (1921). While O'Neill worked on his plays, Boulton halfheartedly tried to fulfill her ambition of writing a story that *Harper's* would publish. Glaspell's success as a writer had always galled her, but now motherhood—a level of creation denied her friend—raised her above such petty jealousies.

Cook eventually returned to Provincetown. Rauh had resolved her quarrels with Light, and possibly Boulton's pleas to O'Neill to intervene and "bring Jig if you can" had some effect.[25] No letters or diaries document Cook's homecoming, but clearly, however deeply his misadventures wounded her, Glaspell would always receive him back in good faith, suppressing her pride and her independence in the name of what she still believed was love. So they spent Christmas quietly, recovering a little of the companionship she longed for, reading, and writing.

———— ··◄∞►·· ————

By January, Glaspell pronounced her play done and asked Boulton to look over this latest work, pouring out her doubts and confiding that she "didn't quite know what to do with it."[26] A little miffed that O'Neill should launch himself on Broadway while she was tied to the Playwrights' Theatre, she too had written with a commercial audience in mind. Boulton read the piece eagerly and declared it "awfully amusing" in her next epistle to O'Neill, who was in New York.[27] Almost immediately after the birth of his son, O'Neill had left to supervise the rehearsals of *Beyond the Horizon*, which John D. Williams—after sitting on the option for two years—had finally decided to produce. Williams was one of the few Broadway producers willing to risk taking on a play that did not appear to be commercial, and O'Neill was in seventh heaven at his professional debut. He offered to press Glaspell's play on the Broadway producer George C. Tyler, his father's oldest friend, who was rehearsing *Chris Christopherson* (which O'Neill would rewrite as *Anna Christie* [1920]) for a trial production in Atlantic City:

> Tell Susan I spoke to Tyler about her play and that he is genuinely eager to have a look at it. He said he had seen three of her plays at different times at the P. P.—*Bernice*, *Woman's Honor* and one other. He said "that girl has a real touch of genius"—(he evidently thinks Susan is as old as Helen Hayes), and he added with a questioning

misgiving: "If the damned Greenwich Village faddists didn't get her into the radical magazine publications class." I didn't disillusion him about Susan being 19 and at the mercy of the faddist world—it was too funny—but I did say she was married to a very sensible man. Upon which Tyler heaved a sigh of relief and ceased to "view with alarm."

The funny end of it aside, her play will be received with gratitude at the Tyler office and given a quick reading, I'm sure of that. . . . If she judges it would be of any use, if she will send me the play (I'd like very much to read it myself, of course) I will put it in Tyler's hand myself and keep asking him if he's read it, to get action. . . . You can at least assure her from me that Tyler, personally, is a fine straight guy—and that's a lot in this man's business. And he sincerely wants—on the strength of her work he has seen and liked immensely—to get a chance to read her play. The outcome is in the lap of the gods of course.[28]

Tyler's assumption that Glaspell was an inexperienced nineteen-year-old tickled both women; they knew from O'Neill that Tyler was so besotted with Helen Hayes, his recent discovery, that he insisted on casting her as the consumptive protagonist in O'Neill's *The Straw* in spite of the playwright's serious misgivings as to her maturity for the role. (Hayes would play the wife in *A Touch of the Poet* when it was produced posthumously in 1958.) Glaspell, aquiver with excitement, spent a couple of weeks revising her play before she sent it off to O'Neill. Presently, Boulton reported his eager reply: "I like her play tremendously and think it has fine chance with him—or anyone else."[29] Her play was in Tyler's hands, "awaiting his first breathing spell."[30]

The sabbatical winter was not proving easy, and O'Neill's praise, almost more than his offer to champion her on Broadway, meant a great deal to Glaspell. Whether all of this met with Cook's approval, we have no way of knowing, but it definitely ran against the grain of his principles. After O'Neill's uptown success with *The Emperor Jones* in November 1920, Cook would bullheadedly seek Broadway recognition for himself and his wife, but in the winter of 1919–20, nauseated by professional infiltration of the theater he had brought into being, he almost certainly disapproved of Glaspell's ambitions.[31]

But Tyler took his time to reply. Boulton wrote to O'Neill on 25 February: "Seriously I do believe that Susan's play would stand a better chance with [John] Williams, than with Tyler. The play struck me as being just a bit 'cluttered' at present, and the ideas and dialogue that clutter it would prove good fun to Williams, while with Tyler they might prove a serious stumbling-block to seeing the real merits of the play. I perhaps influenced Susan into thinking W[illiams] would be even better than T[yler]—and perhaps I shouldn't have done so—but—somehow— I have me doubts about T[yler] caring much about it."[32] Glaspell's hopes were raised, then dashed, with every post. But she followed her friends' advice and submitted the play to Williams, as well as to the Theatre Guild, informing Lulu Huffaker and her husband (of the Guild): "I was glad to hear that the script got to Williams—having it in my head that he might be interested in the play. Probably he'll be the first to turn it down—so much for hunches. I should think I might be hearing from the Theatre Guild very soon now, for Lee S[imonson] said they would have to decide within two weeks." She was desperate to know "the great world's attitude toward *Chains of Dew*."[33]

But as things turned out, the "great world" did not respond favorably. It was judged that *Chains of Dew* was not sufficiently geared to "average intellects and ordinary playgoers . . . [to achieve] a paying popularity" in a commercial Broadway theater, and in both form and content, it was not avant-garde enough to interest the Theatre Guild.[34] This setback disappointed Glaspell. It was not until the summer that, with a little more confidence, she wrote to Huffaker's husband, Eddie Goodman: "I really feel now like getting out my comedy and re-writing it, also writing a new one."[35] She was aware that she had veered too much toward commercial tastes in *Chains of Dew* and did not want to surrender the play to the Provincetown Players; in fact, it was not until 1922, when circumstances obliged her to provide a play for that season's final bill, that she would hand her text to the Players. *Chains of Dew* would be rushed into production once O'Neill's *The Hairy Ape* moved uptown. But O'Neill did not forget the comedy he had tried so hard to place on Broadway, and although he was in Provincetown when *Chains of Dew* was produced, he eagerly asked about its fortunes, complaining to Fitzi that no one had bothered to let him know.[36] However much he used the Players as a stepladder to success and disparaged Cook's skills as a director, he genuinely respected Glaspell as a playwright and was grateful to her for having engineered a hearing for *Bound East for Cardiff* in 1916, thus giving him his first chance to see one of his plays on the stage. Undoubtedly, he felt he had discharged part of that debt by trying to introduce her work to Broadway producers.

Glaspell would continue to support O'Neill. When John Williams, producer of *Beyond the Horizon*, astutely suggested that a "selected audience" of people "who can appreciate the play" would be the best advertising aid, O'Neill turned to her for permission to use the Provincetown Players' list of subscribers.[37] Cook, still smoldering with resentment that O'Neill had not given the first option on *Beyond the Horizon* to the Players, flamed up at this exploitative request; the Washington Square Players, a "sister" group, had always refused to share their constituency, guarding their address list with great secrecy. But as O'Neill had hoped, Glaspell brought Jig round. Boulton, acting as messenger, reported: "[Glaspell] said she thought you surely had a right to use it personally, if you could do so without letting any outsider see it."[38] So it was that a faithful Provincetown audience trooped uptown to the Morosco Theatre, assuring *Beyond the Horizon* a warm reception. The play chalked up 111 performances and won the Pulitzer Prize to boot. Glaspell shared her protégé's delight, but her own failure to reach Broadway with *Chains of Dew* must have been all the more galling.

Chains of Dew is the only one of Glaspell's produced plays that she did not publish. She hurriedly filed the typescript with the Library of Congress on 21 February 1920, and no publisher has ever seen it. Since the play represents an important link in the development of her life and thought, it should be examined in detail. Not produced until 1922, *Chains of Dew* follows from *Bernice* (1919) and furthers Glaspell's exploration of her darkening predicament. The earlier play studies the marriage of an inferior writer to a woman of superior intelligence who would not bow to his demands. *Chains of Dew* examines the emotions of a woman who chooses to sacrifice herself to the needs of her husband. The campaigns promoted by Margaret Sanger and Emma Goldman to inform women about birth control add to the topicality of this personal drama.

Although Glaspell did not participate actively in these campaigns— her desire to have children would have propelled her toward fertility research rather than the dissemination of contraceptive methods—she was well informed of the issue; Rauh would have made sure of that. The

Comstock Law of 1873 had made it illegal to mail obscene matter, a classification that was imposed on information concerning contraceptive techniques by zealots who believed practical knowledge on such a topic should not be allowed to reach the masses. In 1914, Margaret Sanger ran afoul of this law when she used the U.S. postal service to mail her journal the *Woman Rebel* to subscribers and printed a pamphlet with the telling title *Family Limitation*. It was at this time that Emma Goldman, for whom anarchy "was not a mere theory for a distant future" but a "living experience to free us from inhibitions," began lecturing on the subject, giving specific contraceptive instructions.[39] Eventually the law caught up with her and she was arrested; at the public protest organized at Carnegie Hall, the speakers included John Reed and Anna Strunsky Walling, who "dwelt on [the] social and human value [of contraception] as a liberating factor, particularly in the lives of proletarians."[40] (Ironically, in 1932, Walling's daughter would have a child by Glaspell's then companion Norman Matson, thus precipitating the breakup of that relationship.) At a later protest meeting in Union Square, Rauh was among those who distributed pamphlets giving contraceptive advice. As Goldman emphasized in her autobiography, "Birth-control had ceased to be a mere theoretic issue; it became an important phase of the social struggle, which could be advanced more by deeds than by words."[41]

It is unlikely that Glaspell actually helped Rauh hand out pamphlets, but she regarded the subject as sufficiently important to make it figure largely in *Chains of Dew*, thus "cluttering" the first act with ideas, as Boulton noted. Her protagonist, the birth control fanatic Nora, challenges the law forbidding dissemination of contraceptive techniques with the eugenic and social arguments of Sanger and Goldman, but her most effective strategy relies on awakening compassion for the unborn child because of its meager prospects in a large, impoverished family. Glaspell is also anxious to make it clear that the ruling classes, who manage to contain their families to two or three children, monopolize information that is vital to the working classes.[42] She targets this hypocritical behavior in her portrayal of the society matron, Mrs. MacIntyre, who, even though she laments that she will lose the services of her laundress because she is about to "have another," refuses to "talk to those people about— things."[43] (In truth, this Mrs. MacIntyre may well be named after the New York district attorney who was responsible for Goldman's first prison conviction.) Although *Chains of Dew* does not actually purvey any information on birth control devices, it might have attracted Comstock's watchdogs if it had not been for Glaspell's teasing tone and jocular portrayal of Nora's fanaticism. (George Tyler, a man of an older generation, must have been repelled, as Boulton feared, merely by the airing of such a taboo subject.)

Possibly the offices of Goldman's *Mother Earth* offered a model for the offices of the *New Nation*, which double as a center for birth control propaganda. Here the action of the play begins. Nora, in a "flapperish but chaste" gray office dress, is trying to mimeograph a letter, but the machine has a will of its own and dominates the stage, lending a tone of burlesque to the whole act.[44] These unfathomable quirks delight her: "Isn't modern machinery wonderful? So sensitive. Think of how it does its duty! Isn't it touching?," she purrs. (Unfortunately, the actress who played Nora could not cope with the mimeograph, so it became merely "a decoration on its tall latticed table.")[45] The flippant dialogue of this act takes up a number of the topics of the day as it sets the scene for what appears to be a conventional love plot: the dangers of bobbed hair, the differences between the sexes, freedom of speech, the value of truth, poetry versus propaganda, birth control, and the woeful state of the nation.

But the remainder of the play leaves vain topicalities behind as it shatters our expectations of a frivolous romance. We forget the clichés of the first act as we witness the manipulations of man and wife that cruelly reveal the inequality of the sexes that is sanctioned by society. The upshot is that, as the final curtain falls, we taste only the bitterness of a woman's pointless, unappreciated sacrifice.

Seymore Standish, a poet much admired and frequently published by the editors of the *New Nation*, is clearly flirting with Nora. However, according to his friends, he lacks whatever it is that makes for greatness. James O'Brien, an essayist and short story writer from Ireland, is puzzled: "When given so much—why is one left unsatisfied?" He judges Seymore to be "sincere and shrewd" and finally enlightens colleagues and audience with his penetrating wisdom: "But there's one thing sure— If he had that thing—that one misses in him—he'd be a great poet." Seymore does a better job at explaining himself: he is the director of a bank in the barren midwestern town of Bluff City and is duty-bound to make money for his children, ensure serenity for his mother, and escort his wife to society functions. This regimen does not allow time for soul-searching poetry, nor can it possibly provide inspiration; thus, he periodically escapes to New York, where, feted by his courtiers, he plays the part of the "trapped revolutionist" whose return to "bondage" is decreed by fate.

Initially, we feel pity for this poet who has the potential to be great, but Glaspell does not give us time to relish our compassion—very soon, she reveals something of the true Seymore. We find that Nora, O'Brien, and Leon Whittaker, the editor, have all rebelled against what society expected of them; they have freed themselves from the bonds of family and dreary jobs to devote themselves to a cherished cause. Although Seymore listens to their life stories, complaisance in his superior suffering deafens him to their lessons. Superciliously, he contemplates them from his heights: "Dear babes!—I'm so glad you've been so gently handled. It is a bit amusing, though, to see you with this pleased sense of having emancipated yourselves. I hardly know how to talk to you. To me—you don't seem grown-up." Nora is not taken in, but her attempt to deflate him misfires. Her chaffing—"It must be lonely to be the only grown-up person in the world"—meets with his self-pitying outburst—"It is lonely. I see now you've never been up against life. I—I don't know how to talk to you." So, at this stage, Seymore admits he might be weak, endearing himself to us in a confession vibrant with a concern that permeates all of Glaspell's writing: "I just haven't got it in me—the thing that would ride rough shod over all the people who love me. I can't quite believe enough in myself to overthrow their lives in order to right mine." We will learn how to interpret his words when we meet his mother later on in the play. This discussion of Seymore's lack of true greatness is redeemed from the pitfalls of sentimentality by Nora's commonsense bantering and the humor that emerges from her despair at the egocentricism of men. One such episode involves O'Brien, the visiting Irishman.

Nora asks O'Brien to give a speech for the birth control movement and to agree to an interview with one of her coactivists. The young man, who is completely ignorant of birth control, shimmies artlessly:

O'Brien: And what would my mother say? My mother had nine children.

Nora: Your mother had nine children? She'll say, Bless you my fearless lad!

Aware of his distress, she diplomatically changes the subject and inquires into his shopping expedition. This promises to be a good ploy; he is touchingly proud of the red silk stockings he has purchased for his mother. Aghast, Nora asks, "Is your mother like that?" O'Brien blandly explains that his mother had "such a drab life" that he feels he should "enliven" it for her.

> Nora: Will she wear them?
> O'Brien: She'll have to wear them; she wouldn't hurt my feelings.
> Nora: Mother love! And yet there are people who do not believe in birth control.

O'Brien gives another reason for his choice—the name of the color of these stockings is "American Beauty." He wanted something "characteristically American" to show his mother "what sort of environment" he was in.

> Nora: She isn't one to—worry much, is she?
> O'Brien: Oh yes, mother worries a great deal. That's why I'm sending her these.

At this point, Nora rightly gives up on him and returns to her task at the mimeograph. (The stockings caused a commotion on Macdougal Street. Kenton reported: "Throck [Cleon Throckmorton] chased all over town for American Beauty stockings and he found them all right—they came with a bill for $3.75. . . . But they look it—they look it.")[46]

Acts 2 and 3 are set in Seymore's midwestern home. We soon realize that his wife Dotty, properly Diantha (Seymore denies her her name, thus refusing to acknowledge her as a responsible adult), is not the society goose he makes her out to be. During his absence, she has scorned the bridge parties and dinners he had lined up for her and instead has become friends with the English teacher—a representative of the town's intelligentsia—and taken a correspondence course on poetry. She reveals herself to be dissatisfied with the decoration of her home. Removing a picture of the Sistine Madonna was easy, but her education and cultural background leave her stumped for a substitute—a failing she candidly admits. Dotty is quite ready to do without the social life Seymore thinks she thrives on in order to allow him more time for his writing, but he is intent on continuing in his role of the good provider who sacrifices his art for his family. It becomes more and more apparent that his poetry is cheap and facile and that Nora's misgivings as to his worth are valid. Like Craig in *Bernice*, Seymore requires a submissive woman if he is to function at all, in either the public or the private domain. His behavior toward Nora and Dotty shows him for what he is, and the poem he composes, inspired by a rag doll whose hair he has bobbed according to the latest New York style, betrays his utter contempt for women, reducing them to long-haired toys that exist only for his amusement:

> She's in her coffin—she's in her grave,
> Outside her coffin, she was not brave.
>
> What did she have, when she had life?
> She had long hair—a good sound life.
>
> What has she now that she is dead?
> She has long hair —outside her head.
>
> So what is death—and what is life?
> To one who's but—a long-haired wife?

When Nora unexpectedly arrives to canvass for the birth control movement in Bluff City, Dotty immediately follows her lead, accepts the honor of being the president of the town's first Birth Control League, and is delighted that, now that she has other commitments, Seymore will be able to devote more time to his writing. Seymore's mother, who shares Dotty's enthusiastic promotion of birth control, is initially thrilled at the prospect of release from the tedious inactivity to which her son had unwittingly subjected her. In spite of her present life of leisure, she can still remember the anguish of bringing up seven children single-handedly. She has long dodged the boredom of her existence by fashioning rag dolls for church bazaars. Now she promptly offers to make dolls to raise funds for the birth control movement, and the three women become immersed in the founding of the league. She is crushed when Whittaker, the New York editor, unsuspectingly throws light on her son's behavior. As he begs her to free Seymore from bonds imposed by society and family, he innocently discloses that the poet-businessman needs to feel himself "the alien" in order to write poetry—to bridle at the "chains of affection" pulling him back to his family whenever he is with his chosen literary friends—and that this constraint gives him a necessary sense of self-sacrifice and thus moral superiority. The older Mrs. Standish can now understand Seymore's horror at the unprecedented activity of his womenfolk: he is suffering from wounded pride rather than affronted principle. He cannot accept that his wife and mother could be more useful to others than to himself; to him, they are essential agents because, as his dependents, they prove his manhood. Mrs. Standish ruefully concedes: "We must leave him his bondage." She is prepared to sacrifice herself but wonders whether Dotty will be prepared to do likewise: "She's loose. I don't know whether we can catch her—and turn her back into a stumbling block—and a hitching post—and all those necessary things. It's hard to be a wife!" She then asks Dotty whether she loves proselytizing for birth control more than she loves her husband and points out to the young woman that Seymore is lost "without his sacrifice for you." She asks: "Do we want to go skylarking and leave poor Seymore to his freedom? Perhaps we do; it depends on which we value most— ourselves or him." To her daughter-in-law's plea, "If people ought to be free—why can't I be free?," she can only reply, "Because you love an- other person." So awareness of birth control, knowledge that empowers women, does not win the day; the nineteenth-century ethic of feminine sacrifice prevails.

In *Chains of Dew*, Glaspell uses the same structure that had served her so well in *Bernice*: three acts devoid of conventional plot, development, or denouement. True to the Greenwich Village ethic, she is intent on por- traying psychological realism and thus spurns the stock-in-trade devices of the well-made play favored by Broadway. No letter or arrival of a long- lost friend propels the action to an inevitable end. As in life, the climaxes are not satisfactory. The mother's moment of recognition, precipitated by Whittaker's pleas that she help free Seymore from his family chains, is obscured by an ineffectual straining at comedy—a bow in the direction of Broadway. Comedy is, of course, inherent in any dialogue at cross- purposes, but here Whittaker's earnest self-righteousness coupled with the mother's readiness to accept what she had already dimly perceived dull the humor. At this point, the text does not provoke much laughter, and it is difficult to imagine even the best actors bringing it out.

The denouement, or second climax, on which the play ends, is no more satisfactory. Dotty succumbs to domesticity from a sense of duty imposed on her by her mother-in-law and husband. All too briefly, we glimpse the real Dotty struggling to surface, but without Seymore's ap- proval, she cannot stay afloat. Today, regenerated by decades of feminist thought, we can only judge her as too weak, as lacking the courage to go it alone with which Henrik Ibsen endowed his Nora in *A Doll's House*. Glaspell's Nora is frequently linked to her Scandinavian namesake, but the choice of name was probably fortuitous since it is Dotty who is struggling toward freedom—for herself and for Seymore—and she is foiled by his dependency on the limitations imposed by convention.

Ibsen's Nora could categorically affirm that she no longer loved Torvald Helmer; the American Dotty still loves Seymore and therefore puts him before herself. It is only when love has gone or when a lover's feelings are uncertain that Glaspell's protagonists have the courage to strike out on their own. In *Chains of Dew*, the author maintains that the bonds of love enslave a woman as surely as those of motherhood, and she offers no way out. Dotty is not formed by events we are allowed to witness, and thus her final decision cannot be attributed to a development of her personality but must be seen as a result of her prior conditioning. The sacrifice of her own self returns the Standish household to normal, Seymore's ego is appeased, and only the women are aware of Dotty's "voluntary" immolation.

Glaspell is unsparing in her scorn for Seymore, a conceited, half-baked poet who is a caricature of the average husband. His gross inferiority confers on Dotty's final decision the status of tragedy. Unwilling to bend her standards or in any way betray her idealistic commitment to human-ity, Glaspell would never satisfy a box-office audience. She was no Rachel Crothers, whose protagonists are so heroic in their self-denial that ac-cepted morality is easily satisfied.[47] For Glaspell's protagonists, there is no heroism; submission, in life or death—or, as in *The Verge*, a transcen-dence of man-made arbitration—tender the only way out.

Reviewers, accustomed to Glaspell's wit and unconventional handling of social mores in her short plays and in *Inheritors* and *The Verge*—pro-duced before *Chains of Dew*—were not sure how to handle this play. The *New York Herald* reviewer, while having clearly enjoyed the entertain-ment, lamented that the play was "written with saucy disregard of the necessities of dramaturgy."[48] Seeing it merely as a satire on bobbed hair and birth control campaigns, the critic thought it more appropriate for a Broadway audience than for the Greenwich Village coterie. However, he could not quite hide his disappointment at the lack of sex and violence: neither Dotty nor Nora slams doors or brandishes a pistol, and no fatal accident adds to the drama, which is restricted to a woman's voluntary self-immolation. Maida Castellun in the *New York Call* was more percep-tive: "But there is much more implied—among other things the showing up of the male as your only true conservative in matters social and spiritual. . . . As a social iconoclast the female of the species again proves more daring than the male."[49] Burns Mantle, a devotee of the Province-town Players since their founding, tried perhaps a trifle too hard not to let Glaspell down when he effused: "It is a rare mind and a definite talent this playwright discloses whenever she writes anything for the stage." But he too was nonplussed by what he sensed as an unwarranted courting of the popular audience.[50] Alison Smith in the *New York Evening Globe* also responded to the tug of opposing forces in *Chains of Dew*, but she identified those forces not in terms of audience flattery but rather in terms of genre. She saw Glaspell as "wabbling dangerously" between "hilarious satire" and "grim sincerity" and criticized the thematic explosion—the "cluttering" that Boulton relished and that feminist criticism now accepts as characteristic of the "feminine voice."[51] Provincetown friends Ludwig Lewisohn and Heywood Broun, disconcerted by Glaspell's jibbing of both Broadway and Village audiences, deprecated a tendency to rely on symbolism, which they felt had betrayed her.[52] But no reviewer remarked on the primary issue of Dotty's tragedy—it was lost in the staging of the play, which emphasized the situational comedy and the predicament of the businessman-poet. Even for the self-styled bohemians of Greenwich Village, *Chains of Dew* was, after all, the story of a poet, not that of his wife.

We can only speculate about the deeper motives that impelled Glaspell to choose subjects for her plays, but it is surely striking that she created protagonists who play out a drama similar to that going on in her own life. Both Bernice and Dotty give themselves up to wifely obligation. Since Glaspell did so too, she may have considered the play to be a means of reconciling her qualms about her bold choice.

The sabbatical that Glaspell had manipulated Cook into taking did not work out as she had hoped. Although she managed to finish the play she had been composing in New York, to her chagrin it was not snapped up by Broadway. But her main concern had been to save her marriage and shield her husband from both Rauh and the Players' imbroglios. She also dreamed that Cook might finally write the play that would establish him as America's greatest playwright. For most of the autumn and winter, Glaspell must have feared that she had failed miserably, but by the spring of the following year, 564 Commercial Street was outwardly peaceful. Cook was busy with notes for a new play that would demonstrate "the religion of the oneness of men supplanting class-struggle, the oneness of matter and mind, the oneness of all men's mind in the human mind."[53] Convinced that it was possible to reach complete knowledge, a deep subconscious human unity, he turned to historical figures who, he hoped, would lead him toward it. But love and youth were essential, and when those faded, "wine and laudanum" alone could "open the clogged road."[54] He researched the lives of scientists; Paracelsus and Madame Curie absorbed him for weeks; then, nearer home, the Native American tribes of Iowa caught his attention. But the play itself eluded him. Its unusual theme, which he had managed to identify as "the richness of sub-conscious invention," offered ample opportunities for the "dream-like" quality he sought but was hardly the "imaginative impulse" needed to create the "new religion" he was struggling to articulate.[55] Wandering around the house in search of a listener, spouting ideals and maxims, he would disturb his wife at her desk. She was nonetheless gratified that for once her company sufficed him and delighted that his play, *The Spring*, was taking shape.

In the afternoons, she insisted on taking house-hunting trips, and together they scoured the tip of the Cape for a more peaceful dwelling. The previous summer, they had been "much tormented" by the growing traffic "jam[ming] the narrow winding street which faithfully followed the line of the sea, and never meant to be a highway."[56] They did not want their peace disturbed again and, in love with the Truro Valley, settled on an abandoned farmhouse that promised quiet and solitude. Glaspell had the rooms painted, and they were ready to move as soon as the summer hordes became intolerable.

It was then that disaster hit: their collie Nezer came down with distemper. The puppy who had been such an adept pupil, giving Cook enormous pleasure each time he mastered a new trick, was now incapable of performing. He would come to Cook, lay his head on his knee, and listen quietly to the voice he loved. Cook spent hours talking to him, "gently, encouragingly," keeping him in the house, fearful of a "nervous reaction." On 14 April, the Cooks' wedding anniversary, the O'Neills brought over an illegal bottle of whiskey (Prohibition had come into effect in January 1920). But there was no celebration. Jig went upstairs when Nezer's whimpering became unbearable. He had promised Glaspell, "We won't let it go too bad for him," but now proved unequal to the task. O'Neill took over: " 'I'll do this for you, Jig,' Gene said, and Jig and I left them alone in our house while we went and stayed the night in their house."[57] Two days later, after burying Nezer by the sundial, the Cooks, unable to stay in the house with memories of the collie, left for New York. Glaspell, for whom dogs were at least as important as people, would never forget O'Neill's help on that occasion.

A few months later, toward the close of August, the Cooks spent a happier night in the O'Neill home. They had been asked to come for dinner and to listen to the new play O'Neill had written, *The Silver Bullet*. Glaspell was uncertain whether they should return to New York for the winter. The spring and summer had revitalized the intimacy of their marriage, and she feared what winter in New York could bring. She argued that they both needed more time to finish the plays they had started. They had given enough of themselves to the Players. "Now that we had shown our idea, set a number of things in motion, would we not rather return to our work as individuals?," she queried.[58] But the new play, rechristened *The Emperor Jones*, electrified Cook. "Here is a challenge!," he hallooed. "This is what I have been waiting for—a play to call forth the utmost each one can do, and fuse all into unity." He predicted that *The Emperor Jones* would bring the long-awaited "success of the Provincetown Players" and envisioned the play against a Reinhardt-style dome, the horizon stretching away into "pure space."[59] Glaspell marveled at the sudden resurgence of his energy but despaired whenever she thought of him on Macdougal Street. Cook was unperturbed. In an appeasing gesture, he packed the half-finished manuscript of *The Spring*, although he knew he would never touch it in New York. He was convinced it was his duty to reorganize the Provincetown Players and produce *The Emperor Jones*, believing that "Gene knew there was a place where such a play would be produced. He wrote it to *compel* us to the untried, to the 'impossible.'"[60] Ever since the success of *Beyond the Horizon*, Cook had been aching for a play that would be "impossible to produce on Broadway," and he had frequently stimulated O'Neill's creativity by holding forth about the original unity in the minds of humans, which, disrupted by the Apollonian apprehension of death, could only be regained through primitive supernatural forces evoked in the Greek Dionysian theater.[61] These discussions, which inspired Cook's *The Spring* and Glaspell's *Inheritors*, culminated in O'Neill's *The Emperor Jones*, and in their immediate wake came *The Fountain*, *The Great God Brown* (1926), and *Lazarus Laughed*.

CHAPTER SEVEN

Religious Fervor

Once again, Cook left for New York while Glaspell stayed behind to ponder alone the progression of the tides and the fluctuations of human destinies. The summer people returned to their winter lives, and she was at last free to surrender herself to the piecemeal pages of her new long play, *Inheritors*, on which she had spent the mornings of that spring and summer. It was to be "a real American play," as she had explained to Agnes Boulton in January.[1] But she was already distracted by the germ of the play she would write about a woman's frantic need to transcend the patriarchal institutions that surround her. The desire to be recognized both as a creator and as a woman would dominate *The Verge* (1921), the last play she would write for the Provincetown Players.

But the autumn of 1920 was, *nolens volens*, dedicated to *The Emperor Jones*. Cook's enthusiasm had never been more visionary or more determined. He returned to the Players as their rightful overlord, brushing aside Ida Rauh and James Light, the directors of the previous season, and asserting his messianic self with aggressive confidence. Disregarding all protests and negative votes and oblivious to the state of the treasury, he proceeded to erect a dome at the back of the small Macdougal Street stage.[2] Cook had long dreamed of having a dome in his theater, a plaster cyclorama to reflect light and create the illusion of infinity. The Players, more practical, had always denied him on the grounds of cost. But there Cook was, sleeping and eating in the theater, "in a morass of steel netting and iron bars and cement," because, as he explained to Edna Kenton, "*The Emperor* has *got* to have a dome to play against. You see, Edna, it begins . . . thick forest at first . . . steadily thinning out . . . scene after scene . . . to pure space."[3] He was in thrall to the need for light and space; intuitively, he knew that by creating infinity he could transport his audience into the world of Dionysus, of healing religious ritual. And, to a degree, he succeeded: the critics praised lighting effects that were "uncommonly beautiful," and Kenneth Macgowan, a relative newcomer to the avant-garde scene of New York, exulted in the "glorious beauty" created by the dome: "The moment when [Brutus Jones] raises his naked body against the moonlit sky beyond the edge of the jungle and prays, is such a dark lyric of the flesh, such a cry of the primitive being, as I have never seen in the theatre."[4]

Cook had finally realized his ambition of creating dramatic ritual on the stage, of raising an audience above petty individual concerns into a communal spirit of religious exaltation. True, it was not his own play, but it was his faith in O'Neill that had spurred the aspiring playwright to the heights of *The Emperor Jones*, and only Cook's determination to produce the play in the right conditions guaranteed an enthralling spectacle. But during rehearsals, O'Neill, impatient at Jig's lack of professionalism, fumed at his visionary tactics. On one occasion, forgetting Cook's devotion to his talent, he struck viciously at his sponsor, hissing: "You're a rotten producer, and I came to tell you that I've reached a place where I must have more competent direction."[5] He went so far as to ask Broadway producer Arthur Hopkins to help with the production. Glaspell, indignant at this slight from her friend, irately insisted on the true identity of the producer of *The Emperor Jones* in *The Road to the Temple*: "It was [Cook] who produced *The Emperor Jones*. That production is history now. The director's faith and intensity were burned into it, and as he had foreseen, our very limitations forced us to create methods which later took their place in 'the new technique.'"[6]

Cook, humbling himself in the name of theater, absorbed the insult and continued working with O'Neill. With time and success, some of the old friendship and faith were restored, and although O'Neill never publicly acknowledged Cook's part in the glorious achievement of *The Emperor Jones*, he did render homage to Cook in a 1948 interview for the *New Yorker*, affirming that he was "a really imaginative man, imaginative in every way. He was against everything that suggested the worn-out conventions and cheap artificialities of the commercial stage. It's hard to say how much we owe him."[7]

Cook's work was not publicly recognized in 1920, and even those who wanted to celebrate his achievement found themselves overwhelmed by the aftermath of his success. The Playwrights' Theatre was no longer an unknown Greenwich Village playhouse; Fitzi could barely deal with the demand for tickets, and the run was extended again and again, until finally *The Emperor Jones* went uptown, taking with it the better actors. Starry-eyed, Cook succumbed to the fever of Broadway. Kenton was the only member of the Players who, holding fast to their original aims, voted "no" to the move uptown.

The Emperor Jones did more than put the Provincetown Players on the map and settle O'Neill firmly on Broadway. Cook had insisted that the part of the emperor could not be played by a "blacked-up white," and he found Charles Gilpin, a professional actor who had been confined by his color to the vaudeville stage.[8] Thus, the Players scored another first in theatrical history: Gilpin was the first black American to star in a serious play produced by an all-white ensemble.

For O'Neill, *The Emperor Jones* marked the beginning of a friendship that would shape his career. As Broadway welcomed him into its snare, the exalted, amateurish Cook became an embarrassment, and his place as mentor was filled by Kenneth Macgowan, who had reviewed *The Emperor Jones* so enthusiastically. Macgowan had not been a fan of the Provincetown Players, or its playwrights, until *Beyond the Horizon* brought O'Neill to his attention, but he was quick to recognize what Sheldon Cheney had recently taught him. Macgowan had begun his career as an extremely conventional theater critic for the *Boston Evening Transcript* and the *Philadelphia Evening Ledger*. Scornful of the productions of the Boston Toy Theatre and the Chicago Little Theatre, he had preferred the realistic problem play to the innovative ideas presented in Hiram Moderwell's *The Theatre of Today* or Sheldon Cheney's *The New Movement in the Theatre*. His introduction to the work of Adolphe Appia, Edward Craig, and Max Reinhardt did not come about until 1919, when he met Cheney in New York and, converting with the speed of light to New Theatre aesthetics, was appointed editor of *Theatre Arts*.

Meanwhile, O'Neill had been working with the Provincetown Players, slowly absorbing and experimenting with the same European techniques and ideas that struck the young critic with the force of novelty. Thus, the Players, principally Cook and Glaspell, should be given credit for guiding O'Neill toward the historical and the ritual in drama; they primed him for Macgowan's enthusiastic support of the picturesque and the poetic in the theater. A clear example of their influence can be discerned in *The Fountain* (1925), which grew out of conversations with Cook and Glaspell during the sabbatical of 1919–20. In 1922, although the play had still not found a theater, O'Neill believed it to be his best work, second only to *The Hairy Ape*.[9] Four years of tinkering with the original to please prospective producers convinced O'Neill that *The Fountain* was jinxed. Indeed, when the final version, rewritten far from Cook's shamanistic presence, was produced at the Greenwich Village Theatre in December 1925, it was not a success. George Jean Nathan, who had read the manuscript in 1922, lamented the watering-down of the text and went so far as to say "it was not the play [he] had read."[10]

When O'Neill and Macgowan came together, some time after the success of *The Emperor Jones*, the playwright, basking in the critic's admiration of his play, told him he felt "as if I'd known you for a long time and that we were fated for a real friendship."[11] In the spring of 1921, while at work on *The Fountain*, he asked Macgowan for background material on Spain and Columbus's voyage to the New World. He was deeply excited by the concept of the play: "The idea of this Fountain play is so fundamental and deep in the roots of things that the proper expression ought to fall right out of it."[12] In *The Fountain*, O'Neill offers humankind the dream of an enthralling future, "each soul connect[ing] with every other" and each man "in some way one with every man." It was the same kind of apotheosis that Cook sought to offer in *The Spring* (1921). O'Neill's protagonist finally experiences that "keen new sense of the identity of human beings" and learns to transform his desires and his love into what Cook saw as a Dionysian ritual, a "tribal religious feeling" capable of replacing the defunct religion of his day.[13] For Cook, the drama alone could bring about such a spiritual rebirth, which it would achieve by digging back to the roots of the land—hence his interest in the Native American. Macgowan, who never empathized with Cook, expressed similar views in *The Theatre of Tomorrow* (1923). O'Neill, who received his copy of the book directly from the author, approved of his vision of the theater because it corresponded so closely with what he had learned from the Provincetown Players. For Macgowan, the theater was an "instinctive expression of godhead." He trusted that by delving into the past for subject matter the playwright would bring "fresh spiritual qualities" to the drama, and he proclaimed in book form the visions that Cook never considered publishing.[14] Macgowan is believed to have been influential in developing O'Neill's interest in expressionism, the past, and ritual, but Cook and Glaspell were there first and should be given due credit.

O'Neill was not the only inspired playwright in Provincetown during the sabbatical of 1919–20. By the end of that summer, two other plays were crystallizing: Glaspell's *Inheritors* and Cook's *The Spring*. Both plays reach back into the history of America, attempting to link the past to the present and thereby generate a sense of ritual continuity; both testify to the couple's deep involvement with the ideas of Friedrich Nietzsche. Cook and Glaspell embraced as their own his concepts of eternal recurrence and the will to overcome the self. Cook even accepted Nietzsche's perception of woman as the toy of man, although he camouflaged it with current (male) feminist convictions. Having studied in Germany in the 1890s and suffered mystical visions and what we would call today a nervous breakdown, Cook felt justified in writing: "My own mind has been enough like Nietzsche's for him to be one of the few writers with whom I imaginatively identify myself."[15] O'Neill was another addict of Nietzsche. "Zarathustra . . . has influenced me more than any book I've ever read," he freely admitted.[16]

Judging by Cook's notes, *The Spring* was originally to be set entirely in the 1830s in a village of the Sac tribe on Rock River and showed how the white man and his government came to corrupt the pristine tribal life of the Native Americans. But Cook's compulsion to find unity in human-kind and the hope that hypnosis would reveal such a unity led him to shift all but the prologue into modern times. The events of the prologue, foreseen by Nam-e-qua in the waters of the spring, are seen again by Esther Chantland, when they foreshadow a modern tragedy.

Professor Chantland and his daughter Esther are visiting the Rob-bins's country place. Young Elijah Robbins has recently been appointed instructor in Chantland's Department of Psychology at the university and has wild theories about a common deeper soul, a profound, sub-conscious network of communication between men and women. It so happens that Esther has strange powers that her father takes to be signs of insanity; he has forbidden her to practice her gift of automatic writing and treats her like an invalid. Sitting by the spring, Esther sees Native Americans enacting a ritual in which a white youth aims his rifle at a native elder, his future adopted father. Prompted by Elijah, she allows her hand to write automatically and produces a script in Sauk, which only Mr. Robbins can decipher (his grandfather, who had been adopted by the tribal chief, Black Hawk, had taught him Sauk). Elijah is convinced that Esther has the power to help him prove the interanimation of all minds. According to his theory, Esther saw the vision in the spring and wrote in Sauk because she had absorbed ideas emanating from Mr. Robbins's mind. He rejects outright the rival theory of communication with the spirits of the past. In Esther, Elijah sees an unspoiled medium and a highly gifted individual who, tagged as queer, is suffering from the contempt of her family. She is grateful for his recognition of her faculties and falls in love with him. He proposes a partnership whereby his conscious mind will direct her unconscious powers, thus in effect (although neither Cook nor his protagonist seem aware of this) establishing her role as the puppet of his superior intelligence. In spite of Mr. Chantland's death, of which Elijah is accused, Esther is utterly in thrall to him and admits that "I am you and you are me." She accepts that her very life depends on him and that together they will "set sail into [them]selves." She will "go with [him] into that undiscovered country which is not death."[17] Unfortunately, Cook's effort to endow his characters with a poetic language reflecting the profound beauty of intrinsic unity results in a primitive—not to say childish—and highly stilted prose.

Emboldened by O'Neill's successful rejection of traditional act division in *The Emperor Jones*, Cook set his play in seven "highly dramatic and intensely emotional" scenes. He also roped in the services of the young engineer whose silhouette designs had made that play so memorable. Cleon Throckmorton did not disappoint him: the sets were "a real pleasure," the dome again creating the effect of a "faraway" (to borrow Georgia O'Keeffe's term) beyond the immediate location of the action. The reviewer for the *New York Evening Post* was most impressed: "Here again, as did Tolstoy in *Redemption* and Eugene O'Neill in *The Emperor Jones*, an author has disregarded established technique, thrown the conventional divisions to the four winds . . . and produced a piece of sustained emotional and intellectual interest. . . . The dialogue is well articulated and often brushes the poetic."[18]

But today the play fails to excite the reader, largely because Elijah's concept of the deep, underlying "oneness" of humankind is neither proved nor disproved. The rival theory of communication with the dead seems much more likely, if only because we are more familiar with it. But the action of the play leaves the matter of hypnosis and other extraordinary powers nebulous, reducing the plot to a love affair in which the woman surrenders to a man who has convinced her of his superiority. Elijah was Cook's answer to the insipid Craig of *Bernice*.

Elated by the positive reviews, with a hint of a swagger, Cook sent clippings to O'Neill, who was then enjoying family life in Provincetown with Agnes and baby Shane. O'Neill responded effusively:

> I rejoice mightily at this success, not only as an old friend and fellow member of the P. P., but because there has been nothing I have hoped for more, as an observer sticking out for the eternal fitness of things, than that you, who have labored so long and unselfishly for the work of others, should enter into your own kingdom. In fact, this is quite perfect from all angles and I hope you are as satisfied by it as I am.
>
> My own fear has been that the critics of the newspaper genus would, as is their usual custom, find something irresistibly comic in the mere mention of the psychic and give vent to the loud hoots of the empty-minded. But they seem to have risen nobly to the occasion—which is certainly not the least tribute to the intrinsic dramatic power of the play.
>
> Well, the P. P. are sure coming into their own this season, what? We had a hunch they could and would last summer, remember? Now it only remains for Susan's play [*Inheritors*] to finish us up in a blaze of glory. Which it will, depend upon my newly-proved gift of prophecy.[19]

The Spring ran for three weeks, longer than initially intended, in order to accommodate the full houses Cook boasted of in his letter to his daughter, Nilla, in which he also mentioned an offer "to take the play to the Punch and Judy theatre when it closes here at the Provincetown Playhouse."[20] Nothing came of this offer, but Cook, not to be outdone by O'Neill and possibly pressured by Glaspell, had set his sights on Broadway.[21] He spent the next months scheming and maneuvering, and by the end of August, he and Harry Weinberger (a lawyer friend of the Provincetowners) had each "put $1000 into *The Spring*," which was to open at the Princess Theatre on 19 September 1921. Cook was even wondering whether "the Provincetown Players should not put money into *The Spring* as into *Jones*, risking loss and giving share of profits." He asked Glaspell, who had stayed behind on the Cape with his son Harl, what she thought of such a venture. He intimated a hard year ahead when he wrote: "You've no idea what a whirl of decisions, fights, new elements."[22] However, he also gave his approval to Kenton's appointment as publicity agent, thus bringing the Players another step closer to professionalization—and failure.

The Spring did open at the Princess Theatre, and it ran to empty houses for ten days. Cook's dream of Broadway fame—of *The Spring* being followed by Glaspell's *Inheritors* and *The Verge* and "other P. P. plays" sparkling in neon lights—was shattered. Illogically, he felt defrauded by O'Neill, the Players, New York, and Greenwich Village; only Glaspell could share and understand his visions, his ambition. But even she frequently found his demands too taxing.

During that winter in Provincetown, as Glaspell was struggling with her husband's manias and her own low spirits while waiting for word from commercial producers on the fate of *Chains of Dew*, she had confided her idea for a new play to Boulton. The young mother, impressed by Glaspell's intensity, wrote to O'Neill that Glaspell had "an idea for a new long play about which she says she is crazy—a real American play (serious)."[23] The idea of creating a truly "American" work of art has been part of the American psyche ever since James Fenimore Cooper, goaded by his wife, wrote a novel to compete with the fiction imported from Britain. Although Georgia O'Keeffe would mock the concept, featuring skulls on a background of the national colors, writers did not desist in their endeavor. In 1920, in spite of Cook's eager search for the truly "American" play, the theater lacked serious contenders for such a title. It is therefore not surprising that Glaspell felt she should take on the challenge: *Inheritors* would be her response. Filling many a winter's night with her breathless retelling of family lore, of the search for new land and opportunity that resulted in the displacement of the native Sauks, she envisioned a historical, politically committed plot. (Kenneth Macgowan, musing on the contents of the theater of the future, would also advocate the imaginative reworking of the picturesque past.)[24] *Inheritors* was not the only play to grow out of those evenings. Glaspell's words inspired her listeners, pointing the way to hitherto unexplored areas. Cook, his eyes never leaving her expressive features, aglow with intellectual excitement, plotted *The Spring*, and O'Neill, staring into space, drawn by the ritual inherent in the past, mapped out *The Fountain* and *Lazarus Laughed*.

The history of the white man's conquest of the Native Americans had never been a serious subject for the theater, and in the work she was projecting, Glaspell elected to set her forefathers' honest idealism against the bigoted self-satisfaction of the Espionage and Sedition Acts, passed in 1917 and 1918 to protect America from within during the war, which had enflamed her. Close friends had been directly affected—Emma Goldman, Alexander Berkman (and, through him, Fitzi), and the editors and artists of *The Masses*—and everyone had experienced the fear of being prosecuted for sincere, open self-expression. Glaspell, an "anarchist of the spirit" with "the soul of a reformer," as British reviewers would describe her, writhed at the constraints placed on liberties she took for granted, arguing that the stage should be used to attack the evils of her day.[25] In this, she clashed with O'Neill's more disinterested stance. Her later work for the Federal Theatre would show that a committed political theater could indeed be achieved, but in 1919, she was struggling to prove wrong O'Neill's assertion that "as soon as an author slips propaganda into a play everyone feels it and the play becomes simply an argument."[26] All the same, she did not want to fall into the trap of "special pleading" that loomed whenever ideas were not successfully mediated through convincing characters.

On 21 November 1920, Glaspell informed Boulton of her progress: "I've finished the first draft of my play and am beginning to revise it. A big job—for there's much still to do. I hope I'll be better satisfied with it at the end of the second writing than I am at the end of the first."[27] In the rewriting, she paid special attention to characterization, developing the personality of her protagonists through dialogue that Ludwig Lewisohn was to praise for its "verisimilitude" and its "constant ironic and symbolic suppressions and correspondences and overtones."[28]

In *Inheritors*, Glaspell challenged patriarchy more directly than she had ever done before, intimating as always that suffering the punishment it meted out was preferable to stagnating under its laws. The setting is a midwestern college campus founded by the idealist Silas Morton, one of the earliest settlers, and Felix Fejevary, an exiled Hungarian revolutionary whose son is now on the board of trustees. The play opens in 1879 with a discussion of the pioneer days and the importance of learning, and act 1 ends with Morton's decision to bequeath his best land to the building of a college. Act 2 takes place in 1920 and shows how the expansion of the college has brought about financial problems that must now be solved. Felix Fejevary Jr. does his best to convince Senator Lewis that the state should take over the college to assure its future. Lewis agrees but imposes one condition: Professor Holden, a radical idealist and supporter of conscientious objectors, must cease his subversive activities or go. By act 4, Fejevary has persuaded Holden of the advantages of silence, but he is defeated by his niece, the granddaughter of both Silas Morton and Felix Fejevary Sr., who insists on supporting Hindu students in their fight for independence. As the play ends, Madeline Morton leaves for a court hearing, after which, under the Sedition Act, she will undoubtedly be sentenced to prison for her ideals.

This play is a feeling riposte to a historical moment, and although it is the least overtly feminist of Glaspell's plays, the surface plot is merely a thin disguise for her disappointment with patriarchal society, with men's weakness and readiness to forego their ideals under pressure. Indeed, Inez Haynes Irwin, the feminist novelist and noted Greenwich Villager, hailed *Inheritors* as "great muckraking" and its author as a "sage, seer, and a mystic" even though a realist.[29] Discreetly, Glaspell mocks a number of male myths, in particular the myth of male superiority. Just as in *Trifles*, it is the supposedly ignorant women who uncover the clues to a murder, here it is the "inferior sex" as represented by Madeline that has the courage for self-sacrifice. Glaspell's "leading" men, though endowed with some redeeming virtues, are far from being supermen and frequently frustrate the expectations of the female protagonists. In *Inheritors*, Glaspell intelligently refuses to condemn or praise the individual in an outright fashion, and she wavers between Holden, whose predicament is "a terrible judgement on the civilization that has shaped him," and Madeline, although finally coming down on the side of the latter.[30] Holden's pusillanimous decision is excusable only in the light of his wife's costly illness, and Madeline's protest action, although it will bring sorrow on the family, is seen in idealistic terms as an individual's self-sacrifice in the cause of freedom. Glaspell was forever torn by the dilemma facing women who wished to fulfill their potential but were aware of the needs of their families. The young protagonist of her early story "The Rules of the Institution" questions the validity of insisting on freedom when this would hurt so many loved ones: "It seemed that affection and obligation were agents holding one to one's place," but the woman finally decides that "she owed no allegiance to an order that held life in chains."[31] In

Inheritors, Glaspell creates a protagonist whose motivations go beyond an abstract desire for freedom or the "right to love" that she espoused in her novels *Fidelity* (1915) and *Brook Evans* (1928). Madeline fights for the human condition, and as an example of "American womanhood at its best," she is fully up to such a struggle.[32]

O'Neill's prediction of success for *Inheritors* in spite of its "frankly propagandistic" nature and Cook's deep-running confidence in his wife must have rubbed off on the Provincetowners, for Helen Deutsch and Stella Hanau report that "the excitement [provoked by *The Emperor Jones*] was renewed with the fifth bill," which featured Glaspell's play.[33] Glaspell declined to act, but Cook, identifying fully with Silas Morton's resolve to "build a college in the cornfields," was eager to take on Morton's part.[34] For once realistic as to her husband's skills, Glaspell had quietly and tactfully persuaded him that Jasper Deeter, who had joined the Players the previous year, should direct *Inheritors*. Cook was the cardinal inspirer, but he was utterly useless where the details of a production were concerned. He would harangue a "hard-boiled prop man" for hours over the sort of bench he wanted for a play, never answering the simple question first put to him: marble or rustic?[35] The Players' initial intention to give the playwright full control of his or her play had been abandoned during the first New York season, and although we can safely assume that Glaspell would have attended some rehearsals and been available for consultations with director and actors, she preferred to leave the play in their capable hands and continue work on *The Verge*, her next contribution. However, she did insist on casting "the 'just right' actress for Madeline in this play of yellow corn and yellow pollen and revolutionary spirit gone 'yellow.'" Ann Harding, blessed with abundant "pale gold" hair, was given the role.[36] Her debut with the Players proved to be the beginning of a successful acting career, although she never did put herself "under the tutelage of David Belasco," as one persnickety reviewer advised her to do.[37] That review, in a magazine with the improbable title *Zits Weekly Magazine*, set off hoots of derision in the Players' greenroom as older members told of the offer Belasco had once made to Mary Pyne: the Broadway director had demanded she place herself in his hands in return for a promise of stardom. Pyne, who was married to Harry Kemp, refused.[38]

Reviewers who were unanimous in their praise of Ann Harding were also of one mind about the play. Glaspell had fulfilled her ambition: *Inheritors* was recognized as a truly American play. Lewisohn, though admitting that *Inheritors* might not be "a great play," did not stint his praise: "If the history of literature, dramatic or non-dramatic, teaches us anything, it is that Broadway and its reviewers will some day be judged by their attitude to this work. . . . It is the first play of the American theatre in which a strong intellect and a ripe artistic nature have grasped and set forth in human terms the central tradition and most burning problem of our national life quite justly and scrupulously, equally without acrimony or compromise."[39]

The undiluted social protest of *Inheritors*, which so attracted American reviewers, proved almost a liability when the play was staged in England. The Liverpool Repertory Company produced *Inheritors*, under the direction of William Armstrong, in September 1925 and took it to the Everyman Theatre in London in December. Reviews were highly favorable, verging on the ecstatic. Glaspell was acclaimed as the American George Bernard Shaw and set above O'Neill in both achievement and future promise. The London *Times* celebrated the "cleverness and stagecraft manifest in the greater part of [*Inheritors*]" and acknowledged that "the sincerity of the author is evident always, and her knowledge of the stage is so complete, that in spite of seemingly impossible drawbacks, the piece plays excellently throughout."[40] But critics were also quick to point out that an English audience might not understand the root problem of the play, since, as the *Morning Post* loftily observed, it "is one with which we are not very familiar in this country."[41] Likewise, the *Daily Telegraph* critic, reviewing the London performance, revealed his British superciliousness when he praised *Inheritors* for being "as spirited a protest against the intolerance shown in the Land of the Free for any but the 'regular' opinions as is Mr. Sinclair Lewis's *Babbitt*."[42]

In Greenwich Village, *Inheritors* was revived for a "Spring Season" in May 1921 and then forgotten, but its director, Jasper Deeter, could not forget a play he so admired and was to keep it in repertory at his Hedgerow Theatre in Moylan, Pennsylvania, for many years.[43] It was Deeter who introduced Eva Le Gallienne to Glaspell's work. Convinced that a city like New York should have a repertory company, Le Gallienne refurbished a dilapidated Fourteenth Street theater and opened the Civic Repertory Theatre on 26 October 1926. Cook, if he had still been alive, would surely have welcomed her into his inner circle. In her autobiography, *At Thirty-three*, she stated that her main interest was not to compete with the commercial theater but "to widen the *scope* of the word 'theatre' in America."[44] She included *Inheritors* in her first season, putting it into repertory in March 1927, claiming it was "all too little known" and valuing it as "a burning challenge to America, full of indignation against the results of a too rapid, too greedy prosperity, in which the material has become the ultimate goal in complete disregard of spiritual and ethical values."[45] In 1930, Le Gallienne staged Glaspell's *Alison's House* and was rewarded for her faith in the playwright from Iowa when the play won the Pulitzer Prize.

The 1920–21 season had been deeply taxing. Glaspell had hoped to spend Christmas with the O'Neills in Tunis, but nothing came of her plans for a break, and the months dragged on relentlessly. The sabbatical had not solved any problems; in fact, Cook's absence had given the younger Players an opportunity to prove themselves and thus to gain confidence and become more demanding. *The Emperor Jones*, although it eased financial worries, created its own dilemmas. Frustrated ambition lay behind most of the fights Glaspell witnessed and attempted to smooth out, curbing her impatience at having to spend time away from her writing. Even Cook now had his sights on commercial success and popular fame. His high moods were devoted to scheming and designing: he continued to dream of a custom-built theater for the Players, where domes, lighting equipment, and movable spaces would offer infinite possibilities. His lows, however, descending to unbearable depths of disillusionment, disconcerted those Players who unambiguously saw the future in terms of expansion and neon lights. But Cook would talk of taking over any small space and beginning anew. "I am sick of this New York hog-trough!," he would bray at Glaspell, begging: "Let us withdraw into ourselves and form the thing that is ourselves—let come success or failure."[46] One night, he careened out of their dismal rented rooms in New York. A few hours later, she received a cryptic telegram: "I am at the Brevoort writing Greek for the reason that I do not wish to hurt you or be hurt."[47] The success of the Provincetown Players and the threat that Broadway fame could easily impose mediocrity on their work were weakening the tenuous bonds she had cultivated so assiduously during their sabbatical. She felt torn between her own ambition as a writer and the dire need to pamper Cook in all his moods and desires. She still believed that he wanted her to gain recognition as a playwright, but it was becoming clear that he wanted his own success even more and that her soothing, maternal ministrations were essential to his well-being. Glaspell grew more concerned for his weakness as the years passed and observed that it was aggravated by every good review her work received. The writing of *Bernice* and *Chains of Dew* had helped ease the tension building up inside her. By creating Bernice, Craig, Dotty, and Seymore, she had vicariously worked through her own dilemmas and accepted, at least for the time being, that love, just as much as her role as wife, obliged her to conform to certain patterns of behavior. But the chains that she could not—and did not want to—throw off frequently weighed her down.

To compound her misery, Carbon the cat fell ill. She had been left behind, as always, in Provincetown, and once again it was up to the O'Neills to do what had to be done. Glaspell's letter of thanks to Boulton betrayed disproportionate anguish in the very handwriting:

> I know so well that you would give her that loving understanding care animals do not usually get. But I am sorry to have brought this upon you, knowing how hard these things are to one who feels this way. Jig and I thank you more than we have words to say. We have had Carbon almost the whole time we have been together. She seemed a part of our lives—it would have been too terrible to feel she had died uncared for. I cannot think of your letter without crying—how you kept her up in your room—and how she purred. You and Gene seem to help us at these hard times. We'll never forget what you did for us with Nezer.[48]

Once back on the Cape for the summer of 1921, Glaspell gave herself up to the writing of *The Verge*, articulating pent-up frustrations with the man-made world she had inherited. Glaspell's disenchantment with her world is manifest in the very subject of *The Verge*. The story of a woman's struggle with the norms and expectations of society in her effort to create something not more beautiful or more practical but merely different hums with issues that touch the heart of the Provincetown project and vibrates with Glaspell's private dilemmas as woman and writer. Such startling resonances between Glaspell's increasingly fraught position and that of her protagonist justify a conflation of the two women and allow us to see in the language she bestows on Claire a manifestation of her own state of mind. In *The Outside*, she had used a woman's refusal to participate in man's language as a symbol of withdrawal from his world. She would do this again in her novel *The Fugitive's Return*. In *The Verge*, she contains her own dilemma in language that today is recognizably a part of woman's discourse. Luce Irigaray, in her essay "When Our Lips Speak Together" (1977), enjoins women to invent new voices "in order to express all of us everywhere, even in our gaps," for "if we speak to each other as men have been doing for centuries, as we have been taught to speak, we'll miss each other, fail ourselves."[49] Glaspell had intuitively anticipated that same objective as early as 1916: the women of *Trifles* attain understanding only when they accept the significance of their own language. Claire, in *The Verge*, when trying to explain what she is doing in her greenhouse laboratory, is, by definition, attempting the impossible because her domestic audience is composed of upholders of the patriarchy—among them her own daughter. What Claire is doing not only is incomprehensible to the men but simply cannot be articulated in their language. Thus, Claire has recourse to a language that is ranging, repetitive, hesitant, and sometimes designedly incoherent, in which the mind is free to make its own associations; in short, she spontaneously exploits a mode of language that we can now call *écriture féminine*.[50] "Don't listen. That's nothing. This isn't that. I tell you—it isn't that. Yes, I know—that's amorous—enclosing. I know—a little place. This isn't that."[51] Such female "excess and disruption," to use Irigaray's phrase, is precisely what male critics of the 1920s, who left the theater holding their heads in "melancholy resignation," protested.[52] In the words of one such critic, "Nothing pleases the merry, merry Greenwich Villagers so much as a well misdirected idea which nobody quite understands."[53]

Josette Feral, in "Writing and Displacement: Women in Theatre," asks: "What do women say in language? This is an insidious question, often asked, to which Lacanian psycho-analysis provides a ready answer by relegating women to emptiness and nothingness. Women say NOTHING because they have NOTHING to say, and because there is NOTHING to say about whatever they may say, since it means NOTHING."[54] Just so, Claire's scientific experiments can be relegated to the status of a rich woman's hobby and her whole life seen only as an adjunct to that of her husband or lover. Claire has tried marriage twice, hoping to find life in what society condones—wifehood and maternity—but has found only "NOTHING." On the eve of revealing her latest attempt at creation—a new plant that she has hybridized in her greenhouse—and harassed by family and friends, she has come close to insanity, to surrendering what is vital to her sense of herself. In this moment of weakness, she is willing to risk her "by-myself-ness" in an amorous encounter with Tom, the only man who at least tries to understand her predicament. She cries out to him: "That, too, I will give you—my by-myself-ness. That's the uttermost I can give. I never thought—to try to give it. But let us do it—the great sacrilege! . . . But yes—I will, I will risk the life that waits. Perhaps only he who gives his loneliness—shall find. You never keep by holding. . . . Just as I would cut my wrists—Yes, perhaps this lesser thing will tell it—would cut my wrists and let the blood flow out till all is gone if my last drop would make— would make—I want to see it doing that! Let me give my last chance for life to—."[55]

Clearly, to submerge herself totally in a personal relationship is tantamount to suicide, and yet painfully, paradoxically that recourse offers her an escape, not from the punitive mandates of society but from the grandeur, the divinity of her achievements. At one point, she hysterically pleads with Dick, the lover who satisfies her physically but is unaware of her soul: "Yes—hold me. Keep me. . . . Anything—everything—that will let me be nothing."[56] Glaspell, through her protagonist Claire, recognizes that in surrendering herself to a man's love, a woman might find respite from her own self. Closing the doors that might give access to authentic fulfillment and discovery, she will open the one that leads to a miserable peace.

Sybil Thorndike, who at Edith Craig's suggestion played the role of Claire in the Pioneer Players' production of *The Verge* in London in 1925, believed that in Claire, Glaspell had created a genius:

> Claire has a fine, sensitized vision; she sees farther than the conventional people who surround her. . . . She is as daring in her new and extended vision of life as Christ or Buddha. Saint Joan and all the great prophets were daring, so she is misunderstood as they in their generation were misunderstood. . . .
>
> I know . . . that some people believe that Claire kills life, that she represents negation. She is on the contrary affirmative-positive; she experiments with plants, which are the symbol of her desire, not to create something beautiful, but to create some new form more daring than any that preceded it. For her nothing matters if only she succeeds in getting at the truth. She experiments with life, is even prepared to sacrifice it on the chance that something different and more wonderful will arise out of that destruction.[57]

Thorndike insisted that Glaspell's play should be read symbolically. In the same interview, she stated categorically: "*The Verge* is not realistic."

The British actress, herself independent and ambitious but always under a man's influence—first her brother's, then her husband's—validly perceived the dilemma played out in *The Verge*.

Although critics nowadays identify *Trifles* as the play that best exemplifies Glaspell's radical—for her times—feminist stance, it is notable that her peers, the women of the Heterodoxy, seized upon *The Verge*. Their reaction is, ironically, best described by Hutchins Hapgood, who, unable to accept that his women friends could be dissatisfied with man's world, claimed that this play "had little to do with [Glaspell's] nature" and that it was therefore a damning "expression of half-mad feminism." In his autobiography, *A Victorian in the Modern World*, he impudently quotes a member of the Heterodoxy who reported the group's discussion of *The Verge*: "Elise Dufour the dancer, who had never succeeded in getting away from what those women called the mere man's psychology, describing the meeting to me, said, 'It seemed to me, while these women were talking about *The Verge*, that I was in church, that they were worshiping at some holy shrine; their voices and their eyes were full of religious excitement. I was, I think, the only woman not under the spell. I tried at first to say a few things about the play that were in the line of ordinary dramatic criticism, which I thought had a reasonable basis; but when they all glared upon me, as if they thought I should be excommunicated, I spoke no further word.' "[58]

In *Trifles*, Glaspell had appeased men such as Hapgood by silencing her protagonist, but she had offered little to please Heterodoxy women. In *The Verge*, she went beyond an idealistic concern for humanity into the wilderness of woman's predicament. Claire Archer, her protagonist, realizes that the older order—symbolized by a plant she calls the "Edge Vine" that grows in the shape of a cross—has failed her because it has resorted to known patterns of life that have become meaningless; she can destroy the plant, but she recognizes that she is helpless when faced with what it represents—accepted forms and modes of behavior. The new dispensation she hopes for cannot, by its very nature, be articulated.

The play opens in a luscious, overheated greenhouse, an emblem of the socially restricted and shielded space Claire is forced to inhabit. Here she experiments with plants. She believes she can exploit a transplanting technique to create wholly new organisms that are liberated from the previous forms and functions of plant life. But Tom, Dick, and Harry (confidant, lover, and husband) violate her sanctum when they flee the symbolically cold house in search of a more gratifying environment. (O'Neill would use this same conjunction of three weak men in love with a strong woman in *Strange Interlude*.)[59] In the ensuing scenes, Glaspell skillfully highlights the farce and melodrama inherent in the clash between intellectual and popular values, thus, to quote a London reviewer, provoking "hearty laughter at odd moments."[60] Harry's vaudeville instructions to Tom to bring the salt—a "pantomime with the egg-cup and the missing shaker" that is interrupted by Claire sneezing and culminates in Tom's triumphant arrival with a thermometer and the pepper—must have constituted one such moment, raising laughter that distracted from the intensity of Claire's outbursts on "outness—and otherness": "You think I can't smash anything? You think life can't break up, and go outside what it was? Because you've gone in the form in which you found yourself, and you think that's all there is to the whole adventure? And that is called sanity. And made a virtue—to lock one in. You never worked with things that grow! Things that take a sporting chance— go mad—that sanity mayn't lock them in—from life untouched—from life—that waits."[61] Hoping to convince the three men that they should not eat breakfast in a laboratory reserved for experiments with life, Claire tries to express her Nietzschean desire to overcome established patterns and to break through into whatever lies beyond. Only Tom gropes toward an understanding of her disjointed utterances.

In act 2, Claire's sister Adelaide invades her study, a strangely twisted and uncannily lit tower, which is best interpreted as an outward sign of Claire's isolation and her rejection of the world, although it is also a symbol of her disturbed mind. Claire is seen through "a queer bulging window" that separates the audience from the action onstage.[62] Thus, those entering this enclosed space can be construed not only as invaders of Claire's mind but also as a schizophrenic splitting of her thought. Adelaide's mission is to convince her sister to play the part of the dutiful mother and wife, but Claire is too close to transcendence to take heed. Now on the brink of uncovering her latest experiment, the plant she calls "Breath of Life," she is awed by the grandeur of her achievement and staggered by fear of retaliation from the God whose life-giving powers she has appropriated. Claire seeks a haven in the physical consummation of her relationship with the sympathetic Tom, but in deference to her superior spirit, he denies her that ordinary human refuge, bowing down to the imperative of her "by-myself-ness."

The new plant that signals Claire's success in creating a hitherto-unknown form of life is unveiled in the greenhouse in act 3. But the achievement is clearly ambivalent: any organism is condemned to repetition and stagnation unless it continually overcomes itself.

> Breath of the uncaptured?
> You are a novelty.
> Out?
> You have been brought in.
> A thousand years from now, when you are but a form too long
>   repeated,
> Perhaps the madness that gave you birth will burst again,
> And from the prison that is you will leap pent queernesses
> To make a form that hasn't been—
> To make a person new.[63]

Claire is fully conscious of this baleful dilemma. When Tom finally offers her his love, she is appalled at the prospect of losing her independent selfhood and compulsively turns on him and chokes him to death. The murder mimics the suffocating norms of society that inevitably silence the creative urge in those who refuse to conform, but Claire's family sees her convulsive action as final proof of her insanity.

The play ends on a savagely ironic note as Claire chants the hymn "Nearer, My God, to Thee," which Adelaide, intuiting blasphemy, had previously refused to sing in her presence. Claire, a female Faust, is now her own God and cannot be reached by societal structures and compunctions. She has broken out and is existentially free, alone in the transcendental beyond.

During this final act and in her dialogue with Tom in act 2, Claire's language takes on the appearance of free verse, a form that she despises because it is merely "words going into patterns." Glaspell, Cook, and O'Neill were all drawn to the verse plays of Alfred Kreymborg, Harry Kemp, and Edna St. Vincent Millay, and although they were not poets, they did try their hand at introducing poetry—or at least the poetic—into their drama. Only Glaspell acknowledged, through Claire, that "thoughts take pattern—then the pattern is the thing."[64]

The Verge was Glaspell's most ambitious play and best exemplifies the degree to which the Provincetown Players had assimilated and made their own the innovative trends of European theater. As C. W. E. Bigsby points out, "Few writers, before or since, . . . [have] attempted such a radical revisioning of all aspects of theatre."[65] The play's tortured, highly symbolic setting, designed by Cleon Throckmorton, reminded its reviewers of the film *The Cabinet of Dr. Caligari* (1919), released in the United States in the spring of 1921. Kenneth Macgowan somewhat grudgingly acknowledged that *The Verge* was the first example of expressionism on the American stage.[66] Glaspell's treatment of her subject also goes beyond the critique of marriage to which Henrik Ibsen's *A Doll's House* and innumerable Broadway plays had, by 1921, inured the theatergoing public. Claire does not merely slam the door behind her; she encroaches on forbidden territory in her passion to create new life-forms. In a man, her Nietzschean overreaching would be considered a normal function of aggression: in a woman, it amounts to the arrogation of faculties reserved for God—and men. Claire has rejected the roles of wife, mother, and mistress that are available to her and rebels against the suppression of self that society enforces on a woman, only to discover that the penalty is total alienation. Paradoxically, in an age that considered hysteria to be the result of repression, she is repudiated as a hysteric by her family, as well as by most audiences, who have tended to see in her "an almost clinical type for the psychoanalytical laboratory."[67]

Claire may not appear to be a conquering heroine, just as the protagonist of Glaspell's first novel, *The Glory of the Conquered* (1909), ostensibly fails in her self-imposed task. As *The Verge* ends, we cannot doubt that Tennessee Williams's kind stranger is already at the door. But the recognition of Claire's insanity leaves room for a peculiar optimism since she has successfully abandoned the principles of this world for those of her own devising.

O'Neill, writing of his own play *Diff'rent* (1920) for the *New York Herald Tribune*, perfectly caught the mood of *The Verge*: "There is a skin deep optimism and another higher optimism, not skin deep, which is usually confounded with pessimism. . . . The people who succeed and do not push on to a greater failure are the spiritual middle classers. . . . Only through the unattainable does man achieve a hope worth living and dying for—and so attain himself."[68] But O'Neill's men and women never do "attain" themselves. Although O'Neill admitted Nietzsche's influence, he had his own dark vision of the world to work through and, on the whole, was not capable of faith in the human potential to overcome the self.[69] Glaspell brought her positive outlook to the cerebrations of Nietzsche and accepted the doctrine of "over-coming" the self as vital to the development of the human race. In *The Verge*, as in *Inheritors*, a way to reach the perfection of humankind, to transcend man-made institutions, is signaled by woman. Prefiguring Claire, Madeline affirms almost hysterically: "Nothing is to itself. . . . I don't feel alone any more. The wind has come through—wind rich from lives now gone. . . . Then—be the most you can be, so life will be more because you were."[70]

Glaspell took care in *Inheritors* not to be too harsh on her male characters, but in *The Verge*, she is not so generous; she allows each in turn to reveal his inferiority to Claire. Tom, Dick, and Harry, as their names suggest, are stereotypes; they are incapable of helping Claire define herself fully in a patriarchal society or of protecting her from the consequences of transcending it. Harry, the husband, does his utmost to understand her, but his down-to-earth character is an impossible barrier to comprehension and communication. Dick paternally dismisses Claire's strange behavior as "the excess of a particularly rich temperament."[71] And Tom commits the unforgivable error of threatening to hold her back in a bourgeois relationship.

Although the Heterodoxy acclaimed *The Verge* with religious fervor, New York reviewers were not always so enthusiastic. Stark Young, assistant editor of *Theatre Arts Monthly*, reviewed *The Verge* for the *New Republic*. Although he was always ready to praise the Provincetown Players, he found fault with Margaret Wycherley, in the part of Claire, whom he mocked for "Forest of Arden[ing] around like a British Rosalind, as if in fact we were going to have a comedy. . . . She works too hard at it. Her efforts drive out the gods that are visiting this woman and leave only problems and oddities and confusion." He generously recognized that her "neurotic gestures were unfortunately heightened by the gleaming mass of sequins or beads or whatever it was that spread over her gown." But Young, while ignoring the aspects of the play that aroused the Heterodoxy, could still appreciate Glaspell's skill as a dramatist, even though he seemed to find it difficult to articulate his responses without lapsing into a language reminiscent of Claire's: "In the play there is an ominous comedy around something that is isolated, apart, that is driven to eccentricity, but that burns and glows and fascinates by its intensity of living." All the same, for Young, *The Verge* was clearly a valuable "experiment," and he ends his review by berating colleagues who "prattle about new forms in the theatre and then fight any attempt at new material."[72]

The highest praise, which expresses a valuation of the play that remains true to this day, came some years later. Edith Craig, when alerting Sybil Thorndike to Glaspell's play, remarked that, although "*The Verge* contained much that was difficult to understand, it was a play of such uncommon power it might be considered a masterpiece."[73]

The summer of 1921 had not been long enough or sufficiently carefree to dispel the tensions of the previous year. Cook loquaciously pushed for another play from O'Neill of the caliber of *The Emperor Jones*. Whether helping O'Neill drag his canoe up the beach, building a driftwood fire in the evening, or sharing a flagon of bootleg brew, he would relentlessly pester his friend, urging him to write a play for the Provincetown Players so extraordinary that no commercial theater would even consider it and no professional director would want to risk his career on it. Cook commanded a play that he would direct on his small stage, with the blue light illuminating the infinity of his dome. O'Neill humored him, offered him more booze, distracted him with talk of the superior destiny of humankind and the Provincetown Players, and continued to curry favor with professionals who might respond to his ambitions.

Glaspell, a silent observer engrossed in her own creative dilemmas—and more than accustomed to rowdy scenes—would interfere only when the mood became too ugly to tolerate. Even Cook's daughter knew that "some stupendous argument" would inevitably punctuate any meeting between Jig and Gene, and like Glaspell, she took these outbursts in her stride, sensing that "this was their way of bringing out the best of one another." Nilla went even further when, looking back on the Provincetown days, she wrote: "What a pity there is no recording of their battles! *Lazarus* is definitely the outcome of the attacks Jig made on Gene for sticking to the conventional, after the *Emperor*, which had opened the way to new forms."[1] As a grown woman, she could readily voice such a mature understanding of her father, but as an adolescent, she caused her formerly rebellious stepmother a great deal of worry.

Glaspell always enjoyed the company of Nilla and Harl during the summer holidays in Provincetown. They were independent, intelligent children, trained not to disturb adults at work and able to entertain themselves. With Ma-Mie to see to practicalities and discipline, Glaspell had been free to enjoy the privileges of part-time mothering. But now, without Ma-Mie, she felt the burden of responsibility and feared for her stepdaughter's innocence among the self-styled bohemians of Cape Cod. Nilla, now an intractable thirteen-year-old, found any effort to control her actions unbearable; moreover, she was disconcerted by the conflicting standards of behavior imposed on her by different members of the family. She would later write: "What was correct in Iowa was taboo in Provincetown. What was correct in Provincetown got me expelled from school in Chicago."[2] Glaspell, uncertain as to what Mollie, Nilla's mother, expected of her daughter in the way of lipstick and late nights, was overly strict.[3] In this, she was wholeheartedly abetted by Jig, who championed freedom and tolerance only for mental activity as far as his offspring were concerned.

By the time Glaspell returned to New York in the autumn of 1921, she had finished the manuscript of *The Verge* and had accumulated a small fund of energy from which to draw on in mediating between Cook's zaniness and the Players' legitimate aspirations. Although O'Neill would have recommended an uptown director for her play, she could not think of so wounding Jig's vanity. Cook's unwavering belief in his wife's talent precluded any such treachery, especially at a time when he was under attack from many of the younger members of his group who refused to see themselves as part of his supernal project to renew humanity. These younger Players were not steeped in Nietzsche—or in any religious or patriotic values. They identified professional success with material well-being and saw nothing romantic in unheated garrets or bowls of spaghetti. Indeed, they gossiped about his pixilated carryings-on: on West Eighth Street, falling to his knees before designer and actor Charlie Ellis, Cook proclaimed himself unworthy of the dust under Ellis's feet; at another time, Fitzi and a friend came upon him clawing away at the brickwork of a tenement, muttering about "loosening the world."[4] These stories, too odd to be made up, inevitably reached Glaspell by way of those who claimed to love Jig most. Much as she tried to keep him home when he was drinking, he was too strong and too stubborn for her to exercise control over his comings and goings. She did her best to shrug off the stories, explaining to herself and to others that Cook was struggling with his frustration at the failure of the Provincetowners to create a community of superior souls. She was dismayed at her own inability to fully participate in his sorrow and redeemed herself by treating Cook with excessive tenderness during those days of "particular beauty" when, suffering from a massive hangover, he was as dependent and docile as a newborn child.[5]

For some time, O'Neill had been flaunting a manuscript that was well on the way toward completion. When he finally allowed Cook to read *The Hairy Ape*, Cook reacted with the same maniacal enthusiasm with which he had hailed *The Emperor Jones*. The great stager knew intuitively that once again he would be able to stun audiences into mystical fervor. After the success of *The Emperor Jones*, Arthur Hopkins, the Broadway producer, had been so fascinated by the Players' achievement that he enthused over the great heights they could reach if they had more space. But Cook was not clamoring for a larger theater; his imagination inspired more ambitious plans. He responded with his famous drawings of a theater made of domes and light and proudly stated: "The needs of our plays have suggested this new form of theater; the theater will, in turn, suggest new forms of plays."[6] O'Neill, who had benefited most from the Players' obsession with experiment, now grew fainthearted. He chafed at the restrictions imposed by the Provincetown stage and, lacking Cook's vision, sided with Hopkins on the issue of the size of the acting space. He had grown impatient with Cook's proclamations, as well as his refusal to professionalize the theater, and saw no reason why he should keep his dissatisfaction to himself. On 2 January 1922, he confided to George Jean Nathan that he was pleased with his new play and was relying on professional direction, acting, and designing to guarantee its uptown success after a short run at the Playwrights' Theatre.[7] It was not long before rumors took over, and fans of the Players were subjected to a barrage of misinformation. The *New York Tribune* informed its readers on 5 February that Hopkins would direct O'Neill's new play at the Playwrights' Theatre. The news came on 12 February that Cook had started rehearsals, and by 26 February, it was reported that James Light had been appointed stage manager. To add to the confusion, the playbills do not give the name of the director.[8]

James Light belonged to the younger generation; together with Ida

Rauh, he had taken over the reins during Cook and Glaspell's year off, which Glaspell had devised to get away from the Players. Light saw himself as Cook's successor, and being young and arrogant, he did not doubt that he could run a theater much more efficiently than Cook did. A story made the rounds that Cook, in an expansive gesture, had thrown the Provincetown mantle over Light's shoulders. It seems that, on some occasion, Cook had doffed his cape, draping it around the shoulders of one of the younger men—possibly Light—and pronouncing magical words of initiation or succession.[9] Whether or not this tale is true, it does appear that O'Neill seriously considered offering Light the direction of *The Hairy Ape*, thus deeply wounding Cook.[10]

This humiliating insult was badly timed; Light was already in Cook's bad graces, as later letters between Edna Kenton and Cook and Glaspell reveal. The Executive Committee had uncovered proof that Light, using backhanded means, had tried to gain financial support for a new group that would function under the same name and was "unanimous in putting Jimmy out for next year."[11] Cook, suspecting that Gene, his dramatic soul mate, was involved in Light's scheming, knew then that he had failed utterly in his spiritual endeavor; it was not a question of material failure but rather an indication of his inability to revitalize the nation through the group he had created and for which he assumed responsibility. Glaspell now suffered with him and for him, although their strict moral code did not allow them to bring the matter out into the open. In *The Road to the Temple*, Glaspell deals with only Jig's tremendous disappointment, giving reasons so vague that they almost become incongruous—the more so considering that Otto Kahn, the millionaire sponsor of the arts who had already helped the Players in the past (he was responsible for the slightly more comfortable seating at 133 Macdougal Street), had offered considerable financial aid. According to her account, just "at the moment when we were on the verge of financing ourselves, [Jig] pushed the plans for enlargement to the floor" and, "unable to sleep," penned his manifesto. Unnerved by frustrated ideals and fueled by whiskey, he gave way to empty rhetoric and Nietzschean exaltation as he bewailed his failure to inspire friends and followers with the spirit of sacrifice necessary to construct the perfect community he dreamed of. Then, a fallen god, he delivered his verdict: "We give this theater we love good death; the Provincetown Players end their story here."[12] Still unable to sleep, he left the apartment.

Concerned at Jig's protracted absence—he had not been seen at the Brevoort—Glaspell headed for the theater. There she found him sitting alone in the auditorium, the curtain raised and the dome, his contribution to O'Neill's most daring play, *The Emperor Jones*, bathed in the blue light that created infinity—an infinity "that was nothing." She sat beside him, knowing that their feelings could not be articulated, overflowing with tenderness and pity, until "at last he spoke. 'It is time to go to Greece,' he said."[13] Stroking his hand, Glaspell murmured words of assent. For some time now, she had been sweet-talking her husband into moving away from Greenwich Village. She could not bear the lack of respect Provincetowners showed toward their founder or the sympathy and pity they showered on her. Greece offered a haven, and since it presented the extra appeal of history and culture, it was easy to dismiss rumors of political unrest there as the piffling quarrels of feudal lords. Glaspell, of course, could not foresee that Greece would also become a haven for the flood of refugees loosed by King Constantine's advance into Asia Minor. Nor could she foresee the grim trick fate was to play on her: in less than two years, Cook would die in Greece, supposedly a victim of the glanders, a dreadful disease that rarely attacks humans.

Once they had made the decision to go to Greece, Glaspell, afraid that during their absence the younger Players would dispossess them of their theatrical domain, moved quickly to safeguard the work of those hectic, dramatic years. With Kenton's support and driven by a faith that possibly disregarded Cook's wishes, she worked to ensure that his theater would be waiting for him when they returned. Harry Weinberger, the lawyer who had defended Emma Goldman and Alexander Berkman, as well as the editors of *The Masses* when they were tried for printing antiwar propaganda, advised them to incorporate the Players before announcing an interim. Seven people were needed for this, so Cook, Glaspell, Kenton, Fitzi, O'Neill, Cleon Throckmorton, and Weinberger legally took control of the Provincetown Players on 23 February 1922. No other group or individual could thereafter use the name to cash in on their fame. Kenton and Cook drafted an announcement that would be distributed after the last production of that season. One paragraph, addressed "To Our Playwrights," lamented the lack of good plays: "We have given two playwrights to America, Eugene O'Neill and Susan Glaspell: we could have given a dozen by now if the other ten had appeared." This dearth of good plays and the need for "leisure" in which to write them figure as the principal motives for the strange seventeen-month interim—although Kenton, riffling through her collection of playbills, calculated that during their eight seasons, the Players had produced a noteworthy ninety-three plays by forty-seven American playwrights. In the section "To Our Subscribers," Cook flattered his trusting audience: the "faithfully renewed subscription checks" had freed the Players from the "necessity of the box-office appeal," but the subscribers' "sympathy, interest, presence through good bills and bad, appreciation, amusement and curiosity" had been crucial to survival; "lacking these, our adventurous stage must have perished." He appealed to them to accept in the right spirit this seemingly unprofessional decision to "pause": "That impulse in you to escape from routine into what may freshen the spirit and that 'escape' in you which brought us together will interpret the urge in us to flee from our routine for a year."[14] The Provincetown Players Inc. also agreed that Glaspell's *Chains of Dew* would follow *The Hairy Ape* on the sixth and last bill and that the theater would be rented to some trustworthy but unconnected group the following season. Glaspell was reluctant to let *Chains of Dew*— the play Broadway had rejected in 1920—go on in her absence, but the Provincetown Players had promised their subscribers a sixth bill, and there was nothing else on hand. Even so, eager to distance her husband from the snickering Provincetowners, she relinquished control of the production of her play. It is doubtful that Cook ever realized the artistic sacrifice this entailed for her.

Once all of the loose ends were tied up, Cook and Glaspell took berths on the SS *Themistocles*, a small, uncomfortable vessel scheduled to leave on 1 March 1922. In the last days before sailing, both Cook and O'Neill made an effort to return to their old intimacy. They knew that on a deeper level, somewhere beyond ambition and success and failure, they could never be "remote" with each other "because they met in their inner lives." Nilla, who would join her father and stepmother in Greece in 1923, was old enough to remember and interpret their memories and musings. She tells the story of Jig and Gene's last battle of words, which had no witnesses. Jig and Susan, she related, "had dinner with Gene and Agnes and an Italian friend of Agnes who brought a certain wine. The sequence was that Gene and Jig shut themselves behind doors to discuss Dithyramb, Jig thundering that the prose theater was finished, that Gene had no business dying with it, that the dance and dithyrambic mystery were *his*. The talk went on all night, and the whole of the next day.

Neither Agnes nor Susan were told what it had been, but Susan pieced it together from the various quotations Jig made from it in Greece."[15]

That February must have seemed endless to Glaspell; while Cook, at his most genial, was gathering up farewells, she took on all of the practical details of their retreat to the land of his dreams. After they were safely on board the ship, she gave in to the rocking of the waters. Far from any shore, she resigned herself to the ocean's power and dared hope its enfolding isolation would deepen her intimacy with Cook. But Cook preferred historical grammars to the company of his wife. When not engrossed in the heavy tomes he had laboriously carried on board, he was pestering the Greek crew to teach him the modern language. He acknowledged her presence only to browbeat her with disquisitions on Greek history and etymology or on his ever firmer conviction—and fear—that death was closing in on him. When not buried in Greek, he wrote snatches of quasi-imagist verse:

> Beat against me, East Wind
> Wane, Moon;
> Do you think I do not know
> I have to die?[16]

Glaspell could never quite keep up with such mood swings, and, more and more, she felt that she was but a bothersome adjunct to Jig. Indeed, when most despondent, she even questioned her resolve to get him away from the Provincetown Players and, laboring over the revision of *Chains of Dew* (which she had promised to send Kenton), wondered if she had been misguided in her determination to accompany him.

Once they reached the Mediterranean Sea and were approaching Greece, Cook's morbid reflections gave way to febrile excitement. As they rounded the Peloponnesus and neared the port of Pireus, a wild-eyed Jig burst into his wife's cabin again and again, pulling at her skirts to call her attention to the birthplace of Venus, the site where the Venus of Milo was found, or the spot where Sparta lies under the shadow of Mount Elias. Like a child, he could not enjoy his discoveries without an audience, which he was naively prepared to admit: "I want to show you the strange old beauties which are ours. If I can't show them to you they are not very beautiful. They are beauty in vain. And that's why we need God so. As spectator of the beauty we discover in this mainly ugly world. And I, Jig, have weakly become dependent upon Susan, as spectator (there being no God) of the world."[17]

In Athens, Glaspell continued in her role of divine spectator; as long as her husband was not drunk or dejected, she was content to be the mirror reflecting his greatness. It never occurred to her that she was going back on her youthful rejection of the Victorian mores of Davenport and that her family would have been proud of her wifely submission. Climbing up to the Parthenon with Jig, she held back and smiled at the trembling eagerness with which he stroked the marble. As she slowly came up to him, he claimed her for his audience and, turning her first to the west and then to the south, spoke of the wreckage of the Persian fleet at Salamis, the rape of the nymph Aegina by Zeus, and the wall Pericles built to the port of Piraeus. She gazed out at Salamis, Aegina, and Pireus and marveled at the blue of the water and the silhouette of the mountains against the blue of the sky. She asked whether this was where the old Greeks got their feeling for form, and Jig rewarded her query with a thoughtful silence that ended with a brusque, "Let's go some place and get a drink."[18]

Those were the easy days, but one morning, after a lengthy debate over the Provincetown Players, Jimmy Light's supposed treachery, and the lack of news and checks from Kenton and Fitzi, Jig decided to reassert his authority and cable a few telegrams. Suspecting the futility of such a move, Glaspell declared that she was "not in sympathy with hurling these denunciations under the ocean," but he scribbled his violent missives on scraps of paper and pigheadedly stalked off in search of the post office, leaving her alone in a city that, despite all of its myths and monuments, was an alien place.[19] Cook did not return for lunch. Instead, he shared a repast of stew and Hymettus wine with a cabdriver whom he dazzled with stories of the Acropolis. Then, fueled by wine and the spirit of antiquity and completely forgetting the Provincetown Players, he offered to continue the history lesson in situ. The cabbie, suspecting that a good tip or at least another hearty meal would not be difficult to come by, drove along, dangerously twisting backward in his seat in order to continue the conversation with his fascinating fare. But Jig, who had no truck with social barriers in Greece, did not see why he should remain in the passenger seat and heaved himself onto the high seat beside the driver. It was at this point that Glaspell, anxious at Jig's prolonged absence and having ventured out in search of him, spotted her husband's rump precariously perched between passenger seat and driver's elevation. She winced, thinking, "I will have none of this."[20] But her sense of duty and commitment to Jig impelled her to run out and hail the cab. Jig stared down at her and, in that infuriating, abstracted manner he had when displeased, cried out, "Why, *Susan*, how very nice to see you! Get right in." He then turned to the cabdriver and casually gestured, "This is Susan, my friend."[21]

The cabbie drove them around Hadrian's Arch and then, bored now by the American's chatter, deposited them at their hotel. With difficulty, Glaspell cajoled Jig into going upstairs. She counted every step along the long corridor to the safety of their room. Once there, she sat him by the window and tried to get him to focus on the splendors of Mount Hymettus, which rose before them. But Cook refused to be distracted. He obstinately declared that he would sleep in the Acropolis that night. Glaspell's protestations finally got him to bed, and she hoped that, even though they had not had dinner, he would soon be asleep. But after a few minutes, too impatient to wait until she fell asleep, he jumped up, dressed, and set off for the Acropolis. That night, Glaspell did not sleep at all; again, she wondered at the turn her life had taken, asking herself whether it was worthwhile and how long she could stand it. She knew Neith Boyce had plans to visit France—a truly civilized land—that summer and daydreamed of joining her there. She worried what she would do in the morning if Jig did not come back and tried hard to "fall back on the comfortable old truth about God taking care of his children who are in their cups."[22] Around five in the morning, Jig reappeared, exhilarated by his adventure and eager to share it with Glaspell. He spun a yarn about wonderful new friends who had rescued him from robbers but had been too shy to come up to meet her. Undemanding, she accepted his account. When he finally fell into a deep sleep, she sat quietly at his side, watching over him, finding satisfaction in the knowledge that he would always return to her in his need for sympathy and understanding. She looked forward to the coming days that she knew would have that "subtle, fragile, sensitive quality" she loved but did not admit, even to herself, that on those "hang-over days" she was the one in control. Recounting this episode in *The Road to the Temple*, too honest to keep silent as to Jig's drinking, she nevertheless found a way to transform it into a statement of her devotion. Having to look after a helplessly alcoholic husband, she bizarrely suggested, is as fulfilling as nursing a baby: "A woman who has never lived with a man who sometimes 'drinks to excess' has missed one of the satisfactions that is like a gift—taking care of the man she loves when he has this sweetness as of a newborn soul."[23]

In the superficial letters she regularly sent her mother, she was very careful not to mention such dubiously maternal satisfactions or the pangs of anxiety that preceded them. Instead, she wrote of innocuous pleasures, such as the Easter celebrations that, thanks to the intervention of a Greek friend, John Rompapas, they were able to see from a central location. On Easter Saturday, close on midnight, Rompapas recklessly swept them through the surging crowds and into the arms of a young police officer who, awed by the American visitors, escorted them down the center of the street, which was kept open by a police cordon in readiness for the arrival of the royal family. Somehow, Glaspell said, they were shoved onto the platform reserved for royalty. Unfortunately, King Constantine was ill and unable to attend, but Glaspell found herself just ten feet away from the crown prince. The crowd was a constellation of candles, and the ceremonious splendor of a ritual that had never broken with ancient tradition, the bishops and priests enrobed in ornate vestments and enacting age-old gestures and movements, roused Jig into a state of fervent excitement. Rompapas and Glaspell, aware that any agitation on the royal platform could be interpreted as a threat, quieted him as best they could. Once the ceremony was over, Rompapas took them to a tavern where his friends had been waiting for midnight to break the long Lenten fast. Glaspell was grateful for his company; he made sure she was not excluded from the festivities and kept an eye on Jig.[24]

Two and a half months after leaving New York, Cook and Glaspell had received neither word nor money from Macdougal Street. Glaspell anguished over the fate of *Chains of Dew*, and Cook raged at the laxity of socalled friends. One evening, Cook began writing a letter to Kenton, pouring out his frustration in a "basso profundo." Glaspell, warmed by wine, read over his shoulder but refused to be silenced. Seizing Jig's pen, she added lines of her own in a "dramatic soprano." Kenton had never before received "a dialogue, nay, all but a duet in ink" and was duly appreciative.[25] She had mailed ten or more letters before Cook and Glaspell composed their "duet"; the delay in receiving all correspondence was mostly their fault because they had neglected to give a permanent address in their first letter from Athens.

The first of Kenton's epistles to reach them, toward the end of May, was hardly reassuring. It outlined the problems she had faced regarding the production of *Chains of Dew*. Kenton was deeply disappointed and hurt at the Provincetowners' handling of Glaspell's play. It went into rehearsal late because once Cook left, the decks were clear for what she called the "bloodless revolution," with Jimmy Light and Kenneth Macgowan fighting for control and poor Fitzi not knowing whom to appease or how.[26] For a while, it even looked as if Glaspell's *Chains of Dew* would be struck from the program, but Kenton stood her ground, bided her time, and loyally saw the play onto the stage, even though the best actors were either on tour with *The Emperor Jones* or uptown with *The Hairy Ape*. She lamented to Glaspell: "Your play didn't go on under the director, Sue, or with the actors I had so hoped for."[27]

Glaspell agonized over this news, but it was the "bloodless revolution" that enraged Cook. Kenton reported succinctly: "The sailing of the SS Themistocles on March 1st cleared the decks, you see. Jimmy [Light] announced at 4 p.m. March 1 to a table in the Golden Eagle that he was the director."[28] Cook proclaimed his anger, loudly, to anyone who could follow his incoherent mix of modern and ancient Greek laced with American expletives, as well as to Glaspell, who knew there was no consolation to offer.[29]

The postal service eventually established a rhythm of letters and packages; Throckmorton's watercolors for the sets of *Chains of Dew* arrived, providing hours of intensive powwow. It was well known that interiors did not give scope for the best of Throck's talent, and the office and drawing room he had sketched offered little to the imagination. Glaspell was chagrined but did her best to maintain a merry front. But the copy of the cut script of her play, which Kenton had sent with much trepidation, appalled her. Kenton had warned: "If you had been here subtleties and ironies would have stayed in that went."[30] Margaret Wycherly, who had starred in *The Verge* and admired Glaspell's work, told her that throughout the performance she "could feel where things had dropped out— what was you and what wasn't."[31] Glaspell groaned over the scenes and lines that had been jettisoned, the incongruous moments that a dedicated band of thespians could have artfully highlighted, embarrassing the audience into laughter at its faddish posturing.

The next parcel pleased Glaspell: they had begged Kenton to send a copy of *Zarathustra*, a text Cook felt they could not be without. Reading it together brought them closer and helped restore their faith in humanity. Kenton's letters did occasionally convey good news: at the end of June, she wrote that Throck had managed to rescue the weirdly cut lantern that had thrown wild patterns of light on Claire and her tower room in *The Verge*, surreptitiously sneaking it "out of the theater."[32] For Glaspell, this lantern represented the magic of that production and everything she had put into the writing of the play.

Soon after Easter, Cook and Glaspell sailed to Itea, and from there, mounted on mules, they rode up to "the little mountain town" of Delphi, "where the oracle spoke." In 1892, the villagers had been forced to move out of the shielded valley where their ancestors had placed their homes, olive groves, vineyards, and wheat fields. The Greek government, anxious to restore the cultural inheritance of the people and to ensure a market for the currant crop, had ceded excavation rights to the French, and the villagers were offered new homes in a windswept, barren spot, "baldly on the mountain, hanging there" over the spectacular gorge of the Pleistos River.[33]

Archaeologists had unearthed the old Delphi, and Glaspell delighted in walking up the hill, studying the fallen columns of ancient temples, the stone seats of the theater, and the uneven paving of the streets. Glaspell and Cook rented two rooms from the village innkeeper, Athanasius Tchakalós, "a high-class man" whom they promptly employed as "cook, guide, servant, manager." It was not long before they realized that Tchakalós was cheating them, but they decided it was "worth it."[34] His wife had once run a hotel, so they had the luxury of beds in their new quarters (the villagers slept on mattresses thrown on the bare floor) and rudimentary plumbing. They also had wooden tables and chairs and a small balcony where Glaspell would sit, looking down at the steep gorge and out to the bay of Itea.

It was this setting that she would use some years later in the novel *Fugitive's Return* (1929), in which she came to terms with her Greek experience. She had hoped that sharing with Cook the discovery of the ancient culture he had always loved would bring her back into his inner life. Although as a writer, Glaspell was always on the lookout for new material, she had engineered their escape from New York principally to re-affirm herself as wife and keeper of her husband. She suffered, as a mother suffers over a wayward child, to see him dissipating his strength and his talent; tenaciously, she hung on to her faith in him—as only a mother could. Unsurprisingly, Greece disappointed her; not even its beauty could stop Cook from drinking, and thus restore his health and revive his passion. Determined to conquer the land of his dreams, Cook struggled with demotic Greek, and even when lost "deep in the Peloponnesus," he insisted "he understood neither French nor English and finally forced the Greeks to send him to Sparta in Greek."[35] Such command over language empowered him to compensate for what had subconsciously ruffled him in Greenwich Village—Glaspell's success compared to the meager acclaim his plays had enjoyed. Although he always supported his wife's writing, he had now chanced upon the most effective way to deprive her of the power of the word. Refusing to speak French himself, he mocked her efforts in that language and "quite frightened out of [her]" what little she still remembered.[36]

In Athens, American acquaintances and English-speaking Greeks had provided a friendly circle; in Delphi, she was on her own, doubly excluded from his sphere by sex and language. Cook made friends with the locals, practicing his Greek, gulping down the bitter, resinous wine in which they drowned their poverty, and listening to stories of the bandits on the mountain. The village schoolteacher exchanged formal lessons in Greek with Cook—or "Kyrios Kouk" as he was known—for English classes. But Glaspell, thus neglected by Jig, was not without her own resources. Silenced in this strange world just as effectively as the protagonist of *Fugitive's Return* would be, she contrived to make friends with the women of the village, observing them at their tasks, occasionally helping them gather berries around the stones of old Delphi, and learning to spin and weave. It is easy to recognize Glaspell in Irma Lee, the Kyria (Mrs.) of her novel, at moments such as the following: "Though the Kyria did not speak, and understood but little Greek, she and Stamula would communicate with each other at the loom. These difficulties had made them companions, sharing not only the difficulty, but pleasure when the handicap was overcome and communication flowed between them."[37] It seems quite likely that Glaspell initiated the miming that allowed her to communicate with these women, for whom she must have felt compassion and warmth while realizing the huge distance that separated them. She could not resist universalizing such exchanges when she later re-created them: "Talking to each other in this way made them more humorously and more deeply acquainted than if they had been able to talk with words. A thing said by acting seemed to mean, not only the thing said, but something of which it was a part, something underneath."[38]

It took Glaspell five years to put her Greek experience sufficiently behind her to be able to use it in her fiction. In *Fugitive's Return*, she compensates for all of the failures of her life by creating a heroine who bears similar losses but emerges triumphant. Irma Lee, a priggish young midwesterner (Davenport readers recognized the locale),[39] devotes her life to marriage and motherhood, but she loses her husband because she does not care to join in his partying and then loses her daughter to meningitis. Seeing no reason to continue to live, Irma plans to kill herself. She is about to swallow an overdose of sleeping pills when a cousin bursts into her room. For some months, Irma is not sure whether she took the pills or not; she has lost the power of speech, and she lives as if in another world. Mechanically following her cousin's instructions, she sails to Greece, where, regarded as an embodiment of the oracle, she is taken in by the shepherds of Delphi. She is stirred only by the villagers' cruelty toward their animals. Such is her power that boys abandon their favorite sport of stoning birds and families agree not to kill their lambs at Easter. Many months go by; in the graceful Greek tunic she has woven, Irma roams through the ruins of Delphi, a priestess locked in her silence, as spectral a creature as Glaspell must have seemed to the peasants. Irma is jolted out of her mystical existence by a group of villagers torturing a mangy dog. In their language, she cries out, "Did Jesus die for this?" The recovery of the power that speech confers, however, carries with it the loss of her otherworldly status and a return to everyday reality. Irma befriends the deformed Constantina, a rape victim wanted for the murder of her ravisher, and eventually helps her escape from Delphi. They return to her native town, where Irma mothers the young girl into womanhood, thus creating an identity for herself and a reason for living.

This was not the only time Glaspell coupled the need to mother with the loss of speech in her fiction. She would rewrite an early play, *The Outside* (1917), into a story in which the protagonist's recovery of voice and identity results from the adoption of a small child,[40] and a later novel,

The Morning Is Near Us (1939), is a variation on this theme. *Fugitive's Return*, a novel of loss and healing, rehearses Glaspell's feelings of fear, frustration, and guilt during her marriage to Cook. By creating a protagonist who is able to take control of her life, she transforms her experience into a positive memory that she can live with. Curiously, the desire to mother remains inextricably linked with the ability to express oneself and to play a vital role in society even at a time when, to all appearances, she had successfully substituted literary creativity for motherhood. *Fugitive's Return*, a novel by a woman about a woman, hit the best-seller lists, ranking fourth on the same charts that placed Ernest Hemingway's misogynous *Farewell to Arms* in first place.[41]

Fugitive's Return, while it mythologizes Glaspell's experience, relies heavily on the local color of shepherds' lives. The deformed shepherd girl Constantina, the refugee servant Theodora, the innkeeper and his wife, and the mistreated dog are all borrowed from the Delphi she knew. Percy Hutchinson, reviewing the novel for the *New York Times Book Review*, wrote: "So much of an individual is Susan Glaspell one knows in advance that a novel from her pen will not be an ordinary book. . . . The narrative will reflect the individuality of the author." He praised her "almost unearthly sensitiveness to life" but lamented the unevenness of the writing and the meandering of the plot.[42] Experimenting with narrative and chronology, Glaspell structured the novel around the figure of Irma Lee, giving the story of her life through flashbacks that move us disconcertingly from Davenport to Cape Cod to Delphi and from childhood to maturity, intermingling stories from the lives of Greek shepherds. She does not quite control all of these elements, perhaps because in Delphi the figure of Irma Lee, the Kyria, is inexplicably elevated to the status of oracle, with almost supernatural powers. There seems to be no immediate way to account for this transformation, except to the degree that Glaspell's Kyria reflects her own sense of being effectively on the outside in Greece, a ghostly presence in the lives of others. The exalted status of the Kyria also suggests that Glaspell unconsciously modeled her protagonist on Cook and that the eventualities of the plot permit him to fulfill himself in a way that was denied him in life. (Another model was the beautiful Eva Sikelianós, the much revered American wife of the poet Angelos Sikelianós, who befriended Glaspell and Cook.) Either way, the novel becomes an allegory of wish fulfillment and even a kind of apology for her lost life with Cook. The sentimentally elegizing tone that resulted was appreciated by some critics, for example, the reviewer in the *New*

York Evening Sun: "Miss Glaspell is, of course, a poet, and possibly the finest exemplification of the poet's success with the novel."[43]

———— ••◄◦◦◦►•• ————

Glaspell had been aware of the political upheavals in Greece even before booking passage on the SS *Themistocles*, but it never crossed her mind that she would in any way become caught up in them. The crown prince, whose royal platform she had shared at Easter, had been forced to take the throne as George III on his father's abdication after the defeat at Smyrna in August 1922. For many years, in spite of opposition from England and France, the Greeks had dreamed of reestablishing the ancient Greek empire. They claimed Smyrna, in Asia Minor, where the population was largely Greek, and belligerently moved further inland. However, the Turks, resentful of such appropriation (which, in fact, dated back more than 2,000 years) and supported by France, sacked and looted Smyrna. By September, thousands of refugees were pouring into Greece, principally into the port of Salonika. The various relief agencies could not cope with the flood of homeless victims. In Glaspell's eyes, salvation lay in American intervention. "If relief doesn't come on a big scale from America, and very, very quickly, these Greeks driven from their homes by the Turks will have to starve," she wrote to her mother.[44]

Visiting Salonika at the end of September, Cook and Glaspell stayed with Mr. and Mrs. Lamb of the Young Men's Christian Association (YMCA), whom they had met during the Atlantic crossing. Glaspell relished not only the company of these Americans but also the comforts of their cool, American-style apartment. The unwanted sundries that the Red Cross had left behind after World War I had been handed over to the YMCA for distribution to the 35,000 refugees already in Salonika, and Glaspell helped Mrs. Lamb and other American women dispense the meager supplies. The refugees, huddled in barracks outside the city, were a heartbreaking sight: "The barracks are just great bare sheds into which the people can go. There you see them lying on the floor, most of them without any blankets, and with only the clothes they have on." Yet even more refugees docked in Salonika while Glaspell was there,

> mostly women and children, as the men are held prisoner by the Turks. There was simply nothing to be done about them. They had not been expected to arrive here, and anyway it was on too gigantic

a scale for any city to be able to deal with. So they began getting off the ship, exhausted, dazed, hungry people, and there was nothing for them to do but lie down in the streets, and nothing for them to eat. It was the saddest thing I saw in my life and I shall never forget it. They came off so patiently and so trustingly, as if now they had reached their own land, and would be cared for. Saloniki has had much more than its share of refugees, and has been wonderfully good to them, and is now trying to do what it can, but the barracks were full before this ten thousand came. They are getting some of them into buildings, schools, etc. but thousands of them just walk about on the streets, and when too exhausted to stand up, lie down where they can.[45]

Glaspell, moved by this human misery, yearned to participate more actively in the relief effort. Remembering her days on the *Des Moines Daily News*, she thought of trying to capture the agony of the refugees in an article that would spur midwesterners to send money and supplies, but she never did. Possibly embarrassed by Cook's unpredictable behavior around their hosts, she agreed to return to Delphi for their trunks before they established themselves in Athens for the winter. She recognized that they did not have the wherewithal to travel to Italy as she had planned; she also may have feared contradicting Cook, who was eager to meet up with friends he had made that summer when camping on the slopes of Mount Parnassus above Delphi.

One of the Greeks whom Cook had charmed was Leandrus Palamas, the son of "the leading poet of Greece," who invited them to visit him in Agorgiani, "a little town where writers and artists come from Athens."[46] Glaspell welcomed the respite from idyllic primitivism that Leandrus and his sister afforded and was relieved to find that "the Greeks of their sort are cultivated, beautiful people."[47] In Agorgiani, they met other Athenian writers and artists, among them Eva Sikelianós, daughter of Courtland Palmer, a New York philanthropist, and wife of Angelos Sikelianós, a pretentious, eccentric poet.[48] Sikelianós, who evidently had much in common with the mystical Yeats, propounded a philosophy that he called the "Delphic Idea," maintaining that Delphi was one of the sources of wisdom derived from the "Orphic tradition." Thus, he must have been delighted to meet Cook, an American soul mate. They projected a Delphic Festival dedicated to theater and games on the model of the ancient festivals. But Cook had plans for Athens too; he hoped "to establish a vital relation" with a group of students, he said, "perhaps in doing plays." His ever-active mind was busy with blueprints for "some magic lighting" at the surviving stone stage of the ancient theater of Dionysus, and he saw no reason why a "modest little Greek Provincetown," or in fact, a full-blown art theater movement, could not be "compelled to exist"—by him—in modern Athens.[49]

When camping on Parnassus, Glaspell had felt, briefly, that Cook appreciated her company; in Athens, she felt bluntly excluded from his sphere. His unpredictable behavior confused and upset her, especially in front of new friends, and it must have been difficult to understand why he turned on her when irritated by them. Greece refurbished his ego, but it did little for their personal relationship. She considered leaving him there, perhaps joining the Hapgoods in Italy or France, but her sense of duty was too strong. News of her father's death offered an irreproachable excuse to go home. Cook concurred with her; he suggested that she return to Davenport for Christmas. He assured her that he would manage splendidly on his own; Eva Sikelianós would keep an eye on him, and Palamas would help him master Greek in order to translate *The Athenian Women*. He was also anxious for her to check on Nilla. Letters from his daughter had been disconcerting, and he did not approve of the way she was being brought up. Glaspell needed no prodding, and she made it her mission to bring his daughter to him.

The SS *Constantinople* docked in New York at the beginning of December 1922. After spending a few days with Lulu Huffaker, Glaspell boarded a train for Davenport. She dreaded her mother's quizzical eyes. The letters she sent home had not been much more than cursory travelogues, a cover for her anxiety and loneliness. She hoped to avoid the humiliation of acknowledging her disappointment in Cook and wondered whether she could be sufficiently blasé to maintain the fiction of a happy marriage.

She found her mother frail and Davenport, deep in winter snowstorms, as bleak as she remembered it. Letters from Jig did nothing to cheer her; his dependency on her was flattering and fulfilled a deep need, but his mood swings alarmed her. As Christmas approached, he missed her more and more. She was concerned at the wild scrawl she recognized as indicative of drink and depression. "I had no idea what a lost soul I would be without you," he whined. "It is ignoble." His conviction that his own death was imminent horrified Glaspell; it was impossible to constantly shrug off ejaculations such as "I love you, knowing how dead we'll be, for how long, and what a moment only there is left."[50]

Guilt at having left him alone tormented her. Yet she found it difficult to picture the future with Cook; indeed, she failed to see what it could hold for her. His protestations of loneliness in her absence did not quite fill the frame. But she knew she would have to return to Greece and was relieved when Mollie allowed Nilla to accompany her. The girl had been expelled from a Methodist boarding school near Chicago for, among other sins, "telling the Bible teacher what I thought of Jehovah" and had been placed under the care of Great-aunt Fanny, one of the Davenport Cooks, who was as puritan as Ma-Mie had been bohemian.[51] Alice Glaspell worried how her daughter would cope with such a charge, but Susan believed that Nilla would sweeten Cook and hoped she would reprieve her loneliness in Greece.[52] Before they could leave, however, Glaspell had to settle financial matters resulting from her father's death and attend to stocks and property that Jig had inherited from Ma-Mie (she relied on the family law firm, Cook and Balluf, to advise her). Then, after enjoying a few nostalgic days on Cape Cod and in New York, she sailed with Nilla on 21 March 1923.

Cook, who had assured Glaspell he would go to hell to be with her, pulled himself together sufficiently to travel to Palermo in time to meet her ship.[53] He had lost weight and looked older, but it was soon clear that he had lost none of his vivacity. He would not hear of dawdling in Italy or visiting the Hapgoods and the Steeles but insisted on sailing straight back to his beloved new land. He was eager to share with Nilla his Greek discoveries, anxious to save her, as he scrawled in some doggerel verses dedicated to her, from the "bunk and hokum / With which America is doped."[54]

Nilla took instantly to Greece and felt utterly at home in Athens. Whereas Glaspell, in spite of English-speaking acquaintances who welcomed her back, could never love the Frenchified capital, Nilla relished it because "you could loaf in the street, or dance, or sing, or eat, or hear nightingales. There were dark eyes and red wine, palm trees and serenades."[55] But for Glaspell, who was all too conscious of her responsibility as a stepmother, dark eyes, red wine, and serenades could only spell danger. Dashing the young teenager's illusions, she proved no less strict than her Great-aunt Fanny and chaperoned Nilla "carefully and scrupulously."[56] Notwithstanding problems of discipline—which grew with Nilla's expanding circle of Greek admirers—Glaspell enjoyed having the girl with her. She saw the best of Cook in his daughter and loved her spontaneity and fearlessness. She was delighted when Nilla, knowing her weakness for lilacs, picked her a huge bunch, but more important than such signs of affection was the female company Nilla provided, as well as her readiness to enter into small conspiracies aimed at checking Cook's frequently preposterous whims.

Since it was still too cold to return to the summer camp above Delphi on the slopes of Parnassus, Eva Sikelianós recommended Xylocastro, a village on the shores of the Gulf of Corinth. It was here that Glaspell had her first exchange with Nilla concerning love. She had come across her ward sitting on the beach with Eva's fourteen-year-old son, who had his arm around Nilla. Glaspell, who had never adhered to her parents' standards of morality, now scolded Nilla and forbade such assignations. Nilla was baffled because, as she protested, "the heroines of the books [her stepmother] wrote were always meeting people in the woods, even when they were married to someone else."[57] Glaspell's inadequate excuse was that her protagonists were in love and love justified all.[58]

It was in Xylocastro that the Cooks acquired a maid, Theodora.[59] Her unabashed manner and few culinary skills were redeemed in Glaspell's eyes by her refugee status, while Cook, under the spell of the girl's dark features and wild green eyes, agreed to hire her because her name meant "Gift of God." He was to regret that decision; Theodora's officious meddling would soon make him look a fool. When they decided to cross the Gulf of Corinth to Delphi, a mere eighteen miles by boat (instead of the long haul via Patras), Cook arranged for a local fisherman to ferry them over. He knew the man well; he was the only fellow he ever acknowledged as being able to drink and carouse longer and more heartily than he could. The "Captain of the Drunkards" had earned his title by regularly outdrinking the company at weddings and festivals and then leading the dance without a stagger. He was, undoubtedly, "a remarkable man."[60] But Glaspell, claiming she had urgent shopping to do in Patras, flatly refused to sail with him and, moreover, insisted that Nilla go with her. This distrust of his chosen mode of transport infuriated Cook, who hurled insults and swore that he knew what was best for his daughter. For once, Glaspell did not find an ally in Nilla; the youngster was delighted at the prospect of adventure and could not understand why Theodora was horrified that "a great American" should risk his child in the boat of "the most notorious wife-beater in Corinthia."[61] With mixed feelings, Glaspell caught the train to Patras, where she did her shopping—which had not been a vain excuse since commodities such as paper and ink were not readily available in the mountain village—and then she took the ferry to Itea, the port of Delphi. She was vexed to find no one waiting for her and, when the cable she sent to Xylocastro went unanswered, was tormented by the possibility of shipwreck.

Surrounded by his trunks, book boxes, and wine crates, Cook, adamant that "a pact in ouzo" could not be broken, was still waiting on Xylocastro beach for the captain's orange sail.[62] According to Nilla, the captain arrived a week or so late. By this time, Theodora had worked out her strategy; once afloat, she easily got both men drunk on Cook's supplies and surreptitiously turned the boat back to Xylocastro. Undaunted by Cook's barking, she shepherded her charges to the station, where she organized socially acceptable transport—a packed train to Patras and a sardine boat to Itea. But she did not think to wire her mistress, and by this time, the lonesome Glaspell must have been convinced that her husband, stepdaughter, maid, trunks, and books were all at the bottom of the sea.

Cook's arrival did not bring her much reprieve from solitude. He was immediately caught up in the Delphians' wine-drenched celebration of his return, and Nilla went exploring. The girl was fascinated by the ritual of the first wheat harvest: "Lines of horses yoked together were trampling [the wheat] on the stone-paved circles of the threshing floors, and as much of the populace of Delphi as was not drinking with Kyrios Kouk was dancing around in circles after the horses."[63] A few months later, Nilla blissfully participated in the grape harvest, "her bare legs reddening with juice as laughing, singing, there in the sunshine, against the mountain, she danced upon the grapes with bacchanalian joy."[64]

After a few days in Delphi, the family bravely set off on their mules up narrow mountain trails to Agorgiani—a six-hour ride over Parnassus— where they had rented a house.[65] Glaspell was thrown by her mule and stoically explained in a letter to Kenton: "Elbow and knee put out of business, we arrived to find our summer home containing naught but walls and floors. So I lay me down on the latter, and staid there for three weeks, though a few spruce boughs were slipped under me in the interim. That was a wild experience and my elbow has never forgiven the mule."[66]

Agorgiani, today Eptalofos, is but a cluster of houses that cling to the skirts of Parnassus. The valley below, encircled by seven hills, tantalizingly opens out onto the distant plain. The Cooks' house, tucked away at the edge of the village, gave "the feeling of being right in the mountains," and again Glaspell's chief pastime and delight, to judge from her letters to her mother, was to sit on the large balcony and enjoy the shimmering ochers and greens under the deep blue of the sky.[67] The gregarious father and daughter were otherwise employed, studying Greek and making friends. When the temperature rose, they all moved up to Kalania, the summer camp on Parnassus that Glaspell had so loved the previous summer. To-Puppy, a mongrel they saved from vicious baiting, went with them.

The villagers of Delphi and many intellectuals from Athens escaped the summer heat by camping in the huge calyx-shaped valley hidden in the heights of Parnassus called "Kalania of the Kastriotes."[68] Glaspell describes the idyllic beauty of the scene in *Fugitive's Return*: "Here giant spruce trees open for a high meadow, where peasants grow lentils and grain, and harvest wood for their winter. . . . Above [Irma Lee] moved the great flocks and the music of their bells would come through the deep music of the trees. Here was the world nobly proportioned; here was majesty, and after a time she could rest, as if taken by a great mother."[69]

The previous summer, Athanasius Tchakalós, the servant who was cheating them, had helped Cook choose the ideal spot for their tent. They pitched it "under a great spruce tree" at some distance from the shepherds' huts to ensure privacy and quiet. They had their own spring, and their quarters were enfolded in the boughs of the spruce, as giant as Merlin's tree, which made "a sort of tent outside the tent." Not content with the work of nature, Cook made "little bowers of the spruce boughs, for seats, and places to lie down in the day time" and extra spruce huts for sleeping quarters.[70] (Glaspell preferred to sleep separately from Cook.) Now he added new huts for Theodora and Nilla and a kitchen "in a clump of tree" for the maid; he put up shelves and pegs for supplies and maneuvered stones to form a two-burner stove. A fever of building overtook him; the place was so beautiful, he said, it deserved to be made more so by his striving: "The air, the light, the breeze, the sun, the color and fragrance are fit for the dwelling-place of gods."[71] He rolled the largest stones he could find into camp to create walls, terraces, steps, maintaining that this was how temples had been built. To Hapgood, he boasted that he had fashioned "a stone-wall cloister-fortress on the mountainside."[72] Even when Glaspell pleaded with him to rest, to eat, he would not stop. He was getting thinner and thinner and more cantankerous in his behavior and would not hear of traveling to Athens to see a doctor.

The lazy monotony of Glaspell's summer days was broken toward the end of August by a visit from William J. Rapp, secretary of the Athens

YMCA.[73] That winter, the young man had fallen under the spell of Jig's charm, finding in him a father figure or maestro; he shared Cook's enthusiasm for all things Greek and was quite carried away by his capacity to bring history to life. He suggested that the Cooks climb Parnassus with him. The previous summer, Glaspell, afraid that the altitude would bring back her heart troubles, had refused to go any higher than Kalania, but now, motivated by Rapp's urging and her own desire to conquer the mountain, she agreed. Accompanied by Athanasius and the mule drivers, they trekked up the tortuous path until they reached "a hidden sort of place, in magnificent rocks" surrounded by fragrant spruce woods, where they made their first camp. Wrapped in blankets to protect her from the cold night air, Glaspell slept soundly. The following day, they climbed to the foot of the peak, where they made camp with a shepherd who greeted them joyfully and plied them with goats' milk and roasted lamb. Glaspell was fascinated by the water supply—"a great cake of ice tilted so it dripped into a bucket." Leaving the mules behind, they headed for the summit on foot, reaching it in time to watch the sunset. Glaspell was so deeply moved that she knew she could never satisfactorily describe the spectacle. "There is no use trying to tell how magnificent it is," she wrote to her mother. It was "an experience that will be a delight all my life."[74]

As they gazed at Greece spread out before them, two eagles circled ominously, casting a shadow on the little group; only Jig was unmarked by the foreboding that descended on them. He cut a lonesome figure there on the summit of Parnassus; tall and lean against the darkening sky, his long white hair and beard set off by black brows and mustache, he had the air of a bygone prophet. Rapp watched him with humble admiration, but Glaspell resolved to get him to a doctor and to trim his hair and beard. The gloom left her only when the eagles returned to their nest lower down the slope and she spotted an eagle's feather on the scant grayish moss. The feather she kept as trophy and talisman; the moss she added to her other samples.

Glaspell had reason to worry about Jig's health. His moods had always swung from the extremes of enthusiasm to the depths of dejection, but good company and immersion in a flagon of wine and a new project usually succeeded in keeping him on an even keel. Now he refused to eat and drank more than was good for him. He would sit beside Glaspell as she read under the spruce boughs, the fire gone from his words as he spoke of failure and destruction. It was at such times, "from the depth of my insanity," that he looked back to the Provincetown Players, recriminating himself, and them, for his failure to "have written America."[75] When he turned his eyes on her softly, begging for explanation and understanding of his aborted genius, she felt that she too had failed him. Perhaps if she had been less engrossed in her writing, had known how to present him to the world, had been more passionate, had never rejected him, had been able to give him the child he wanted of her, things might have been different. One night he came into her hut and sat beside her. In one of the rare scenes in *The Road to the Temple* in which Glaspell speaks directly of herself, she recounted that moment:

> "I do not want to live beyond sex," Jig said to me. . . . He was unhappy because it was not as it had been in the first years. "We who were those mad lovers. . . ." Was not that one of the things we had to accept, I said. After years together, something goes, yet is all loss? Does not something also come? He did not care for that way of looking at it, he said. He was the lover. In his loving was all of himself, and without it himself was impoverished. He had a rare gift for romantic, intense love. It created a world in which his spirit could be. More than once he said to me, "But we will lie alone so long in our graves. . . ." To succeed in love is the greatest beauty in life. Love is fulfilment, and the great ordeal. We have our failures. Yet I think he always knew I loved him.[76]

Cook's drinking and ill-health must have affected his virility, provoking such scenes of recrimination and guilt that Glaspell could rarely have felt sufficiently relaxed to want sex. His constant references to death would have lent morbidity to such encounters, and he hated to have his manhood questioned. During the months he was alone in Athens, he had sweated through nightmares that revealed a deep sexual insecurity, as well as matrimonial fears: he dreamed of his wife "copulating with other men. It's not nice of you—when I want you so much. You do the things I have always wanted you to want to do with me—and you explain that that is what you have always wanted and I not. What kind of inside-out 'transference' is this dreaming? Or why didn't you tell me what you wanted and didn't get from me?"[77]

The passing of time and the inevitability of death possessed his mind; coauthoring *Tickless Time* (1918) and constructing a sundial had only lulled his fears. One day, entertaining his Agorgiani disciples with ouzo, he planted death squarely in their midst when he declared that he had

George Cram Cook, in shepherds' attire, with Delphi villagers
(Courtesy of the Billy Rose Theatre Collection, New York Public Library
for the Performing Arts, Astor, Lenox, and Tilden Foundations)

come to Parnassus to die. Slopping out the alcohol, he decreed that it was hard to die alone and that each man should choose a partner with whom to defeat the randomness of death. Finally, after a moment of dramatic suspense, he invited the village doctor to be his companion in the journey "from life to death." The next day, the priest called on Glaspell and Cook and "gently admonished" the Kyrios; the doctor had a family and patients to care for—"he was not free to die."[78] Once the holy man had gone, Jig roared with laughter as he played the incident out for his wife. But although she pretended to share his amusement, Glaspell was surely wounded that her husband would prefer the doctor to herself as a partner in that last act. She could only interpret his choice as a sign that in spite of all of her efforts they were moving away from each other. The old intimacy she strove to recover would never return, and inevitably, she gave in to the guilt that tormented her more and more.

The shepherd Elias Scarmouches, who by now considered Kyrios Kouk an honorary native of Parnassus, took him down to the town of Amphissa and rigged him out in traditional shepherds' garb. For Glaspell, this must have signified Cook's ultimate rejection of America, and of her, but knowing his temper, she humored him and admired the white woolen tights, the fitted black tunic with its full short skirt, the skull cap, and the half-shoes with pom-poms. She assured him that "as he walked, white hair and beard under the small white cap, he seemed some other kind of high-priest clothed in authority."[79] In his shepherd costume, Kyrios Kouk, taking Nilla with him, went down to Agorgiani for the festivities of the Virgin on 15 August 1923. Glaspell preferred to stay in Kalania; although by now she did understand a lot of what was said around her, she found Cook's all-male drinking parties tedious and sensed that he did not want her with him.

Alone in the camp—except for Athanasius and his wife, who remained to look after her—Glaspell had an august visitor, Argyros Kastritis, the Man of the Silver Fortress, the last of the Bandit Kings. Parnassus was a land beyond the law; the police did not venture up the mountain, and the bandits ruled, extorting sheep and supplies from local villagers. Athenians had warned Cook and Glaspell of the danger of camping in bandit territory, but the Delphians shrugged off any possible threat. Athanasius argued that the outlaws would not want to risk government intervention by attacking Americans. Moreover, prepared to ply them with cigarettes and wine, he claimed to know how to maintain good relations. On the whole, the bandits kept away, and although Glaspell soaked up the stories of robberies and abductions, she did not fear that the "lystes" were near when "dried spruce boughs snapped in the night." But the Bandit King, curious about the American woman who was not afraid to remain in his territory without her man and protector, visited Kyria Kouk in her spruce hut. He surprised Glaspell at her typewriter, which was perched on a piece of flat rock Cook had rolled in front of the spruce bough seat he had fashioned for her. Startled, she looked up to see the Bandit King silhouetted against the deep blue of her doorway. He bowed, and she, sensing material for a story, motioned for him to enter. She offered him a cigarette; he took the pack. Somehow, using mime as much as words, they started to talk about the valley of Kalania, the heart of Parnassus; Kastritis knew all of its secrets and loved its very essence. Glaspell recreated his noble spirit in Nondas, protagonist of "The Faithless Shepherd" (1926), who discovered "those inmost places" that she too loved, "where mountain shadowed mountain, the places where great sombre shadows lay below, while little cloud shadows moved softly across the upper sunshine."[80] Kastritis, animated by wine and cigarettes, may have mimed for her the experience of "the star that one instant stood upon the mountain and in that same instant ceased to be" that thrilled Nondas. He perhaps conjured up what she too had seen and admired: "There was a night—the second night it was after full moon—when the whole way up the mountain the moon was just behind the edge, and one by one, or sometimes three by three, the trees of the edge stood against the climbing moon—a night when there were trees on the moon."[81]

Glaspell savored the sensitivity and naïveté of Kastritis and was not afraid of the murderer the law did not dare confront. When he got up to go, she asked him to come again, but he slipped out in silence, quickly disappearing into the spruce trees. For some reason, Glaspell wanted to keep the visit to herself, but the conspicuous depletion of their cigarette store, when discovered by Jig, brought on a loud interrogation that obliged her to own up. Kyrios Kouk was proud that his wife had known how to deal with the fearsome brigand and encouraged her to write his story.

Glaspell had been struck by the poignancy of Kastritis's fascination with her typewriter and the mysterious signs it imprinted. She correlated his wonder with her desire to interpret the symbols carved into ancient stone slabs that she found at the Temple of Apollo. She took up the challenge of translating the inscriptions and, notwithstanding her scant knowledge of old Greek, traced the letters, trying to penetrate their secret.[82] Some of the excitement she felt when examining these stones went into the story of Nondas, the innocent shepherd forced into banditry by the tawdry philistinism of his comrades. Nondas is awakened to the beauty of the world surrounding him when, as a boy, he recognizes letters that the priest had taught him carved by the ancients into fallen stones:

> There were only six different letters, and three of them he knew. He liked this word which he half knew, and wished he knew what it meant, why it had been cut in stone, and why all those great stones, looking as if they had once made something, but not making anything now, were here alone on the mountainside. His fingers followed each letter until finger-tips knew the cuts—cuts smooth with age. Then, poppies brushing his slowly moving hand, he was idly looking about—those rich lower slopes of Parnassos, the great olive groves far below, plowland and vineyard stretching up and up, here and there small fields of grain—and everything moving just a little; he heard the bells of his father's flock, heard faintly the waters of

the Castalian spring. Things smelled good; though it was dawn he felt warm inside, and as if he could dance and sing—and as if he could cry.[83]

"The Faithless Shepherd," not written to order, is one of Glaspell's finest short stories. In it, she contrasts the harmony of nature with man's pernicious jealousies as she examines the fate of the young shepherd who seeks to share his knowledge of beauty. Although the bandit on his mountain inspired the narrative, we can also read the story as a parable of Cook and the Provincetown Players, the good shepherd as sacrificial victim. Glaspell wrote from the heart, polishing her sentences, to achieve a gem she could never have produced without her sojourn in Greece. Although she intended to write a collection of pieces about Greece, to be published in one volume, the project never materialized; instead, she absorbed and transformed her Greek experience into the novel *Fugitive's Return*.

They stayed in Kalania until late September, when the days got short and the nights too cold for comfort. Cook, content that the mountain could not be beautified further, was calmer and better company. He was delighted at Nilla's progress with the Greek language and spent hours with her, painstakingly drawing charts to show how the old tongue had developed into the new. In the evenings, they gathered wood for a fire, throwing on dead spruce boughs to make a huge, comforting blaze. Nilla, who had a sweet tooth, made hot chocolate, which they sipped sybaritically before going to bed. At such peaceful moments, Glaspell could write to Neith Boyce: "I think you will never be sorry if you come to Greece. I cannot recommend it for comforts and conveniences, but I call it the most rewarding country I know anything about. We have lived around in villages, with peasants, and endured more hardships than one need endure. After all it is not necessary to lie on the floor, for you can confine yourself to places where there are beds. . . . Anyway you must come, and wander all around through Greece. The food is all right enough—the plumbing's awful; but you will feel things you never felt before—or so it has been with me."[84]

Leaving Kalania for the winter was made more difficult by the problem posed by Jig's bird, "a young wild bird . . . a field-jack" that, attracted by the motion of Jig's hand as he wrote, had hopped onto his table and sat there, fearlessly watching.[85] Jig, seeing himself as a modern St. Francis, was delighted; he talked to the bird and invited it to share their meals. The only quarrel with Jig that Glaspell admits to in *The Road to the Temple* was occasioned by this bird. Cook had spent the afternoon pouring his soul out in an indignant letter to one of the Provincetown Players. Such purgative letters were very rare now and usually effective, but that day, Jig emerged scowling from his tent and refused to eat. The bird observed him; suddenly, Jig took a piece of bread and threw it, frightening the creature away. When Glaspell protested, "Jig seized my arm and I looked up into the blaze of rage, of hate, it seemed, in his eyes."[86] Frightened at his outburst, she was unable to fathom the source of his anger or his resentment against her, until it became clear that his hostility was aimed at the Provincetown Players and that she too was guilty of not understanding what he was about. Nilla, not blessed with much tact, tried to quiet him, at which he grabbed his revolver and set off for Delphi.

This was the last straw for Glaspell, whose nerves were much frayed by Jig's cantankerous behavior. Although in *The Road to the Temple* she denies any serious intention of leaving Cook and joining the Hapgoods and the Steeles in France, she clearly contemplated such a move on more than one occasion. This time, she did write a desperate letter to Hutch and Neith, but before she could take further action, Jig returned in a contrite mood.[87] It was mid-September by then and time to head down, but Jig could not leave his field-jack, which had refused to migrate with the flock. Finally, he constructed a cage and managed to lure the bird into it; he walked down the mountain to Delphi, carrying the cage, so his bird would not be too frightened.

In Delphi, they took the same house they had occupied the previous year, and Glaspell settled in to absorb once again the mythic blessedness of the center of the ancient world. The women she had made friends with welcomed her noisily, inviting her and Nilla to take part in the wine making. Her command of Greek had grown, although she steadfastly refused to study the grammar, arguing that she wanted "to write [only] in the English language." Jig, in one of his expansive, friendly moments, boasted: "She says she doesn't know [Greek], but she understands everything."[88] The Greek village community was, of course, strictly divided by sex; the men were interested in Glaspell, but from afar, and even with perfect knowledge of Greek, she would have found it virtually impossible to establish friendships with them. That was Cook's sphere—the world of the wine shops, the world of men. Glaspell had no household chores since Athanasius and his wife took care of everything for them and did not derive much enjoyment from the company of Delphi wives and mothers once the novelty of the age-old methods of housekeeping wore off. She spent most of her time alone. Nilla was engrossed in her Greek studies—she now had a tutor, a student from the University of Athens—and in her numerous admirers.

"I have my times of something like loneliness, yet even that is not without its interest—rather pleasant to be lonely in Delphi," Glaspell confided to Kenton.[89] After a couple of hours at the typewriter, she would go for a long walk up to the theater through the ruins of the temple and, following the excavated streets of old Delphi, on to the Castalian spring. The burnished quiet of the old stones scattered in the rich vegetation soothed her but frequently induced a depressing intimation of her own insignificance and a need for the reassurance of friends.

Although Glaspell usually did not participate in Cook's activities— scorning the satisfactions of retsina and ouzo, she refused to belong to the "Delphic Players" that he was intent on forming among his rowdy tavern associates—at times she did join in, but not always willingly. On one such occasion, when Athanasius had been unable to lure Cook home for dinner from Andreas's wine shop, she went to get him. Characteristically, in *The Road to the Temple*, she attempts to disguise the pathetic scene with a veneer of mystical grandeur: "The commotion stopped as I stood in the door. 'I've been alone all day, Jig,' I said. 'Won't you come home and keep me company for dinner?' He stood up; he held out his hands, as if realization was growing. 'Why—Susan,' he said. 'It is Susan.' With ceremony and feeling he took my hands. A strangeness about it, and everyone watching."[90] Cook went home with her but refused to eat; he had left good companions at Andreas's who were perhaps hungry. He went back for them, returning with eleven men. Athanasius, who had prepared dinner for three, was faced with the task of dividing the loaves and the fishes. He "shook his head darkly" and advised the Kyria against feeding feckless shepherds.[91]

Elias Scarmouches, who had overseen Cook's acquisition of shepherds' garb (an exploit that Athanasius had also frowned on), convinced his American friend to hold another party—but with more select guests. He supervised the invitation list, while an irate Athanasius worked at the fire. They would have a picnic at the Castalian spring. This time, Glaspell and Nilla went along readily, for they both loved the spot. There was plenty of wine and food, and a fiddler and a piper played for Nilla and the shepherds as they danced in the moonlight. A gay pagan procession marched past the temple, through the cemetery, and into the town that night, with Elias, a step behind the musicians, bearing the lord of the flies: the head of the sacrificed lamb on a pole. The next day, officers arrived from Amphissa to inform the revelers that they had violated martial law. Athenian papers had carried stories of a royalist uprising on Parnassus. Political turmoil seemed so distant from Delphi that no one had imagined that the decree ordaining martial law could apply there; the activities of counterrevolutionaries in Athens bent on overthrowing the government that had forced Constantine to abdicate after the Asia Minor fracas seemed irrelevant to the shepherds. The coup was quickly quelled, and Greece continued its stormy path away from constitutional monarchy. Mussolini's 1923 attack on the Greek islands in the Adriatic also passed unnoticed in Delphi.

Life in Delphi, except for the occasional party, was extremely quiet and routine, and it was this that Glaspell most enjoyed. She would walk down to the Castalian spring to fill containers with the clear water that gushed down the gorge and spend long hours reading or just musing there, sitting in the cavities of the reddish-gray rock face, which secured her in a comforting skein of historical continuity. The ritual of locking up in the evening, when Athanasius handed her the keys and left for the night, fulfilled a deep longing, giving her a sense of satisfaction, "of a household which one keeps safe, that it may move on its destined way."[92] She would chat a moment with Jig and frequently join Nilla on the porch, where they had "some of our best talks . . . —of Greece, of people she knew at home, of the things she wanted to do."[93] No one asked what she was doing or would like to do, but Glaspell was too wrapped up in her charges, husband and stepdaughter, to give much thought to herself. Jig's health was increasingly on her mind; he was tired, haggard, and thin, and she feared dysentery. He drank grossly, but he refused to listen to her remonstrations or even to talk of traveling to Athens to see an American doctor.

Nilla's schooling—or lack of it—was another source of worry. Glaspell had promised Mollie that the girl would go to school, but Cook insisted that she would receive a better education from talking to local shepherds and studying ancient inscriptions. However, he eventually agreed that she should enroll in the American College for Girls in Phaleron.[94] Glaspell accompanied Nilla to the school, stopping in Athens to see to the shopping necessary to set up the new boarder. She took the opportunity to consult an American doctor about Jig's condition and brought back "medicine and a diet."[95] Although she was seriously concerned about Jig's health, she could not bring herself to confide fully in her mother and, writing from Athens, admitted merely that "George is not very well. I feel worried about him—some bowel trouble."[96]

During her absence, the unexpected arrival of two Americans, one of them a reporter after a story, rekindled some of Jig's zest. Whereas Glaspell showed little enthusiasm for his plans to form a theater group in Delphi and revive the Pythian games in the crumbling stadium, these young men applauded wholeheartedly. Glowing with their acclaim, Jig again saw the world as a riot of opportunities. Zanily, he asked Glaspell whether she would prefer to "become co-proprietress of [a] hotel at the Castalian Spring, director of the theater of Delphi and mayoress of the village, or . . . grass-widow of monk in the monastery of Prophet Elijah."[97] But the past continued to torment him, and he inquired of her: "Why, with so much beautiful power, was I nothing? Say exactly in answer if you can. Because you know, best loved of my whole life, these are real questions, such as we would ask from beyond the grave."[98]

Glaspell had no satisfying answer to such questions and was glad when the fond and foolish Bill Rapp announced he would accompany her to Delphi. Rapp's admiration soothed Jig's ego, and the boyish playfulness they indulged in was always calculated to show off Jig's physical prowess. When Rapp left them, Glaspell was downcast; not sure whether she could cope with Jig's moods, she dreaded being alone with him and counted the days until Nilla's return for the winter vacation. Jig's newest mania did nothing to alleviate her depression: he had taken to inspecting the graveyard, learning about burial customs, while she lay in her room nursing a cold she had brought back from Athens alongside poor To-Puppy, who was also coughing.

The ugly little dog they had rescued from the cruelty of the villagers of Agorgiani grew seriously ill; other dogs in Delphi were dying from some mysterious sickness, and To-Puppy, never very strong, had clearly become infected. Caring for him brought Glaspell and Jig closer. He put aside his plans for the Delphic Players and spent more time with her. Christmas passed quietly. Although Greece had officially adopted the Gregorian calendar earlier that year, the villagers could not yet accept celebrating Christmas thirteen days early. Cook and Glaspell complied with the local custom, especially since Nilla would then be with them.

On one of the last days of December, when the wind howled, they recovered their old intimacy. They talked of what they had wanted from life and what they had obtained as if they were "lovers who had been long separated." They accepted that To-Puppy would die, and then Jig asked the dark question that Glaspell would never forget: "We've grown together—way down deep. We are one. How can one of us go and—That *other* one. *What is that other one going to do?*"[99] Jig then gave her instructions for his burial there in Delphi. Refusing to listen, she started to cry, and he could do nothing to comfort her. She was aware of "a strange doom in Jig's blood" and knew she was helpless to combat it.[100]

After To-Puppy died, Jig and Athanasius buried him, and the three sat together, taking small comfort from the griddle cakes they had taught the Greek to make. Glaspell was desolate but more worried than ever about Jig, who clearly had a fever. The next day, the village doctor, braving an unusual snowstorm, pronounced that Cook had the grippe. Jig also had an unexpected visitor: his bird, which had escaped a few weeks previously, returned to the warmth of their home, bringing companionship and reassurance. But when Nilla, accompanied by two teachers, arrived for Christmas, Jig barely had the strength to look up. He was delirious, and when he suffered a bowel hemorrhage, Glaspell lost all faith in the local doctors and wired for the American she had talked to in Athens. After examining Cook, Dr. Marden was evasive in his diagnosis; he suspected typhus and advised them to leave for Athens in the morning, even at the "risk [of] collapse on the way."[101] But by morning, Athens was out of the question; Jig, almost unconscious, was covered in "big purple blotches" and had difficulty breathing. Glaspell would never know how she lived through that week; she could neither sleep nor eat in her effort to keep him in life. But Cook died at midnight, on Wednesday, 14 January 1924.

The villagers insisted that everything be done according to their tradition, which to Glaspell seemed "crude, and very different from our way," although she recognized the love that impelled them.[102] They washed Cook's body in wine, dressed him in his shepherds' garb, and, covering him with the spruce boughs he loved, buried him with the rites of the Greek Orthodox Church. Thus, Jig Cook, the man whose religion was Nietzsche, Zarathustra, and himself, was laid in "the crude little graveyard whose wall is an ancient wall" where Delphi had always buried its dead. At the request of the poets Palamas and Sikelianós, the Greek government gave permission for one of the stones from the Temple of

Apollo to be used as a headstone. Glaspell, who thought the burial ceremonies unseemly, was quite disarmed by this honor. She wrote to her mother: "I had no idea and neither had Jig—how much he was valued in Athens, both among the Greeks and by the Americans here."[103] It was further proposed that Jig's body be moved to one of the ancient tombs of the temple; Glaspell knew he would have liked that, "and somehow it would seem so lasting."[104]

After the funeral, Glaspell and Nilla left Delphi. Nilla returned to school, and the kindly teachers found adequate lodgings for Glaspell nearby. She sat desolately looking "across the Attic plain to the Parthenon" as she gradually acknowledged that "there is no place in the world where I can go and find [Jig]."[105] She dreaded returning to Davenport so broken by death and would gladly have joined the Hapgoods and the Steeles in France. "It would be easier to begin anew there than to return to America without Jig," she wrote to her old friend Lulu Huffaker. But she knew her mother needed her: "What else is there for me to do? Mother does need me—and there are so few reasons for living. . . . I start to do things, then just sit looking at Jig's things."[106] The closeness of Nilla, the daughter she had brought across the ocean to Jig, must have consoled her somewhat. She believed that Nilla had done "so wonderfully" at her Greek that it would be a pity to interrupt her studies, but Mollie insisted on her daughter's prompt return. Although she sympathized with Nilla's bitter disappointment, Glaspell understood the mother's concern; she had come to love Nilla, but she had also observed how headstrong she was—how like her father, in fact. Now that the father was no longer there, she acknowledged that she must relinquish the daughter. However, the bond that had grown between them would never be broken; Nilla would spend many vacations with her in Provincetown, as would her son Sirius, whom Glaspell helped through Harvard.

As Glaspell waited for a ship to take her from Greece, she began to create a mythical Jig. Once Dr. Marden had satisfied her that she was in no danger from the terrible disease, his diagnosis could only help her: alcohol had nothing to do with Jig's death; he had died of the glanders, a disease normally contracted by horses that was only rarely transmitted to dogs and so to humans.[107] (She could hide even from herself the recognition that Cook's destructive drinking would have killed him before long.) Jig Cook, spurned by his fellows in the Provincetown Players, had sacrificed his life caring for a beloved dog. Of course, this theory does not explain why Jig had been losing weight for almost a year, had lost his appetite, and had constantly complained of exhaustion, but Glaspell perceived the mythical viability of such a death. Thus, she could write to her mother and friends with the assurance that no blot would tarnish George Cram Cook's name. She had buried the obstreperous megalomaniac who drank too much and would remember only the man who, some fifteen years previously, had dazzled her with his grasp of the universe and dazed her with his kisses. In what was perhaps a conscious replay of her first novel, *The Glory of the Conquered* (1909), she made it her duty to "make Jig realized by more people" and determined to write "something about him—perhaps a book— . . . a memorial, and I hope to make it the best thing I ever wrote."[108] Her hagiographical study, *The Road to the Temple*, would appear three years later, in 1927.

Hutchins Hapgood, in his autobiography *A Victorian in the Modern World*, was not fooled by either Dr. Marden's diagnosis of glanders or Glaspell's attempts to apotheosize her husband. Discreetly acknowledging Cook's fatal drinking, he wrote: "For Susan Glaspell my respect and admiration grew immensely; it is a difficult position to be the wife of a man who is driven by a daemon, a position from which any mortal woman might, however great her love, shrink in dismay or turn away in weariness; but it was a position which she maintained with a serene and radiant dignity."[109]

Aptly enough, Glaspell arranged for passage to America on the SS *Byron*, departing on 21 February 1924. Before she left Greece, she arranged with Leandrus Palamas for the publication of *The Athenian Women* in a parallel English-Greek edition. C. Carthaios, a young poet, completed the translation Jig had not been able to finish. Eva Sikelianós took upon herself the organization of the Delphic Festival that Cook had conceived in conversation with his friends and eventually pulled it off in May 1927.[110] But Glaspell did not attend the festival. "When I go to Delphi I would rather go alone," she would say, "and find it as much as possible as when we were there."[111]

CHAPTER NINE

Betrayal of Trust

The leaden weeks in Greece before she sailed and the long crossing gave Glaspell time to mourn and to map out a new life for herself. She wrote to Hutchins Hapgood, articulating not only what she thought her life should be from that moment on but also what she expected from Jig's friends: "And you will all help me to come through to the place where I can perhaps make Jig realized by more people, and especially more deeply realized by all of us. And you will all do what you can to keep his memory in the life he loved."[1] She could not foresee that a new amour would distract her from the self-imposed task of finding "the form that will make [Jig's life] count for the most" or that her friends had already forgotten how profoundly her husband had influenced their lives.[2]

Although the previous spring she and Jig had voted for termination of the lease on Macdougal Street, Glaspell knew they had been outvoted and that Kenneth Macgowan, goaded by Eugene O'Neill, planned to resurrect the Provincetown Players. So, willfully misreading Edna Kenton's newsy letters, she counted on a warm welcome, a stage for the plays she would write, and support for her agenda: the mythologizing of George Cram Cook. But when her ship docked in New York on 16 March 1924, she was disappointed on all counts. Kenton plunged her straight into the dispute with the ensemble that, she alleged, was illegally using the name of the Provincetown Players and moreover had delivered itself into the hands of men who had betrayed Cook. And O'Neill—whom Glaspell trusted—was not there to greet her; Kenton derisively attributed his absence to a "sense of guilt over Jig," but according to the ever-placating Fitzi, "Gene was drunk when he was down [in New York]. . . . Not an escape from Susan, but over his work, Edna, over his work."[3] Whatever the reason, he was not there when she needed him most, nor did he make any effort to support her or explain the situation until it was too late.

It was not until May that O'Neill, perhaps spurred on by Agnes Boulton or perhaps simply responding to the old ties that existed between him and Glaspell, eventually got in touch. It was a feeble attempt to explain "that I tried my damnedest to have everything worked out as I knew you and Jig would have wished it. . . . As for Jig—when I heard of his death, Susan, I felt suddenly that I had lost one of the best friends I had ever had or ever would have—unselfish, rare and truly noble! And then when I thought of all the things I hadn't done, the letters I hadn't written, the things I hadn't said, the others I had said and wished unsaid, I felt like a swine, Susan. Whenever I think of him it is with the most self-condemning remorse. It made me afraid to face you in New York." Seeking to exonerate himself, he assured her that a memorial tablet for Jig would be placed in the theater and ended with a stark request for absolution, ruined by a piqued inversion of responsibility: "This is a frightfully poor attempt at writing what I want to say to you. Forgive it. I wish you could have come out to see us here. Why didn't you? It made us feel you didn't want to see us."[4]

Guided by her maternal feelings toward O'Neill, Glaspell accepted this apology for his silence and extended it to his intrigues.[5] As befits a mother, she refused to lose faith in O'Neill and now turned to him and Boulton, hoping they would contribute to a collection of memoirs on Cook. O'Neill replied that both he and Agnes would do so gladly (though their pieces never materialized) and that they hoped to see much of her in Provincetown. He said her letter had made them "feel close" to her and assured her: "We love you very much, Susan."[6] But Glaspell spent most of the summer in Truro, and although Boulton visited her a number of times, O'Neill only saw her once.[7]

In the same letter, O'Neill informed Glaspell of what she already knew from Kenton: Macgowan had successfully transformed the Provincetown Players Inc. from a membership to a stock company; he had then "sold" the Players' assets to a newly formed group, which took the name of the Experimental Theater Inc. This group was to perform at the Provincetown Playhouse. Neither Kenton nor Glaspell's objections to this de facto appropriation of the Provincetown name served any purpose except to embitter relations with Macgowan. Finally, Jimmy Light and Stark Young, at Macgowan's insistence, were incorporated in this "new" venture, which had mobilized to exploit the old name and prestige. Macgowan, O'Neill, and Robert Edmond Jones made up the "Triumvirate" that was to rule the new players.

The whole "slimy" business was made intolerable for Glaspell and Kenton by Light's continued presence in the group.[8] But the final straw for Glaspell was Macgowan's brazen demand that Kenton forego all of her rights in the new stock company. At this, Glaspell wrote an indignant open letter to Fitzi, reminding her of Kenton's dedication to the Players, her tireless playreading, and her loyalty to Cook's ideal. Exasperated by the Players' continued disdain for a past she held sacred, she signed off: "Fitzie, and all of you, for this letter is for all of you, from very deep down, I am through."[9]

Although Macgowan managed to appropriate the Provincetown name, he lost Glaspell. Astutely recognizing in her a useful link to the past—if nothing more, an invaluable bait for old subscribers—he had wanted an option on her work.[10] Glaspell had looked forward to supplying a new theatrical ensemble with plays; she had even had in mind a play about Cook that would honor his name and memory. But she did not feel she could work with those who did not value the ideals and the achievement of their leader. For lack of a reverential stage, she severed all relations with the new Players and decided instead to publish Jig's writings. Macgowan's open-armed acceptance of Light and his virulent rejection of Kenton wounded her more than the quibble over the Provincetown name. Assuring Kenton that Cook would have wanted the theater itself to continue as the Provincetown Playhouse, she agreed with O'Neill that it was in itself a monument to its founder.[11]

After spending a few cold, dreary weeks in Davenport with her mother, Glaspell, accompanied by Lulu Huffaker, retired to Provincetown to wait for the summer. Her first task, once safely ensconced in the little house on Commercial Street, was to go through Cook's papers. At this time, the long "musical table" acquired a new function. It had sagged under the weight of bowls of punch and had listened unperturbed as Cook and his followers took the American drama in hand. Now it held his flourishes and squiggles and all of the scraps on which diligent, industrious penmanship disintegrated into a sprawling cacography—a reflection of his struggle to transcend known boundaries. Although Glaspell spent hours reading, annotating, construing, and sorting, she found it impossible to structure her husband's thoughts into a coherent shape suitable for distribution to the general public.

But Glaspell did find enough poems for a collection and, trusting to old ties, asked Floyd Dell to advise her on publication. Kenton and Dell both contributed pieces on Cook,[12] and Glaspell added an account of the two years in Greece. Using the three memoirs as an introduction to the poems, she offered the volume to George H. Doran of New York. *Greek Coins*, by George Cram Cook, appeared in late 1925.[13]

While piecing together the edition of Cook's poems, Glaspell continued her struggle with his biography.[14] Her sudden intense involvement with Norman Matson, a younger writer, made the task more pressing and much more tortuous. In her mind, she had created for Cook the legend of a prophet unknown to his community and had cast herself as the widow who, having sustained him in life, would foster his memory after death. For a time, there seemed to be no way for her to deal with the loss of faith that her precipitate relationship with Matson implied.

Norman Matson was in Mary Heaton Vorse's entourage in Provincetown in the summer of 1924. A handsome, promising writer, still mourning the recent death in childbirth of his companion, Matson was certainly not denied female company. But he was particularly attracted to Glaspell; her slender, grief-stricken figure and sad hazel eyes, coupled with her fame as a playwright and her natural desire to help any young man who showed a spark of literary ambition, drew him to her. Once again, Glaspell's maternal instincts were awoken, but more than mothering was involved. During the last years, Cook's drinking had attenuated his virility, and now Glaspell found herself desired by, and desiring, a neatly bearded young fellow with dazzling blue eyes who promised abandonment and joy. Glaspell gave in, and Matson, otherwise homeless, moved into the cottage that Cook had so lovingly made comfortable for her.

Biography could not countenance such betrayal.[15] Eventually, after burning at least one draft of the manuscript of Cook's life, Glaspell solved the problem by erasing her grief and her guilt from the text, enabling Cook's voice, which she quoted from the turgid jottings of his life, to dominate.[16] Thus, in *The Road to the Temple*, she is the silent companion, the ideal wife dedicated to her oracle. Composing *The Road to the Temple* gave her an opportunity to deconstruct her dilemmas with Jig, order her feelings, and absolve herself of her supposed deficiencies with regard to him. An indication of the extent to which she refashioned herself to fit the myth she created can be found in these words to Matson:

Norman Matson
(Courtesy of the Berg Collection of English and American Literature,
New York Public Library, Astor, Lenox, and Tilden Foundations)

"I have concealed [*The Road to the Temple*] from my mother. She is so frail and nervous, I hate to have her read the things I say about myself."[17]

Glaspell had initially intended to write only about Cook's Greek exploits, but as she noted to Kenton, "Greece begins in Iowa."[18] Relying on memory, family lore, and Jig's own scrappy notes, she remade his life into a pilgrimage to Greece, where the simple shepherds recognize the godliness that sophisticated New Yorkers had scorned.[19] The effect is a hagiography that today's reader dismisses as pathetically romantic and that, when published, did little to establish Cook's place in the history of American drama.[20] The few chapters (less than a tenth of the book) dedicated to the Provincetown Players give no sense of Cook's achievement, nor do they satisfactorily explain his departure for Greece. Upton Sinclair's conclusion was utterly damning: after reading Glaspell's "pious tribute," he concluded "that Jig cast in his poetical fortunes with Bacchus, and prohibition had made these rites too expensive in America."[21] Glaspell tied her own hands when she accepted the principles by which Cook had insisted they act in 1922 when Light's machinations had been made known to them.[22] So, for all her devotion, she gives the reader a strong impression that Cook was peeved by the Provincetown Players' failure to acknowledge his creative and directorial achievements.

But not all readers were as cynical as Upton Sinclair. J. B. Priestley, noting the unusual biographical structure of *The Road to the Temple*, concluded that "the result is a disjointed, jerky, frequently annoying record, which is, however, extremely vivid and lifelike."[23] And the young May Sarton enthusiastically recorded in her journal in 1928: "I am reading Susan Glaspell's *The Road to the Temple*. It is too unpruned to be art, but it's great as a chunk of life. The more I read biography, the more I love it."[24]

Thus, a history of the Provincetown Players was still to be written. Kenton, who was not as intimately involved as Glaspell, clung tenaciously to her faith in Cook's vision of a truly American theater. She alone, perceiving the significance of placing his Players on a wider stage, searched for a way to turn Macgowan's annexation of their name to the greater glory of George Cram Cook: "The longer I have thought this out the clearer it has become. [The use of the name of] the Provincetown Playhouse will make for confusion and exploitation . . . *until the history of the Provincetown Players and the history of Jig is written*. Then the ambiguous name becomes the line of cleavage . . . the precise point at which the Provincetown Players ended their career."[25] When in 1928 Fitzi and Light, who had taken the theater over from Macgowan's Triumvirate, tried to publish a leaflet on the history of the Provincetown Players, Kenton dashed off her own spirited account.[26] She turned to Glaspell for help in finding a publisher, convinced that her book would stop "these people . . . exploiting the whole adventure."[27] Although she abandoned the idea, the history is now available in the *Eugene O'Neill Review*.

But Fitzi went ahead with her project.[28] She enraged Glaspell when she invited her to contribute a brief statement to what she declared would be an account of "the fourteen years of our existence." Fitzi was stupidly unaware that her letter was a conglomerate of insults to Glaspell's sensibilities. The letterhead did not mention the Experimental Theater; instead, "Provincetown Playhouse" dominated the sheet. Light figured at the head of the executive staff, and Glaspell, cofounder of the Provincetown Players, was lumped together with "friends and former members." She was given two weeks to submit her piece, for the leaflet was about to go into print, thus suggesting that she had been added as an afterthought to a list of possible contributors.[29] Glaspell, "hating to take up that old fight," replied tersely: "I cannot write the article you suggest."[30] Giving further proof of insensitivity, Fitzi and the new board of directors insisted that they were an "offshoot of the group that disbanded in 1924" and thus had the right to use the name of the Provincetown Players, but at the same time, they speciously asserted that they did not in fact use the name.[31] Glaspell controlled her irritation and, recognizing that further correspondence would achieve nothing, laid the matter to rest.

The usurpers disbanded a few months later, in December 1929, and in 1931, two of their number, Helen Deutsch and Stella Hanau, published *The Provincetown: A Story of the Theatre*. A photograph of George Cram Cook on the frontispiece appeased Glaspell, and Macgowan's introduction, in which he apologizes for his part in the confusion of the past, vindicated Kenton's stand on the matter of the name:

> I remember the irritation I felt when Jig Cook and Susan Glaspell and Edna Kenton refused to let us continue the name of the Provincetown Players, and the pleasure we all took in seeing the public ignore their wishes. Yet now I know that the three were right, and I understand why the later attempt of Fitzi and Jimmy Light to return to first principles was doomed. . . . The heart of the Provincetown Players was the spirit which Jig Cook felt in his friends as well as in himself, and which he nourished and dramatized. The secret of their success was that they gave no thought to success. The secret of their failure—or rather their fulfillment—was again their success.[32]

But continuity is implicit in this history, and Cook emerges as nothing more than a quixotic dreamer who trusted in his power to "cross visions with facts" and so "breed miracles."[33] But at last, Cook's spirit was recognized as the force that held the early adventurers together. The same volume consistently ignored Glaspell's part in the success of the Provincetown Players. It was left to her friend Mary Heaton Vorse, writing her memoir *Time and the Town* in 1942, to turn the spotlight on her, if only summarily: "Not enough has been said about Susan Glaspell and her quality of enthusiasm. . . . The plays she contributed were all based upon an understanding of the life of the country—some witty, some ironical, some tragic. Nor without her would George Cram Cook's intensive work in the theatre have been possible. Her constant encouragement and her humor as well as her irony were the things which nourished him and made his never-ending tasks possible."[34]

In the summer of 1924, just months after returning from Greece, Glaspell and Norman Matson became lovers. They never took formal wedding vows, but they certainly considered themselves married until Matson chose to end the relationship in 1932. Born in 1893 of Norwegian immigrants, the thirty-one-year-old Matson was seventeen years younger than Glaspell. Good features and relative youth made him arrogant, and, proud of his virile figure, he thought nothing of deprecating Glaspell's older friends. Hutchins Hapgood's autobiographical *The Story of a Lover* elicited the swaggering comment: "He writes with his feet and his elbows—what a dreadful fellow he is! . . . How does a Socialist-journalist with a protruding stomach make love?"[35] Nonetheless, he welcomed Glaspell's efforts to promote his novels through old connections. She sent the manuscript of his autobiographical *Day of Fortune* to Victor Gollancz, then her British editor, and when the book was published in America, she had complimentary copies despatched to Sherwood Anderson and Theodore Dreiser, praising it as "indeed an American novel."[36]

Eager to help him toward success, Glaspell wrote a play, *The Comic Artist* (1927), with Matson. Since it was conceived and written mostly by him, however, its publication on both sides of the Atlantic passed unnoticed, as did the eventual stage productions.[37] This play, in which passion and ambition contrive to ruin the lives of two brothers, lacks the clear thought that characterizes Glaspell's work, and the hallmark of her writing, the determined woman who consciously molds her own life, is absent.

Susan Glaspell
(Courtesy of the Berg Collection of English and American Literature,
New York Public Library, Astor, Lenox, and Tilden Foundations)

But her ardor for Matson did inspire Glaspell to write *Brook Evans*, a novel that settled comfortably into second place on the *New York Herald Tribune* best-seller list in August 1928 and sold more copies than any of her previous works.[38] In England, her plays had been published by Ernest Benn, an extension of the trade journal firm, Benn Brothers. Victor Gollancz was responsible for the new, hugely successful imprint, and in 1927, he formed his own company, making "every possible effort to get anyone I want away from [Benn]," as he boasted self-righteously to one author.[39] His letters to Glaspell, full of admiration for her work, easily convinced her to offer him *Brook Evans*, which became the first novel to be published in Gollancz's distinctive yellow cover on 19 April

1928. The terms of the contract were excellent: Gollancz increased his initial advance of £125 to £400, thus buying out the serial rights that Stokes in New York had been anxious to acquire.[40] He also insisted on publishing in advance of Stokes so that the novel would indeed be the first on his list. To Glaspell's delight, by 10 April, he had already sold 5,000 copies by subscription.[41] The excellent sales, both in America and England, led Paramount Pictures to film the novel, changing the title to *The Right to Love*.[42]

Glaspell had asked Gollancz not to forget that *Brook Evans* should be dedicated to Matson, the model for the lover from Iceland who teaches Brook the value of sensual love.[43] Although the novel argues that no person can be complete without love—a theme that runs through Glaspell's fiction—it also broaches an emotional minefield she had so far avoided: the relationship between mother and daughter. As a review of *Brook Evans* in *Oxford Magazine* correctly recognized, "It penetrates so deeply into the thing that is so casually and so truly supposed to be woman's function in life—motherhood—that nobody having read it can think quite so casually of that function again."[44]

As the novel opens, Naomi, bound by the intensity of first love, conceives a child, but before she can marry Joe, a threshing machine maws him to pieces. Rather than bear the shame of having an illegitimate grandchild, her parents marry her off to Caleb Evans, a good but dour man who has just bought land in Colorado. Although Caleb, the suitor she had previously rejected, treats the baby Brook as his own child, Naomi can never reward him with anything more than sullen acquiescence. As Brook grows older, her stepfather's puritan disapproval of larks and laughter outlaws her love for Tony, a Catholic neighbor. But Naomi, vicariously reliving her own blighted passion, arranges for the couple to meet. Brook, mistakenly attributing the reunion to Tony's desire, agrees to accompany him to California, although she is fully aware that her mother will miss her and Caleb will be pained. When Tony confesses her mother's part in his plans, she is so hurt by such unwarranted meddling that she only wants to "punish, defeat her mother, even though it took her own love."[45] Abandoning the luckless Tony, she joins a missionary friend on her way to Turkey. When we next see Brook, she is in Paris, the widow of an English captain killed in the war, and is planning to marry an elderly friend of her dead husband, the staid Colonel Fowler. She then meets ardent Erik Helge from Iceland and is carried away by his candescent blue eyes and fiery words. She finally understands why her mother had tried to push her into Tony's arms so many years before and can now resolve the exasperation her mother's tense, excessive love had always provoked.

Glaspell, recognizing that her success had helped make up for so many frustrations in Alice Keating Glaspell's life, poured into this novel the conflict with her mother that she had always stifled. She now acknowledged that her mother's vicarious life had shamed and pained her, even as it impelled her into the wider world. Poor Alice, who had taken such inordinate pride in her daughter's early literary achievements, now identified with Naomi, the wicked mother—according to traditional moral codes—and was offended by *Brook Evans*. She expressed her hurt in a letter to her daughter but then apologized: "I did not realize the story and after I read the different reviews I thot [*sic*] differently."[46] Alice never met her second son-in-law, Norman Matson; for some reason, perhaps blushing at his youth, Glaspell had not brought them together. He never accompanied her on the Christmas trips to Davenport and tactfully addressed his letters to "Mrs. Matson."

The chief criticism leveled at *Brook Evans* is that the last section of the novel, which discusses Brook's son's reaction to her sudden marriage to Erik Helge, is somewhat redundant. Evans, at eighteen, returns to America to the farm where Naomi's family still resides, and by the brook where his mother was conceived, he comes to accept the fact that she has deserted him for love. But Victor Gollancz found this return to the beginning or "reconciliation," as he termed it, reminiscent of a "symphony." For him, the novel was "technically . . . remarkable" and the construction "nearly perfect."[47] After publication, he sent Glaspell extracts from the reviews, commenting wryly: "This will rather interest you: that women as a whole both like and understand the book far more than do men. . . . The general view undoubtedly is that the novel, great in its earlier pages, falls off at the end, but that is not my view. I think the critics who take this line have misunderstood the basic conception."[48] Perhaps if Glaspell had written more consciously of mother-daughter relationships, she would have avoided the final coda that disgruntled the critics or she might well have created a daughter rather than a son for Brook. Nonetheless, in this novel, women and their feelings are at the center, and the given role of a mother—to prepare a virgin bride for her future master—is brutally brushed aside. No wonder Alice Keating Glaspell flinched when she read it.

The slopes of Mount Parnassus had been beneficial for all of the ailments that plagued Glaspell during her marriage to Cook, and most important, she lost her fear of heart problems and grew stronger. But now, in her fifties, her teeth and bladder were giving her trouble. On her way to Davenport, still favoring Chicago doctors, she would visit her brother Ray and submit to the manipulations of dentists and other practitioners. Her mother's health also gave her cause for worry: in December 1928, Alice Keating Glaspell, now senile, failed to recognize her daughter.[49] Glaspell returned to Provincetown after Christmas knowing she could do nothing. On 15 February, a telegram alerted her that her mother was much worse, and two days later, Ray cabled that she had died painlessly. Glaspell did not go to Davenport for the funeral; Ray and Frank, aware of her frail health, excused her, "for . . . Susie is always worse than she says."[50]

During the rest of 1929, still smarting from her mother's censure of *Brook Evans*, Glaspell struggled to justify her love life in a new play, *Alison's House*, which she submitted to the Theatre Guild. History repeated itself when the Guild returned the play, echoing the 1915 rejection of *Suppressed Desires* by its parent company, the Washington Square Players.[51] But this time, there was no Jig Cook to conjure up a company to produce her work. However, in spite of the fracas with the successors of the Provincetown Players, Glaspell had not lost touch with other theatrical contacts, and she offered *Alison's House* to Eva Le Gallienne, director of the Civic Repertory Theatre. The two women had struck up a firm friendship following the Civic Repertory production of *Inheritors* in 1926. Glaspell admired Le Gallienne's determination "to create a theatre for the service of the People" and recognized in her work a continuation of Cook's spirit.[52] Le Gallienne, drawn by the quiet realism of *Alison's House*, put the play into rehearsal; she would play the role of the protagonist, Elsa, herself.

In spite of the difficulties in finding a theater for *Alison's House*, the play won the 1931 Pulitzer Prize for drama. Although most critics, quite understandably, did not read the play "as a woman" would and thus distorted its meaning, Glaspell still exulted over the award.[53] She wished Cook—and O'Neill, whose Pulitzers for *Beyond the Horizon* and *Anna Christie* had aroused carefully hidden twinges of jealousy—could celebrate with her. When Lee Shubert, who controlled the greatest commercial theater empire New York had ever known, offered to move *Alison's House* to the Ritz Theatre, Glaspell could at last forget the cruel disappointment inflicted by Broadway's indifference to *Chains of Dew*. She rejoiced that all of her rebellions and her earlier bid to move away from the limited Provincetown stage had been vindicated.[54] If her parents had still been alive, they might now accept that she had refused to become Davenport's second Alice French and even understand her determination to marry Cook, as well as her attachment to Matson.

Alison's House is best interpreted as a personal expression of a dilemma that Glaspell had not quite worked out of her system with the writing of *Fidelity* (1915): once again, she attempts to justify her marriage to Cook, which broke up his family unit, and argues that love is all-important in a woman's life.[55] But in the words of a diffident critic, the play was "based, so rumor has it, on certain incidents in [Emily Dickinson's] life."[56] Such reports were all the more credible because certain aspects of *Alison's House* are clearly reminiscent of Dickinson's life: the character Alison Stanhope, who died eighteen years before the play opens, physically resembled Dickinson and always wore white.[57] Her poetry, not published during her lifetime, was written on scraps of paper sewn together and zealously guarded by her sister Agatha, who discloses, as she dies in act 2, a portfolio of passionate love poems that the family members fight over in act 3. And three members of the family have known adulterous passion, thus echoing Dickinson's supposedly unconsummated love and the Austin Dickinson and Mabel Loomis Todd affair. As if ratifying the rumors, *Alison's House* opened at the Civic Repertory Theatre on 1 December 1930, coinciding almost exactly with the centenary of Dickinson's birth. However, literary history has insisted on interpreting the play as an account of Dickinson's life that the literary estate of the poet forced the author to modify, but no documents support the case, although other writers were indeed forbidden to quote from Dickinson's published poems and letters.[58]

Klaus Lubbers contends that *Alison's House* was "stimulated by the Dickinson criticism of that year," but even his bland statement is inaccurate. Glaspell had not been stimulated by the "criticism of that year" for the simple reason that her play was written *before* that year.[59] In April 1930, she wrote to Barrett Clark (an old friend from the Provincetown days and biographer of O'Neill) confessing her disappointment at the Theatre Guild's rejection of *Alison's House* and considering the effect of publishing the play before it reached the stage. She wrote: "Of course I would love to see it as a book, but hesitate a little, wondering whether publication before production is good for the play's chances."[60] Quite clearly, if in April the play had already been rejected by a theater and been considered for publication, it must have been completed sometime before.

According to the rumors that Glaspell had fashioned her play around the life of Dickinson, she had been obliged to change the locale and the name by the Dickinson family.[61] However, Dickinson's niece Martha Dickinson Bianchi wrote to her Houghton Mifflin editor on 20 October 1930, saying, very much in passing, "I hear reports of a play built around her [Emily Dickinson] which is to be produced in New York (so I am told)."[62] Bianchi does not appear to be angry or perturbed, and there is no evidence that she took action to stop the play. The date of the letter, especially when we consider that in April Glaspell was writing to Barrett Clark about a play entitled *Alison's House*, makes it impossible to argue that she *changed* the name and the location because of a direct prohibition issued by Bianchi.

Glaspell must have come to Dickinson quite independently of the critical flurry of 1930. She had long admired the Amherst poet; in a scene of poignant irony, when success and failure are rubbing shoulders in *The Glory of the Conquered* (1909), the protagonist quotes "a little poem" beginning, "Success is counted sweetest."[63] Clearly the verses had made a mark on Glaspell; she would have read them in *A Masque of Poets*, an 1878 collection of anonymous poems published in the No Name Series by T. Niles. "Success is counted sweetest" had generally been attributed to Ralph Waldo Emerson: the world had not yet heard of Emily Dickinson. But by the late 1920s, Dickinson and her presumed love affair had become the property of all. In *The Life and Letters of Emily Dickinson* (1924), Martha Dickinson Bianchi affirmed that "there is no doubt that two predestined souls were kept apart only by her high sense of duty, and the necessity for preserving love untarnished by the inevitable destruction of another woman's life."[64]

Already won over by Dickinson's poetry, Glaspell now experienced a more personal bond: she identified with the poet, seeing in her a victim of society's stranglehold on women. But whereas Dickinson had purportedly submitted to the strict codes of acceptable behavior, Glaspell rebelled. A New Woman empowered by love, she dared to take Cook from Mollie Price and gave little thought to the scandalmongers of Davenport. To all appearances, Glaspell had assimilated—and atoned for—this sin, but adulterous love and its consequences still haunted her. Thus, the secret in Dickinson's life "possessed" her. As Mary Heaton Vorse was to write: "Seeing Susan in those days when she was first plunging her mind into Emily Dickinson's story was seeing a creative force at work."[65]

For all of her political activism, Vorse did not forget her friends and must have shared with Glaspell an interview she gave to poet and critic Genevieve Taggard. Taggard, who was then writing a biography of Dickinson, hoped that Vorse, whose childhood had been spent in Amherst, would be able to reveal the secret of the poet's forbidden love. Taggard refused to accept Bianchi's insinuation that Dickinson had loved a married man, stating categorically that "Emily would never have allowed herself to fall more than a little in love with an already married man. Her spirit was fastidious; she was incapable of such treachery against the kind of love she was for ever glorifying for all her married friends."[66] When Vorse reported this to Glaspell, she gave her yet another reason for writing *Alison's House*: the need to show Taggard, and other like-minded prudes, that adulterous and unmarried love can also be sacred.

Glaspell had always grasped the didactic possibilities inherent in the theater; she understood that a skillfully developed idea could excite an audience and lead to public discussion of the evils that plague society. The Pulitzer Prize committee recognized this when it selected *Alison's House* as "the American play . . . best represent[ing] the educational value and power of the stage."[67] Glaspell saw in Dickinson's life the ideal vehicle for the heightened expression of the dilemma she had presented in so much of her writing: the conflict that inevitably arises when an individual has to choose between private and public good and the inexorable outcome in which the woman is the victim. In *Alison's House*, which takes place on the last day of the nineteenth century, she creates a foil to the Dickinson character: a younger woman, the poet's niece Elsa, who, in a replay of Glaspell's earlier novel *Fidelity*, had eloped with a married man. The newly discovered cache of Alison's poems allows the family to understand Elsa and to accept her back into their midst. Critics, reading Dickinson into the play, construed it as arguing for the public character of an artist's work; they did not acknowledge, or maybe dismissed as too trivial, Glaspell's preoccupation with the right to love.

In both *Trifles* and *Bernice*, Glaspell had drawn attention successfully to her protagonists' fate by resorting to the patriarchal strategy of denying a woman's presence, but in this play, it is not the long-buried Alison Stanhope but her niece Elsa who holds our attention and sympathy. Eventually, as the clocks chime in the New Year, signaling a new century, Elsa's father relinquishes the package of poems to Elsa, accepting that Alison "said it—for women" and thus giving his sister to the world, recovering his daughter, and embracing the new order of the twentieth century, which affirms the individual's right to self-fulfillment.[68]

Away from the experimental aura of the Provincetown Players and consumed by the urge to affirm the power of love and thereby vindicate her own marriage—and her relationship with Matson—Glaspell was content to express a family drama in realistic, Chekhovian terms. According to a reviewer in the *Los Angeles Times*, the play is "a drama of intense realism, a realism which somehow exudes the spirit of a real America, an America which still bears herself with dignity and reverence."[69] As in *Inheritors*, she had indeed captured a facet of America and its changing values, but the intensity is based more on her passionate involvement with her characters' dilemmas than on the realism with which they are portrayed.

As in all of Glaspell's plays, there is more talk than action, and most critics disapproved of this imbalance.[70] However, the characters are more in control of what they say than in any of her earlier plays. They do not fumble for words or fall into the patterned rhythms of poetry; they are confident, self-assured people who established their place in the family and society long before the play began. Doubt and hesitation are, of course, reflected in their speech patterns, but the characters are fully articulate, and any variation in their speech is a response to the plot and not a quest for new forms of expression, as was the case with Claire Archer in *The Verge*.

Glaspell knew that the raw impulses of humankind frequently have to be restrained and would gladly have retained some of the Victorian veneer of respectability even while insisting on a woman's right to love and happiness. Although she was obviously sympathetic to Elsa's predicament—which was, after all, her own—Glaspell's ambivalence toward the new morality runs through *Alison's House*. It allowed Richard Dana Skinner, writing for *Commonweal*, to uphold "the central idea" of the play, which he vexatiously summarized as "a ringing and revolutionary challenge to all the Narcissistic self-worship, all the irresponsibility, all the stupendous egotism and all the unchained eroticism which modern life has set up as its all too easily achieved ideal."[71] Such a resounding condemnation of Elsa's "irresponsible" act must have felt like a personal indictment to Glaspell, but it is also a measure of Skinner's inability to interpret the play, which, for all of Glaspell's distrust of twentieth-century crassness, does finally come down on Elsa's side—on the side of the woman and love. Richard Lockridge of the *New York Sun*, although he did not fully identify the conflict, showed himself to be more sensitive than Skinner when he recognized that Glaspell had found "in the struggle between centuries, between ideals . . . the material for . . . clear and moving drama."[72]

The excellent sales of *Brook Evans*, followed by the $1,000 Pulitzer Prize, gave a huge boost to Glaspell's finances. At a time when even Greenwich Village bohemians were beginning to feel the Depression and practiced hoboes such as Harry Kemp were becoming desperate, she was planning to travel abroad. A delightful trip with Matson to Norway and France in 1925 had helped Glaspell forget the nightmare of chasing after Cook in foreign cities, and in the spring of 1932, fortified by prosperity and the illusion of love, she set off with her companion for Mexico. Before leaving, Glaspell had mailed Gollancz the manuscript of her next novel, *Ambrose Holt and Family*, which had "absolutely delighted" him.[73] A variation on the plot of *Chains of Dew*, this novel returns to the theme of the pretty wife who is trapped in a marriage to a somewhat worthless writer. In order to make him happy, she must surrender her hopes of becoming a complete human being. The earlier play had undoubtedly arisen from her life with Cook, but she possibly rewrote it as a novel to stifle doubts regarding her present situation with Matson. Their relationship, suffering from her triumphs and his miffed male vanity, was becoming more and more tense, even though (with some help from her) between 1926 and 1930 he had published a novel or play every year.[74]

Thanks to Victor Gollancz, the British were now reading Glaspell's novels and discussing her plays, which avant-garde groups such as the Pioneer Players, the People's National Theatre, the Gate Theatre, and the Lena Ashton Players had performed in London throughout the 1920s. The Liverpool Repertory Theatre had produced *Inheritors* and *Alison's House*, and the Cambridge Festival Theatre, having staged *Woman's Honor* and *Inheritors*, was to perform *Alison's House* in early 1932. English audiences did not object to the "talky" quality of Glaspell's plays that certain American critics had found tiresome. J. K. Prothero, in a review of the 1925 London production of *The Verge*, had claimed: "The success of Shaw at the Chelsea Palace has demonstrated the possibilities of the

Susan Glaspell, circa 1930
(Courtesy of the Museum of the City of New York)

drama of ideas and there is little doubt in my mind that as keen and as paying an audience would be found for Susan Glaspell as for G.B.S."[75] Prothero was not the only critic so taken with Glaspell. Herbert Farjeon of the *Westminster Weekly*, writing in his column "Odds and Ends" after the British publication of her plays, enthused that "Susan Glaspell, an American playwright, [is] immeasurably superior to all other American playwrights, and perhaps superior to any playwright alive."[76]

Encouraged by such reviews and drawn by the magnet of the world's cultural capital, Glaspell convinced Matson in the autumn of 1931 to travel to England with her and spend the winter in London. Leaving her house to Edmund Wilson, an accredited Provincetown habitué, she rented the novelist Richard Hughes's house at 21 Lloyd Square, about half a mile from King's Cross. Sheltered from the hubbub and fog of London, she wrote easily all morning and thus doubly enjoyed spending an evening at the theater or an afternoon wandering through museums and galleries.

The London literary world lionized her. She was not the brash, loud American everyone feared; precise, yet gentle and sensitive, almost waif-ishly slender and sporting a stylish "wind-blown" haircut, she appealed to all. The London *Times* reported on 18 December that Mrs. Gollancz was "at home on Wednesday afternoon" to receive Glaspell; other guests included novelists Rose Macaulay and Elizabeth Bowen.[77] Mr. Ould of PEN was anxious to have Glaspell grace official dinners, and the American Woman's Club honored her "as one of America's outstanding women writers" at a reception held on 20 January 1932.[78] Luminaries of the theater world were invited to give speeches; Eva Le Gallienne, Nancy Price (founder of the People's National Theatre), and Edith Craig ex-tolled Glaspell's plays, and Glaspell offered a "modest account" of her part in the founding of the Provincetown Players.

The People's National Theatre, about to put *Trifles* into rehearsal, asked Glaspell to act in the play. Although she assured everyone that she was no actress, Glaspell was sufficiently flattered to accept the role she had created in Provincetown sixteen years previously. As a foreigner, however, she needed Home Office approval to act in Great Britain, but this took so long that when permission was finally granted, a British actress had already started rehearsing, and Glaspell, secretly relieved, refused to take the part from her. But she was tickled by the sensational headlines that appeared in the New York, Davenport, and Des Moines papers, in which the insignificant episode erupted into an international scandal.[79] Most accounts mentioned, but only in passing, that her husband accompanied her, thus exacerbating Matson's resentment at being merely a sleeping partner.

Matson yearned for the more arty ambience of Paris, so Glaspell gave in and the couple flew to France on 27 February. This was Glaspell's first flight; although she was eager for the experience, she was "holding [her] breath" in anticipation hours before.[80] In Paris, roving Americans quickly drew them into their Depression-diminished circle, which nonetheless still contained many old comrades. Among these was Anna Strunsky Walling, "one of the most consistent and sincere socialists of America," who was chaperoning her nineteen-year-old daughter, Anna, a student at the Sorbonne.[81] The Wallings had been among the earliest Greenwich

Villagers, and although they were not active members of the Province-town Players, they had faithfully supported the venture from the dreadful seats of the little auditorium.

After some weeks, unable to write in a hotel room, Glaspell decided to return to America; she sailed with Anna in May, but Matson, wholly absorbed in the charms of Paris, insisted on remaining behind. The younger Anna Walling, quite happy to exchange her duenna mother for the worldly gentleman friend, also stayed on. It is impossible to tell whether Glaspell suspected a rival in the younger Anna, but when Matson rejoined her in Provincetown that summer, she soon realized that she had lost her lover. She was hurt because he no longer desired her, and she could not countenance his shallowness when he declared that his affair with Anna was just a passing whimsy. Leaving him in her Province-town cottage, she sought solace in Boston and Maine.

Matson's callousness amazed Glaspell. She suffered almost more for Anna's sake than for her own when he wrote: "That life flows into me from her you know. It doesn't change, doesn't need to change the you-and-me at all. Why should it? Even if it shipwrecks her—it's her choice."[82] He wanted sex with Anna but insisted this relationship would not affect his love for Glaspell. No self-respecting woman could accept such an in-sult, and Glaspell was adamant: "You say life flows into you through her. Then you must have her."[83] The situation was complicated—as Glaspell had suspected it soon would be—by Anna's pregnancy. Glaspell insisted she would do whatever was necessary and urged against an abortion. It was then that Matson showed his true colors: he left Provincetown for New York, taking with him $600 from Glaspell's account, only to start showering her with complaints about his miserable new life. He nonsen-sically demanded a divorce and then thanked fate that they had never been legally married since he realized what a divorce would cost. His let-ters imply that she should shoulder all expenses, that she should, in fact, continue to support him financially. Bitterly resenting the eight years he had spent with her, he complained that the friends he had once merrily mocked had now turned against him: "You must one day try to see my life as it was for me. It was Susan's house, Susan's Cape; and—really—Susan's friends. When, as I've told you before, I about got an assignment from *Cosmo*, the managing editor said, 'Good idea: but get *her* to do it. He's nobody.' So now 'my friends'—but they were yours all the time: every-thing was yours, the houses, the writing, the money-making, the success, the friends. That was my fault, no doubt. But a man's not a woman. Our generation sometimes lost sight of that fact." His feminism, just like Hutchins Hapgood's, was not up to the task of dealing with an emancipated woman; nor was he above directing cruel digs at the woman he had loved: "You'll be back at work soon. Why not a short story at first? And—if you haven't—go on the wagon, just for the sensation. . . . You have the Cape, your friends, your house—and—your great gift for writing."[84]

To find one's world suddenly empty is heartrending; to be rejected for a nineteen-year-old when approaching sixty is a grievous blow to a woman's pride. But Glaspell was totally selfless when she assured Anna Strunsky Walling that Matson would be good to her daughter. She appealed to her not to forget the close friendship that had grown between them during the crossing of the Atlantic. "As I grow older I think friendship between women is a thing to cherish," she wrote.[85] Such friendships never figured largely in her writing, and in her life, except for Lulu Huffaker, whom she had known since adolescence, there were no significant women. Neith Boyce and Mary Heaton Vorse, circumscribed by their own family problems, never had the time for real intimacy with other women. Agnes Boulton had, for a time, provided companionship and the warmth of new motherhood, but she was younger and she was Eugene O'Neill's wife. Matson entered Glaspell's life at a time when she desperately needed to be valued, and in 1932, even as he was destroying the stability he had helped create in her life, she acknowledged that "Norman was God's gift to me. When Jig died, and I came home from Greece, I thought of myself as the observer. I thought I will try to be brave, and I will write, because I love life, and want to celebrate it in expression[, as a ritual (crossed out)]. Then Norman came, and loved me, and instead of seeing life from death, again I saw it from life. I was again in life. That I owe to Norman. And never will I forget it."[86]

CHAPTER TEN

Writing Is a Lonely Business

Norman Matson's smug affront affected Glaspell deeply. The Province-town crowd, however, never wholly sympathetic toward the handsome, would-be novelist, was not surprised at his defection. Mary Heaton Vorse, who lately had avoided Glaspell, proved an efficient friend, aiding the sorry dissolution of an affair she had never blessed. Literary critic Edmund Wilson, previously merely a cobeliever in the desirability of destroying accepted ideas in order to make way for new concepts, be-came a congenial companion for nights of doleful confidences. Here was another "old fashioned American idealist," and he too was grieving (his wife Margaret Canby died in the summer of 1932).[1] His rotund form, neat in a natty business suit, was frequently seen striding "up-along" Commercial Street. Whenever Glaspell spotted him on her forlorn walks with Tucker—the dog that Wilson later said was "always likely to bite you"—she would bear down on him eagerly, armed with an account of her latest wrangle with Matson.[2]

April 1933 was a month of crises: Matson's baby was due, and he managed, without Glaspell's aid, to get *The Comic Artist* produced at the Morosco Theatre in New York. Provincetown residents were faced with the spectacle of Glaspell "going to pieces."[3] An added insult in her eyes was the fact that Cleon Throckmorton, who had designed the sets for *The Verge*, was responsible for the scenery of this play she had "co-written" and to which she now fervently wished she had never lent her name. A few years later, when her novel *The Morning Is Near Us* was about to come out, she asked her publisher to strike *The Comic Artist* from a list of her plays printed in the book.[4]

But Matson's gratuitous insults did not stop there. He pestered her with patronizing inquiries about her health and writing and wholly failed to understand that friendship, as much as love, depends on trust. Glaspell was indignant when Norman and Anna planned to invade her territory and spend the summer on the Cape; she saw their togetherness as a jibe at her solitude. And she was enraged when Matson sent her a list of things he wanted from the house, including an antique spinning wheel that she had bought during the early days of their relationship.

For a time, unable to see her way forward and finding no gratification in writing, Glaspell took refuge in boisterous company. She spent her first winter without Matson struggling to keep the house reasonably warm and, according to Wilson, "drinking constantly" with Knobby, a woman friend staying with her.[5] Wilson, who also found solace in Provincetown partying, nonetheless expressed bitter contempt for the "female inebriates" of his circle.[6] He snootily disparaged Glaspell's dinner parties, famed for her abundant bootleg liquor. One guest, Commander Donald B. MacMillan, who had led the Crocker Land Expedition in the Arctic in 1913–17 and who did not drink, refused the "drinks made up with alky which [Langston Moffett had] forgotten to cut" and was offended when Glaspell insisted on calling him "darling." He departed early, leaving Wilson and others to the uncut "alky."[7] At another party, according to one witness, more amenable guests "had gotten themselves around the room by hanging on to furniture, like a slowed-up moving picture or an animal act."[8]

Thus, Wilson was relieved when Glaspell "united on an alcoholic basis" with Langston Moffett "of Washington D.C. and Provincetown"; he could now walk out without fear of Tucker nipping at his elegantly trousered leg. He was also saved from Glaspell's confidences and her tiresome repetitiveness when she drank too much. According to Wilson, Provincetown reckoned this new alliance "was a great thing for the rest of them, because now Susan and Langston could listen to each other where they had previously made other people listen to them."[9]

Moffett, nearly thirty years Glaspell's junior, albeit a family man, proved to be a devoted disciple prepared to share her lonely hours. In May 1935, driving her home one night after an evening of freely flowing bootleg followed by intimate revelations, he stopped the car in the middle of the highway to admire the harbor and the golden, glistening ocean under the moon. Moffett, who later admitted he had imbibed five drinks, "draped" himself over the wheel, while Glaspell rehearsed scenes for a novel she was plotting about a woman who rejects the intellectual world of her ex-husband.[10] This sorry spectacle was interrupted by a couple of state troopers who unceremoniously arrested Moffett and escorted Glaspell home. When the case was heard ten days later, her friends and supporters jammed the courtroom. As soon as Moffett completed his testimony, Glaspell sprang up and insisted the judge hear her out. She had been a law-abiding resident of Provincetown for twenty-three years, she declaimed, and she would not be treated like a petty criminal by the forces her tax money paid for. Ida Rauh, who had defended the Provincetown Players so brilliantly in a New York courtroom some twenty years earlier, could not have done better. The charges against Moffett were dismissed, and Glaspell and her friends rejoiced self-righteously, mocking the zeal of the inexperienced troopers.[11] For all of Wilson's jibing and Matson's sarcastic comments, this must have been an isolated incident; Glaspell, the wife and companion for many years of a man inspired—and destroyed—by liquor, was not generally known to assuage her sorrows by indulging in excessive drinking.[12]

Glaspell's stepdaughter, Nilla, now reappeared in her life. After a couple of restless years under her mother's guardianship, Nilla had returned to Greece to marry the poet Nicholas Proestopoulos, by whom she had a son, Sirius, in 1927. In 1931, after an amicable divorce on the grounds of incompatibility, Nilla joined Gandhi's movement for Indian independence, the first American to be admitted to his ashram. Although Gandhi introduced her to the Koran, thus granting her a vocation that would occupy her for the next twelve years—the study and translation of that holy book—she soon grew restless in his irenic presence, declaring her desire "to fly and attend orchestra dances." After "a series of disturbances and a period in a padded cell," she was eventually deported from India by the British authorities.[13] On the return voyage to the United States in 1933, she fell in love with the ship's steward, Albert N. Hutchins, and, believing him to be a writer in search of material for a book, married him as soon as they left the boat. The intensity of her feelings blinded and deafened her to the fact that the man "couldn't even speak good English, much less write." Annulment proceedings in December 1936 hit the papers: Nilla refused to speak before reporters, adopting a Gandhian attitude of passive resistance until the courtroom was cleared of the press.[14]

Glaspell had always loved Nilla, even when she was a trying adolescent, so she was delighted to have her and six-year-old Sirius stay through the summer of 1933. Harl, who had grown into an unpredictable young man, joined them. Glaspell dug out Nilla and Harl's old buckets and spades and dedicated her afternoons to building sandcastles with her stepgrandson. To her disappointment, Sirius preferred his uncle's motorbike to the tame pleasures of the beach, and, placing little faith in Harl's driving skills, Glaspell predicted an accident. As she expected, both riders eventually took a bad tumble, although luckily no serious damage was done. Glaspell perhaps hoped that Nilla, who was involved in theatrical and dance ventures in New York, would allow her to take care of the boy, but, to her disappointment, Sirius was sent back to Greece to his father and did not return to the States until after World War II. Nilla stayed until 1939, when she left to cover the Albanian front for American and Greek newspapers. She eventually made her way to Teheran, where she was cultural attaché in the U.S. embassy, director of the Persian State Theaters, and censor of all performances.[15] She died in Austria in 1982 and was buried in Delphi, beside her father.[16]

During these years, Glaspell, deep in her own personal depression, was indifferent to the plummeting value of her savings and the stocks left her by Jig. Writing no longer offered satisfaction. Halfheartedly, goaded by the recognition that she had not been able to transform her lover into a revered writer—a power she had bestowed on Bernice in the play of that name—she tried to convert *Bernice* into a novel. But she was not satisfied and hoped for a movie contract for one of her short plays or perhaps the novel *Ambrose Holt and Family*. She was rescued from this mood of apathy and dejection by the Federal Theatre.

Glaspell joined the roll of Federal Theatre appointees in September 1936, enthusiastically throwing herself into the job of organizing and directing the Midwest Play Bureau. She was confident that she would find herself among dedicated people intent on founding a truly American theater— the task that had supposedly defeated the Provincetown Players and broken George Cram Cook. She wrote to Barrett Clark, who had congratulated her on the appointment: "If I can find some good plays from the soil or from the experiences of recent years, I will feel that we are doing something for the theatre in helping build it up through this part of the country."[17]

That spring, she had enjoyed the Federal Theatre's magnificent New York season. One of the four Arts Projects promoted by the Works Progress Administration (WPA) as part of President Theodore Roosevelt's effort to put the unemployed back to work, the Federal Theatre was particularly successful in New York in early 1936. A very young Orson Welles directed *Macbeth* for John Houseman, codirector of the New York City Negro Unit. Welles transported Shakespeare's witches to the Caribbean, where, aided by jungle drums and African dancers, they created unforgettable moments described by Brooks Atkinson as "logical and stunning and a triumph of theatre art."[18] Another production that gripped Glaspell's attention was the first successful living newspaper, *Triple-A Plowed Under*. Combining theater with newspaper, this daring new form presented the plight of the American farmer, who was suffering from low prices, government intervention, and greedy middlemen.[19]

The New York season had scored with new plays too. Hallie Flanagan, future director of the Federal Theatre, had so charmed T. S. Eliot during her 1934 visit to England that he promised her "another *Sweeney*... a play, not yet named, about Thomas à Becket."[20] Thus, the world premiere of *Murder in the Cathedral* was produced by Edward Goodman under the auspices of the New York Federal Theatre "Popular Price" Project in March 1936. Remembering how Cook and Glaspell had thrilled to the tribal ritual of the Yiddish theater, Lulu Huffaker, proud of her husband's success, insisted that her friend see this production. The religious ritual of Eliot's poetry enthralled Glaspell, and the pale cyclorama sky, in which infinity yielded to ominous oppression, recalled for her those moments of experiment and play when Cook triumphantly threw light on his beloved dome, creating the illusion of unending space.

In August 1935, Hallie Flanagan, a "wild little woman" with "matted reddish hair," tremendous self-confidence, and no experience in the commercial theater, after swearing to "protect and defend the Constitution of the United States against all enemies foreign and domestic," was appointed director of the Federal Theatre.[21] Flanagan had studied playwriting with George Pierce Baker at Harvard and theater organization, acting, and producing techniques in Europe on a Guggenheim Fellowship; she then worked at Grinnell and Vassar Colleges, creating a theater in which she could test the provocative new ideas she had brought back from Europe. When offered the challenge of directing the Federal Theatre, Flanagan immediately came up with bold but feasible suggestions for employing the actors and stagehands that the rise of cinema, combined with the Depression, had left jobless. She recognized the need for a theater organized along lines quite different from the national theaters she had seen in Europe. Although her theater had to be "national in scope," it also had to be "regional in emphasis and American in democratic attitude."[22] Normal practice was inverted: instead of starting with a play, a director, a theater, and the money necessary to hire the best actors, she commanded thousands of unemployed actors across the country and had at her disposal funds for minimal wages, although little else. Most theater people refused to believe that such a system could function, let alone produce dramatic art. But Flanagan, after careful study of the material at hand and the audience to be reached and ravished, organized what one of her actors still believes—and hopes—"*can* and *will* be the model for our National Theatre in the future."[23]

Flanagan wanted plays by American playwrights, plays about life in America. George Cram Cook, almost twenty years earlier, had created a tiny theater in which American playwrights could experiment; Flanagan attempted just that, but on a national scale, declaring: "If the plays do not exist we shall have to write them."[24] Glaspell, Pulitzer playwright, charged with the same idealism that had fired her husband, was the obvious choice to lead the hunt for new plays about the Midwest by midwesterners.[25]

So, in September 1936, responding to Flanagan's urging that she direct the Midwest Play Bureau, Glaspell took a pleasantly anonymous room at the Hotel Eastgate on Chicago's East Ontario Street, a couple of blocks from the Federal Theatre offices on East Eerie Street.[26] The WPA Arts Projects for the Midwest had taken over the top floors of an empty building close to Lake Shore Drive. Frequently, when the lake winds threatened to whisk her right out of Chicago and onto the vast midwestern prairies, Glaspell had to stop on her way to work and cling to iron railings until some strong soul helped her on her way. But even after she was safely behind her desk, life was still far from serene. Personal ambitions, political infighting, and "complete lack of planning," plus the constant threat of censorship from overzealous self-styled authorities, would tempt her to resign again and again.[27]

One of Glaspell's battles was fought over *Big White Fog* by Theodore Ward, which played from 7 April to 30 May 1938. Centering on the figure of Marcus Garvey, this play had to be severely tailored to the tastes of bureaucrats in Washington, D.C. Irwin Rubinstein, legal counsel for the Federal Theatre, and Emmet Lavery, director of the Play Department, feared that "like many scripts dealing with Negro problems, [it] requires the exercise of considerable discretion."[28] Previously, Lavery had lamely advised that the play would receive permission for production only "if a director could properly temper the outright sales appeal for Communism—which appears, however, in only one scene."[29]

When Glaspell arrived in Chicago, George Kondolf, a prestigious New York producer, was director of the Federal Theatre in Chicago. Anxious to find new plays for his own use as well as for the Federal Theatre, he had started building up a play bureau even before Glaspell's appointment.[30] One of her first tasks was therefore to make quite clear to the New York offices and to her colleagues in Chicago exactly what she was prepared to do. She spurned a proposal to dramatize *Gone with the Wind* as stubbornly as she later refused to handle the paperwork involved in sending off, in duplicate, triplicate, or quadruplicate, production permission requests that had to be signed by an ever-increasing number of local and regional bigwigs.[31] Alleging lack of staff, she firmly declined responsibility for the administrative side of performances and eventually won a measure of independence. In a memorandum that she sent to Flanagan on 6 November 1936, Glaspell stated her priorities: to collect manuscripts and published plays on the Midwest or by midwesterners; to select "producible manuscripts" and develop them with their authors; and to recommend these to the theaters in the region and, in cases of outstanding merit, to Hiram Motherwell, director of the Play Policy Board.[32] She succeeded in gathering a group of faithful playreaders whom she put to work reading and criticizing the countless scripts that poured in from farmers and shop clerks eager to gain thespian immortality.

Each reader was faced with two scripts a day, which were frequently "utterly hopeless." Although at first glance, "the duties seemed hardly onerous," Glaspell demanded that the reader prepare a careful commentary, which was sent to the author when the script was returned.[33] She insisted that the comments be constructive, never cruel, and urged readers "to find something—anything—that suggested merit."[34] Once a week, enveloped in her long wool cardigan and gaining inspiration from an occasional sip out of the coke bottle she kept on her desk, Glaspell met with her readers to discuss their reports. Guiding them in writing their commentaries, always anxious that they recognize and formulate the dramatic rules that created good theater, she helped them couch criticism in friendly terms. One conclusion they quickly reached—corroborating Glaspell's Provincetown experience—was that "playwrights do not easily learn their craft in a vacuum."[35] These meetings had the air of a postgraduate seminar, with Glaspell as mentor, the kindly professor whose influence would remain forever with her little flock.[36]

Whenever a reader was lucky enough to come across a promising piece, it was read by others and then by Glaspell. One such play was *The Great Spirit* by Edwin B. Self, a dramatization, from the Native American point of view, of the betrayal of Native American leader James Logan by land-hungry whites. Two of Kondolf's readers had approved this script just before Glaspell arrived in Chicago. One of them, Alice Gerstenberg, a playwright Glaspell knew from Greenwich Village days, tersely reported: "Audiences may not enjoy being reminded of shameful history but this play should be forced upon them in all communities from coast to coast, year in and year out 'lest we forget' through the ages."[37] Glaspell agreed with Gerstenberg; she rejoiced that a play about the Midwest, showing true feeling, had been dropped so propitiously into her lap. Flanagan, who read the script during a visit to Chicago in December 1936, was not quite so enthusiastic, although she did admit that the play had "fine moments."[38] Glaspell would have enjoyed revising the piece herself, taking care to keep the "beauty and poetry" while correcting the numerous technical flaws.[39] But "play-doctoring" was not her task; she entered into a drawn-out, frustrating correspondence with the author, who eventually agreed to allow the play to be rewritten, with the proviso that his name precede that of the coauthor.[40]

Glaspell had already chosen a "play doctor"; from the Federal Theatre lists, she had picked Ann Grosvenor Ayres, who had been responsible for a summer production of *The Comic Artist* at Westport some years previously. Already estranged from Matson, Glaspell had wanted as little as possible to do with the play she had cowritten and, as Ayres reminded her, had run from photographers and interviewers.[41] Now she hoped that this woman, who had struck her as highly competent, would take on the job of converting *The Great Spirit* into "the genuinely American classic" her readers had detected in the play.[42] But in spite of Glaspell's wholehearted efforts to placate the author and convince her superiors, this attempt at dramatizing American history was eventually rejected by the Federal Theatre.

Despairing of finding suitable plays in the mailbox, Glaspell turned to old friends for recommendations. Barrett Clark, whose recent biography of O'Neill Glaspell had praised, made various suggestions. He sent her a copy of Edgar Lee Masters's *New Salem*, which had never been produced. Although Clark recognized that this episodic play needed to be pulled into shape, he was sure that Masters would "take suggestions—at least from you."[43] But a careful reading of the play did not impress Glaspell, who failed to see how it could "go into form for the theatre" without complete rewriting; disappointed, she replied that she "fear[ed] that Mr. Masters is not a playwright."[44] She also begged plays of Professor E. C. Mabie, director of the Iowa University Theatre and the first Federal Theatre regional director for the Midwest, but with no success.[45]

During Glaspell's first year in Chicago, Professor R. W. Cowden of the University of Michigan invited her to sit on the panel of judges for the Avery Hopwood Drama Awards. An invitation extended the previous year had followed her from Provincetown to New York but had not reached her in time.[46] Now, particularly interested in finding potential Federal Theatre scripts, Glaspell gladly accepted, and early in May 1937, she received the entries. Twenty plays competed for the Avery Hopwood Awards in the Major and Minor categories that year. She read and reread the texts conscientiously, speaking the lines and moving around her hotel room as if she were back on the Provincetown stage, and finally made out her order of preference. Cowden soon informed her that there had been no discrepancy of opinion among the judges;[47] thus, in the Minor Awards, first place had gone to her choice, *Honors at Dawn*, by a student who used the alias "Corona." Glaspell had immediately recognized and identified with the author's major preoccupation: the personal struggle for integrity within the larger social context. She saw "real possibilities" in the author, although she found the play "faulty as it stands." More important, she reckoned it "says something in feeling," and she recognized that innate "sense of the theatre" so essential to a playwright.[48] Thus, the first prize of $250 went to "Corona," the as yet unknown Arthur Miller, then a student at the University of Michigan.

In Chicago, Glaspell was surrounded by aspiring young artists who saw her as not only the director of the Play Bureau but also the cofounder of the legendary Provincetown Players and winner of a Pulitzer Prize. In spite of the distance such prestige and a generation gap inevitably established—her once chestnut hair was now turning gray—her gentle manner drew the young men, and her determined stand against Federal Theatre bureaucracy convinced them they could rely on her support. She hoped to discover new writers and nurture them as she had Sinclair Lewis, George Cram Cook, Eugene O'Neill, and Norman Matson.[49]

Although Alice Gerstenberg, Sidney Blackstone, and Fannie McConnell (who would marry Ralph Ellison) were already reading scripts when she took on the Play Bureau, Glaspell needed more readers to cope with the plays that kept flooding in. When Arnold Sundgaard, fresh from the

Yale University Drama Department and desperate for work, came to see her in November 1936, she pulled strings to hire him as a playreader. In order to qualify for work in the Federal Theatre, Sundgaard had to apply for relief with the local WPA office; luckily, he had worked as a dishwasher at a hospital while he was a student and thus fulfilled WPA requirements. In less than a week, he was reading plays for Glaspell, who, seeing in him a future playwright, encouraged him to write, assigning the "bad plays" to him, which presumably allowed him more time for his own work.[50]

One day, Glaspell brought in the first issue of a new magazine, *Midwest*; the "broad, bold photograph of the prairies" on the cover inspired "some kind of theatrical vision" that she did her best to communicate to her playreaders. No doubt recalling how Silas Morton in *Inheritors* had created a better variety of corn, she saw the golden prairie as a "wonderful setting" for a play on the life of the Midwest. Her words hypnotized Sundgaard, who "began to grope [his] way toward a free-wheeling story" of the westward expansion.[51] Combining dialogue with folk songs and dance, he told the national tale of innocence and exploitation in *Everywhere I Roam*, quite accidentally hitting on the format of epic theater.[52]

Glaspell saw promise in the young playwright whose readiness to try new forms was like a breath of fresh air to her. Judiciously, maternally, she alternated criticism and flattery, thus spurring Sundgaard on, until in the spring of 1937, she confidently affirmed that *Everywhere I Roam* was fit for production. The play now had to be approved by George Kondolf, director of the Chicago project. Kondolf was a Broadway man, so arrogantly paternalist in his contempt for experimental theater that he was incapable of sharing Sundgaard's scope of vision, and, not surprisingly, he rejected the play.[53] Glaspell, although she must have expected difficulties, was even more disappointed than the young playwright. As she indignantly told him the verdict, she sucked vigorously on the straw in her coke bottle, coloring decorously, from anger and possibly from the bourbon she poured into the bottle on particularly stressful days. Although on the surface she maintained an affable relationship with Kondolf, she rarely agreed with him on theater matters and had little respect for his opinions; "intellectually and aesthetically" their views were totally opposed.[54]

In spite of Kondolf's rejection of *Everywhere I Roam*, Glaspell did not give up on her vision of a play of the Midwest. In an interview published in April 1937, she spoke of a proposed spectacle that would be more than a pageant; it would be a "wedding of several forms," relating the story of the transformation of the frontier into an industrialized farming community.[55] The outline and the production plan, on which Federal Theatre writers, especially Sundgaard, had worked, were ready. The project, under the name *Midwest*, met with Flanagan's approval. In the autumn of 1937, she proudly announced that the "symphonic drama being compiled by Susan Glaspell and other Midwest dramatists" would be "the big event of the spring."[56] But Glaspell left the Federal Theatre before *Midwest* could be put into production, and the project was forgotten.

The Federal Theatre had obtained from Eugene O'Neill (as well as George Bernard Shaw) the right to produce his plays for the minimal royalties of $50 a week. In October 1937, the Chicago project staged O'Neill's *The Straw*, which the Greenwich Village Theatre had performed in 1921. Thus, Glaspell was reminded of her old friend, whose marriage to Carlotta Monterey following his divorce from Boulton had totally removed him from her circle. Glaspell explained to her young followers that *The Straw* was based on O'Neill's bout with tuberculosis and that writing the play had been very painful for him.[57] Fifteen years later, the talky three acts and tragic love story seemed dated to her, and she wondered whether a more contemporary play could be written about syphilis.

A cure for syphilis had been discovered in 1906, but the "French disease" was still taboo, as, of course, was discussion of it. Nevertheless, in 1936, Thomas Parron, surgeon general of the United States, instigated a nationwide drive to eradicate the disease, and many states, including Illinois, passed legislation approving mandatory prenuptial blood tests. Although Chicago's mayor was perhaps better known in Federal Theatre circles for censoring plays he had not read, he supported this campaign.[58] Hoping to endear the Federal Theatre to the mayor, Glaspell conceived the idea of a dramatic piece in the form of a living newspaper on the subject of syphilis. Readers and playwrights involved in the Chicago project nodded general approval, but Sundgaard, Glaspell's special protégé, was the one who set to work, and, after long hours in libraries and lengthy consultations with medical experts, he produced the outline that would become *Spirochete*. With his mentor's encouragement, he gave the material theatrical shape, assimilating Glaspell's suggestion that the dry statistics and scientific facts be interspersed with the human story, with sketches portraying the "effect on employment, on love affairs, on marriage and on children."[59] Flanagan, when shown the script, wanted such personal material removed, but Glaspell, with characteristic tenacity that belied her fragile appearance, was adamant, and the episodes were retained.[60] She also launched a battle to make Sundgaard the play's copyright holder.

Under the WPA Arts Project guidelines, a writer employed by the Federal Theatre automatically surrendered copyright of his or her work to the government, but, Glaspell argued, Sundgaard was employed as a reader, not a writer, and he had written the script on his own time.[61] Nevertheless, Flanagan insisted the copyright of *Spirochete* belonged to the Federal Theatre. Glaspell resolutely took the case before the Dramatists' Guild, which responded immediately by threatening to refuse to grant the Federal Theatre permission to produce plays by Guild members. Glaspell won the case, thus ensuring Sundgaard payment of fees for productions of *Spirochete*, which, like many other Federal Theatre plays, was performed in various cities almost simultaneously. He reminisced: "For a very brief period of about six weeks I was making a lot of money."[62] At the time, he did not know the extent to which Glaspell had intervened, and he later lamented that he "was never able to express [his] gratitude for this act of generosity and courage."[63]

In Chicago, *Spirochete* was produced by Harry Minturn, a man of the old school, with whom neither Glaspell nor Sundgaard saw eye to eye. According to Sundgaard, "he represented the kind of theatre that we . . . didn't stand for really."[64] But he surprised both of them where *Spirochete* was concerned. Sundgaard had initially titled his living newspaper *Dark Harvest*, and it was Minturn who rejected such a euphemism, suggesting they use the generic name of the coiled bacteria that causes the disease: the spirochete.[65] Minturn "thought we should come out boldly and call it for what it was," adding that "it was time to stop whispering about it and start talking about it—out loud." Sundgaard was so impressed that he not only accepted the new title but used Minturn's words for the final line of the play.[66] Minturn also supported Glaspell on the inclusion of the human-interest scenes and wrote to Flanagan: "While much of the material we have used in our present version is of historical record, we thought it advisable to lend dramatic and romantic interest by the use of certain scenes . . . taken from actual case histories."[67] Flanagan, generally supportive of any theatrical experiment, hesitated to back *Spirochete*, claiming that since it dealt with such delicate matter, no producer or director should be forced to stage it.[68]

The stuffiness of the Chicago crew disheartened Glaspell, and the red tape sickened her. Assuring Flanagan that "the difference between what I have on the Federal Theatre [$200 a month] and what I could make through my own work is considerable," she repeatedly threatened to resign.[69] But she struggled on, compelled by a desperate faith in the possibility of creating a people's theater that would vindicate Cook's spirit. Whenever she sensed an opening for a fellow idealist who would help her transform the Chicago unit into a truly visionary theater, she approached Flanagan. But, oblivious of Federal Theatre political bickering, Glaspell was rarely successful in such maneuvering. In the autumn of 1937, she was greatly excited by Helen Tieken's work at the Hull House Theater, and she was keen—in vain—to add Tieken to the Federal Theatre ranks to work on a Children's Theatre.[70]

There were other disappointments. Garrett Leverton, Northwestern University theater director, had staged a production of *Alison's House* with such flair that Glaspell was eager to convince him to work for Uncle Sam. She longed to bring more life to the Chicago project, and she believed that a local director would draw audiences and shore up the Federal Theatre against the city's critics, who, she feared, suffered from "a WPA antagonism almost impossible to break down."[71] But Flanagan, who could not afford to offend Kondolf and Minturn, chose to ignore Glaspell's suggestion. Eventually, Leverton was offered an appointment at a ridiculously low salary, which he refused. Glaspell felt slighted, and although her "feeling about the Federal Theatre" remained "as strong as ever," she once again questioned the wisdom of her commitment.[72]

But Glaspell did get on well with Kay Ewing, an assistant director who had spent a year as acting director with Flanagan's Experimental Theatre at Vassar. Ewing was appointed to assist Minturn in the Chicago production of Sinclair Lewis's *It Can't Happen Here*. She later wryly recounted that this was her "first exposure to a typical old master of 'show-bizz,' and his first . . . to a brash young academic."[73] Harold Kopel, designer and technician, had arrived with Ewing, and with them, Glaspell could at least joke about the commercial convictions of Kondolf and Minturn and moan over their lack of vision.

From among the plays submitted by midwestern writers, Glaspell had selected *Within These Walls*, a play about a Trappist monastery by the Iowan Marcus Bach, and had somehow convinced the Chicago fusties to accept it for the Blackstone Theatre.[74] Casting had not been easy; Ewing had to make do with "left-over actors and vaudevillians" who were too old to play in the musical review *O Say, Can You Sing*, a satire on the Federal Theatre. Both Glaspell, who frequently attended rehearsals, and Ewing were delighted to see how well these actors, considered by many to be third class simply because they were on relief, adapted "to Stanis-lavsky's 'effective memory' techniques." Faithful to the old Provincetown tenets, Glaspell invited the author to attend rehearsals and share with the actors his experience as a novice in a Trappist monastery. Bach, delighted at Ewing's production, "wondered how [they] had ever assembled a bunch of actors who could be such *perfect* monks."[75]

During one performance, Glaspell and Ewing looked in on the already darkened theater and were taken aback by the rows of empty seats. When the lights went on, they realized that nuns from a local convent filled the auditorium, their black cowls and habits making them invisible in the dark.

Glaspell's public duties as director of the Midwest Play Bureau in-cluded presiding over official functions, giving speeches, and, in gen-eral, making the work of the Federal Theatre known in Chicago. She always stressed how delighted she was to be back in the Midwest, where her roots were, and told audiences that she saw no reason why Chicago should not become "one of the greatest theatrical centers of the world."[76] The Federal Theatre, she insisted, "gives young American playwrights of promise the best opportunity that has been offered them" because it caused "better American plays to be written." By the end of 1937, more than 800 plays had been read in the Chicago bureau, and hundreds more awaited their turn. Glaspell loved to tell the story of the Provincetown Players, how young American playwrights had been given their chance, and how Eugene O'Neill had been discovered. On one occasion, at a luncheon for businesswomen, her playreaders were embarrassed when she "rambled on about the city's indifference to [its] many artists." Alice Gerstenberg suggested that Glaspell was "somewhat tight," but to Sund-gaard, she could do no wrong. He thought "the speech sounded like something that might well have been uttered by Jig Cook."[77]

In April 1938, Glaspell finally abandoned her dream of continuing Cook's work in the theater and handed in her resignation. Even before her decision was made official, aspirants to the position of director of the Play Bureau were clamoring for the appointment. Her idealistic vision of the theater had clashed frequently with the go-getting, practical concerns of those who wielded power, but it was the battle over the copyright of *Spirochete*, on top of the constant hassle of administrative hurdles, that convinced Glaspell that she was wasting her time. During long evenings in her room at the Hotel Eastgate or in the small apartment she later rented in her brother's building, she had managed to overcome the writer's block that had gripped her since 1932 and to plot out a new novel. She was now anxious for homey Provincetown days and the peace to pull her ideas into shape.

In July 1938, a few months after Glaspell left the Federal Theatre, Flanagan expressed her pleasure at what the Chicago project had achieved. She praised the "courage to cling to a program largely made up of new plays," but although she mentioned the directors by name, Glaspell's contribution to finding these new plays went unnoticed.[78] The Federal Theatre, the inevitable victim of red-baiting and partisan politics, was "voted out of existence" by Congress just a year later.[79]

During her time in Chicago, Glaspell did not join in with the bohemian spirits who gravitated to the North Side, where the *Poetry Magazine* crowd mingled nightly with WPA artists and writers, Sundgaard, Nelson Algren, Richard Wright, and John Huston among them. She was older and the director of the Play Bureau, an appointed position, but more important, a natural fragility, accentuated by Matson's falseness, kept her away from noisy youth. She spent most of her free time with her brother Ray and his wife Flossie, taking delightful long walks with their dog. Although she was homesick for Provincetown, she lingered in Chicago even after resigning from the Federal Theatre, spending most of the winter of 1939 there.

As Glaspell grew older, the mystery of motherhood obsessed her. The mother became virginal, a Madonna, her whole being acquiring significance from her child. One day, when she was still with the Federal Theatre, the readers were engaged in a discussion on how a woman should pose for a photograph, and Glaspell, according to Sundgaard, insisted that "the best pose for a woman is when she is a mother and holding a baby in her lap. In focusing on the baby—wanting to hold her forward so the baby looks good—the mother herself looks beautiful. In that transcendent act of love and self-effacement she becomes the object of adoration."[80] Glaspell had always wanted a baby; she had never overcome her disappointment and deep sorrow at the loss of Cook's child in 1913. The baby clothes she had gathered at the time still filled her bottom drawer in Provincetown. She loved Nilla and Harl but knew that, however much they turned to her for affection and help at difficult moments, she was not their mother. She pondered maternal love, her mother's daily sorrows and frustrations, and the monstrous dilemma that the choice between a husband and a child must pose. She identified a mother's supreme sacrifice as the obligation to deny love to her child in order to satisfy her husband. The man trapped in such a ghastly triangle could smooth the way with love for his wife, and, more important, for the child, even if it was not his.

This had been Caleb's way out in *Brook Evans*. Now, giving the screw another twist, Glaspell explored the conditions that could lead to such a situation and the effect on a daughter. Unable to accept that a mother would not love her child, Glaspell wove the story of *The Morning Is Near Us*, again using the absent woman as her focal point, in this case the mother, Hertha Chipman, who is dead. The intricate plot, contorted into startling sinuosities, is gradually disclosed to the unsuspecting reader and to Hertha's daughter, Lydia. Most discreetly, Glaspell tells a horror story of child rape, incest, adultery, murder, and madness, played out against a backdrop of desire for love, understanding, and forgiveness. The horrors suffered by the absent Hertha in the past are overshadowed by Lydia's need to understand why her parents sent her away when she was a child. The inevitable revelations fall on her with mechanical precision, almost destroying the hopeful, intuitive belief in parental love she had clung to all of her life. Her father, the sole possessor of the full story, must now, to all intents and purposes, return from the dead—from internment in a psychiatric institution—to give Lydia the assurance that she was indeed loved as a child and thus arm her with the confidence she needs to continue in life and to bring up the two children she has adopted. In spite of the horrors Glaspell manages to pack into this novel, she conveys such an atmosphere of generosity and friendship that the Chipmans, together with their relatives and neighbors, seem to form an ideal community struggling to do the right thing. Initial opposition to Lydia is soon dispelled; provincial narrow-mindedness fades under Lydia's charm, and we find ourselves hoping for a sequel to tell us how she and her adopted children fare after the mysteries of her past have been cleared away.

In this novel, Glaspell returns to the fears that haunted her throughout her adolescence and early adulthood. Although there can be no doubt that Lydia Chipman's wandering life is modeled on that of Nilla Cook, the overbearing fear of being an alien in one's own community comes from Glaspell's experience—whether imagined or real. Despite Davenport's social distinctions, there is no evidence that her childhood and youth were violently unhappy. Elmer Glaspell may have been dour and

strict with the children, while his wife dreamed of a more genteel existence, pinning all of her hopes on her daughter, but as far as we know, the
family experienced no overt trauma. Was this precisely the reason Glaspell was so frequently driven to imagining waifs and strays, adopted
children and absconding fathers? Was this how she brought excitement
into her life? Or was it symbolic of some seemingly insignificant childhood experience that caused a deep-seated feeling of rejection, heightened now by Matson's faithlessness?[81]

The disappointments Glaspell suffered destroyed neither the idealism
that characterizes all of her writing nor her natural optimism; she borrowed the title of *The Morning Is Near Us* from Euripides, consciously
evoking the hope of dawn, which sheds light on the truth. The novel
marked her return to the world of literature; a decade had gone by since
the critical and financial successes of *The Road to the Temple*, *Brook Evans*,
and *Alison's House*. In March, Stokes, her publisher, delighting in the good
sales—the Literary Guild had selected *The Morning Is Near Us* as its April
1940 Book of the Month—gave a party in Glaspell's honor at the Al-
gonquin Hotel in New York. For once, Glaspell could freely enjoy the
limelight without fear of offending a male partner, but years of self-
effacement made it impossible for her to do so. The guests were charmed
by the elegant, fashionably permed, poised writer who was so reluctant
to speak about herself or her novel.[82] As Edmund Wilson would callously
say, she "seemed much better for her years in the West, seemed to have
resigned herself to become an old lady."[83]

The Morning Is Near Us was indeed highly successful. Victor Gollancz,
always a Glaspell fan, published it under his imprint in London. The *New
York Herald Tribune* reported on 14 April 1940 that the novel was ninth on
its list of best-sellers.[84] Royalties came in steadily, substantiating Glaspell's earlier claim that she could make a better living by her writing than
by working for the Federal Theatre. More than 100,000 copies were sold
by mid-1940, and Glaspell was negotiating movie rights with Columbia
Pictures. Dissatisfied with its original offer of a 10 percent advance of
$2,500, she coolly turned to Metro-Goldwyn-Meyer, at which Columbia
raised the advance to $10,000, which was paid on 3 September 1940.
Glaspell was relieved that her finances were secure and delighted that this
tale of mystery and love had recaptured her readers.

Her satisfaction did not last long. Rumors of German belligerence
turned into dismal reality in the autumn of 1939, and Glaspell saw history
repeat itself as America debated pacifism and preparedness. Her fan-

tasies of abandoned children turned into nightmares filled with Belgian and Dutch families trudging down unending roads. Her conscience demanded she write something that might alleviate the suffering, but when she approached her agent, he cynically dismissed her idealism with advice not to "worry about the war."[85] Nonetheless, unable to ignore the carnage, Glaspell did write a short piece, *Cherished and Shared of Old*, a naive children's story that she dedicated to her young neighbors, Karl and Susan Marie Meyer. In keeping with Glaspell's passé Nietzschean idealism, the war turns out to be the means of reestablishing the friendship of two older women, one a native midwesterner, the other, a German immigrant. *Cherished and Shared of Old* was published by Julian Messner in 1940; *Redbook* offered $1,000 for the story.

While working for the Federal Theatre, Glaspell had, for the first time in her life, come up against "the real world"—the nine-to-five world of administration, bureaucracy, petty jealousies, and ambition. She had, of course, witnessed egotistical, self-promoting behavior among the Provincetown Players, but it had been easier to dismiss because of the "spirit of play" that pervaded everything they did. Cook's dream, the desire to create an American theater, was on a smaller scale, and such mundane matters as pecuniary or professional advantage, by the very nature of the Players, did not at first enter into the scheme of things. It was taken for granted that friends would help each other in bad moments, and rents were low in Greenwich Village. Not so in Chicago. Although Hallie Flanagan was imbued with a visionary ideal of the theater, she was conscious that she was using taxpayers' money to put people to work. Very little of her idealism filtered down to hungry professional actors and stagehands, and even less filtered up to senators and congressmen charged with keeping an eye on political purity, as well as accounts.

Glaspell was not happy working with such truncated idealism; in spite of the horrible circumstances of Cook's death, the treachery of the new Players, and Matson's betrayal, she still clung to her youthful faith that humankind can "shape the better world of [our] dreams."[86] But in Chicago, she began to question her creed; her doubts grew and threatened to overcome her as World War II dragged on and America's intervention became inevitable, but the buoyancy of her faith held her, and she came through to a belief in the existence of "the good."[87] Glaspell described this struggle in the novel *Norma Ashe* (1942).

Not surprisingly, Glaspell's protagonist is a mother, Norma Ashe, and the scene is the home, where so many battles are fought and so many spirits laid low. Norma Ashe had excelled at the local Pioneer College and won a scholarship to the University of Chicago. In language reminiscent of *The Verge*, Glaspell tells us that her young heroine is "chosen" by "their teacher" and resolves that after his death she will study and "pass on the torch." Overpowered by the gravity of her ideals, Norma vows she will not "fail life that waited to be moulded by the dream of what life might be."[88] But during the summer vacation, as she eagerly awaits the autumn term, Norma meets Max Utterbach, a traveling salesman, and falls in love. For the first time, wiser for her experience with Matson, Glaspell openly equates love with "sex appeal."[89] Max Utterbach, whose very name binds him to the banal, boasts of no positive qualities except for a winning smile and a charming manner. Before she knows how it has happened, Norma Ashe is Mrs. Utterbach, beguiled into marriage, ensnared in a vacuous social circle imposed by her husband's growing prosperity, and then, after his death at a "bad moment," broken by widowhood and poverty.[90]

In this novel, Glaspell gives us her clearest analysis of marriage. Norma Ashe, at the beginning of her romance with Max, asks: "Was it a *trap*?"[91] In *Ambrose Holt and Family* and *Chains of Dew*, Glaspell's protagonists fight the limitations that marriage imposes on them but never question the love that binds them to worthless husbands. Neither woman will hurt her lord and master by spiritual rebellion, and we are to understand— although we may find it difficult to believe—that both do, in fact, find happiness in matrimony. Norma Ashe, in spite of several years of depressing wifehood, still has the guts to fight for her right to be a person. She can say to Max: "I am more than a wife." And when, incredulous, he asks, "*What* more—for heaven's sake?," she has the right answer, "Myself."[92]

The relationship between Max and Norma is examined minutely. In keeping with Glaspell's roll of male characters, Max is intrinsically weak and unscrupulous. His willpower depends on his wife's satisfaction and approving smile. Excuses are, of course, made for him: he is racked by the knowledge that his mother died in circumstances of abject poverty, circumstances he could have remedied. Oedipally, he identifies Norma with his mother: she must cuddle and coddle him as only a mother can. In return, she is rewarded with a satisfactory sex life and a sparkling diamond ring.

The most poignant moments in the novel come when Norma is pregnant with her first child—a child that is stillborn. Norma had high hopes for this son: he would go to the university, and "what wasn't realized through her would come through him. Nothing would be lost."[93] This son was to carry on the torch her teacher had bequeathed to her; her worthiness would be proved by her childbearing capacity. But, ironically, Norma's first child dies, her second, Fred, grows up to be a bootlegger, and her daughter, Lorna, gives up on the social niceties the Utterbachs set such store by and marries beneath her. Glaspell, still haunted by the dull resentment her mother's stolen pleasures had aroused in her, denies Norma the vicarious gratification that would give some sense to her life.

When Max dies in an accident, Norma is left with a huge house and two children. She sets up a boarding establishment, which, as the district deteriorates and the building decays, descends to utter seediness. The first section of the novel shows the aging Norma struggling with mounting bills, insistent creditors, a leaking roof, and insolvent lodgers. She has completely forgotten her youthful idealism and her later immersion in the "right" social crowd. It is a world of misery and poverty, both spiritual and real, and Glaspell demonstrates her skill at creating a lifelike picture of people struggling to make ends meet.

Glaspell had, from *Trifles* onward, been aware of the trap marriage could become for an intelligent woman. But she had firmly believed that love would gild the cage, transforming confinement into rapture. In *Norma Ashe*, she dismisses love and rejects the gilding as cheap and spurious. But Glaspell's idealism prevails; through a series of unlikely encounters, Norma wins back her faith in the "oneness" of humanity and argues that our puny, individual efforts count in the grandiose scheme of betterment. The leap into transcendental otherness that Claire's plant "Breath of Life" had taken could also be achieved by humankind. Norma conveys this optimism, not to her children, but to a student who is still unspoiled by the world. Unfortunately, Glaspell does not end the novel here; in a sorry twist of self-doubt, Norma's new faith is shattered when she learns that her beloved teacher had frequently laughed at his pupils and that he had committed suicide. Norma is thrown back into gloom and despair, from which she is rescued by death, but not before she happily returns to the conviction of "oneness" and a belief in goodness, exemplified by the shining sun, which illuminates her last moments as she lays her head down on the notebooks she filled with adolescent fervor so many years previously.

Glaspell's need to reaffirm the idealism that had brought her and Cook together dominates this novel and at times controls the language, which becomes nebulous and romantically vague as it attempts to express an absolute faith in the inexpressible potential of the human race to "make the thrust and—."[94] Although Norma finally reclaims her faith, a pall is thrown on this seemingly optimistic ending by a reminder that she, as much as her fellow students, betrayed her "teacher" in one way or another. Somewhere beyond that enthusiastic idealism, Glaspell hides a realistic core that enables her to understand failure and that colors all of her writing with a characteristically uneasy ambivalence.

Norma Ashe was, of course, published in England by Victor Gollancz; in America, for the first time, Glaspell's novel was not published by Stokes, her publisher since 1909. Stokes had transferred its rights to Glaspell's novels to Lippincott in 1941.[95] In September 1942, just as *Norma Ashe* was to be published, Lippincott notified her that it planned to surrender the metal plates of her books, except for *The Road to the Temple* and *The Morning Is Near Us*, to the war effort. Glaspell, although she contributed to the war effort—she had donated the plaque put up in her husband's memory at the Provincetown Theatre and gave generously to the Greek War Relief Association and the National War Fund—was deeply shaken at the thought that her novels might never be reprinted. She begged Lippincott to reconsider and to keep the plates for *Brook Evans* and, if at all possible, *Ambrose Holt and Family* and *The Fugitive's Return*. She hoped that the publication of *Norma Ashe*, "what seems to me my best novel," would arouse interest in her previous work.[96] But her longer fiction was clearly doomed: not one novel was reprinted after its initial success had died down.[97]

The woodstove in the unpretentious cottage at 564 Commercial Street in Provincetown had always stymied Glaspell, and after her brother Ray's death in 1942, she chose to escape the Provincetown blizzards in New York, taking rooms at the Halley Chambers on Washington Square West. But as soon as spring beckoned, Glaspell spryly exchanged the gray concrete of Manhattan for Provincetown's tree-lined streets, slipping back into her long-established routine of writing, pottering about in the garden, walking Tucker's successor, and socializing. She was a charter member of the Provincetown Civic Association and deployed considerable energy in working to preserve the natural environment of her town and supporting the school and the theater, legatee of the original Wharf Theatre. In the evenings, friends would gather around Cook's legendary musical table, just as in the old Provincetown days.

In the 1940s, Glaspell's companions, although not enmeshed in a fraternal theatrical enterprise, were mostly literary, artistic folk, and, following in the footsteps of the previous generation, they valued Provincetown as an ideal place for work. John Dos Passos and his wife, who lived opposite Glaspell's cottage, liked to drop in, as did Edmund Wilson. The young Paul Chavchadze would come begging her to correct his prose, only to chafe at the kindly critique she offered him.[98] Drawing the curtains "in observance of the dim-out," these liberal intellectuals would try to "persuade [themselves that] a room temperature of 65 would toughen [them] up a bit." One such night, Glaspell, who was reading André Maurois's *I Remember, I Remember,* lamented the fate of France, at which Katy Dos Passos recalled Walt Whitman's "O Star of France." Taking *Leaves of Grass* off Glaspell's shelves, she read the poem, which, although first published in 1870, struck them all as still meaningful in 1942. This moment stimulated Glaspell to expand on the value of the past. "Time does not dim what is real. . . . The past does not lose its voice, but is there to speak to us," she pronounced. She welcomed Whitman's lines as "a gift from the timeless" and urged "those who now write, and all who read, [to] seek the truth that will lead to peace on earth, good will to men."[99]

Firmly convinced of the value of the written word but aware of the more immediate power of the stage, Glaspell wrote a play about America's involvement in the cause of freedom and democracy. *Springs Eternal,* like most of her writing, is a meditation on the theme of evolution and achievement, but in this her last play, Glaspell raises the stakes, admitting that the future of the world is imperiled.[100] Her idealism is so unworldly that she can offer a solution: a declared pacifist is inspired by a friend's book—by the written word—to enlist and thereby contributes to the struggle for democracy and freedom. Glaspell does not doubt that his heroism will save humankind. Although she at no point condones the war, she accepts its inevitability as part of the process of improving the

Susan Glaspell, circa 1940
(Courtesy of the University Libraries, The University of Iowa)

world. After all, as one of the characters blandly reassures the recruit, "an awful lot of those guys you'll be shooting at deserve to die."[101]

In *Springs Eternal*, Glaspell places the fate of humanity in the hands of men, relegating women to the drudgery of homemaking. Although she had never declared herself a feminist, she had always supported the importance of so-called trifles, challenging women to determine their own space. But now, carried away by the persuasive arguments of the defenders of the patriarchy, she argued that women should stay at home, stay married, and look after their menfolk. *Springs Eternal* is best read as an apology for America's decision to enter World War II, but even as such, it is not convincing.

Early in 1944, Glaspell sent the manuscript to her old friend Lawrence Langner of the Theatre Guild. She pointed out that *Springs Eternal* was not a collaboration, as *The Comic Artist* had been, and should therefore receive his full attention.[102] Nevertheless, Langner stalled. When he finally gave his verdict, he dismissed the play as a "conversation piece" that recounted something "most of us have gone through . . . [arriving] at the conclusions two or three years ago."[103]

Glaspell was devastated; she had dreamed of a glorious return to the theater with a play that would point the way toward the salvation of the world. But she knew she must not give in to her disappointment, and, as she did so many times in her life, she unobtrusively put into practice a maxim she must have worked out as a young woman, crudely expressed by one of the characters in *Springs Eternal*: "I suppose the only thing we really have is the thing we're going to do."[104] Her refusal to give in led her to rewrite *Springs Eternal*, converting the play into a novel, *Judd Rankin's Daughter*.[105] Once again, she urged all writers—specifically those who were closest to her, Wilson and Dos Passos—to give America the book that would save humankind from despair. Her protagonist, Judd Rankin, does just that.

Rankin's memoirs of the Midwest dispel his grandson's traumatic experience of war. On his return from the Pacific front, young Judd Mitchell finds it impossible to return to everyday life; he has forfeited his faith in humankind and blames his father, an intellectual whose writing he now reckons only "lights dead faces," for not in some way preventing the war.[106] Disillusioned by his parents' impotence in the face of the world's inhumanity, he turns back to his roots. His grandfather had written an account of life in the Midwest, *The Jenkses*, in which he self-protectively negated the truth of feelings, thus leaving his readers "unsatisfied."[107] But a sequel, prompted by his daughter Frances, who wants her father to be "as big as he might have been," is so full of truth that on reading it, Judd no longer feels alone and can, once again, reach out to his parents and to life.[108]

The secret that Rankin reveals to his grandson, however, is not revealed to the reader. His truth is allowed to rest in obscurity, although Glaspell intimates that it stems from his relationship with Cousin Adah. When the novel opens, Cousin Adah is dying in an impersonal hotel room, accompanied by Frances Rankin Mitchell and an adolescent soldier with whom Cousin Adah has promised to share the secret of her life—a vital truth that will enable him to get through the war. Cousin Adah dies before she can impart her wisdom, and it is left to Frances and her father to bring this woman who joyously believed that "we should be happy and make everyone else we can happy" before us.[109] In *Alison's House*, Alison's message to the world is recovered through her poetry; in this novel, it is Frances Rankin Mitchell who takes over from the silenced, invisible woman and, by inspiring her father to write his truth, begets serenity—if not for the world, at least for the men in her life.

In her last novel, Glaspell acknowledges that, in a patriarchy, it is up to the men to act—be it by the sword or by the pen; she limits women to the role of passive inspirer or muse. For the first time, she has created male characters we can admire. Len Mitchell, Frances's husband, is an esteemed critic who has the courage to stick to his principles, and Judd Rankin, her father, proves himself a successful writer.

In *Judd Rankin's Daughter*, Glaspell is still immersed in that battle between the values of the past and the present that had always brought a note of ambivalence to her writing. Her unworldly solution to all problems—from local bigotry to shell shock—requires us to recognize that we are all part of the same scheme of things, of a Whitmanesque "oneness" that welcomes all creeds and races and thus makes loneliness unthinkable. The model for this idyllic community was Cape Cod, where social life was "like a great loosely-woven fishnet" that lured all types of men and women and where it was possible for minds to meet, mingle, and coexist.[110]

Judd Rankin's Daughter was published by Lippincott on 24 October 1945. Gollancz, still Glaspell's faithful advocate, accepted the novel but insisted the title be changed, fearing the English public would consider it reminiscent of a bad western. After much thought, Glaspell suggested *Prodigal Giver*, which suited her British publisher, who brought out the novel the following year. It was well received on both sides of the Atlantic, just missing the 1945 Metro-Goldwyn-Mayer Award. According to one American reviewer, Glaspell's writing had not lost its "quality of youth" and she had produced an "attractive" and "wise" novel.[111] A British reviewer, although miffed that Judd Rankin and Cousin Adah's secret is never revealed, considered it "a most accomplished novel in which marital and family relations are maintained on a friendly basis (such a nice change) and the noblest sentiments find expression through homely speech."[112]

Once *Judd Rankin's Daughter* was off her hands, Glaspell began writing a novel about an actress who hoped to return to the theater, but it was a novel she would never complete. As she grew older, and more lonely, she depended more and more on the company of her characters, experiencing particular pleasure when they surprised her by acquiring an identity and life of their own.[113] She would rehearse their lines as if they were actors on a stage, speaking out loud, trying to hear not only their words but also the personalities behind the words. One morning, Francelina, her maid, was horrified to hear voices coming from the bathroom and called out to inquire whether her mistress needed help. Enraged, Glaspell burst out of the bathroom, accusing poor Francelina of having ruined her concentration for the day.

Dr. Hiebert, Provincetown Greenwich Villagers' favorite doctor, had introduced Francelina to Glaspell in 1940. The daughter of a Portuguese fishing family, she was devoted to her mistress and grateful for the job. Despite her recent favorable portrayals of woman as mother and wife, Glaspell was sympathetic to Francelina's unhappy marriage and helped pay for her divorce.[114] As the years went by, Glaspell needed domestic help more and more; Francelina came in the mornings and afternoons, doing the shopping on her way, thus saving Glaspell from the horror of riding the bus that jounced up and down Commercial Street. Francelina also did the cleaning and the cooking, a cheese soufflé, salad, and chocolate mousse being her mistress's favorite menu. She also learned to prepare Glaspell's afternoon highball, vodka watered down with orange juice and a slice of lemon, which she would silently place on Glaspell's desk if she was writing in the afternoon. Glaspell would then put down her cigarette, cool her hands on the glass, take an occasional sip, and allow the characters to come to life. Her maid did not dare interrupt such moments of creative meditation. But if neighbors dropped in, Glaspell gladly abandoned her typewriter, exchanging fictional characters for the lively company of Mr. and Mrs. Ball or Christine Foster. Old friends, when they were in Provincetown, did not forget her either. Maddy L'Engle, who had a house close by, came regularly. But as Glaspell grew older, her dog and three cats became her most trustworthy companions.

Glaspell had always relied on her writing to bring in sufficient money, and she still owned property in Davenport, which brought in regular sums of about $25 a month. Notwithstanding the advances on novels that she deposited in her accounts at the West Side Savings Bank and the Manhattan Savings Bank, the interest on her savings was rarely significant. *The Morning Is Near Us* had helped her recover financially after her Federal Theatre stint, and now *Judd Rankin's Daughter*, which by January 1946 was in its third printing and had sold 15,500 copies, enhanced her finances. That same year also brought an advance of £150 from Gollancz for her new novel and $50 from Curtis Brown for a reprint of "A Jury of Her Peers."

The old farmhouse in Truro, with its cabin where she had loved to write, was now the home of Harl Cook, a wild young man who—like his father—found it hard to settle down. He delighted in terrifying placid Provincetowners as he roared down Commercial Street on his motorbike or flashed by on his roller skates. Glaspell saw Jig in him—not the Jig she had known intimately but that younger man she had admired when she was reporting on Davenport society for the *Weekly Outlook*.

An even younger version of Jig appeared in Provincetown in the summer of 1946. Glaspell was overjoyed to receive her stepgrandson, Sirius Cook Proestopoulos, who at eighteen was a veteran of the Greek civil war, having fought the communist guerrillas who planned to overthrow the German, Italian, and Bulgarian invaders. He soon dropped his last name because it was too much of a tongue twister and, under Glaspell's guidance, passed the entrance exams for Harvard. To Sirius, Glaspell seemed laconic and even-tempered; his exploits, even when they irritated her, inevitably acquired heroic proportions when she described them to others. The dog-sharks he had left on the kitchen floor after a midnight swim—which in private provoked terse criticism for cruelty to animals—became, to Sirius's amazement and relief, the excuse for public boasts of his athletic prowess. On one occasion, however, Sirius did manage to embarrass his stepgrandmother. He had accompanied her to a community meeting at which the speaker accused the Greek right wing of fascism. Sirius, whose grandfather would have done the same under such circumstances, thundered his disagreement, calling the speaker a liar. Glaspell rapidly rose to explain and excuse her volatile charge; she believed in free speech and knew that Sirius spoke from experience, an experience not shared by the speaker. Her reasonableness cooled all tempers, and the meeting continued, but Sirius recognized that he had trodden on dangerous ground, for his stepgrandmother's convictions had always been far removed from the right. In spite of this political clash, Glaspell loved the young student and helped him as best she could, often presenting him with a check or a gift. She enjoyed his company during vacations and was always happy to join him and Harl for a drink (which she had learned to water down remorselessly), as she puffed away at her Philip Morrises.[115]

In 1947, Glaspell, now seventy-one, was ailing. She could not see well and suffered from anemia. Nonetheless, she continued writing, the self-imposed discipline of so many years serving her well. The summer, as always, brought crowds to Provincetown, and old friends enlivened her evenings, Katy and John Dos Passos among them. Katy's unexpected death on 12 September 1947 shook the whole community. Driving up the Cape, Dos Passos was suddenly blinded by the setting sun and crashed into a parked truck. Katy, thrown into the windshield, "the top of her head practically sliced off, as though with a scalpel," died immediately.[116] John Dos Passos lost his right eye.

Dazed by the sudden loss of her friend, Glaspell attended the funeral service at Katy's house, the Arequipa, at 571 Commercial Street, opposite her own cottage. Crossing the street, she remembered the promise she had extracted from Katy when the younger woman bought the plot of land adjoining her home: while she lived, Katy was not to build anything or grow anything that would obstruct Glaspell's view.[117] Glaspell had sold this plot, where Cook had once desperately tried to grow vegetables, to Maddy L'Engle, who in turn sold it to Katy in 1945. She had been sure that Katy, so much younger, would outlive her.

That December, Glaspell made out her last will and testament. She was fast losing weight, and Francelina worried that she looked more and more "like a doll," fragile and paper-thin.[118] Glaspell told her she had cancer and assured her that no amount of food would help her now. She relied more and more on Francelina, knowing there was no one else she could turn to. One afternoon, going through her possessions as she tried to clear out the accumulations of a lifetime, she came across a beaded stocking her mother had made to wean her from the habit of sucking her thumb. She gave this to Francelina, who treasured the gift. Francelina helped her dispose of papers, letters, diaries, and such, for Glaspell did not like the thought of anyone digging into her life. The University of Iowa had, in 1946, asked for the privilege of storing her papers; she apparently did not even bother to reply.[119]

As 1948 advanced, Glaspell's health deteriorated visibly. Sirius visited her in July; she was lying on the couch downstairs and seemed to him extremely frail. She was too weak to read and spent her time dozing, with the radio for company. But she did manage to write out a check for Sirius, as she questioned him about his progress at Harvard and his plans for the future.

On the evening of 27 July, Glaspell, now very weak, turned for the last time to her maid and murmured: "I'm dying." She was fully conscious to the last and died quietly in Francelina's arms. Francelina sat with her until morning, when she called Maddy L'Engle.

Glaspell died of viral pneumonia and an embolism. The Protestant Episcopal Church, to which she had turned in her later years, remembering the kindness of the Episcopalian missionaries at the American College for Girls in Phaleron, held a quiet funeral service, and her ashes were scattered near Truro.[120] The Truro farmhouse had been her favorite refuge from the summer bustle of Provincetown, and her little cabin, where she had worked on *Alison's House* and written the novels inspired by her love for Norman Matson, was a symbol of peace and security.

Glaspell's will offered few surprises; she bequeathed all of her possessions to Harl and Sirius, and if they should die within thirty days of her death, to Nilla. Francelina White, her maid, was to receive $500, as was Florence Glaspell, Ray's widow.[121] She had no other close friends or relatives.

In an unpublished essay drafted toward the end of her life, Susan Glaspell, who had "the soul of a reformer," sought to articulate the impulse that led her to write.[122] Rejecting the easy answers—"because it's my business, because I want to make money, because I want to be important"—she concluded that the only satisfactory answer was "Because I want to!" But even that did not fully convince her. For Glaspell, writing was "a lonely business," an enervative, tormenting task; after a morning's work, she was "burned out—all spent" from the strain of bringing characters to life, balancing her creative power against their individuality. She argued that a worthwhile book had to "shed a light on life; to clarify" and declared that "the best books take us a little farther into understanding, into tolerance, to a keener amusement and to warmer sympathies."[123]

Glaspell's plays and novels do bring us closer to the dilemmas of the people of her time, and although women have now obtained the vote and much else has changed since she started writing, her work still "help[s] us in understanding ourselves,"[124] thus making it all the more difficult to accept that her voice has been silenced for so long. Critics of her era recognized Glaspell's worth as a writer and her vital role in the daily operation and artistic development of the Provincetown Players. Glaspell contributed eleven plays to the Provincetown stage, and at the time, her name was coupled with that of Eugene O'Neill. British critics tended to consider her the better dramatist "because she seems . . . to have a surer grasp of what she wants to do."[125] In America, Ludwig Lewisohn declared: "The Provincetown group produced Susan Glaspell and Eugene O'Neill and disappeared."[126]

Glaspell's part in the management of the Players has been very rarely acknowledged; in her demanding relationship with George Cram Cook, she was the counselor, confidante, and guardian angel—mother and mistress—who empowered him to galvanize others. Oliver Saylor, writing while Cook was still alive, praised Glaspell's "rare imagination," while at the same time regretting that it "sometimes bows to the latter and lesser master," and paid tribute to the "courage, daring and insight" she brought to the Players.[127]

As a playwright, Glaspell wrote for a specific audience: the fellow intellectuals and bohemians who subscribed to the Provincetown Players' bold adventure in creating an American drama. Her plays were compared to those of George Bernard Shaw and Anton Chekhov and were frequently dismissed as too talky and highbrow. But her novels, written, like her short stories, to please a wider audience, often reached the best-seller lists. In spite of such popular appeal, the critics responded well to her novels, ranking her with Willa Cather, Ellen Glasgow, Edith Wharton, and even Virginia Woolf. Arthur Hobson Quinn admitted condescendingly: "That the effort to find the right basis for the relations of men and women should engage the attention of women novelists, is natural, for the problem seems of more moment to them, and in some ways, is of more significance to women than to men." All the same, he declared Glaspell "a novelist of high rank," regardless of her sex.[128]

Glaspell's voice was silenced in the 1950s because her women—and her men—did not conform to postwar consumer society role models, which converted women into pretty dolls and men into brave, successful businessmen. Except in *Judd Rankin's Daughter*, Glaspell created forceful women who dare to risk all for love while maintaining more than a measure of independence; her men are ineffective, weak, and entirely dependent on women. Thus, perhaps it is not surprising that producers preferred to ignore her plays and editors forgot her novels.

Over the last thirty years, feminist literary criticism has worked to recover lost women writers. Unfortunately, in the case of Susan Glaspell, emphasis on one play, *Trifles*, and the short story that grew from it, "A Jury of Her Peers," has obscured her other writing and her contribution to the Provincetown Players and the Federal Theatre. My years with Glaspell have convinced me that this self-effacing woman who was brought up to revere men as her superiors but who never doubted her own power to transform the world can teach us much about the relations between men and women. In particular, in her plays and novels, she values the woman who, recognizing the transient nature of love, is not afraid to strike out on her own journey of improvement.

Notes

Abbreviations

BRBML	Beinecke Rare Book and Manuscript Library, Yale University, New Haven, Connecticut
BRTC	Billy Rose Theatre Collection, New York Public Library for the Performing Arts, New York, New York
Deutsch and Hanau, *PP*	Helen Deutsch and Stella Hanau, *The Provincetown: A Story of the Theatre* (1931; reprint, New York: Russell and Russell, 1972)
FTPC	Federal Theatre Project Collection, Copyright Drama Collection, Manuscript Division, Library of Congress, Washington, D.C.
GA	Gollancz Archives, London, England; courtesy of Livia Gollancz
GCC	George Cram Cook
GCCP	George Cram Cook Papers, Berg Collection of English and American Literature, New York Public Library, Astor, Lenox, and Tilden Foundations, New York, New York
Glaspell, *B*	Susan Glaspell, *Bernice* (London: Ernest Benn, 1924)
Glaspell, *I*	Susan Glaspell, *Inheritors*, in C. W. E. Bigsby, ed., *Plays by Susan Glaspell* (Cambridge: Cambridge University Press, 1987)
Glaspell, *RT*	Susan Glaspell, *The Road to the Temple* (New York: Frederick A. Stokes, 1927)
Glaspell, *SD*	Susan Glaspell, *Suppressed Desires*, in Barbara Ozieblo, ed., *The Provincetown Players: A Choice of the Shorter Works* (Sheffield, Eng.: Sheffield Academic Press, 1994)
Glaspell, *V*	Susan Glaspell, *The Verge*, in C. W. E. Bigsby, ed., *Plays of Susan Glaspell* (Cambridge: Cambridge University Press, 1987)
HTC	Harvard Theatre Collection, Nathan Marsh Pusey Library, Harvard University, Cambridge, Massachusetts
Kenton, "PPPT"	Edna Kenton, "The Provincetown Players and the Playwrights' Theatre, 1915–1922," carbon copy of typescript, BRBML

MBPP	Minute Book of the Provincetown Players, Province-town Players File, BRTC
RBML	Rare Book and Manuscript Library, Butler Library, Columbia University, New York, New York
RFTP	Records of the Federal Theatre Project, Records of the Work Projects Administration, RG 69, National Archives, Washington, D.C.
Sarlós, *JCPP*	Robert Károly Sarlós, *Jig Cook and the Provincetown Players: Theatre in Ferment* (Amherst: University of Massachusetts Press, 1982)
Sarlós Papers	Robert Károly Sarlós Papers, Department of Special Collections, University of California Library, Davis, California
SG	Susan Glaspell
SGP	Susan Glaspell Papers, Berg Collection of English and American Literature, New York Public Library, Astor, Lenox, and Tilden Foundations, New York, New York

Introduction

1. Sigmund Freud, *The Standard Edition of the Complete Psychological Works of Sigmund Freud*, trans. and ed. James Strachey (1957; reprint, London: Hogarth Press and the Institute of Psycho-Analysis, 1975), 11:130.

2. Kathleen Barry, "Toward a Theory of Women's Biography: From the Life of Susan B. Anthony," in Teresa Iles, ed., *All Sides of the Subject: Women and Biography* (New York: Teachers College Press, Columbia University, 1992), 28.

3. James Agate, *"The Verge*: A Play by Susan Glaspell," in *The Contemporary Theatre* (London: Chapman and Hall, 1926), 100.

4. R. Ellis Roberts, *The Guardian*, 17 July 1925; "Personalities and Powers: Susan Glaspell," *Time and Tide*, 27 March 1925.

5. Virginia Woolf, "The New Biography," *New York Herald Tribune*, 30 October 1927, reprinted in *Granite and Rainbow* (New York: Harcourt Brace and World, 1958), 149, 150.

6. Leon Edel, "The Figure under the Carpet," in Marc Pachter, ed., *Telling Lives: The Biographer's Art* (Washington, D.C.: New Republic Books / National Portrait Gallery, 1979), 24.

7. Friedrich Nietzsche, *Thus Spoke Zarathustra*, trans. R. J. Hollingdale (Harmondsworth, Eng.: Penguin, 1987), 41.

8. Susan Glaspell, "The Rules of the Institution," *Harper's Monthly Magazine*, January 1914, 208.

9. Ibid.

10. Lawrence Langner, *The Magic Curtain* (London: Harrap, 1952), 70.

11. Virginia Woolf, *Orlando* (1928; reprint, Harmondsworth, Eng.: Penguin, 1967), 218.

Chapter One

1. A photograph of this portrait is in an album in Ines Haynes Irwin Papers, Schlesinger Library, Radcliffe College, Cambridge, Massachusetts.

2. William Bradford, *Of Plymouth Plantation*, in Nina Baym, ed., *Norton Anthology of American Literature* (New York: Norton, 1989), 1:60.

3. Glaspell family genealogies can be found in Susan Glaspell and Belle Dodge-James (Alice Keating Glaspell's cousin), comps., "Genealogies: Jewett, Ricker, and Chipman Family Histories," SGP. For a detailed account of the Glaspell family, see Elsie Spry Davis, comp., "Glaspell: Relatives of James Glaspell (1789–1847) and Wife Jane Stathem (1792–1860)," Susan Glaspell File, Davenport Public Library, Davenport, Iowa.

4. Ronald N. Satz, "Indian Policy in the Jacksonian Era," in Leonard Dinnerstein and Kenneth T. Jackson, *American Vistas, 1607–1877* (New York: Oxford University Press, 1983), 156.

5. Glaspell, *I*, 110.

6. Julie Jensen, "Rich, Robust History," *Quad City Times*, 4 July 1976.

7. Harry E. Downer, *History of Davenport and Scott County, Iowa* (Chicago: S. J. Clarke, 1910), 1:598.

8. Marie Meyer, "Glaspell Family One of First to Found Village School System in City," *Davenport Democrat*, 27 December 1936.

9. Silas Glaspell's obituary, *Davenport Democrat*, 26 April 1881.

10. Ibid.

11. Ibid.

12. Ibid.

13. Mrs. Keating to Alice Keating, 30 August [?], SGP.

14. Although Susan Glaspell gave her birth date as 1 July 1882 (*Twentieth Century Authors* [1942]), Marcia Noe, in *Susan Glaspell: Voice from the Heartland* (Macomb: Western Illinois University Press, 1983), 13, has proved conclusively that Glaspell was born in 1876.

15. Octave Thanet (Alice French), *The Man of the Hour* (1905; reprint, New York: Arno Press, 1977), 34.

16. Lawrence H. Larsen, "Urban Iowa One Hundred Years Ago," *Annals of Iowa* 49, no. 6 (Fall 1988): 456.

17. Susan Glaspell, *Fugitive's Return* (New York: Frederick A. Stokes, 1929), 118.

18. Maria to Susan Ricker Glaspell, January 1881, SGP.

19. Elmer Glaspell to Alice Glaspell, 8 October 1882, SGP.

20. Minutes of the Ladies Harmonie Society, 3 September 1896 (thanks to Betty Gorshe for this source). *Weekly Outlook*, 19 June 1897, reports that the Etude Club "will enter upon a systematic course of study that will place it well to the front among the musical organizations of city and state" and gives the program of the club's latest performance, which includes Glaspell's solo.

21. Elmer Glaspell to SG, 15 January 1920, SGP.

22. Ibid., 20 May 1918.

23. Ibid., 23 October 1897 (essential punctuation added).

24. Ibid., 15 January 1920.

25. Susan Glaspell, "The Escape," *Harper's Monthly Magazine* December 1919, 36.

26. Elmer Glaspell to SG, n.d., SGP.

27. Downer, *History of Davenport*, 601.

28. "Susan Keating Glaspell," *Des Moines Daily News*, 3 May 1903.

29. Alice Keating Glaspell to SG, 24 February 1909, SGP.

30. SG to Alice Keating Glaspell, 12 March 1909, SGP.

31. Ibid., 18 June 1922.

32. Susan Glaspell, "The Return of Rhoda," *Youth's Companion*, 26 January 1905, 40.

33. SG to Alice Keating Glaspell, 17 October 1924, SGP. Emphasis in quotations throughout is reproduced as in the original unless otherwise specified.

34. Ibid., 12 September 1923.

35. Alice Keating Glaspell to SG, 27 September 1927, SGP.

36. Ray Glaspell to SG, 17 February 1929, SGP.

37. Florence Glaspell to SG, February 1929, SGP.

38. Floyd Dell, *Moon-Calf* (1920; reprint, New York: Sagamore, 1957), 219.

39. See George McMichael, *Journey to Obscurity: The Life of Alice French* (Lincoln: University of Nebraska Press, 1965); Clarence A. Andrews, *A Literary History of Iowa* (Iowa City: University of Iowa Press, 1972); and Susan C. McQuin, "Alice French's View of Women," in *Books at Iowa* (Iowa City: University of Iowa Press, 1974), 20, 34– 42.

40. Elmer Glaspell to SG, 23 October 1897, SGP.

41. Dell, *Moon-Calf*, 212.

42. *Weekly Outlook*, 1 July 1896, 27 February 1897.

43. Noe, *Susan Glaspell*, 87 (n. 8).

44. "Social Life," *Weekly Outlook*, 10 October 1896.

45. Ibid., 10 July 1897.

46. "The News Girl on the Congress of Mothers," *Des Moines Daily News*, 1 June 1900; "Social Life," *Weekly Outlook*, 24 July, 27 February 1897.

47. "Social Life," *Weekly Outlook*, 17 July 1897.

48. Ibid., 14 November 1896.

49. "In and Out of Town," *Weekly Outlook*, 21 August 1897.

50. Graduation from an accredited high school such as Davenport High School qualified a student to enter the junior year at Drake University.

51. *Drake University Bulletin*, June 1900, 17; Charles J. Ritchey, *Drake University through Seventy-five Years, 1881–1956* (Des Moines, Iowa: Drake University, 1956), 90.

52. Charles Blanchard, *Building for the Centuries: A Memorial of the Founders and Builders, Semicentennial, 1881–1931* (Des Moines, Iowa: Drake University, 1931), 89.

53. Ritchey, *Drake University*, 79.

54. "Drake University and Its Possibilities," *Des Moines Daily News*, 4 September 1900, reports 1,593 students in 1896 and augurs 1,800 for 1901.

55. *Drake University Bulletin*, June 1900, 26.

56. Blanchard, *Building for the Centuries*, 21.

57. "Profs Remember Susan Glaspell, Pulitzer Winner," *Des Moines Times-Delphic*, 7 May 1931, clipping, Susan Glaspell File, Drake University, Des Moines, Iowa.

58. Dorothy Fowler Heald on Susan Glaspell, quoted in unidentified clipping, n.d., SGP.

59. Ibid.

60. Ritchey, *Drake University*, 104.

61. Susan Glaspell, "The Philosophy of War," *The Delphic*, October 1898, 7–10. According to the Susan Glaspell File, Drake University, Des Moines, Iowa, *The Delphic* published the following works by Glaspell: "His Literary Training," January 1898, 83–85; "The Tragedy of a Mind," February 1898, 98–102; "The Philosophy of War," October 1898, 7–10; "In Memoriam" (obituary of Margaret Craig), February 1899, 126–29; and "Bismarck and European Politics" (essay), March 1899, 147–50. "The Unprofessional Crime," February 1900, 109–12, is not mentioned in the list at Drake or in Mary E. Papke's *Susan Glaspell: A Research and Production Sourcebook* (Westport, Conn.: Greenwood Press, 1993), which also omits "His Literary Training." The Drake files also contain a copy of Glaspell's "From the Pen of Failure," *Quax* (1905), 215–18 (an annual published by the junior class).

62. Glaspell, "Philosophy of War," 8.

63. "Philomathian Anniversary," *The Delphic*, March 1898, 123.

64. Glaspell, "Bismarck and European Politics."

65. "Oratorical Contest," *The Delphic*, December 1898, 86.

66. "Locals," *The Delphic*, December 1898, 86; January 1899, 113.

67. "The Oratorical Contest," *The Delphic*, March 1899, 157.

68. Ritchey, *Drake University*, 102.

69. Glaspell's student record for 1897–98 shows grades mostly in the high 80s and 90s, except for a 38 in modern history and a 40 in "Hugo" (Records Office, Drake University, Des Moines, Iowa) (thanks to Joyce Onnen for this source).

70. "Senior Class Day," *The Delphic*, June 1899, 247.

71. Blanchard, *Building for the Centuries*, 183.

72. The *Des Moines Daily News* claimed to be the first Iowa paper to hire women reporters. See Andrews, *Literary History of Iowa*, 169.

73. Gladys Denny Schultz, "Susan Glaspell," in Johnson Brigham, ed., *A Book of Iowa Authors by Iowa Authors* (Des Moines: Iowa State Teachers Association, 1930), 112.

74. Helen Woodward, *The Lady Persuaders* (New York: Obolensky, 1960), 64.

75. "The News Girl on the Business Girl," *Des Moines Daily News*, 5 May 1900.

76. "The News Girl on the Congress of Mothers," *Des Moines Daily News*, 1 June 1900.

77. "The News Girl on the Iowa Politician," *Des Moines Daily News*, 12 May 1900.

78. "Mrs. Hossack May Yet Be Proven Innocent," *Des Moines Daily News*, 12 December 1900. See also Patricia L. Bryan, "Stories in Fiction and in Fact: Susan Glaspell's 'A Jury of Her Peers' and the 1901 Murder Trial of Margaret Hossack," *Stanford Law Review* 49, no. 6 (1997): 1293–1363.

79. For a detailed analysis of Glaspell's coverage of this case and her transformation of it into a play, see Linda Ben-Zvi, " 'Murder, She Wrote': The Genesis of Susan Glaspell's *Trifles*," *Theatre Journal* 44, no. 2 (May 1922): 141–62, reprinted in Linda Ben-Zvi, ed., *Susan Glaspell: Essays on Her Theater and Fiction* (Ann Arbor: University of Michigan Press, 1995), 19–48.

80. *Twentieth Century Authors* (1942), 541.

81. Ibid.

82. Most biographical sources state that Glaspell earned a higher degree at the University of Chicago, but her record there shows only that she registered for the summer quarter in 1902, taking two literature courses taught by Oscar Lovell Triggs.

83. See Floyd Dell, *Homecoming: An Autobiography* (New York: Farrar and Rinehart, 1933), 171; Hutchins Hapgood, *A Victorian in the Modern World* (1939; reprint, Seattle: University of Washington Press, 1972), 376; and GCC to Mollie Price, 26, 27 December 1907, GCCP.

84. Richard J. Storr, *A History of the University of Chicago: Harper's University—The Beginnings* (Chicago: University of Chicago Press, 1966), 187.

85. Susan Glaspell, "The Girl from Down-Town," *Youth's Companion*, 2 April 1903, 160.

86. "Susan Keating Glaspell," *Des Moines Daily News*, 31 May 1903. Insofar as I have been able to ascertain, only three stories by Glaspell appeared in *Youth's Companion*: "The Girl from Down-Town," 2 April 1903, 160–61; "The Return of Rhoda," 26 January 1905, 40; and "The Boycott on Caroline," 22 March 1906, 137–38.

87. Susan Glaspell, "For Love of the Hills," *Black Cat*, October 1905, 2.

88. Susan Glaspell, "At the Turn of the Road," *The Speaker*, September 1907, 361.

89. Glaspell, *RT*, 248.

90. Susan Glaspell, "For Tomorrow: The Story of an Easter Sermon," *Booklovers Magazine*, 5 March 1905, 563.

91. Susan Glaspell, *Lifted Masks and Other Works*, introduction by Eric S. Rabkin (1912; reprint, Ann Arbor: University of Michigan Press, 1993), 256.

92. The *Ladies' Home Journal* published the following stories by Glaspell: "A Boarder of Art," October 1912, 10–11, 92–93; "Whom Mince Pie Hath Joined Together: The Story of a Starving Girl and a Thanksgiving Dinner in Paris," November 1913, 10, 71–73; and "Looking after Clara," August 1914, 9, 35–37.

93. The following stories by Glaspell appeared in *Harper's Monthly Magazine*: "The Rules of the Institution," January 1914, 198–208; "The Manager of Crystal Sulphur Springs," June 1915, 176–84; "Unveiling Brenda," June 1916, 14–26; "The Hearing Ear," December 1916, 234–41; "Beloved Husband," April 1918, 675–79; "The Busy Duck," November 1918, 828–36; "Pollen," March 1919, 446–51; "The Escape," December 1919, 29–38; and "The Nervous Pig," February 1920, 309–20.

94. Glaspell, "Pollen," 449.

Chapter Two

1. Glaspell, *RT*, 18.

2. Ibid.

3. Ibid., 194.

4. Floyd Dell, *Homecoming: An Autobiography* (New York: Farrar and Rinehart, 1933), 153; *Des Moines Daily News*, 31 May 1903.

5. George Cram Cook's 1902 curriculum vitae stated: "Born Davenport, Iowa, October 7th, 1873. A.B. University of Iowa, 1892. A.B. Harvard, 1893. Heidelberg, 1894. Université de Geneve, 1894–95. Instructor in English, University of Iowa, 1895–99. Served in 50th Iowa Vol. Inf. April–September 1898. Editorial writer, *Davenport Democrat*, 1901. Publications: *Hampton Roads*, played in 1897. 'Verses and Essays,' *Weekly Outlook*, 1897–98. 'Two Views of Whitman,' *The Dial*, 1897. 'Company B. of Davenport,' *The Company*, 1898. 'Kipling: An Appreciation,' *Contemporary Club Papers*, 1899. 'A Glimpse of Florentine Art,' *The Whitney Club*, University of Iowa, 1899. *In Hampton Roads*, Rand & McNally, 1899. 'A Mexican Masterpiece,' *The Two Republics*, 1900. 'Concerning Beaucaire,' *National Magazine*, 1902. 'Elves,' *Century Magazine*, 1902" (Department of Special Collections, Stanford University Libraries, Stanford, California).

6. "Hell with S," annotation in Cook's notes for an autobiography, GCCP.

7. Glaspell, *RT*, 168.

8. Dell, *Homecoming*, 152.

9. GCC to Charles Eugene Banks, [late November or December 1907], GCCP.

10. Floyd Dell, *Moon-Calf* (1920; reprint, New York: Sagamore, 1957), 247.

11. Ibid., 156.

12. Glaspell, *RT*, 194.

13. Ibid., 191.

14. Dell, *Moon-Calf*, 248.

15. Susan Glaspell, "For Tomorrow: The Story of an Easter Sermon," *Booklovers Magazine*, 5 March 1905, 565.

16. George Cram Cook, *Evolution* (Davenport, Iowa: Contemporary Club, 1907), 20–22. Glaspell used this passage in *The Road to the Temple*, 197–98. On 17 December 1906, Cook wrote to Mollie Price that he had "about finished my paper on Evolution." The paper was refused by the *Scientific American* (GCC to Price, 8 March 1907, GCCP). Cook decided to read it to the Contemporary Club on 27 December 1906, which then published it.

17. Glaspell, *RT*, 182.

18. Upton Sinclair, *Money Writes!* (New York: Albert and Charles Boni, 1927), 167.

19. George Cram Cook, *Some Modest Remarks on Socialism* (Davenport, Iowa: Contemporary Club, 1910), 6, 10.

20. Glaspell, *RT*, 179.

21. GCC to Mollie Price, 27 December 1907, GCCP. By this time, Cook was already flirting with Susan Glaspell.

22. Ibid., 23 August 1906.

23. Ibid., 30 November 1907.

24. Ibid., 18 February 1907.

25. Ibid., 26 November 1907.

26. Ibid., 29 November 1907.

27. Ibid., 2 December 1907.

28. Ibid., 17 December 1907.

29. GCC to SG, 10 December 1907, GCCP.

30. GCC to Mollie Price, 26 December 1907, GCCP.

31. Ibid., 3 January 1907.

32. Glaspell, *RT*, 200.

33. Ibid., 201.

34. SG to Alice Keating Glaspell, 12 March 1909, SGP.

35. "Miss Glaspell back from Paris," *Davenport Democrat*, 8 June 1909.

36. SG to Alice Keating Glaspell, 12 March 1909, SGP.

37. See Barbara Ozieblo, "Can a Woman Amount to Anything?: The American Woman's Kunstelroman at the Turn of the Century," in María José Alvarez Mauriño et al., eds., *Fin de siglo: crisis y nuevos principios* (León, Spain: Secretariado de Publicaciones de la Universidad de León, 1999), 291–97.

38. Susan Glaspell, *The Glory of the Conquered: The Story of a Great Love* (New York: Frederick A. Stokes, 1909), 268.

39. Ibid., 57.

40. Ibid., 32.

41. Ibid., 182.

42. Ibid., 82.

43. *Brook Evans* (1928), the novel inspired by Glaspell's love for Norman Matson, is about love—not about marriage as a solution to a woman's struggle for survival in a patriarchal world.

44. Glaspell, *Glory of the Conquered*, 262.

45. Ibid., 160.

46. Ibid., 189.

47. Ibid., 50.

48. GCC to SG, 10 December 1907, GCCP.

49. Ibid.

50. Dell, *Homecoming*, 170.

51. Hutchins Hapgood, *A Victorian in the Modern World* (1939; reprint, Seattle: University of Washington Press, 1972), 376–77.

52. Jane Tompkins, *Sensational Designs: The Cultural Work of American Fiction, 1790–1860* (New York: Oxford University Press, 1985), xvii.

53. Unidentified clipping signed "S. P. B. M.," n.d., SGP.

54. "Miss Glaspell Speaks before Tuesday Club," *Davenport Democrat*, 9 June 1909. The program of the Tuesday Club gives the date as 1 June 1909.

55. Dell, *Homecoming*, 173.

56. Mollie Price to Floyd Dell, spring 1909, Floyd Dell Papers, Newberry Library, Chicago, Illinois.

57. George Cram Cook, *The Chasm* (New York: Frederick A. Stokes, 1911), 19; Susan Glaspell, *The Visioning* (New York: Frederick A. Stokes, 1911), 160–61.

58. Glaspell, *The Visioning*, 418.

59. Ibid., 420.

60. Glaspell, *RT*, 62.

61. GCC to Mollie Price, 27 December 1907, GCCP.

62. Glaspell, *RT*, 293.

63. GCC, Holograph Diaries, 1898–1919, GCCP.

64. Susan Glaspell, "At the Source," *Woman's Home Companion*, May 1912, 5–6.

65. Susan Glaspell to editor, "Buy Books That the People Want," *Davenport Democrat*, 16 February 1910.

66. E. M. Sharon, "Denies That He Is Book Censor," *Davenport Democrat*, 18 February 1910.

67. Glaspell, "Buy Books That the People Want."

68. Susan Glaspell, "Finality in Freeport," *Pictorial Review Combined with Delineator*, 17 July 1916, 32.

69. GCC, "Political Aspects of the Library Board," GCCP.

70. Dell, *Homecoming*, 201.

71. Glaspell, *RT*, 208.

72. Susan Glaspell, *Fidelity* (1915; reprint, London: Jarrolds, 1924), 375.

73. Ibid., 158.

74. Ibid., 167.

75. Ibid., 267.

76. Ibid., 242.

77. Nilla Cram Cook, *My Road to India* (New York: Lee Furman, 1939), 8–9. According to Nilla Cook, Mollie had been spotted bowing to an ancient statue of Buddha on the school grounds. The local papers thereupon reported that the schoolchildren were taught to bow to a statue of the Kaiser. Mollie was arrested but was released on bail thanks to the efforts of Upton Sinclair. Proclaiming her pacifist convictions, she refused to dismiss a German teacher because of his nationality. Boyland was closed, and Mollie was tried for pacifism.

78. Ibid., 47.

79. Jack Reed, *The Day in Bohemia*, in Mabel Dodge Luhan, *Movers and Shakers*, vol. 3 of *Intimate Memories* (1936; reprint, New York: Kraus Reprint, 1971), 174.

80. SG to Charlotte Rudyard, editor of *Harper's Monthly Magazine*, April 1913, Susan Glaspell File, University Libraries, University of Iowa, Iowa City, Iowa.

81. Cook explained to Floyd Dell: "They won't let justices marry people any more in New Jersey. Our prejudice against the theological would probably bar preachers even if their prejudice against marrying divorced persons did not bar me. Hence the mayor. It's his first job" (13 April 1913, Floyd Dell Papers, Newberry Library, Chicago, Illinois).

82. Ibid.

83. Glaspell, *RT*, 238.

84. Ibid., 239.

85. Ibid., 230.

86. Ibid., 231.

87. Ibid., 239.

88. Ibid., 231.

89. Ibid., 232.

90. Ibid., 233–34.

91. Ibid., 234.

92. Hapgood, *Victorian in the Modern World*, 373.

93. See Dee Garrison, *Mary Heaton Vorse: The Life of an American Insurgent* (Philadelphia: Temple University Press, 1989), 85–86.

94. John Reed, "The Traders' War," *The Masses*, September 1914, 16–17.

95. *New Republic*, 4 December 1915, 108.

96. Max Eastman, Floyd Dell, and Art Young were charged under section 3 of the Espionage Act of 1917 with obstructing the war effort by publishing pacifist and anarchist articles in *The Masses*. Although the editors were acquitted, the magazine was denied distribution through the mails. It was reorganized as *The Liberator*, which was more cautious in its opposition to the war. For more details, see Leslie Fishbein, *Rebels in Bohemia: The Radicals of "The Masses," 1911–1917* (Chapel Hill: University of North Carolina Press, 1982), 15–29.

97. GCC to SG, February 1913, GCCP.

98. Hapgood, *Victorian in the Modern World*, 375.

99. Ines Haynes Irwin, "Adventures of Yesterday," 416, typescript, Ines Haynes Irwin Papers, Schlesinger Library, Radcliffe College, Cambridge, Massachusetts.

100. GCC to SG, 8 January 1915, GCCP.

101. Marsden Hartley, "Farewell Charles," in Alfred Kreymborg et al., eds., *The New Caravan* (New York: Norton, 1936), 557.

102. Hapgood, *Victorian in the Modern World*, 376.

103. Susan Glaspell's copy of *Our Mr. Wrenn*, SGP.

104. Luhan, *Movers and Shakers*, 143.

105. Ibid.

106. For more information on the Heterodoxy, see Judith Schwarz, *Radical Feminists of the Heterodoxy: Greenwich Village, 1912–1940* (Norwich, Vt.: New Victoria Publishers, 1986). See also Irwin, "Adventures of Yesterday."

107. Floyd Dell, *Women as World Builders: Studies in Modern Feminism* (Chicago: Forbes, 1913), 19.

108. Hutchins Hapgood, "Women in Society III: New Sex and Domestic Relations," unidentified clipping, n.d., Hutchins Hapgood and Neith Boyce Papers, BRBML.

109. Glaspell, *The Visioning*, 327. Glaspell's heroine wishes she lived in a state where women could vote; it seems only fair to ascribe a similar approval of suffrage to Glaspell. In an interview with Alice Rohe (*New York Morning Telegraph*, 18 December 1921), Glaspell asserted that she was "interested in all progressive movements, whether feminist, social or economic . . . but I can take no very active part other than through my writing. One can't work with too many things. . . . When one has limited strength one must use it for the thing one feels most important."

Chapter Three

1. Glaspell, *RT*, 249.

2. Lawrence Langner, in his autobiography *The Magic Curtain* (London: Harrap, 1952), 76, admits that this performance by Sam Eliot and Robert Edmond Jones, among others, took place but denies that it marked the birth of the Provincetown Players. His account identifies the play as Lord Dunsany's *Gods of the Mountain*, but Kenneth Macgowan reports that it was *The Glittering Gate* in *Footlights across America: Toward a National Theater* (New York: Harcourt Brace, 1929), 56.

3. GCC to SG, 26 January 1915, GCCP.

4. Langner, *Magic Curtain*, 94.

5. Thomas H. Dickinson, *The Insurgent Theatre* (New York: B. W. Huebsch, 1917), 176.

6. Glaspell, *RT*, 248.

7. *New York Herald*, [20 February 1915], and *New York Times*, [20 February 1915], quoted in Langner, *Magic Curtain*, 96.

8. Mabel Dodge Luhan, *Movers and Shakers*, vol. 3 of *Intimate Memories* (1936; reprint, New York: Kraus Reprint, 1971), 142.

9. Floyd Dell, "The Science of the Soul," *The Masses*, July 1916, 30–31.

10. Ernest Jones, *Years of Maturity, 1901–1919*, vol. 2 of *Sigmund Freud: Life and Work* (London: Hogarth Press, 1955), 62–63; Nathan G. Hale Jr., *Freud and the Americans: The Beginnings of Psychoanalysis in the United States, 1876–1917* (New York: Oxford University Press, 1971), 5.

11. Jones, *Years of Maturity*, 63. Jones eventually convinced Freud to transcribe the lectures, which were published in English translation in the *American Journal of Psychology* in 1910.

12. Max Eastman, "Exploring the Soul and Healing the Body," *Everybody's Magazine* 32 (June 1915): 750.

13. Hutchins Hapgood, *A Victorian in the Modern World* (1939; reprint, Seattle: University of Washington Press, 1972), 383; Sandor Ferenczi in *New York Times*, 5 June 1927, quoted in Frederick J. Hoffman, *Freudianism and the Literary Mind* (1945; reprint, Baton Rouge: Louisiana State University Press, 1967), 66.

14. Hapgood, *Victorian in the Modern World*, 384.

15. For a full discussion of Eastman's and Dell's reconciliation of Freud's and Marx's teachings, see Leslie Fishbein, "Freud and the Radicals: The Sexual Revolution Comes to Greenwich Village," *Canadian Review of American Studies* 12, no. 2 (Fall 1981): 173–89.

16. Hoffman, *Freudianism and the Literary Mind*, 58. William L. O'Neill, in *The Last Romantic: A Life of Max Eastman* (New York: Oxford University Press, 1978), 58, argues that Eastman, who needed quick money, deliberately simplified psychoanalysis in his articles for the popular *Everybody's Magazine* in order to make the subject accessible.

17. Glaspell, *RT*, 250; Ray Lewis White, ed., *Sherwood Anderson's Memoirs* (1942; reprint, Chapel Hill: University of North Carolina Press, 1969), 339.

18. Hale, *Freud and the Americans*, 411.

19. Glaspell, *RT*, 250.

20. Ibid.

21. Ludwig Lewisohn, *The Drama and the Stage* (New York: Harcourt Brace, 1922), 104.

22. Max Eastman, "A New Journal," *The Masses*, April 1914, 9.

23. Charles F. Oursler, "Behind the Madman's Dreams," *Technical World* 21 (April 1914): 207, quoted in Hale, *Freud and the Americans*, 410.

24. Glaspell, *SD*, 41, 37.

25. Ibid., 42.

26. Ibid., 45.

27. Ibid., 36.

28. Ibid., 51, 50.

29. Edwin Tenney Brewster, "Dreams and Forgetting: New Discoveries in Dream Psychology," *McClure's Magazine* 29 (October 1912): 719.

30. Ibid., 715.

31. Glaspell, *SD*, 39.

32. Ibid., 716–17 (emphasis added).

33. W. David Sievers, *Freud on Broadway: A History of Psychoanalysis and the American Drama* (New York: Hermitage House, 1955), 27.

34. Hale, *Freud and the Americans*, 400, 405; Hugo Munsterberg, "The Third Degree," *McClure's Magazine* 24 (October 1907): 614–22.

35. Glaspell, *SD*, 50.

36. Sigmund Freud, *Five Lectures on Psycho-Analysis*, in *The Standard Edition of the Complete Psychological Works of Sigmund Freud*, trans. and ed. James Strachey (1957; reprint, London: Hogarth Press and the Institute of Psycho-Analysis, 1975), 11:27.

37. Edna Kenton to Carl Van Vechten, 15 July 1915, Carl Van Vechten Papers, BRBML.

38. Quoted in Lois Palken Rudnick, *Mabel Dodge Luhan: New Woman, New Worlds* (Albuquerque: University of New Mexico Press, 1984), 96–97.

39. Luhan, *Movers and Shakers*, 45.

40. Ibid.

41. Ibid., 310.

42. Neith Boyce did eventually finish the fairy-tale version of the amours of Mabel Dodge and Jack Reed, entitled *The Faithful Lover* (typescript in Hutchins Hapgood and Neith Boyce Papers, BRBML, along with the versions of *Constancy*). The minutes of a 22 November 1916 meeting indicate that the Provincetown Players rejected *The Faithful Lover* by a majority of eight to three.

43. Boyce, *Faithful Lover*, typescript, Hutchins Hapgood and Neith Boyce Papers, BRBML.

44. The years given in the text for plays written by the Provincetown playwrights are those of the first production.

45. Hiram Kelly Moderwell, "The Art of Robert Edmond Jones," *Theatre Arts Magazine* 1, no. 2 (February 1917): 52.

46. Glaspell, *RT*, 251. Sarlós, in *JCPP*, suggests late summer for this performance, giving 15 July 1915 as the possible date.

47. Glaspell, *RT*, 251.

48. Ibid., 91.

49. Ibid., 94.

50. Mary Heaton Vorse, *Time and the Town: A Provincetown Chronicle* (New York: Dial Press, 1942), 118.

51. Ibid., 119.

52. GCC to SG, 15 March 1913, GCCP.

53. George Cram Cook, *Change Your Style*, 6, 1, typescript, Papers of Eugene O'Neill (MSS 6488-b), Clifton Waller Barrett Library of American Literature, Special Collections Department, University of Virginia Library, Charlottesville, Virginia.

54. Ibid., cast list and p. 3.

55. Luhan, *Movers and Shakers*, 89.

56. Dee Garrison, *Mary Heaton Vorse: The Life of an American Insurgent* (Philadelphia: Temple University Press, 1989), 84.

57. The church raids were initiated at the Ferrer Center, where anarchists, Industrial Workers of the World members, feminists, and other revolutionary spirits met to discuss how to bring about the new millennium. See Paul Avrich, *The Modern School Movement: Anarchism and Education in the United States* (Princeton, N.J.: Princeton University Press, 1980), 189.

58. Glaspell, *RT*, 252.

59. Garrison, *Mary Heaton Vorse*, 100.

60. Susan Glaspell, "Joe," *The Masses*, January 1917, 9.

61. SG to Alice Keating Glaspell, December 1915, SGP.

62. Glaspell, *RT*, 251.

63. GCC to SG, 15 February 1916, GCCP.

64. *Suppressed Desires* was performed at the Liberal Club on 5 March 1916, according to a printed announcement in SGP. Kenton mentions a performance at Ira Remsen's studio in "PPPT," 7.

65. Sarlós (*JCPP*, 20) claims that a notice in the *Provincetown Advocate* (8 June 1916) mentioning "carpenters, who are making sundry interior changes" to the fish-house dispels the myth that all of the work was carried out by the Players themselves. They may well have had local help, but as in their later theaters, most of the work was done by Cook and his followers.

66. For details of the size of the Wharf Theatre, see Sarlós, *JCPP*, 200–202.

67. Glaspell, *RT*, 307.

68. Kenton, "PPPT," 9.

69. Mary Heaton Vorse, "Playhouse History II," typescript, Archives of Labor and Urban Affairs, Walter P. Reuther Library, Wayne State University, Detroit, Michigan. The fire is also described in Louis Sheaffer, *O'Neill: Son and Playwright* (London: J. M. Dent and Sons, 1969), 347, where it is blamed on Myra Carr, who had hung some costumes too close to the stove. According to Vorse's account, Carr used the smaller shed on the wharf, and it was that shed that burned down in a fire caused by an oil stove.

70. Glaspell, *RT*, 255.

71. For an account of Glaspell's transformation of her experience as a reporter in 1900 into the play *Trifles*, see Linda Ben-Zvi, " 'Murder, She Wrote': The Genesis of Susan Glaspell's *Trifles*," *Theatre Journal* 44, no. 2 (May 1992): 141–62, reprinted in Linda Ben-Zvi, ed., *Susan Glaspell: Essays on Her Theater and Fiction* (Ann Arbor: University of Michigan Press, 1995), 19–48.

72. Glaspell, *RT*, 256.

73. Susan Glaspell, *Trifles*, in C. W. E. Bigsby, ed., *Plays by Susan Glaspell* (Cambridge: Cambridge University Press, 1987), 35–45.

74. Hapgood wrote to Dodge on 1 July 1916 that "Terry Carlin and O'Neill (son of James O'Neill)" were in Provincetown and that O'Neill enthusiastically took part in the theatricals (in Luhan, *Movers and Shakers*, 478).

75. Harry Kemp, "Out of Provincetown: A Memoir of Eugene O'Neill," *Theatre Magazine* 51 (April 1930): 22, reprinted in Mark W. Estrin, ed., *Conversations with Eugene O'Neill* (Jackson: University Press of Mississippi, 1990), 95–102.

76. Ibid. Gary Jay Williams has identified this play as *The Movie Man*, which was not published until 1950. See Gary Jay Williams, "Turned Down in Provincetown: O'Neill's Début Re-Examined," *Eugene O'Neill Newsletter* 12, no. 1 (1988): 17–31, for a full discussion of O'Neill's beginnings with the Provincetown Players.

77. Arthur Gelb and Barbara Gelb, *O'Neill* (1962; reprint, New York: Harper and Row, 1973), 334. For George Pierce Baker's influence on O'Neill and the rewriting of *Bound East for Cardiff*, see Paul Voelker, "Success and Frustration at Harvard: Eugene O'Neill's Relationship with George Pierce Baker (1914–1915)," in Marc Maufort, ed., *Eugene O'Neill and the Emergence of American Drama*, Costerus, n.s., vol. 75 (Amsterdam: Rodopi, 1989), 25.

78. Kenton, "PPPT," 12.

79. Glaspell, *RT*, 254.

80. Ibid.

81. Harry Kemp, "Stray Cats, Purple Cabbages, and a Shaky Throne: It Is the Unforeseen and Unrehearsed Incidents in a Play That Make It or Break It," *Theatre Magazine* 48 (May 1927): 64.

82. Throughout *The Road to the Temple*, Glaspell understates her own achievements and undervalues her role in the Provincetown Players. For her account of the first meeting with O'Neill, see *RT*, 253–54.

83. Edna Kenton, "The Provincetown Players and the Playwrights' Theater," *Billboard* 5 (August 1922): 7. In Kenton's unpublished history of the Players, O'Neill's arrival is further embellished: Glaspell hails Carlin from her window and, on hearing

of the trunkful of plays, calls out: "Too many. Make him understand that. But ask him to come here tonight with just one—the best one—to read" (Kenton, "PPPT," 11–12). Glaspell's own account is straightforward and represents her as totally undiscriminating; she instructs Carlin to "tell Mr. O'Neill to come to our house at eight o'clock to-night, and bring some of his plays" (*RT*, 253). Sheaffer in *O'Neill: Son and Playwright*, 346, relies on Glaspell's *The Road to the Temple* for his account of O'Neill's introduction to the Players.

84. Glaspell, *RT*, 256.

85. This phrase was used by Edna Kenton in the *Boston Evening Transcript*, 27 April 1918, and quoted by Glaspell in *RT*, 245. It was originally used by Cook in one of the Provincetown circulars.

86. Vorse, *Time and the Town*, 116, 117, 124.

87. Neith Boyce to her father, 17 August 1915, quoted in Sheaffer, *O'Neill: Son and Playwright*, 343.

88. Glaspell, *RT*, 253.

89. Ibid.

90. Ibid., 244.

91. Ibid., 257.

92. Ibid., 265, 266. Glaspell assures her readers that the Players were "never so poor we couldn't have wine for these parties." It is therefore most likely that on an occasion such as the founding of their theater, Cook would have put one of his kegs of wine at the disposal of his friends.

93. MBPP, 5 September 1916.

94. Ibid., 11.

95. According to Glaspell's account, the Players launched their New York career on $245 (*RT*, 258). Kenton in "PPPT" states that eight of the wealthiest members subscribed $30 each, a sum that was added to the $80 profit from the fifth summer bill, resulting in a still meager total of $320.

96. Kenton, "PPPT," 22.

Chapter Four

1. Glaspell, *RT*, 258.

2. Ibid., 259.

3. GCC to SG, 12 September 1916, GCCP.

4. Ibid., 20 September 1916.

5. Glaspell, *RT*, 260.

6. Ibid.

7. For detailed descriptions of the first Macdougal Street theater, see Kenton, "PPPT"; Deutsch and Hanau, *PP*; and Sarlós, *JCPP*, 202–3.

8. Deutsch and Hanau, *PP*, 19.

9. Kenton, "PPPT," 27A.

10. Ibid., 30.

11. GCC to Frank Shay, 17 March 1920, Hutchins Hapgood and Neith Boyce Papers, BRBML.

12. Susan Glaspell, "A Jury of Her Peers," *Everyweek*, 5 March 1917, and "The Hearing Ear," *Harper's Monthly Magazine*, December 1916, 234–41.

13. "The Provincetown Players, Season of 1916–17," Provincetown Scrapbook, Hutchins Hapgood and Neith Boyce Papers, BRBML.

14. Kenton, "PPPT," 30.

15. Sam Hume's exhibition of the "New Stagecraft" in Cambridge, Massachusetts, included a number of Robert Edmond Jones's designs. Emily Hapgood saw the exhibit in New York and was so fascinated by Jones's work that she asked him to design New York Stage Society productions, thus launching his career.

16. Deutsch and Hanau, *PP*, 20. According to Deutsch and Hanau, the members of the New York Stage Society were distinctly hostile, frequently making the Players feel that "they were indulging in the most commonplace of amateur theatricals" (ibid.). The Players considered the performances for the Stage Society to be more nerve-wracking than those for "friends and fellow-torch-bearers." Sarlós, contradicting Kenton, argues that there could only have been fifty nonsociety members and that performances must have been mixed. Sarlós contends that the Stage Society subscriptions "probably saved the Provincetowners' enterprise from still birth" (*JCPP*, 68).

17. Deutsch and Hanau, *PP*, 20.

18. MBPP, 22 November 1916.

19. Louise Bryant to Jack Reed, [November/December 1916], John Reed Papers, shelf mark bMS 1091 (261), by permission of the Houghton Library, Harvard University, Cambridge, Massachusetts.

20. MBPP, 27 November 1916.

21. Louise Bryant to Jack Reed, [November/December 1916], John Reed Papers, shelf mark bMS 1091 (261), by permission of the Houghton Library, Harvard University, Cambridge, Massachusetts.

22. Kenton, "PPPT," 45.

23. "Provincetown Players Offer Three More Plays," *New York Herald*, 18 November 1916.

24. Ibid.

25. Kenton, "PPPT," 45; Sarlós, *JCPP*, 80.

26. Glaspell, *RT*, 265–66.

27. Of all of the people I interviewed, only Ana Matson Hamburger believed that alcohol had been a problem for Glaspell (during the end of Glaspell's relationship with Norman Matson); Miriam Hapgood DeWitt, Madeleine L'Engle, and Sirius Cook all assured me that Glaspell did not drink.

28. Kenton would write of *Before Breakfast*: "It was deliberate experiment for a definite result" ("PPPT," 47).

29. Eugene O'Neill, *Before Breakfast*, in John Lahr, ed., *The Collected Plays of Eugene O'Neill* (London: Jonathan Cape, 1988), 111.

30. Sarlós, *JCPP*, 70; Deutsch and Hanau, *PP*, 23; Arthur Gelb and Barbara Gelb, *O'Neill* (1962; reprint, New York: Harper and Row, 1973), 322–23.

31. In his analysis of *Beyond the Horizon* in *Contour in Time: The Plays of Eugene O'Neill* (New York: Oxford University Press, 1972), 119, Travis Bogard recognizes O'Neill's debt to T. C. Murray's *Birthright*, a two-act tragedy O'Neill saw on the bill of short plays that opened the Irish Players' New York season in November 1911. He does not mention Boyce's *The Two Sons*, which clearly reverberated in O'Neill's imagination.

32. Alfred Kreymborg, *Troubadour: An Autobiography* (New York: Boni and Liveright, 1925), 306, 308.

33. Ibid., 308.

34. This is according to Kreymborg (ibid.). The MBPP on 8 November 1916 does not record any argument over whether *Lima Beans* should be accepted: the text "was read by the author. Balloting of this play resulted in 14 votes for it, 3 against and 2 provisional. It was therefore declared accepted." Later at the same meeting, "it was suggested that the 3rd bill might be better balanced if *Lima Beans* were substituted for *Joined Together*, the latter to be used for a later bill. A vote taken by ballot resulted in a

vote of 9 to 3 in favor of this substitution." *Lima Beans* was included in the third bill on 1–5 December 1916, when Reed was not in New York; Louise Bryant wrote to him on 14 November 1916: "I am just home from Kreymborg's—the first rehearsal of *Lima Beans*. There were several disappointing girls there—not one would do, went through the part with Carlos Williams. He is fine. They will rehearse here Thursday with more new girls" (John Reed Papers, shelf mark bMS Am 1925 [197] (111), by permission of the Houghton Library, Harvard University, Cambridge, Massachusetts).

35. Kreymborg, *Troubadour*, 308–9.

36. Ibid., 309.

37. Kenton, "PPPT," 40.

38. Gerhard Bach, "Susan Glaspell: Provincetown Playwright," *Great Lakes Review* 4, no. 2 (1978): 35. See also Sarlós, *JCPP*, 88 and chap. 6.

39. Bach, "Susan Glaspell," 36.

40. Kreymborg, *Troubadour*, 312.

41. Ibid., 320.

42. Heywood Broun in *New York Tribune*, 31 March 1918.

43. Deutsch and Hanau, *PP*, 31.

44. Kenton, "PPPT," 89.

45. Edmund Wilson, *Shores of Light: A Literary Chronicle of the Twenties and Thirties* (New York: Farrar, Straus and Giroux, 1952), 683, 748.

46. Edna St. Vincent Millay to Cora B. Millay, November 1919, in Allan Ross Macdougall, ed., *Letters of Edna St. Vincent Millay* (New York: Harper and Brothers, 1952), 90.

47. Joan Dash, *A Life of One's Own: Three Gifted Women and the Men They Married* (New York: Paragon House, 1988), 144.

48. Heywood Broun in *New York Tribune*, 25 November 1918.

49. Dash, *Life of One's Own*, 146.

50. Edna St. Vincent Millay, *Aria da Capo*, in Barbara Ozieblo, ed., *The Provincetown Players: A Choice of the Shorter Works* (Sheffield, Eng.: Sheffield Academic Press, 1994), 222.

51. See William Shakespeare, *Midsummer Night's Dream*, 5.1.

52. In the 1924 edition of *Aria da Capo* (ed. Grace Adams [New York: Appleton, 1924], 39), Millay added advice to amateur players on how to stage her play. She refers to the original Provincetown production: "Instead of wings and back-drop the Provincetown Players cleverly utilized painted screens, the height varying from 6 to 10 ft., these being set right and left of the stage in such a manner as to give the effect of depth and distance." In the stage instructions, she indicates that "the curtain rises on a stage set for a Harlequinade, a merry black and white interior."

53. Bach, "Susan Glaspell," 35–36. Bach gives 1918 as the year the play was written; *Aria da Capo* was first performed by the Provincetown Players in December 1919 and published by Harper in 1920.

54. Kenton, "PPPT," 45, 27.

55. Ibid., 49.

56. Floyd Dell, *Homecoming: An Autobiography* (New York: Farrar and Rinehart, 1933), 266. See also Louise Bryant to Jack Reed, 2 December 1916, John Reed Papers, shelf mark bMS Am 1925 (197), by permission of the Houghton Library, Harvard University, Cambridge, Massachusetts. Bryant arrogantly affirms that the only good plays done by the Provincetown Players were her own *The Game* and O'Neill's *Bound East for Cardiff*, although "the only thing wrong with [Reed's] *Freedom* was that some of them didn't know their lines."

57. Quoted in Sarlós, *JCPP*, 72.

58. Ibid.

59. According to the MBPP, Glaspell read the play on 17 January 1917, and it was unanimously accepted at the 31 January 1917 meeting and performed on 9–14 March 1917.

60. John Corbin, "Little Theater Plays," *New York Times*, 11 November 1917.

61. Jacques Copeau, quoted in Norman H. Paul, "Jacques Copeau Looks at the American Stage, 1917–1919," *Educational Theatre Journal*, March 1977, 68.

62. Susan Glaspell, *The People*, in *Trifles and Six Other Short Plays* (1926; reprint, London: Ernest Benn, 1929), 43.

63. Ibid., 34, 35, 39.

64. Ibid., 39.

65. M. H. Hedges, "Miss Glaspell's Vision of Life," *The Nation*, 4 April 1923.

66. Deutsch and Hanau, *PP*, 24.

67. Isaac Goldberg, *The Drama of Transition: Native and Exotic Playcraft* (Cincinnati: Stewart Kidd, 1922), 475.

68. SG to Louise Bryant, 21 December 1916, John Reed Papers, shelf mark bMS Am 1091 (999), by permission of the Houghton Library, Harvard University, Cambridge, Massachusetts.

69. *Family Pride* was read at a meeting on 27 December 1916, unanimously accepted on 17 January 1917, and performed, under the title *Close the Book*, on 2–6 November 1917.

70. Corbin, "Little Theater Plays." Corbin applauds Glaspell for "striking at the vagaries of the abnormal psychologist [in *Suppressed Desires*] and the equally abnormal new-moralist."

71. Susan Glaspell, *Close the Book*, in *Trifles and Six Other Short Plays*, 49.

72. Glaspell, *RT*, 287.

73. Susan Glaspell, "A Rose in the Sand: The Salvation of a Lonely Soul," *Pall Mall* (1927), 45–51.

74. Ibid., 48.

75. Ibid., 51.

76. Susan Glaspell, *Woman's Honor*, in *Trifles and Six Other Short Plays*, 82–102.

77. Ibid., 97.

78. Glaspell, *B*; *Chains of Dew*, typescript, Library of Congress, Washington, D.C.; and *Ambrose Holt and Family* (New York: Frederick A. Stokes, 1931).

79. Goldberg, *Drama of Transition*, 475.

80. *New York Evening Globe*, 22 May 1918.

81. Interview in *New York Tribune*, 13 February 1921, reprinted in Oscar Cargill, ed., *Eugene O'Neill and His Plays* (London: Peter Owen, 1962), 104.

82. George Cram Cook, *The Athenian Women* (Athens: Estia, 1926), 8.

83. "Provincetown Players Announcement for the Third New York Season, 1918–1919," Hutchins Hapgood and Neith Boyce Papers, BRBML.

84. Aristophanes, *Lysistrata*, trans. Alan H. Sommerstein (Harmondsworth, Eng.: Penguin, 1987), 200.

85. Ibid., 221.

86. Ibid., 227.

87. Glaspell, *RT*, 415. It is important to remember that the only translation available at this time was by Benjamin Bickley Rodgers, a Victorian version that suppressed the fun and obscenity.

88. George Cram Cook, *Athenian Women*, 4.

89. Ibid., 6.

90. Ibid., 4.

91. Ibid., 204.

92. Ibid., 224.

93. GCC to Ida Rauh, n.d., GCCP; Heywood Broun in *New York Tribune*, 4 March 1918.

94. Glaspell, *RT*, 273.

95. GCC to SG, 24 May 1918, GCCP.

96. "Art Is Stove In," *New York Sun*, 5 April 1917.

97. Edna Kenton, "Unorganized, Amateur, Purely Experimental," *Boston Evening Transcript*, 27 April 1918. Robert Károly Sarlós believed that Cook's resentment was not called for since Kenton spoke very highly of the group's producer (*JCPP*, 94), but the context implies that she was referring to Nina Moise, not to Cook, whose official title was director of the Provincetown Players.

98. GCC to SG, 24 May 1918, GCCP.

99. Kenton, "Unorganized, Amateur, Purely Experimental," 9.

100. Jefferson Machammer, "The Stage and Its People," *New York Tribune*, 12 February 1922.

101. John Corbin, "The One-Act Play," *New York Times*, 19 May 1918.

102. John Corbin in *New York Times*, 26 May 1918.

103. "Who Is Susan Glaspell?," *New York Times*, 26 May 1918.

Chapter Five

1. Agnes Boulton, *Part of a Long Story: Eugene O'Neill as a Young Man in Love* (London: Peter Davies, 1958), 166.

2. Mary Heaton Vorse, *Time and the Town: A Provincetown Chronicle* (New York: Dial Press, 1942), 134.

3. Glaspell, *RT*, 298–99. Glaspell does not specify what sort of questionnaire it was.

4. GCC to SG, [May 1918], GCCP.

5. Kenton comments wryly: "We were lucky in that year of mass hysteria not to have been jailed for [staging *The Athenian Women*]" ("PPPT," 95).

6. "Provincetown Players Announcement for the Third New York Season, 1918–1919," Hutchins Hapgood and Neith Boyce Papers, BRBML.

7. Friedrich Nietzsche, *Thus Spoke Zarathustra*, trans. R. J. Hollingdale (Harmondsworth, Eng.: Penguin, 1987), 52.

8. Glaspell, *RT*, 257.

9. Eugene O'Neill, "What the Theater Means to Me," in Oscar Cargill, ed., *Eugene O'Neill and His Plays* (London: Peter Owen, 1962), 107.

10. Ibid.

11. Friedrich Nietzsche, *The Birth of Tragedy*, trans. Walter Kaufmann (New York: Vintage Books, 1967), 62.

12. Arthur Gelb and Barbara Gelb, *O'Neill* (1962; reprint, New York: Harper and Row, 1973), 364.

13. Boulton, *Part of a Long Story*, 163–64.

14. Ibid., 32–33.

15. GCC to SG, 11 September 1918, GCCP.

16. Glaspell, *RT*, 300.

17. Alice Keating Glaspell to SG, 8 October 1918, SGP.

18. Glaspell, *RT*, 300.

19. GCC to SG, 20 September 1918, GCCP.

20. Ibid.

21. MBPP, 21 April 1918.

22. Deutsch and Hanau, *PP*, 80.

23. Alexander Berkman, *Prison Memoirs of an Anarchist* (1912; reprint, Pittsburgh, Pa.: Frontier Press, 1970), 63.

24. Ibid., 10.

25. M. Eleanor Fitzgerald to Erwin Piscator, 1 January 1950, quoted in *In Memory of Fitzi*, edited and issued by Pauline H. Turkel, New York, on Fitzi's death in 1955, Provincetown Players File, BRTC.

26. Both Fitzgerald and Goldman feared that if Berkman were released on bail, he would be "in danger of being kidnapped and spirited away to California" (Emma Goldman, *Living My Life* [1931; reprint, New York: Dover, 1970], 2:630).

27. Turkel, *In Memory of Fitzi*.

28. Deutsch and Hanau, *PP*, 81.

29. Turkel, *In Memory of Fitzi*.

30. Deutsch and Hanau, *PP*, 81.

31. Allen Churchill, *The Improper Bohemians: A Re-creation of Greenwich Village in Its Heyday* (1959; reprint, London: Cassell, 1961), 210.

32. Deutsch and Hanau, *PP*, 45.

33. For detailed measurements of the stage and auditorium, see Sarlós, *JCPP*, 203–4.

34. Kenton, "PPPT," 113.

35. Glaspell, *RT*, 224.

36. Ibid.

37. James W. Flannery, *W. B. Yeats and the Idea of a Theatre: The Early Abbey Theatre in Theory and Practice* (Toronto: Macmillan, 1976), 63.

38. Nathaniel Hawthorne, preface to *The Marble Faun* (New York: Signet, 1961), vi. Van Wyck Brooks coined the phrase "a usable past" in his reevaluation of American literature, "On Creating a Usable Past," *The Dial* 64 (April 1918): 337–41.

39. Nietzsche, *Birth of Tragedy*, 76.

40. Deutsch and Hanau, *PP*, 21.

41. Ibid., 26.

42. Jacques Copeau, "An Essay on Dramatic Renovation," in Marie-Hélène Dasté and Suzanne Maistre Saint-Denis, eds., *Les Registres du Vieux Colombier* (Paris: Gallimard, 1974), 1:23, quoted in John Rudlin, *Jacques Copeau* (Cambridge: Cambridge University Press, 1986), 6.

43. For an analysis of the aims of the original Players, see Arnold Goldman, "The Culture of the Provincetown Players," *American Studies* 12, no. 3 (Autumn 1978): 291–310.

44. Quoted in Churchill, *Improper Bohemians*, 207; Glaspell, *RT*, 264.

45. Deutsch and Hanau, *PP*, 41–42.

46. Kenton, "PPPT," 129.

47. Ibid., 128. Nilla Cook, in an 18 December 1963 letter to Robert Károly Sarlós, attributes the "failure" of the Provincetown Players to "the lightness with which the new generation of Bohemians, Greenwich Villagers, treated the things which had been so serious to the older" and places most blame on director James Light (Sarlós Papers).

48. Glaspell, *RT*, 91, 37.

49. Churchill, *Improper Bohemians*, 213.

50. Ibid., 262.

51. Ibid., 204; Sarlós, *JCPP*, 106. Sarlós interviewed and corresponded with a number of the younger Players and concluded that it was not just a generation gap that troubled their relations with Cook. Although Sarlós is careful not to deny Cook's role as "prime mover and sustainer" of the Provincetown Players, he implies that his

"lack of gift in the crafts of the theater," coupled with his pride, prevented him from attaining the place in the theater world that his zeal and energy merited.

52. Glaspell, *RT*, 224.

53. Ibid., 277.

54. Ibid., 276–77.

55. Ibid., 122.

56. Hutchins Hapgood, *A Victorian in the Modern World* (1939; reprint, Seattle: University of Washington Press, 1972), 375.

57. Glaspell, *RT*, 264.

58. Eugene O'Neill, *The Fountain*, in John Lahr, ed., *The Collected Plays of Eugene O'Neill* (London: Jonathan Cape, 1988), 462.

59. *New York Tribune*, 23 December 1918.

60. Maxwell Bodenheim, "Roughneck and Romancer," *New Yorker*, 6 February 1926, 17.

61. *New York Tribune*, 5 January 1919.

62. Eleanor Flexner, *The Woman's Rights Movement in the United States* (Cambridge: Harvard University Press, 1973), 285.

63. Alice Rohe in *New York Morning Telegraph*, 18 December 1921.

64. Elizabeth Cady Stanton, Susan B. Anthony, and Matilda Joslyn Gage, eds., *History of Woman Suffrage*, vol. 1, *1848–1861* (1881; reprint, New York: Arno and New York Times, 1969), 806.

65. Crystal Eastman, "Now We Can Begin," *Liberator* 3, no. 12 (December 1920): 23.

66. Inez Haynes Irwin, "Adventures of Yesterday," 414, typescript, Inez Haynes Irwin Papers, Schlesinger Library, Radcliffe College, Cambridge, Massachusetts.

67. SG to Eleanor Fitzgerald, 7 May 1929, Susan Glaspell File, BRTC.

68. Floyd Dell's autobiographical protagonist in *Moon-Calf* proclaims: "I merely want a girl that can be talked to and that can be kissed, and I want it to be the same girl" ([1920; reprint, New York: Sagamore, 1957], 253). He was clearly not aware that his choice of pronouns betrayed him.

69. Max Eastman, *Enjoyment of Living* (New York: Harper and Row, 1948), 35.

70. Ellen Kay Trimberger, "Feminism, Men, and Modern Love: Greenwich Village, 1900–1925," in Ann Snitow et al., eds., *Powers of Desire: The Politics of Sexuality* (New York: Monthly Review Press, 1983), 139.

71. Hutchins Hapgood, *The Story of a Lover* (New York: Boni and Liveright, 1919), 91–92 (initially published anonymously). One of Hapgood's affairs was savagely derided by Theodore Dreiser in his story "Esther Norn," in *A Gallery of Women* (New York: Horace Liveright, 1929), 2:723–75. Like so many of the Greenwich Village men, Hapgood needed a feminine muse to massage his ego. His gaze fell on the beautiful Mary Pyne, one of the better Provincetown actresses. But Mary was married to the hobo poet Harry Kemp—she was his legitimate muse, and although he never had the wherewithal to supply basic needs, he loved her dearly. Mary contracted tuberculosis and, nursed by both Dreiser and Hapgood, died in 1920.

72. Hapgood, *Victorian in the Modern World*, 320.

73. Glaspell, *RT*, 156.

74. Ibid., 174.

75. Florence Kiper, "Some American Plays from the Feminist Viewpoint," *Forum* 51 (June 1914): 921–31.

76. Ibid., 931.

77. Arthur Pollock, "About the Theater," unidentified clipping, n.d., Provincetown Players Scrapbook, 1916–20, HTC.

78. Sarlós, *JCPP*, 98–99.

79. "Funereal Drama and Childish Skit in the Village," *New York Herald*, 24 March 1919.

80. Ibid.

81. See Trimberger, "Feminism, Men, and Modern Love," for a clear account of the discrepancies between what the men and women of Greenwich Village sought from love and marriage.

82. Glaspell, *B*, 11.

83. Ibid., 18.

84. Ibid., 15.

85. Ibid., 17.

86. Ibid., 17, 52.

87. Ibid., 53.

88. Ibid., 55.

89. Ibid., 54.

90. Ludwig Lewisohn, *The Drama and the Stage* (New York: Harcourt Brace, 1922), 105.

91. Glaspell, *RT*, 297, 294.

92. Glaspell, *B*, 28, 27.

93. Ibid.; John Corbin, "Seraphim and Cats," *New York Times*, 30 March 1919.

94. Glaspell, *B*, 11.

95. Ibid., 9.

96. "Funereal Drama and Childish Skit in the Village"; Corbin, "Seraphim and Cats."

97. *Boston Evening Transcript*, 31 March 1919.

98. Agnes Boulton to Eugene O'Neill, 8 February 1920, Agnes Boulton Papers, HTC.

Chapter Six

1. Arthur Gelb and Barbara Gelb, *O'Neill* (1962; reprint, New York: Harper and Row, 1973), 316.

2. Edna Kenton, "Provincetown and Macdougal Street," in George Cram Cook, *Greek Coins* (New York: George H. Doran, 1925), 24.

3. Kenton, "PPPT," 58.

4. Edna Kenton, "The Provincetown Players and the Playwrights' Theater," *Billboard*, 5 August 1922.

5. Sarlós, *JCPP*, 52. In a more recent article (" 'Write a Dance': *Lazarus Laughed* as O'Neill's Dithyramb of the Western Hemisphere," *Theatre Survey* 29, no. 1 [May 1988]: 37–49), Sarlós examines the relationship between Cook and O'Neill in greater depth, specifically analyzing Cook's influence on *Lazarus Laughed*.

6. Nilla Cook to Robert Károly Sarlós, 5 February 1975, Sarlós Papers.

7. Eugene Solow, "America's Great Woman Dramatist: Susan Glaspell," *The World*, 9 February 1930.

8. Linda Ben-Zvi, "Susan Glaspell and Eugene O'Neill," *Eugene O'Neill Newsletter* 6, no. 2 (1982): 21–29, and "Susan Glaspell and Eugene O'Neill: The Imagery of Gender," *Eugene O'Neill Newsletter* 10, no. 1 (1986): 22–27.

9. Ludwig Lewisohn, *Expression in America* (London: Thornton Butterworth, 1931), 392.

10. Isaac Goldberg, *The Drama of Transition: Native and Exotic Playcraft* (Cincinnati: Stewart Kidd, 1922), 472–73.

11. Agnes Boulton, *Part of a Long Story: Eugene O'Neill as a Young Man in Love* (London: Peter Davies, 1958), 282–83. Louis Sheaffer gives a slightly different account of how the coast guard station was acquired by the O'Neills in *O'Neill: Son and Playwright* (London: J. M. Dent and Sons, 1969), 446, 455.

12. Boulton, *Part of a Long Story*, 280.

13. Gelb and Gelb, *O'Neill*, 393.

14. Boulton, *Part of a Long Story*, 296.

15. Ibid., 290.

16. Ibid., 163.

17. Glaspell, *RT*, 244.

18. Ibid.

19. Ibid., 278–79.

20. Ibid., 280–81.

21. Ibid.

22. Ibid., 278.

23. Agnes Boulton to Eugene O'Neill, [November 1919], Agnes Boulton Papers, HTC.

24. Boulton, *Part of a Long Story*, 303.

25. Agnes Boulton to Eugene O'Neill, n.d., Agnes Boulton Papers, HTC.

26. Ibid., n.d.

27. Ibid., 13 January 1920.

28. Travis Bogard and Jackson R. Bryer, eds., *Selected Letters of Eugene O'Neill* (New Haven: Yale University Press, 1988), 103. Bogard and Bryer identify the play as "possibly *Inheritors* or *The Verge*, written in Provincetown in 1919–20," but Boulton's comments on the play point to *Chains of Dew*, which was not produced by the Provincetown Players until 1922 (Agnes Boulton to Eugene O'Neill, n.d., Agnes Boulton Papers, HTC). Undated letters from Glaspell to Edward Goodman also identify the play as *Chains of Dew* (Edward Goodman Papers, BRTC).

29. Eugene O'Neill to Agnes Boulton, n.d., Eugene O'Neill Papers, HTC (October–November 1921 is suggested as a possible date, but O'Neill's comment clearly predates his letter supposedly dated 16 February 1920).

30. Eugene O'Neill to Agnes Boulton, 16[?] February 1920, in Bogard and Bryer, *Selected Letters of Eugene O'Neill*, 115.

31. Cook's detractors accused him of avidly seeking Broadway fame for his plays. According to his daughter—obviously not an impartial witness and probably too young at the time to understand much—the Provincetowners forced him to take plays to Broadway to give the younger actors a chance after the success of *The Emperor Jones* (Nilla Cook to Robert Károly Sarlós, 5 February 1975, Sarlós Papers). Compare Nilla's account to that of Susan Jenkins Brown, secretary for the Provincetown Players during the 1919–20 season, who was "not an admirer of Jig Cook's abilities." According to Brown, *The Spring* was moved uptown at Cook's insistence, "abetted by the loyal Susan," and this was "hard on the Players" (Susan Jenkins Brown to Robert Károly Sarlós, 17 February 1965, Sarlós Papers).

32. Agnes Boulton to Eugene O'Neill, 25 February 1920, Agnes Boulton Papers, HTC.

33. SG to Edward Goodman, [February 1920], Edward Goodman Papers, BRTC.

34. Burns Mantle, "Plays of the Week—*Chains of Dew*," *New York Mail*, 29 April 1922.

35. SG to Edward Goodman, [spring–summer 1920], Edward Goodman Papers, BRTC.

36. Eugene O'Neill to Eleanor Fitzgerald, 27[?] May 1922, in Bogard and Bryer, *Selected Letters of Eugene O'Neill*, 169.

37. Eugene O'Neill to Agnes Boulton, 29 January 1920, in Bogard and Bryer, *Selected Letters of Eugene O'Neill*, 110.

38. Agnes Boulton to Eugene O'Neill, 31 January 1920, Agnes Boulton Papers, HTC.

39. Emma Goldman, *Living My Life* (1931; reprint, New York: Dover, 1970), 2:556.

40. Ibid., 569.

41. Ibid., 571.

42. James Reed, *The Birth Control Movement and American Society: From Private Vice to Public Virtue* (1978; reprint, Princeton, N.J.: Princeton University Press, 1983), 100.

43. All quotations in this discussion are from *Chains of Dew*, typescript, Library of Congress, Washington, D.C.

44. Edna Kenton to SG and GCC, 5 May 1922, Edna Kenton Papers, HTC.

45. Ibid.

46. Ibid.

47. In *He and She* (1911; reprinted in Arthur Hobson Quinn, ed., *Representative American Plays, 1767–1923* [New York: The Century, 1925]), Rachel Crothers discusses a woman's right to pursue a career, but the protagonist eventually gives up an important commission to care for her daughter. *A Man's World* (1909; reprinted in Judith E. Barlow, ed., *Plays by American Women, 1900–1930* [New York: Applause, 1985]) argues against the double standard because inevitably it is the woman who suffers because of it. In both cases, the protagonist denies her own right to happiness and thus satisfies convention.

48. "Susan Glaspell's *Chains of Dew* Is Sharp Satire," *New York Herald*, 28 April 1922.

49. Maida Castellun, "The Plays That Pass," *New York Call*, 30 April 1922.

50. Mantle, "Plays of the Week—*Chains of Dew*."

51. Alison Smith, "The New Play," *New York Evening Globe*, 28 April 1922; Josette Feral, "Writing and Displacement: Women in Theatre," *Modern Drama* 27 (December 1984): 550.

52. Ludwig Lewisohn, "Aftermath," *The Nation*, 24 May 1922; Heywood Broun in *New York World*, 28 April 1922.

53. Glaspell, *RT*, 294.

54. Ibid., 295.

55. Ibid., 292.

56. Ibid.

57. Ibid., 284.

58. Ibid., 286.

59. Ibid.

60. Ibid., 287.

61. Sarlós, *JCPP*, 52, 124.

Chapter Seven

1. Agnes Boulton to Eugene O'Neill, 14 January 1920, Agnes Boulton Papers, HTC.

2. For a detailed account of how the dome was built, see Sarlós, *JCPP*, 204–6.

3. Glaspell, *RT*, 288.

4. Kenneth Macgowan in *New York Globe*, 4 November 1920, quoted in Deutsch and Hanau, *PP*, 67.

5. Harry Kemp, "Out of Provincetown: A Memoir of Eugene O'Neill," *Theatre*

Magazine 51 (April 1930): 22, 23, 60, reprinted in Mark W. Estrin, ed., *Conversations with Eugene O'Neill* (Jackson: University Press of Mississippi, 1990), 95–102.

6. Glaspell, *RT*, 289.

7. Hamilton Basso, "Profiles: The Tragic Sense," *New Yorker*, 28 February 1948, 40.

8. Glaspell, *RT*, 287.

9. Eugene O'Neill to George Pierce Baker, 3 April 1922, in Travis Bogard and Jackson R. Bryer, eds., *Selected Letters of Eugene O'Neill* (New Haven: Yale University Press, 1988), 165. When working on *The Hairy Ape*, O'Neill wrote to Baker that it was "with the possible exception of *The Fountain* . . . my best play" (166).

10. George Jean Nathan, "Eugene O'Neill," in Alan S. Downer, ed., *American Drama and Its Critics: A Collection of Critical Essays* (Chicago: University of Chicago Press, 1965), 85–86. Nathan was tickled by the reaction to the Native Americans in *The Fountain*; he notes a "general dissatisfaction with the American Indian as O'Neill has presented him," since the American public was used to the idea that "the only things American Indians were capable of saying to one another were either 'Ugh!' or 'Big Chief Bushwah has spoken!'" (88). Cook and Glaspell, who respected the native culture, may have imbued in O'Neill a similar courtesy, which he evinced by endowing his Native Americans with "a measure of intelligible discourse" (87).

11. Eugene O'Neill to Kenneth Macgowan, 18 March 1921, in Jackson R. Bryer, ed., *"The Theatre We Worked For": The Letters of Eugene O'Neill to Kenneth Macgowan* (New Haven: Yale University Press, 1982), 20.

12. Ibid., 29 March 1921, 22.

13. George Cram Cook, *The Spring* (New York: Frank Shay, 1921), 49–50; Glaspell, *RT*, 249.

14. Kenneth Macgowan, *The Theatre of Tomorrow* (London: T. Fisher Unwin, 1923), 177, 262.

15. Glaspell, *RT*, 223.

16. Arthur Gelb and Barbara Gelb, *O'Neill* (1962; reprint, New York: Harper and Row, 1973), 121.

17. George Cram Cook, *The Spring*, 50, 138, 140.

18. P. F. R., *"The Spring," New York Evening Post*, 3 February 1921.

19. Eugene O'Neill to GCC, 5 February 1921, in Bogard and Bryer, *Selected Letters of Eugene O'Neill*, 148.

20. GCC to Nilla Cook, 11 April 1921, GCCP. Although O'Neill's suggested name, Playwrights' Theatre (Glaspell, *RT*, 258), was accepted and initially used by the Provincetowners, the theater was popularly known as the Provincetown Playhouse.

21. See chap. 6, n. 31.

22. GCC to SG, 27 August 1921, GCCP.

23. Agnes Boulton to Eugene O'Neill, 14 January 1920, Agnes Boulton Papers, HTC.

24. Macgowan, *Theatre of Tomorrow*, chap. 17.

25. R. J., "An Anarchist of the Spirit (The Plays of Susan Glaspell)," *Spectator* (London), 16 January 1926; A. D. Peters, "Susan Glaspell: New American Dramatist," *Daily Telegraph* (London), 19 June 1924.

26. Oscar Cargill, ed., *Eugene O'Neill and His Plays* (London: Peter Owen, 1962), 110.

27. SG to Agnes Boulton, 21 November 1920, Eugene O'Neill Collection, BRBML.

28. Ludwig Lewisohn, *"Inheritors," The Nation*, 6 April 1921, reprinted in *The Drama and the Stage* (New York: Harcourt Brace, 1922), 110.

29. "Inez Haynes Irwin Turns Light on Susan Glaspell," unidentified clipping, n.d., SGP.

30. Lewisohn, *The Drama and the Stage*, 110.

31. Susan Glaspell, "The Rules of the Institution," *Harper's Monthly Magazine* 128 (January 1914): 208.

32. Peters, "Susan Glaspell: New American Dramatist."

33. Deutsch and Hanau, *PP*, 79.

34. Glaspell, *I*, 13.

35. Susan Jenkins Brown to Robert Károly Sarlós, 17 February 1965, Sarlós Papers.

36. Kenton, "PPPT," 168.

37. Anonymous, "Provincetown Play Is Poor," *Zits Weekly Magazine*, 26 March 1921.

38. Theodore Dreiser would make good use of this episode when he retold the story of Mary Pyne, Harry Kemp, and Hutchins Hapgood in "Esther Norn," in *A Gallery of Women* (New York: Horace Liveright, 1929), 2:723–75.

39. Lewisohn, *The Drama and the Stage*, 107.

40. *The Times* (London), 28 September 1925.

41. *Morning Post* (London), 26 September 1925.

42. *Daily Telegraph* (London), 29 December 1925.

43. Sarlós, *JCPP*, 228 (n. 36).

44. Eva Le Gallienne, *At Thirty-three: Autobiography* (London: John Lane, Bodley Head, 1934), 202.

45. Ibid., 205.

46. Glaspell, *RT*, 309.

47. GCC to SG, n.d., telegram, Susan Glaspell Papers, HTC.

48. SG to Agnes Boulton, [after 1921], Eugene O'Neill Collection, BRBML.

49. Luce Irigaray, *This Sex Which Is Not One*, trans. Catherine Porter and Carolyn Burke (1977; reprint, Ithaca, N.Y.: Cornell University Press, 1985), 213, 205.

50. See Marcia Noe, "*The Verge: L'Écriture Féminine* at the Provincetown," in Linda Ben-Zvi, ed., *Susan Glaspell: Essays on Her Theater and Fiction* (Ann Arbor: University of Michigan Press, 1995), 129–42.

51. Glaspell, *V*, 89.

52. Irigaray, *This Sex Which Is Not One*, 76; G. D. Cummins, "A London Letter: The Situation Unchanged," *Yorkshire Post*, 3 April 1925.

53. Weed Dickinson, "*The Verge*—Bad Insanity Clinic," *New York Evening Telegraph*, 15 November 1921.

54. Josette Feral, "Writing and Displacement: Women in Theatre," trans. Barbara Kerslake, *Modern Drama* 27 (December 1984): 551.

55. Glaspell, *V*, 89.

56. Ibid., 92.

57. G. D. Cummins, "*The Verge*: Miss Thorndike's Views on Her New Play," *Yorkshire Post*, 13 February 1925.

58. Hutchins Hapgood, *A Victorian in the Modern World* (1939; reprint, Seattle: University of Washington Press, 1972), 377.

59. Linda Ben-Zvi, "Susan Glaspell and Eugene O'Neill," *Eugene O'Neill Newsletter* 6, no. 2 (1982): 21–29, and "Susan Glaspell and Eugene O'Neill: The Imagery of Gender," *Eugene O'Neill Newsletter* 10, no. 1 (1986): 22–27.

60. "Pioneer Players: Last Subscription Performance," *Morning Post* (London), 20 March 1925.

61. Glaspell, *V*, 65.

62. Christine Dymkowski notes, "It is most unusual for a playwright to separate characters from the audience with an actual physical barrier rather than a merely imagined fourth wall" ("On the Edge: The Plays of Susan Glaspell," *Modern Drama* 31, no. 1 [March 1988]: 101).

63. Glaspell, *V*, 96.

64. Ibid., 88.

65. C. W. E. Bigsby, ed., introduction to *Plays by Susan Glaspell* (Cambridge: Cambridge University Press, 1987), 19.

66. Mardi Valgemae, *Accelerated Grimace: Expressionism in the American Drama of the 1920s* (Carbondale: Southern Illinois University Press, 1972), 179. Kenneth Macgowan described Throckmorton's set as "expressionistic"; he first used the term with reference to a whole play apropos O'Neill's *The Hairy Ape* (1922) ("The New Play," *New York Evening Globe*, 15 November 1921).

67. Isaac Goldberg, *The Drama of Transition: Native and Exotic Playcraft* (Cincinnati: Stewart Kidd, 1922), 475.

68. Eugene O'Neill, "Damn the Optimists!," *New York Tribune*, 13 February 1921, quoted in Cargill, *Eugene O'Neill and His Plays*, 104. Although O'Neill never saw *The Verge*, he may well have read *The Glory of the Conquered*; since he shared Glaspell's enthusiasm for Nietzsche's doctrine of self-perfection, it is not surprising to find in his writing words that describe her feelings.

69. See Emory Elliott, ed., *Columbia Literary History of the United States* (New York: Columbia University Press, 1988), 1110, which states: "Glaspell's Claire Archer achieves stature apart from the men in her life, as O'Neill's women never do."

70. Glaspell, *I*, 156.

71. Glaspell, *V*, 65.

72. Stark Young, "Susan Glaspell's *The Verge*," *New Republic*, 7 December 1921, reprinted in Montrose J. Moses and John Mason Brown, *The American Theatre as Seen by Its Critics, 1752–1934* (New York: Cooper Square Publishers, 1967), 252–55. Significantly, when *The Verge* was rediscovered recently by the London Orange Tree Theatre, the reviews were just as mixed as in 1921. For Jeremy Kingston, *The Verge* is "demented in spirit . . . turgid in dialogue . . . opaque nonsense" ("Growing Pains," *The Times* [London], 3 April 1996), whereas for Michael Billington, it is a "heavily symbolic but deeply fascinating work about the female capacity for innovation" and "a pioneer work of feminist drama" ("*The Verge*," *The Guardian*, 1 April 1996).

73. Cummins, "*The Verge*: Miss Thorndike's Views."

Chapter Eight

1. Nilla Cook to Robert Károly Sarlós, 5 February 1975, Sarlós Papers.

2. Nilla Cram Cook, *My Road to India* (New York: Lee Furman, 1939), 4.

3. Ibid., 9, 16.

4. Arthur Gelb and Barbara Gelb, *O'Neill* (1962; reprint, New York: Harper and Row, 1973), 493.

5. Glaspell, *RT*, 324.

6. Ibid., 307.

7. Eugene O'Neill to George Jean Nathan, 2 January 1922, in Nancy L. Roberts and Arthur W. Roberts, *"As Ever, Gene": The Letters of Eugene O'Neill to George Jean Nathan* (London: Associated University Presses, 1987), 47.

8. Eugene O'Neill to Kenneth Macgowan, 22 January 1922, in Jackson R. Bryer, ed., *"The Theatre We Worked For": The Letters of Eugene O'Neill to Kenneth Macgowan* (New Haven: Yale University Press, 1982), 33. (Bryer annotates this letter thus: "Arthur Hopkins collaborated with James Light in directing *The Hairy Ape* for the Provincetown Players.")

9. Deutsch and Hanau mention the incident without giving a name: "One night

[Cook] removed the great cloak he wore, and threw it dramatically over the shoulders of one of the younger men" (*PP*, 55). Robert Károly Sarlós, who interviewed both Jasper Deeter and James Light, records that Light did not mention the incident, whereas Deeter did, considering himself the "heir apparent." As Sarlós points out, the timing in Deeter's account does not coincide with that in Deutsch and Hanau's, and Light does seem the more likely candidate, given his longer association with the Players (since 1917), his leadership during Cook and Glaspell's sabbatical, his cooperation on the dome, and Cook's bitterness toward the onetime votary when he learned of his designs on the Players (Sarlós, *JCPP*, 134, 227 [n. 33]).

10. Sarlós, *JCPP*, 139.

11. Edna Kenton to GCC and SG, 13 May 1922, Edna Kenton Papers, HTC.

12. Glaspell, *RT*, 309–10.

13. Ibid., 310.

14. The full text of the announcement is reproduced in Deutsch and Hanau, *PP*, 91–93, and, in a slightly different version, in Sarlós, *JCPP*, 142–45.

15. Nilla Cook to Robert Károly Sarlós, 28 August 1974, Sarlós Papers.

16. George Cram Cook, "Beat against Me, East Wind," in *Greek Coins* (New York: George H. Doran, 1925), 89. The lines reproduced here are scrawled in his handwriting at the end of a probably unsent letter from Cook to Kenton.

17. GCC to SG, 15 December 1922, GCCP.

18. Glaspell, *RT*, 314.

19. Ibid., 321.

20. Ibid.

21. Ibid.

22. Ibid., 323.

23. Ibid., 324.

24. SG to Alice Keating Glaspell, 25 April 1922, SGP.

25. Edna Kenton to SG and GCC, 19 June 1922, Edna Kenton Papers, HTC.

26. Ibid., 5 May 1922.

27. Ibid.

28. Ibid.

29. GCC to Edna Kenton, 14 July 1922, Papers of Susan Glaspell (MSS 7629), Clifton Waller Barrett Library of American Literature, Special Collections Department, University of Virginia Library, Charlottesville, Virginia.

30. Edna Kenton to SG and GCC, 5 May 1922, Edna Kenton Papers, HTC. To Kenton, the greatest loss was an exchange between Dotty and Seymore toward the end of the third act. Dotty and Nora had replaced a picture of the Sistine Madonna with posters unequivocally advocating birth control—one showing a poverty-stricken mother with nine children; the other, a happy mother with two. In the typescript of act 3, Seymore takes the posters down and returns the picture of the Madonna—which Dotty had come to identify with her thwarted existence—to its original place, saying, "That's the stuff—put her right back where she was before. Just as if nothing had ever happened." Although the symbolism of these pictures can hardly be considered subtle, Kenton clearly perceived that it framed the development of the action and imposed a unity of theme that was lost when the scene was omitted.

31. Edna Kenton to SG and GCC, 15 May 1922, Edna Kenton Papers, HTC.

32. Ibid., [?] June 1922.

33. Susan Glaspell, *Fugitive's Return* (New York: Frederick A. Stokes, 1929), 49.

34. GCC to Hutchins Hapgood, 29 October 1923, Hutchins Hapgood and Neith Boyce Papers, BRBML.

35. Glaspell, *RT*, 317.

36. Ibid.

37. Glaspell, *Fugitive's Return*, 64.

38. Ibid., 65.

39. "Story of a Woman Who Came Back," *Davenport Times*, 2 November 1929.

40. Susan Glaspell, "A Rose in the Sand: The Salvation of a Lonely Soul," *Pall Mall* (1927), 45–51.

41. *Fugitive's Return* was on the best-seller list in the *Baltimore Evening Sun* on 15 November 1929, along with *A Farewell to Arms* and *All Quiet on the Western Front*; the *Detroit News*, 17 November 1929, placed *A Farewell to Arms* first and *Fugitive's Return* fourth.

42. Percy Hutchinson, "A Sensitive Novel by Susan Glaspell," *New York Times Book Review*, 11 October 1929.

43. "The Color of a Life," *New York Evening Sun*, 7 December 1929.

44. SG to Alice Keating Glaspell, 29 September 1922, SGP.

45. Ibid.

46. Kostis Palamas (1859–1943) was a major figure in the revival of modern Greek poetry and the establishment of the demotic movement. Best known for his lyrical verse (as in *The King's Flute*, 1910), he also wrote drama, epic poetry, and literary criticism. See C. A. Trypanis, *Greek Poetry from Homer to Seferis* (London: Faber and Faber, 1981), 654–61.

47. SG to Alice Keating Glaspell, 15 September 1922, SGP.

48. Angelos Sikelianós (1884–1951), poet and dramatist, the central figure of the Generation of 1905, is best known for his autobiographical poem *The Visionary* (1907). See Trypanis, *Greek Poetry*, 672–76.

49. GCC to William Rapp, 5 July 1922, private papers of Sirius and Valentina Cook.

50. GCC to SG, 15 December 1922, GCCP.

51. Nilla Cram Cook, *My Road to India*, 12.

52. Glaspell was wrong, at least as far as Cook's attitude toward his daughter was concerned. In an undated letter to Hutchins Hapgood, Nilla wrote: "As to Jig, he was a perfect stranger to me until long after he had died. There was considerable antagonism between us, as far as I can see, because I was young. The few months we lived together he was rarely if ever sober" (Hutchins Hapgood and Neith Boyce Papers, BRBML). This letter was probably written between 1934 and 1939 when Nilla was in the United States in response to queries from Hapgood, who was writing his autobiography, *A Victorian in the Modern World*.

53. GCC to SG, February 1923, GCCP.

54. George Cram Cook, "Nilla Dear," in *Greek Coins*, 114.

55. Nilla Cram Cook, *My Road to India*, 16.

56. Ibid.

57. Ibid., 19.

58. Nilla had too many admirers to be in love with any one of them at this time, and despite her radical upbringing, her vivid imagination fueled innocent theories on childbirth, virginity, and sex that Glaspell, burdened by her Puritan inheritance, did nothing to dispel. It was Floyd Dell who, some years later, told her about the ovum and the sperm (Nilla Cram Cook, *My Road to India*, 46).

59. This girl would later serve as Glaspell's model for her namesake, the untamed, delightful Theodora in *Fugitive's Return*.

60. Nilla Cram Cook, *My Road to India*, 24.

61. Ibid.

62. Ibid.

63. Ibid., 31.

64. Glaspell, *RT*, 407.

65. The Tchakalós family holds that Athanasius took Cook and Glaspell to Agorgiani to protect them from the brigands, who had threatened to capture the two Americans and hold them for ransom (author interview with Fanis Tchakalós, Delphi, May 1995).

66. SG to Edna Kenton, 29 October 1923, Edna Kenton Papers, HTC.

67. SG to Alice Keating Glaspell, 12 June, 5, 15 July 1923, SGP.

68. According to Glaspell's explanation to her mother, kalania are huts, and the Kastriotes are the people of Delphi.

69. Glaspell, *Fugitive's Return*, 235.

70. SG to Alice Keating Glaspell, 18 June 1922, SGP. See also GCC to Hutchins Hapgood, 29 August 1923, Hutchins Hapgood and Neith Boyce Papers, BRBML.

71. GCC to Hutchins Hapgood, 28 August 1923, Hutchins Hapgood and Neith Boyce Papers, BRBML.

72. Ibid.

73. Bill Rapp was so entranced by George Cram Cook that on his return to America he sought out Mollie Price, Cook's second wife, and eventually married her.

74. SG to Alice Keating Glaspell, 26 August 1923, SGP.

75. Glaspell, *RT*, 386.

76. Ibid., 388–89.

77. GCC to SG, 15 December 1922, GCCP.

78. Glaspell, *RT*, 378–79.

79. Ibid., 388.

80. Ibid., 7.

81. Susan Glaspell, "The Faithless Shepherd," *The Cornhill* 60 (January 1926): 7.

82. At times, Glaspell shared her discoveries with Jig, who delighted in reading indecent intent into seemingly innocent letters (*RT*, 409–10).

83. Glaspell, "Faithless Shepherd," 2.

84. SG to Neith Boyce, 29 August 1923 (in a letter from GCC to Hutchins Hapgood), Hutchins Hapgood and Neith Boyce Papers, BRBML.

85. GCC to Hutchins Hapgood, 29 August 1923, Hutchins Hapgood and Neith Boyce Papers, BRBML.

86. Glaspell, *RT*, 397.

87. SG to Hutchins Hapgood and Neith Boyce, August 1923, Hutchins Hapgood and Neith Boyce Papers, BRBML.

88. GCC to Edna Kenton, 14 July 1922, Papers of Susan Glaspell (MSS 7629), Clifton Waller Barrett Library of American Literature, Special Collections Department, University of Virginia Library, Charlottesville, Virginia.

89. SG to Edna Kenton, 29 October 1923, Edna Kenton Papers, HTC.

90. Glaspell, *RT*, 411.

91. Ibid.

92. Ibid., 420.

93. Ibid., 421.

94. The American College for Girls, run by American Episcopalian missionaries in Smyrna, had been forced to close down the previous year; in the autumn of 1923, it reopened in Phaleron, near Athens, taking students from upper-class families, both old Greeks and refugees.

95. SG to Alice Keating Glaspell, 2 December 1923, SGP.

96. Ibid., 19 December 1923.

97. GCC to SG, 27 November 1923, GCCP, reprinted in Glaspell, *RT*, 423.

98. Glaspell, *RT*, 424.

99. Ibid., 431.

100. SG to Lucy Huffaker Goodman, [January–February 1924], Edward Goodman Papers, BRTC.

101. Glaspell, *RT*, 439.

102. SG to Alice Keating Glaspell, 21 January 1924, SGP.

103. Ibid.

104. SG to Lucy Huffaker Goodman, [January–February 1924], Edward Goodman Papers, BRTC. Cook was not moved into the temple precinct. His grave is in a shaded corner of the cemetery, marked by an ancient, rough slab; Nilla Cook was buried beside him.

105. SG to Hutchins Hapgood, January 1924, Hutchins Hapgood and Neith Boyce Papers, BRBML; SG to Lucy Huffaker Goodman, [January–February 1924], Edward Goodman Papers, BRTC.

106. SG to Lucy Huffaker Goodman, [January–February 1924], Edward Goodman Papers, BRTC.

107. Since no autopsy was performed, it is impossible to determine the cause of death. Family lore, based on Glaspell's letters, accepts Dr. Marden's diagnosis of the glanders. However, Glaspell's account does not mention pain in the joints, inflammatory swelling, ulcers discharging a thick mucous or sanguineous fluid, or swelling of the lymphatic glands—all of which are symptoms of the disease.

108. SG to Lucy Huffaker Goodman, [January–February 1924], Edward Goodman Papers, BRTC; SG to Hutchins Hapgood and Neith Boyce, [late January 1924], Hutchins Hapgood and Neith Boyce Papers, BRBML.

109. Hutchins Hapgood, *A Victorian in the Modern World* (1939; reprint, Seattle: University of Washington Press, 1972), 268. Not everyone was as discreet and understanding as Hapgood. A few years after Cook's death, Glaspell was very upset by the "damaging matter" in Upton Sinclair's *Money Writes!* (SG to Norman Matson, n.d., SGP). Sinclair, who admired Glaspell's work, considering her "a dramatist of power" and *Inheritors* "an almost Socialist drama," came down heavily on Cook—and Glaspell—in his criticism of *The Road to the Temple*: "I cannot recall ever having read a greater piece of nonsense from the pen of an emancipated woman. The plain truth, which stares at us between every line of the closing narrative, is that poor Jig Cook, a poet who pinned his faith to Bacchus instead of to Minerva, was at the age of fifty a pitiful white-haired sot, dead to the Socialist movement, dead to the whole modern world, wandering about lost among dirty and degraded peasants. He died of an infection utterly mysterious to his wife—who apparently knows nothing of the effects of alcohol in destroying the cells of the liver and breaking down the natural immunity of the body" (*Money Writes!* [New York: Albert and Charles Boni, 1927], 167, 169).

110. Although the poet Sikelianós is generally credited with the idea of the Delphic Festival and with its organization, correspondence indicates otherwise. John Pararas of the Athenian YMCA wrote to Bill Rapp on 24 June 1924 informing him that the members of the Euripides George Cram Cook Club had visited Cook's tomb that Easter and that Pararas had suggested to the Delphians that they honor the American by holding athletic games at the stadium and producing a classical drama at the ancient theater every Easter. On 15 May 1925, Eva Sikelianós wrote that the date for the festival had been fixed for April–May 1926 and that it would include an exhibition of arts and crafts, especially weaving. An article offering similar information appeared in the *Morning Post*, 13 May 1925, stating that "a portion of the games will be given in honor of the late George Cram Cook, a remarkable American poet, who lived and died last year at Delphi, and has already become a saint and hero in the eyes of the peasants of Parnassos." (These letters are in the private papers of Sirius and Valentina Cook.)

111. SG to Neith Boyce, [early 1926], Hutchins Hapgood and Neith Boyce Papers, BRBML.

Chapter Nine

1. SG to Hutchins Hapgood, 28 January 1924, reprinted in Hutchins Hapgood, *A Victorian in the Modern World* (1939; reprint, Seattle: University of Washington Press, 1972), 492.

2. SG to William Rapp, 2 October 1924, private papers of Sirius and Valentina Cook.

3. Edna Kenton to Eleanor Fitzgerald, 28 October 1924, Edna Kenton Papers, RBML; Kenton to SG, 27 May 1924, Edna Kenton Papers, HTC (quoting Fitzi).

4. Eugene O'Neill to SG, 26 May 1924, Papers of Eugene O'Neill (MSS 6488-b), Clifton Waller Barrett Library of American Literature, Special Collections Department, University of Virginia Library, Charlottesville, Virginia. The plaque O'Neill mentions was—at his urging—eventually put up, with an inscription of Glaspell's choice taken from one of Cook's verses: "And we will make the cold world / Flame and music / The dance of flame / Obedient to dream." During World War II, Glaspell donated the bronze plaque to the war effort, according to an undated, untitled, and unsigned essay in SGP.

5. O'Neill, as Kenton pointed out, had not had a play produced since *The Hairy Ape* in early 1922 and was eager to find a theater that would accept his work unquestioningly. He had indeed spurred Macgowan to take over the Provincetown Players, and he blamed Kenton for unnecessarily complicating matters. For her part, Kenton had no respect for either O'Neill or Macgowan. See Edna Kenton to Eleanor Fitzgerald, 28 October 1924, Kenton to SG, 29 October 1924, and Kenton to Harry Weinberger, 3 November 1924, Edna Kenton Papers, RBML; and Kenton to GCC and SG, 17 November 1923, Edna Kenton Papers, and Eugene O'Neill to Kenton, 26 May 1924, Eugene O'Neill Papers, HTC.

6. Eugene O'Neill to SG, 3 June 1924, Papers of Eugene O'Neill (MSS 6488-b), Clifton Waller Barrett Library of American Literature, Special Collections Department, University of Virginia Library, Charlottesville, Virginia.

7. Eugene O'Neill to Kenneth Macgowan, August 1924, in Jackson R. Bryer, ed., *"The Theatre We Worked For": The Letters of Eugene O'Neill to Kenneth Macgowan* (New Haven: Yale University Press, 1982), 56.

8. Kenton uses the phrase "it was slimy" in her letter to SG, 28 October 1924, Edna Kenton Papers, RBML. Light had latched onto Macgowan, who saw in Light a useful worker, sometime in 1923; Light directed most of the new Players' productions, including the revival of O'Neill's *The Emperor Jones* and *All God's Chillun Got Wings* (both in May 1924). The latter was a new play that, in its study of a woman unable to cope with the restrictions imposed by society, owed much to Glaspell's *The Verge*.

9. SG to Eleanor Fitzgerald, 31 May 1924, Susan Glaspell Papers, HTC.

10. Edna Kenton to SG, 28 May, 2 June 1924, Edna Kenton Papers, HTC; Kenton to SG, 29 October 1924, Edna Kenton Papers, RBML.

11. SG to Edna Kenton, [October 1924], Edna Kenton Papers, RBML; Eugene O'Neill to Kenton, 26 May 1924, Eugene O'Neill Papers, HTC.

12. William Rapp and Neith Boyce did write the memoirs Glaspell asked for, but for some reason, they were not included in her publication. The typescripts of William Rapp's "An American Apollo" and "American to Stage *Prometheus* in Delphi's Ancient Theatre" are in the private papers of Sirius and Valentina Cook; "A Self-

Made Greek Hero from America" appeared in the *New York Herald Tribune*, 3 January 1926. Neith Boyce's "Iowa to Delphi" is in the Hutchins Hapgood and Neith Boyce Papers, BRBML.

13. For reviews of *Greek Coins*, see Babette Deutsch, *Bookman* 62 (February 1926): 726, and *The Dial* 80 (March 1926): 253. Dell's comments in "A Seer in Iowa" (in George Cram Cook, *Greek Coins* [New York: George H. Doran, 1925], 9–16) are particularly illuminating concerning his relationship with Cook. The fullest evaluation of Cook's literary production can be found in G. Thomas Tanselle, "George Cram Cook and the Poetry of Living, with a Checklist," in *Books at Iowa* (Iowa City: University of Iowa Press, 1976), 1–37.

14. SG to Arthur Ficke, 16 April [1927], Arthur Ficke Papers, BRBML.

15. Hapgood was not afraid to point out that Glaspell had "left out of the [*Road to the Temple*] the finest thing in Jig's spirit" (*Victorian in the Modern World*, 500).

16. SG to Edna Kenton, 12 January [1926], Papers of Susan Glaspell (MSS 7629), Clifton Waller Barrett Library of American Literature, Special Collections Department, University of Virginia Library, Charlottesville, Virginia.

17. SG to Norman Matson, November 1926, SGP.

18. SG to Edna Kenton, [October 1924], Edna Kenton Papers, RBML.

19. Ann Larabee's analysis of *The Road to the Temple* in "Death in Delphi: Susan Glaspell and the Companionate Marriage," *Mid-American Review* 7, no. 2 (1987): 93–106, shows Glaspell reclaiming patriarchal history through a reconstruction of Cook as the essential American male, thus allowing her to control her husband, but it leaves out the inevitable feelings of guilt that afflict the partner of an alcoholic and ignores Glaspell's relationship with Matson, which flourished as she wrote *The Road to the Temple*.

20. Although Herschel Brickell wrote that "few books of the spring have met with such unanimously enthusiastic praise from critics as this one" ("Books on Our Table," *New York Evening Post*, 25 March 1927), other critics were more skeptical. The reviewer for the *Times Literary Supplement* (London) believed that "it would have achieved its purpose better either if it had been a great deal more formal as biography or if it had been presented in quite another way" (18 November 1926). It took a woman reviewer to intuit Glaspell's hidden subtext: "Without intention on her part, in this generous rendition of tribute to her husband, she has given also the measure of a woman worthy to have been his companion on the Temple road" (Gretchen Mount, "Extraordinary Biography," *Detroit Free Press*, 8 April 1927).

21. Upton Sinclair, *Money Writes!* (New York: Albert and Charles Boni, 1927), 169.

22. Nilla Cook wrote to Robert Károly Sarlós: "Susan went out of her way in *The Road to the Temple* to keep to matters of principle. Jig would not want an old breach of trust to be revived for the sake of explaining how he left friends high and dry, which is what his departure for Greece amounted to. . . . I feel you should be included in the trust which Susan and Jig left with me. Perhaps you can reconcile 'good taste' with history and so find a solution" (28 August 1974, Sarlós Papers). Sarlós's account in *JCPP* is impartial; he attempts to understand and justify the actions of Cook, O'Neill, and Light.

23. J. B. Priestley, "Strange American," *Daily News* (London), 10 November 1926.

24. May Sarton journal, 1928, May Sarton Papers, Berg Collection of English and American Literature, New York Public Library, Astor, Lenox, and Tilden Foundations, New York, New York (thanks to Susan Sherman for this source).

25. Edna Kenton to SG, 24 May 1924, Edna Kenton Papers, HTC.

26. This was not the first such proposal; in 1924, Harry Kemp prefaced his new volume of plays (*Boccaccio's Untold Tales* [New York: Brentano's, 1924], 1–10) with a brief history of the Provincetown Players. Alfred Kreymborg, while writing his auto-

biography (*Troubadour: An Autobiography* [New York: Boni and Liveright, 1925]), turned to Kenton for information on the history of the Provincetown Players, as did Herschel Brickell of the *New York Evening Post*, who saw a best-seller in the project. Kenton, shrewdly refusing to surrender her collection of playbills and miscellanea, directed them to already published material (Edna Kenton to SG, 24 May 1924, Edna Kenton Papers, HTC).

27. Edna Kenton to SG, 1 January 1929, Edna Kenton Papers, Fales Collection, Elmer Bobst Library, New York University, New York, New York.

28. The "good-sized book" that Fitzi planned to publish never materialized. An eight-page leaflet, containing brief statements by various people connected with the theater and a list of plays produced since 1915, was published to mark the move of the Provincetown Playhouse to the Garrick Theater for the 1929–30 season (Provincetown Scrapbook, Provincetown Players File, BRTC). In December 1929, the theater, a financial failure, closed down.

29. Eleanor Fitzgerald to SG, 6 April 1929, Edna Kenton Papers, Fales Collection, Elmer Bobst Library, New York University, New York, New York.

30. SG to Edna Kenton, 30 April 1929, Edna Kenton Papers, Fales Collection, New York University, New York, New York; SG to Eleanor Fitzgerald, 16 April 1929, Susan Glaspell File, BRTC.

31. Experimental Theater to SG, 29 May 1929, Susan Glaspell File, BRTC.

32. Deutsch and Hanau, *PP*, x.

33. Ibid., 83.

34. Mary Heaton Vorse, *Time and the Town: A Provincetown Chronicle* (New York: Dial Press, 1942), 124.

35. Hutchins Hapgood, *The Story of a Lover* (New York: Boni and Liveright, 1919); Norman Matson to SG, October 1926, SGP.

36. SG to Victor Gollancz, 25 January 1927, GA; SG to Theodore Dreiser, 9 June 1928, Theodore Dreiser Papers, Rare Book and Manuscript Library, University of Pennsylvania, Philadelphia, Pennsylvania.

37. Glaspell submitted *The Comic Artist* to Lawrence Langner, hoping for a production by the Theatre Guild (SG to Lawrence Langner, 17 December [1926], Lawrence Langner Papers, BRBML). She also tried to interest Sybil Thorndike in the play, but to no avail (Curtis Brown to SG, 11 January 1927, SGP). *The Comic Artist* was published in England by Benn and in New York by Stokes in 1927 and produced in London in 1928 at the Strand Theatre. The New York Morosco Theatre produced it in 1933; the performance was reviewed in the *New York Herald Tribune* on 9 August 1933. Glaspell also wrote *The Good Bozo* with Matson, but it was never published (SG to Victor Gollancz, 27 December 1927, GA).

38. The best-seller listings of the *New York Herald Tribune* for the week ending 12 August 1928 rate *Brook Evans* second, after John Galsworthy's *Swan Song*. Brentano's included *Brook Evans* among the six best-selling novels for the week ending 4 August 1928.

39. Victor Gollancz to Dorothy Sayers, 1933, quoted in Ruth Dudley Edwards, *Victor Gollancz: A Biography* (London: Victor Gollancz, 1987), 162.

40. SG to Victor Gollancz, 6 February, 14 March 1928, GA.

41. Victor Gollancz to SG, 10 April 1928, GA.

42. *The Right to Love* was directed by Richard Wallace and produced and distributed by Paramount in 1931, with a screenplay by Zoe Aikins.

43. SG to Victor Gollancz, 14 March 1928, GA.

44. I. R. M., "Three Novels by Women," *Oxford Magazine*, 14 June 1928, 627.

45. Susan Glaspell, *Brook Evans* (New York: Frederick A. Stokes, 1928), 208.

46. Alice Keating Glaspell to SG, 16 July 1928, SGP. The letter in which Alice first

articulates her feelings on *Brook Evans* has not survived—perhaps an indication of how hurt Glaspell was by it.

47. Victor Gollancz to SG, [February–March 1928], SGP.

48. Victor Gollancz to SG, 18 May 1928, GA.

49. Marcia Noe, *Susan Glaspell: Voice from the Heartland* (Macomb: Western Illinois University Press, 1983), 58.

50. Ray Glaspell (SG's brother) to SG, 21 February 1929, SGP.

51. SG to Barrett Clark, April 1930, Barrett Clark Papers, BRBML.

52. Eva Le Gallienne, *At Thirty-three: Autobiography* (London: John Lane, Bodley Head, 1934), 198. Le Gallienne opened the Civic Repertory Theatre on 14th Street in 1926, hoping to provide good theater at modest prices. She was convinced that New York needed a repertory theater and that such a theater could be subsidized by private capital. Curiously, the dilapidated theater she took over was the old French Opera House that Edna Kenton had urged George Cram Cook to rent in 1918. Dreaming of a luminous and plastic acting space and seeing no hope of converting the old theater into his dream, he had rejected it.

53. Jonathan Culler, *On Deconstruction* (London: Routledge and Kegan Paul, 1983), 64. For a full account of the critical reception of *Alison's House*, see Mary E. Papke, *Susan Glaspell: A Research and Production Sourcebook* (Westport, Conn.: Greenwood Press, 1993), 94. Although in general critics did not consider *Alison's House* the best play of the year, Brooks J. Atkinson stated that Glaspell deserved the Pulitzer Prize, if not for *Alison's House*, then for some other work ("Pulitzer Laurels: *Alison's House* as the Most Unsatisfactory Dramatic Award Made during the Past Few Years," *New York Times*, 10 May 1931). But Barrett H. Clark fully approved the Pulitzer committee's choice ("The End of the Season in New York," *Drama* 21 [June 1931]: 7).

54. *Alison's House* played at the Civic Repertory Theatre on 14th Street in New York, with Eva Le Gallienne in the role of Elsa, until the announcement of the Pulitzer Prize in May 1931. The play was then moved to the Ritz Theatre on Broadway. Gail Sondergaard took over as Elsa after the first week. *Alison's House*, in spite of the Pulitzer, was not commercially successful and was withdrawn after forty-one performances. See Burns Mantle, ed., *The Best Plays of 1930–31 and the Year Book of the Drama in America* (New York: Dodd, Mead, 1931), 222, and Papke, *Susan Glaspell*, 84.

55. C. W. E. Bigsby, ed., *Plays by Susan Glaspell* (Cambridge: Cambridge University Press, 1987), 28. Bigsby perceptively points out that Glaspell "still felt it necessary to engage in a debate with her own past and with a morality which, if scarcely irrelevant, had lost a great deal of its immediacy."

56. Richard D. Skinner, *Our Changing Theatre* (New York: Dial Press, 1931), 148. See also John Chamberlain, "A Tragi-Comedy of Idealism in Miss Glaspell's Novel," *New York Times Book Review*, 12 April 1931, which boldly asserts: "Her recent play *Alison's House*, based as it is on the life of Emily Dickinson . . . " According to an anonymous reviewer in *Outlook*, the rumors were "assiduously circulated by Miss Le Gallienne's press department and others" (12 December 1930).

57. Katharine Rodier draws our attention to the parallels between Emily Dickinson and Alison Stanhope in "Glaspell and Dickinson: Surveying the Premises of Alison's House," in Linda Ben-Zvi, ed., *Susan Glaspell: Essays on Her Theater and Fiction* (Ann Arbor: University of Michigan Press, 1995), 195–218.

58. According to Marcia Noe, Glaspell was stymied in her desire to portray the poet onstage by the Dickinson family, who "refused to allow Susan to use the family name or any of Emily Dickinson's poems in the play" (*Susan Glaspell*, 59). Arthur E. Waterman, Glaspell's first biographer, concludes that Glaspell was inspired by Genevieve Taggard's biography of Emily Dickinson but does not annotate his statement (*Susan Glaspell* [New York: Twayne, 1966], 86). Klaus Lubbers, in *Emily Dickinson: The*

Critical Reception (Ann Arbor: University of Michigan Press, 1968), 149, records that Josephine Politt, who wrote *Emily Dickinson: The Human Background of Her Poetry* in 1930, was not allowed to quote Dickinson's poems.

59. Lubbers, *Emily Dickinson*, 157.

60. SG to Barrett Clark, April 1930, Barrett Clark Papers, BRBML.

61. See Waterman, *Susan Glaspell*, 87.

62. Martha Dickinson Bianchi to Mr. Greenslet, 20 October 1930, Martha Dickinson Bianchi Papers, shelf mark bMS Am 1091 (999) by permission of the Houghton Library, Harvard University, Cambridge, Massachusetts (thanks to Elizabeth Falsey for this source).

63. Susan Glaspell, *The Glory of the Conquered: The Story of a Great Love* (New York: Frederick A. Stokes, 1909), 140. In Glaspell's novel *Ambrose Holt and Family* (New York: Frederick A. Stokes, 1931), 262, Blossom, the protagonist, receives a box of books that includes Taggard's *The Life and Mind of Emily Dickinson* and Virginia Woolf's *A Room of One's Own*.

64. Martha Dickinson Bianchi, *The Life and Letters of Emily Dickinson* (London: Jonathan Cape, 1924), 47.

65. Vorse, *Time and the Town*, 124.

66. Genevieve Taggard, *The Life and Mind of Emily Dickinson* (New York: Knopf, 1930), 120. Although Taggard's biography appeared in May 1930, her interview with Mary Heaton Vorse would have taken place well before then. Glaspell's letter to Barrett Clark shows that *Alison's House* was written before 1930, thus the play could not have been "inspired" by the biography (as stated by Waterman in *Susan Glaspell*). However, I do not discount the possibility of indirect inspiration via Vorse.

67. Mantle, *Best Plays of 1930–31*, 222.

68. Susan Glaspell, *Alison's House* (New York: Samuel French, 1930), 150.

69. Katherine T. von Blon, "*Alison's House* Presented," *Los Angeles Times*, 22 February 1933.

70. See, for example, Brooks J. Atkinson, "The Play—Discussion of an Artist," *New York Times*, 2 December 1930, and "Pulitzer Laurels"; Stewart Beach, "The Editor Goes to the Play," *Theatre Magazine* 53 (February 1931): 24–26; and Charles Morgan, "*Autumn Crocus*'s Author Tries Again," *New York Times*, 13 November 1932.

71. Richard Dana Skinner, "The Play—Pulitzer Award," *Commonweal*, 20 May 1931.

72. Richard Lockridge, "Play of a Poet," *New York Sun*, 2 December 1930.

73. Victor Gollancz to SG, 3 March 1931, GA.

74. At least one of Matson's novels, *Flecker's Magic* (1926), won E. M. Forster's approval (*Aspects of the Novel* [1927; reprint, Harmondsworth, Eng.: Penguin, 1962], 118–21).

75. J. K. Prothero, "The Drama: Over the Top," *G. K's Weekly*, 11 April 1925.

76. Herbert Farjeon, "Odds and Ends," *Westminster Weekly*, 7 February 1926.

77. *The Times* (London), 18 December 1931.

78. *New York Times*, 21 January 1932.

79. The *Davenport Democrat* reported protests by English actors and affirmed that "several American performers already have been ordered to go home" (22 January 1932).

80. SG to Richard Hughes, 27 February 1932, Lilly Library, Indiana University, Bloomington, Indiana.

81. Hapgood, *Victorian in the Modern World*, 426.

82. Norman Matson to SG, 16 July 1932, SGP.

83. SG to Norman Matson, n.d. (reply to letter of 16 July 1932), SGP.

84. Norman Matson to SG, [late 1932], SGP.

85. SG to Anna Strunsky Walling, [summer 1932], SGP.

86. Ibid.

Chapter Ten

1. Leon Edel, "Edmund Wilson in the Thirties," in Edmund Wilson, *The Thirties: From Notebooks and Diaries of the Period* (New York: Farrar, Straus and Giroux, 1980), xx.

2. Wilson, *The Thirties*, 486.

3. Ibid., 342.

4. SG to Horace W. Stokes, 15 April 1939, SGP.

5. Wilson, *The Thirties*, 307.

6. Ibid.

7. Ibid., 485.

8. Ibid.

9. Ibid., 475.

10. Reports of this incident can be found in unidentified clippings in the Provincetown Players File, Museum of the City of New York, New York, New York. See Glaspell's "first six chapters of unfinished novel," typescript, SGP.

11. Unidentified clipping, 24 May [1935], Provincetown Players File, Museum of the City of New York, New York, New York.

12. When I interviewed them in August 1987, both Sirius Cook and Madeleine L'Engle insisted that Glaspell was not known to drink excessively. Francelina White Hubbard (author interview, 22 August 1987), Glaspell's maid during the last eight years of her life, admitted that Glaspell liked to have a "highball" on her desk when writing in the afternoons but insisted that she never saw her mistress drunk.

13. "Davenport Girl, Nilla Cook, Once Follower of Gandhi," *Des Moines Register*, 31 January 1948.

14. "His Girl Disciple Does a Gandhi and Clears the Court," unidentified clipping, 2 December 1936, Provincetown Players File, Museum of the City of New York, New York, New York.

15. "Iran's Censor—Iowa's Nilla Cram Cook," *Des Moines Tribune*, 24 May 1945.

16. "Nilla Cram Cook, 74; A Writer and Linguist," *New York Times*, 13 October 1982.

17. SG to Barrett Clark, 7 October 1936, Barrett Clark Papers, BRBML.

18. John O'Connor and Lorraine Brown, *The Federal Theatre Project: "Free, Adult, Uncensored"* (London: Eyre Methuen, 1980), 8.

19. A projected living newspaper, *Ethiopia*, had been canceled by the White House for political reasons. See Hallie Flanagan, *Arena: The Story of the Federal Theatre* (1940; reprint, New York: Limelight Editions, 1969), 65, and Willson Whitman, *Bread and Circuses: A Study of the Federal Theatre* (New York: Oxford University Press, 1937), 94–96.

20. Flanagan, *Arena*, 6.

21. John Houseman, *Run-Through: A Memoir* (New York: Simon and Schuster, 1972), 174–75; Flanagan, *Arena*, 29.

22. Hallie Flanagan, "Art and Geography," p. 4, typescript of article submitted to *Magazine of Art*, 8 July 1938, Articles by Hallie Flanagan #3, National Office File, RFTP.

23. John McDermott to author, 30 May 1993.

24. Hallie Flanagan, "Federal Theatre Tomorrow," *Federal Theatre* 2, no. 1 (1937): 6.

25. Arnold Sundgaard seems confused as to how and why Glaspell joined the Federal Theatre. In one letter, he writes that Flanagan "persuaded" her to join (Sundgaard to Joanne Bentley, 26 March 1984, box 16, folder 129, Hallie Flanagan Davis Papers, Vassar College Library, Poughkeepsie, New York), but in an interview for the George Mason University archives, Sundgaard said: "I wouldn't be surprised if [Glaspell] may have gone to Hallie Flanagan with that idea [to search for American playwrights]. Because when she wrote to me, that's obviously what she was doing" (Arnold Sundgaard, interview with John S. O'Connor, 5 September 1976, Oral Interviews, p. 34, FTPC). It seems most likely, however, that somebody like Edward Goodman, or perhaps Jasper Deeter, an old Provincetowner now directing for the Federal Theatre, suggested Glaspell's name to Flanagan, who then asked her to take on the Midwest Play Bureau. I have found no correspondence between Flanagan and Glaspell regarding the appointment.

26. In April 1936, Flanagan was dismayed at how poorly the Federal Theatre was developing in the Midwest; by the summer of 1936, regional adviser E. C. Mabie, initially so enthusiastic, had resigned, as had the regional director, Thomas Wood Stevens. See Jane de Hart Mathews, *The Federal Theatre, 1935–1939: Plays, Relief, and Politics* (Princeton, N.J.: Princeton University Press, 1967), 29–43, 59, 90, and Joanne Bentley, *Hallie Flanagan: A Life in the Theatre* (New York: Knopf, 1988), 206–7.

27. John McGee to Hallie Flanagan, 10 November 1936, Illinois Correspondence, National Office File, RFTP.

28. Irwin A. Rubinstein and Emmet Lavery to Harry Minturn, att. Susan Glaspell, 20 December 1937, Midwest Play Bureau, National Office File, RFTP.

29. Emmet Lavery to George Kondolf, 8 November 1937, Midwest Play Bureau, National Office File, RFTP. For a full account of censorship in the first years of the Federal Theatre, see Whitman, *Bread and Circuses*, chap. 7.

30. George Kondolf to Hallie Flanagan, 23 June 1936, Illinois, Kondolf, George, Dramatic Director, National Office File, RFTP.

31. Hiram Motherwell to SG, 19 November 1936, and David Lane to SG, 9 December 1936, Midwest Play Bureau, National Office File, RFTP.

32. SG, George Kondolf, and John McGee to Hallie Flanagan, 6 November 1936, memorandum, Midwest Play Bureau, National Office File, RFTP.

33. Arnold Sundgaard to author, 15 June 1993. See also Sundgaard's "Susan Glaspell and the Federal Theatre Revisited," *Journal of American Drama and Theatre* 9, no. 1 (Winter 1997): 1–10.

34. Arnold Sundgaard to author, 15 June 1993.

35. Ibid.

36. "Like several of the great teachers I had known in college, and never saw again, she was a profound influence in and on my life" (Arnold Sundgaard to author, 15 June 1993).

37. Alice Gerstenberg, report on *The Great Spirit*, 20 July 1936, FTPC. Gerstenberg founded the Playwrights' Theatre in Chicago in 1922; her one-act *Overtones* had been performed by the Washington Square Players in 1915. See Stuart J. Hecht, "The Plays of Alice Gerstenberg: Cultural Hegemony in the American Little Theatre," *Journal of Popular Culture* 26, no. 1 (1992): 1–16.

38. Hallie Flanagan to SG and John McGee, 22 December 1936, Midwest Play Bureau, National Office File, RFTP.

39. Ann Grosvenor Ayres to SG, 17 April 1937, FTPC.

40. Edwin B. Self to SG, 25 May 1937, FTPC.

41. Ibid., 17 April 1937.

42. Sydney Blackstone's report, 26 July 1936, FTPC.

43. Barrett H. Clark to SG, 21 October 1936, Barrett Clark Papers, BRBML.

44. SG to Barrett H. Clark, 28 November 1936, Barrett Clark Papers, BRBML.

45. SG to E. C. Mabie, 29 October 1936, 4 January 1938, University of Iowa Libraries, Iowa City, Iowa.

46. R. W. Cowden to SG, 18 October 1935, SG to Cowden, 3 February 1936, and Cowden to SG, 21 October 1936, Department of Rare Books and Special Collections, University of Michigan Library, Ann Arbor, Michigan.

47. E. C. Cowden to SG, 31 May 1937, Department of Rare Books and Special Collections, University of Michigan Library, Ann Arbor, Michigan. The other two judges were Allardyce Nicholl and Percival Wilde.

48. SG to R. W. Cowden, 14 May 1937, Department of Rare Books and Special Collections, University of Michigan Library, Ann Arbor, Michigan.

49. See, for example, John T. Frederick to SG, memorandum on "our young men who are trying to write plays," 19 April 1938, SGP.

50. Arnold Sundgaard, Oral Interviews, p. 5, FTPC.

51. Arnold Sundgaard to author, 15 June 1993.

52. Arnold Sundgaard, Oral Interviews, p. 8, FTPC.

53. Sundgaard's *Everywhere I Roam* was produced on Broadway, directed by Marc Connelly, in December 1938; Robert Edmond Jones designed the sets.

54. Arnold Sundgaard, Oral Interviews, p. 6, FTPC.

55. A. R. Crews, "Susan Glaspell and the Federal Theatre," *Northwestern University Information: The Drama* 5, no. 31 (April 1937): 4.

56. Hallie Flanagan, "Work in Progress," fall 1937, p. 2, typescript, Articles by Hallie Flanagan #3, National Office File, RFTP.

57. Arnold Sundgaard to author, 15 June 1993.

58. *Model Tenement* by Meyer Levin, a play about a rent strike, was canceled at the last moment on orders from Washington, D.C., allegedly because Chicago's mayor disapproved of it. For more detailed information, see Meyer Levin, *In Search: An Autobiography* (Paris: Author's Press, 1950), 80–85, and Flanagan, *Arena*, 135–36.

59. SG to Harry Minturn, 28 February 1938, memorandum, *Spirochete*, National Office File, RFTP.

60. Hallie Flanagan to Harry Minturn, 22 March 1938, *Spirochete*, National Office File, RFTP. See also Emmet Lavery to Flanagan, 3 March 1938, Flanagan, Hallie, #1, National Office File, RFTP. Lavery, a Chicago director, also supported Glaspell in this.

61. "Mrs. Flanagan pointed out that if plays were written on time paid for by the Government, such plays would be Government property. However, research may be done on Government time with the play written outside, in such cases the play ownership being retained by the writer who could be paid royalties by the Government while remaining in its employ" (Conference Report, 1 May 1936, Midwest Play Bureau, National Office File, RFTP).

62. Arnold Sundgaard, Oral Interviews, p. 12, FTPC.

63. Arnold Sundgaard to author, 15 June 1993.

64. Arnold Sundgaard, Oral Interviews, p. 9, FTPC.

65. Arnold Sundgaard to author, 15 June 1993. See Emmet Lavery to Harry Minturn, 21 March 1938, and Sundgaard's notes on the play, sent to Flanagan by Minturn, 1 March 1938, *Spirochete*, National Office File, RFTP. *Spirochete* played in Chicago from 29 April to 4 June 1938.

66. Arnold Sundgaard to author, 15 June 1993.

67. Harry Minturn to Hallie Flanagan, 1 March 1938, *Spirochete*, National Office File, RFTP.

68. Marion Brooks to Emmet Lavery, 16 May 1938, memorandum, Living Newspaper, Syphilis, National Office File, RFTP.

69. SG to Hallie Flanagan, 17 September 1937, Midwest Play Bureau, National Office File, RFTP. See also ibid., 18 April 1938. Glaspell's income during these years was augmented by the small but steady royalties she received from productions of her own plays; see, for example, her correspondence with Stanley Richards, supervisor of contracts and play rentals, 25, 27 January 1937, Chicago, Illinois, National Office File, RFTP.

70. SG to George Kondolf, 23 November 1937, Illinois, Kondolf, George, Dramatic Director, National Office File, RFTP.

71. SG to Hallie Flanagan, 7 September 1937, Midwest Play Bureau, National Office File, RFTP.

72. Ibid., 17 September 1937.

73. Katherine Ewing Hocking to author, 8 October 1993.

74. *Within These Walls* by Marcus Bach played at the Blackstone Theatre from 28 January to 13 February 1937.

75. Katherine Ewing Hocking to author, 8 October 1993.

76. Susan Glaspell, carbon copy of unsigned essay, [late autumn 1937], SGP.

77. Arnold Sundgaard to author, 15 June 1993.

78. Hallie Flanagan's speech at Federal Theatre Project Meeting, 15 July 1938, Chicago, Flanagan, Hallie, Speeches, #1, National Office File, RFTP.

79. Flanagan, *Arena*, 363.

80. Arnold Sundgaard to author, 24 August 1993.

81. The other possibility that comes to mind is that Glaspell either knew or suspected that she had been adopted and was reluctant to disclose the fact. Or perhaps her mind played with the possibility of adoption or mistaken identity as she romantically dreamed of being rescued from provincial poverty by the proverbial knight on a white steed—through whom she would satisfy her mother's expectations. Although now we accept her year of birth as 1876, Glaspell frequently gave it as 1882; our only proof (surely convincing) is the Scott County census of 1880, which lists a four-year-old Susie Glaspell. Is this simply a case of vanity, or was Glaspell unsure of the year of her birth? And why return to the themes of adoption and motherhood at the age of sixty-odd?

82. Isobel Patterson, "Turns with a Bookworm," *New York Herald Tribune*, 31 March 1940.

83. Wilson, *The Thirties*, 707.

84. "What America Is Reading," *New York Herald Tribune*, 14 April 1940.

85. Alan C. Collins of Curtis Brown to SG, 19 June 1939, SGP.

86. Susan Glaspell, *Norma Ashe* (Philadelphia: J. B. Lippincott, 1942), 271.

87. Ibid., 348.

88. Ibid., 70–71.

89. Although it is one of the minor characters, a cynical writer, who makes the equation between love and "sex appeal" (*Norma Ashe*, 289), Glaspell is clearly admitting the power of sex in this novel and how it can ruin a woman's life.

90. Ibid., 196.

91. Ibid., 96.

92. Ibid., 164.

93. Ibid., 144.

94. Ibid., 274.

95. Contract, 19 November 1941, SGP.

96. SG to George Stevens of Lippincott, 7 September 1942, SGP.

97. Glaspell's collection of short stories, *Lifted Masks*, was reprinted by the University of Michigan Press in 1993.

98. Paul Chavchadze was the author of *Family Album*, 1949.

99. "Susan Glaspell Says We Need Books Today as Never Before," *Chicago Sunday Tribune*, 6 December 1942, typescript, SGP.

100. Susan Glaspell, *Springs Eternal*, manuscript, SGP.

101. Ibid., act 3.

102. SG to Lawrence Langner, n.d., Lawrence Langner Papers, BRBML.

103. Lawrence Langner to SG, 3, 19 May 1944, Lawrence Langner Papers, BRBML.

104. Glaspell, *Springs Eternal*, act 3, 13.

105. Susan Glaspell, *Judd Rankin's Daughter* (Philadelphia: J. B. Lippincott, 1945).

106. Ibid., 241.

107. Ibid., 157.

108. Ibid., 158.

109. Ibid., 49.

110. Ibid., 127.

111. Lewis Gannett, "Books and Things," *New York Herald Tribune*, 8 December 1945.

112. Daniel George, "Ultimate Truth," *Tribune* (London), 10 May 1946.

113. Susan Glaspell, "On the Subject of Writing," typescript, SGP.

114. Author interview with Francelina White Hubbard, Provincetown, 27 August 1987.

115. Author interviews with Sirius and Valentina Cook, New York, 6, 19 August 1987.

116. Virginia Spencer Carr, *Dos Passos: A Life* (Garden City, N.Y.: Doubleday, 1984), 455.

117. Ibid., 439.

118. Author interview with Francelina White Hubbard, 22 August 1987.

119. From April 1946 to March 1948, the University of Iowa repeatedly asked Glaspell to deposit her manuscripts and papers there. I have not been able to find any replies from her.

120. *Provincetown Advocate*, 29 July 1948; *New York Herald Tribune*, 28 July 1948.

121. *Provincetown Advocate*, 5 August 1948. Francelina White Hubbard remembers receiving $1,000, not $500 (author interview, 22 August 1987).

122. A. D. Peters, "Susan Glaspell: New American Dramatist," *Daily Telegraph* (London), 19 June 1924.

123. Susan Glaspell, "On the Subject of Writing," 1–2, typescript, SGP.

124. Ibid.

125. *Westminster Gazette*, 2 January 1926.

126. Ludwig Lewisohn, *Expression in America* (London: Thornton Butterworth, 1931), 392.

127. Oliver Sayler, *Our American Theatre* (New York: Brentano's, 1923), 99.

128. Arthur Hobson Quinn, *American Fiction: An Historical and Critical Survey* (New York: Appleton Century Crofts, 1936), 718, 717. See also George Snell, *The Shapers of American Fiction* (New York: Dutton, 1947), 140.

Select Bibliography

For an extensive bibliography of works by and about Susan Glaspell, see Mary E. Papke, *Susan Glaspell: A Research and Production Sourcebook* (Westport, Conn.: Greenwood Press, 1993).

Manuscript Collections

The main repository of Susan Glaspell's and George Cram Cook's papers is the Berg Collection of English and American Literature, New York Public Library, Astor, Lenox, and Tilden Foundations, New York, New York. A few letters are held by Sirius and Valentina Cook. The other collections listed below hold correspondence and various materials of interest, primarily concerned with the Provincetown Players and the Federal Theatre.

Ann Arbor, Michigan
  Department of Rare Books and Special Collections, University of Michigan
    Library
Bloomington, Indiana
  Lilly Library, Indiana University
Cambridge, Massachusetts
  Harvard Theatre Collection, Nathan Marsh Pusey Library, Harvard University
    Agnes Boulton Papers
    Susan Glaspell Papers
    Edna Kenton Papers
    Eugene O'Neill Papers
    Provincetown Players Scrapbooks
  Houghton Library, Harvard University
    Martha Dickinson Bianchi Papers
    John Reed Papers
  Schlesinger Library, Radcliffe College
    Ines Haynes Irwin Papers
Charlottesville, Virginia
  Clifton Waller Barrett Library of American Literature, Special Collections
    Department, University of Virginia Library
    Papers of Susan Glaspell
    Papers of Eugene O'Neill

Chicago, Illinois
  Newberry Library
    Floyd Dell Papers
    Eunice Tietjens Papers
  University of Chicago
    Records Office
Davenport, Iowa
  Davenport Public Library
    Susan Glaspell File
  Putnam Museum
Davis, California
  Department of Special Collections, University of California Library
    Robert Károly Sarlós Papers
Des Moines, Iowa
  Drake University
    Susan Glaspell File
    Records Office
Detroit, Michigan
  Archives of Labor and Urban Affairs, Walter P. Reuther Library, Wayne State
      University
    Mary Heaton Vorse, "Playhouse History I"
    Mary Heaton Vorse, "Playhouse History II"
Fairfax, Virginia
  Special Collections and Archives, Fenwick Library, George Mason University
    Federal Theatre Project Collection
Iowa City, Iowa
  University Libraries, University of Iowa
    George Cram Cook File
    Susan Glaspell File
London, England
  Gollancz Archives
  Theatre Museum
New Haven, Connecticut
  Beinecke Rare Book and Manuscript Library, Yale University
    Barrett Clark Papers
    Arthur Ficke Papers
    Hutchins Hapgood and Neith Boyce Papers
    Edna Kenton, "The Provincetown Players and the Playwrights' Theatre,
      1915–1922"
    Lawrence Langner Papers
    Eugene O'Neill Collection
    Carl Van Vechten Papers
    Edmund Wilson Papers
New York, New York
  Berg Collection of English and American Literature, New York Public Library,
      Astor, Lenox, and Tilden Foundations
    George Cram Cook Papers
    Susan Glaspell Papers
    May Sarton Papers
  Fales Collection, Elmer Bobst Library, New York University
    Edna Kenton Papers

Museum of the City of New York
  Provincetown Players File
Rare Book and Manuscript Library, Butler Library, Columbia University
  Edna Kenton Papers
Billy Rose Theatre Collection, New York Public Library for the Performing Arts
  George Cram Cook File
  Susan Glaspell File
  Edward Goodman Papers
  Provincetown Players File
Philadelphia, Pennsylvania
  Rare Book and Manuscript Library, University of Pennsylvania
  Theodore Dreiser Papers
Poughkeepsie, New York
  Vassar College Library
  Hallie Flanagan Davis Papers
Stanford, California
  Department of Special Collections, Stanford University Libraries
Washington, D.C.
  Copyright Drama Collection, Manuscript Division, Library of Congress
  Federal Theatre Project Collection
  National Archives
  Records of the Federal Theatre Project, Records of the Work Projects
  Administration

Works by Susan Glaspell

BIOGRAPHY

The Road to the Temple. New York: Frederick A. Stokes, 1927.

NOVELS

The Glory of the Conquered: The Story of a Great Love. New York: Frederick A. Stokes, 1909.
The Visioning. New York: Frederick A. Stokes, 1911.
Fidelity. 1915. Reprint, London: Jarrolds, 1924.
Brook Evans. New York: Frederick A. Stokes, 1928.
Fugitive's Return. New York: Frederick A. Stokes, 1929.
Ambrose Holt and Family. New York: Frederick A. Stokes, 1931.
The Morning Is Near Us. New York: Frederick A. Stokes, 1939.
Cherished and Shared of Old. New York: Julian Messner, 1940.
Norma Ashe. Philadelphia: J. B. Lippincott, 1942.
Judd Rankin's Daughter. Philadelphia: J. B. Lippincott, 1945.

PLAYS

Plays. Boston: Small, Maynard, 1920. (*Trifles, Suppressed Desires, The People, Close the Book, The Outside, Woman's Honor, Bernice, Tickless Time.*)
Chains of Dew. Typescript, Library of Congress, Washington, D.C., 1920.

The Comic Artist (with Norman Matson). London: Ernest Benn, 1927.

Alison's House. New York: Samuel French, 1930.

Plays by Susan Glaspell. Edited by C. W. E. Bigsby. Cambridge: Cambridge University Press, 1987. (*Trifles, The Outside, The Verge, Inheritors*.)

SHORT STORIES

In addition to the short stories listed in Papke, *Susan Glaspell*, see the following.

"His Literary Training." *The Delphic* January 1898, 83–85.

"The Unprofessional Crime." *The Delphic* February 1900, 109–12.

"From the Pen of Failure." *Quax* (1905), 215–18.

Lifted Masks and Other Works. Introduction by Eric S. Rabkin. 1912. Reprint, Ann Arbor: University of Michigan Press, 1993.

Works on Susan Glaspell

Alkalay-Gut, Karen. "Jury of Her Peers: The Importance of Trifles." *Studies in Short Fiction* 21, no. 1 (1984): 1–9.

Andrews, Clarence A., and Marcia Noe. "Susan Glaspell of Davenport." *The Iowan* 25 (Summer 1977): 46–53.

Bach, Gerhard. "Susan Glaspell: Provincetown Playwright." *Great Lakes Review* 4, no. 2 (1978): 31–43.

———. "Susan Glaspell: Supplementary Notes." *American Literary Realism, 1870–1910* 5 (1972): 71–73.

———. "Susan Glaspell (1876–1948): A Bibliography of Dramatic Criticism." *Great Lakes Review* 3, no. 2 (1977): 1–34.

———. *Susan Glaspell und die Provincetown Players: Die Aufange des modernen amerikanischen Dramas und Theaters*. Frankfurt am Main: Peter Lang, 1979.

Bach, Gerhard, and Claudia Harris. "Susan Glaspell: Rediscovering an American Playwright." *Theatre Journal* 44, no. 1 (March 1992): 94–96.

Ben-Zvi, Linda. "Susan Glaspell and Eugene O'Neill." *Eugene O'Neill Newsletter* 6, no. 2 (1982): 21–29.

———. "Susan Glaspell and Eugene O'Neill: The Imagery of Gender." *Eugene O'Neill Newsletter* 10, no. 1 (1986): 22–27.

———. "Susan Glaspell's Contributions to Contemporary Women Playwrights." In *Feminine Focus: The New Women Playwrights*, edited by Enoch Brater, 147–66. New York: Oxford University Press, 1989.

———, ed. *Susan Glaspell: Essays on Her Theater and Fiction*. Ann Arbor: University of Michigan Press, 1995.

Bryan, Patricia L. "Stories in Fiction and in Fact: Susan Glaspell's 'A Jury of Her Peers' and the 1901 Murder Trial of Margaret Hossack." *Stanford Law Review* 49, no. 6 (1997): 1293–1363.

Carpentier, Martha C. "Susan Glaspell's Fiction: *Fidelity* as American Romance." *Twentieth Century Literature* 40, no. 1 (Spring 1994): 92–113.

Crawford, Bartholomew V. *Palimpsest* 11, no. 12 (December 1930): 517–21.

Dymkowski, Christine. "On the Edge: The Plays of Susan Glaspell." *Modern Drama* 31, no. 1 (March 1988): 91–105.

Fetterly, Judith. "Reading about Reading: 'A Jury of Her Peers,' 'The Murders in the Rue Morgue,' and 'The Yellow Wallpaper.'" In *Gender and Reading: Essays on*

Readers, Texts, and Contexts, edited by Elizabeth A. Flynn and Patrocinio P. Schweickart, 47–64. Baltimore: Johns Hopkins University Press, 1986.

Friedman, Sharon. "Feminism as Theme in Twentieth Century American Women's Drama." *American Studies* 25, no. 1 (Spring 1984): 69–89.

Gainor, J. Ellen. "A Stage of Her Own: Susan Glaspell's *The Verge* and Women's Dramaturgy." *Journal of American Drama and Theatre* 1 (Spring 1989): 79–99.

Goldie, Grace Wyndham. *The Liverpool Repertory Theatre, 1911–1934.* London: University Press of Liverpool, 1935.

Gould, Jean. *Modern American Playwrights.* New York: Dodd, Mead, 1966.

Hedges, Elaine. "Small Things Reconsidered: Susan Glaspell's 'A Jury of Her Peers.'" *Women's Studies: An Interdisciplinary Journal* 12, no. 1 (1986): 89–110.

Hedges, M. H. "Miss Glaspell's Vision of Life." *The Nation,* 4 April 1923.

Kolin, Philip C. "Therapists in Susan Glaspell's *Suppressed Desires* and David Rabe's *In the Boom Boom Room.*" *Notes on Contemporary Literature* 18, no. 4 (November 1988): 2–3.

Larabee, Ann. "Death in Delphi: Susan Glaspell and the Companionate Marriage." *Mid-American Review* 7, no. 2 (1987): 93–106.

Lewisohn, Ludwig. *The Drama and the Stage.* New York: Harcourt Brace, 1922.

——. *Expression in America.* London: Thornton Butterworth, 1931.

Makowsky, Veronica. *Susan Glaspell's Century of American Women: A Critical Interpretation of Her Work.* New York: Oxford University Press, 1993.

Marshall, Norman. *The Other Theatre.* London: John Lehman, 1947.

Noe, Marcia. "Reconfiguring the Subject/Recuperating Realism: Susan Glaspell's Unseen Woman." *American Drama* 4, no. 2 (Spring 1995): 36–54.

——. "Region as Metaphor in the Plays of Susan Glaspell." *Western Illinois Regional Studies* 4, no. 1 (1981): 77–85.

——. "'A Romantic and Miraculous City' Shapes Three Midwestern Writers." *Western Illinois Regional Studies* 1 (1978): 176–98.

——. *Susan Glaspell: Voice from the Heartland.* Macomb: Western Illinois University Press, 1983.

——. "Susan Glaspell's Analysis of the Midwestern Character." *Books at Iowa* 27 (November 1977): 3–20.

Ozieblo, Barbara. "Love and Envy in Provincetown: Susan Glaspell, George Cram Cook, and Eugene O'Neill." In *Amor, Odio y Violencia en la Literatura Norteamericana,* edited by José Antonio Gurpegui, 215–34. Alcalá de Henares, Madrid: Servicio de Publicaciones de la Universidad de Alcalá de Henares, 1994.

——. "Rebellion and Rejection: The Plays of Susan Glaspell." In *Modern American Drama: The Female Canon,* edited by June Schlueter, 66–76. London: Associated University Presses, 1990.

——. "Susan Glaspell." In *American Drama,* edited by Clive Bloom, 6–20. London: Macmillan, 1995.

Papke, Mary E. *Susan Glaspell: A Research and Production Sourcebook.* Westport, Conn.: Greenwood Press, 1993.

Radel, Nicholas F. "Provincetown Plays: Women Writers and O'Neill's American Intertext." *Essays in Theatre* 9, no. 1 (November 1990): 31–43.

Rohe, Alice. "The Story of Susan Glaspell." *New York Morning Telegraph,* 18 December 1921, 4.

Shafer, Yvonne. "Susan Glaspell: German Influence, American Playwright." *Zeltschrift für Anglistik und Amerikanistik* 4 (1988): 333–38.

Smith, Beverly A. "Women's Work—Trifles?: The Skills and Insights of Playwright Susan Glaspell." *International Journal of Women's Studies* 5, no. 2 (1982): 172–84.

SELECT BIBLIOGRAPHY

Sundgaard, Arnold. "Susan Glaspell and the Federal Theatre Revisited." *Journal of American Drama and Theatre* 9, no. 1 (Winter 1997): 1–10.

Sutherland, Cynthia. "American Women Playwrights as Mediators of the 'Woman Problem.'" *Modern Drama* 21 (1978): 319–36.

Waterman, Arthur E. *Susan Glaspell*. New York: Twayne, 1966.

———. "Susan Glaspell (1882?–1948)." *American Literary Realism 1870–1910* 4, no. 2 (1971): 183–91.

———. "Susan Glaspell and the Provincetown." *Modern Drama* 7 (September 1967): 174–84.

———. "Susan Glaspell's *The Verge*: An Experiment in Feminism." *Great Lakes Review* 6, no. 1 (1979): 17–23.

Memoirs, Autobiographies, and Biographies of Susan Glaspell's Contemporaries

Adams, Samuel Hopkins. *A. Woollcott: His Life and His World*. New York: Reynal and Hitchcock, 1945.

Atkins, Elizabeth. *Edna St. Vincent Millay and Her Times*. New York: Russell and Russell, 1964.

Barnes, Djuna. *A Book*. New York: Boni and Liveright, 1923.

———. "The Days of Jig Cook." *Theatre Guild Magazine* 31 (January 1919): 33.

Benn, Ernest. *Happier Days*. London: E. Benn, 1943.

Bentley, Joanne. *Hallie Flanagan: A Life in the Theatre*. New York: Knopf, 1988.

Boulton, Agnes. *Part of a Long Story: Eugene O'Neill as a Young Man in Love*. London: Peter Davies, 1958.

Bowker, Gordon. *Malcolm Lowry Remembered*. London: Ariel Books/BBC, 1985.

Brevda, William. *Harry Kemp: The Last Bohemian*. London: Associated University Presses, 1986.

Broe, Mary Lynn. *Silence and Power: A Reevaluation of Djuna Barnes*. Carbondale: Southern Illinois University Press, 1991.

Browne, Maurice. *Too Late to Lament: An Autobiography*. London: Victor Gollancz, 1955.

Carr, Virginia Spencer. *Dos Passos: A Life*. Garden City, N.Y.: Doubleday, 1984.

Cheney, Anne. *Millay in Greenwich Village*. Tuscaloosa: University of Alabama Press, 1975.

Clark, Barrett H. *Eugene O'Neill: The Man and His Plays*. 1926. Reprint, New York: Dover, 1947.

Clurman, Harold. *The Fervent Years: The Story of the Group Theatre and the Thirties*. London: Dennis Dobson, 1946.

Commins, Dorothy, ed. *"Love, Admiration, and Respect": The O'Neill-Commins Correspondence*. Durham: Duke University Press, 1986.

Cook, Nilla Cram. *My Road to India*. New York: Lee Furman, 1939.

Cowley, Malcolm. *Exile's Return: A Literary Odyssey of the 1920s*. 1934. Reprint, London: Bodley Head, 1961.

Crotty, Frank. *Provincetown Profiles and Others on Cape Cod*. Barre, Mass.: Barre Gazette, 1958.

Dash, Joan. *A Life of One's Own: Three Gifted Women and the Men They Married*. New York: Paragon House, 1988.

Dell, Floyd. *Homecoming: An Autobiography*. New York: Farrar and Rinehart, 1933.

———. *Moon-Calf*. 1920. Reprint, New York: Sagamore, 1957.

DeWitt, Miriam Hapgood. "The Provincetown I Remember." *Provincetown Art Association and Museum Summer 1987 Guide* (1987), 7–13.

Douglas, George H. *Edmund Wilson's America*. Lexington: University Press of Kentucky, 1983.

Eastman, Max. *Enjoyment of Living*. New York: Harper and Brothers, 1948.

——. *Great Companions: Critical Memoirs of Some Famous Friends*. London: Museum Press, 1959.

Edwards, Ruth Dudley. *Victor Gollancz: A Biography*. London: Victor Gollancz, 1987.

Ferber, Edna. *A Kind of Magic: Autobiography*. London: Victor Gollancz, 1963.

Field, Andrew. *Djuna: The Life and Times of Djuna Barnes*. New York: Putnam's, 1983.

Flanagan, Hallie. *Arena: The Story of the Federal Theatre*. 1940. Reprint, New York: Limelight Editions, 1969.

——. "Did I Consider the Theatre a Weapon?" In *Women of Valor: The Struggle against the Depression as Told in Their Own Voices*, edited by Bernard Sternsher and Judith Sealander, 151–55. Chicago: Ivan R. Dee, 1990.

Gelb, Arthur, and Barbara Gelb. *O'Neill*. 1962. Reprint, New York: Harper and Row, 1973.

Goldman, Emma. *Living My Life*. 2 vols. 1931. Reprint, New York: Dover, 1970.

Gould, Jean. *The Poet and Her Book: A Biography of Edna St. Vincent Millay*. New York: Dodd, Mead, 1969.

Groth, Janet. *Edmund Wilson: A Critic for Our Time*. Athens: Ohio University Press, 1989.

Hapgood, Hutchins. *A Victorian in the Modern World*. 1939. Reprint, Seattle: University of Washington Press, 1972.

Hartley, Marsden. "The Great Provincetown Summer." Manuscript, Beinecke Rare Book and Manuscript Library, Yale University, New Haven, Connecticut.

Herring, Phillip. *Djuna: The Life and Work of Djuna Barnes*. New York: Viking Penguin, 1995.

Hodges, Sheila. *Gollancz: The Story of a Publishing House*. London: Victor Gollancz, 1978.

Houseman, John. *Run-Through: A Memoir*. New York: Simon and Schuster, 1972.

Jones, Ernest. *Sigmund Freud: Life and Work*. London: Hogarth Press, 1955.

Kemp, Harry. *More Miles: An Autobiographical Novel*. New York: Boni and Liveright, 1926.

——. *Tramping on Life: An Autobiographical Narrative*. London: Heinemann, 1923.

Kreymborg, Alfred. *Troubadour: An Autobiography*. New York: Boni and Liveright, 1925.

Langner, Lawrence. *The Magic Curtain*. London: Harrap, 1952.

Le Gallienne, Eva. *At Thirty-three: Autobiography*. London: John Lane, Bodley Head, 1934.

——. *With a Quiet Heart*. New York: Viking, 1953.

Ludington, Townsend. *John Dos Passos: A Twentieth Century Odyssey*. New York: Dutton, 1980.

——. *Marsden Hartley: The Biography of an American Artist*. Boston: Little, Brown, 1992.

Luhan, Mabel Dodge. *Movers and Shakers*. Vol. 3 of *Intimate Memories*. 1936. Reprint, New York: Kraus Reprint, 1971.

McMichael, George. *Journey to Obscurity: The Life of Alice French*. Lincoln: University of Nebraska Press, 1965.

Marcaccio, Michael D. *The Hapgoods: Three Earnest Brothers*. Charlottesville: University Press of Virginia, 1977.

Middleton, George. *These Things Are Mine: The Autobiography of a Journeyman Playwright*. New York: Macmillan, 1947.

Morley, Sheridan. *Sybil Thorndike: A Life in the Theatre*. London: Weidenfeld and Nicholson, 1977.

O'Neill, William L. *The Last Romantic: A Life of Max Eastman*. New York:: Oxford University Press, 1978.

Paluka, Frank. *Iowa Authors: A Bio-Bibliography of Sixty Native Writers*. Iowa City: Friends of the University of Iowa Libraries, 1967.

Rosen, Robert C. *John Dos Passos: Politics and the Writer*. Lincoln: University of Nebraska Press, 1981.

Rudnick, Lois Palken. *Mabel Dodge Luhan: New Woman, New Worlds*. Albuquerque: University of New Mexico Press, 1984.

Schanke, Robert A. *Eva Le Gallienne: A Bio-Bibliography*. London: Greenwood Press, 1989.

Sheaffer, Louis. *O'Neill: Son and Artist*. London: Paul Elek, 1973.

——. *O'Neill: Son and Playwright*. London: J. M. Dent and Sons, 1969.

Sinclair, Upton. *The Cup of Fury*. New York: Cannell, 1956.

——. *Money Writes!* New York: Albert and Charles Boni, 1927.

Sprigge, Elizabeth. *Sybil Thorndike Casson*. London: Victor Gollancz, 1971.

Stevens, Holly, ed. *Letters of Wallace Stevens*. London: Faber and Faber, 1967.

Tarbell, Roberta K. *Marguerite Zorach: The Early Years, 1808–1920*. Washington, D.C.: Smithsonian Institute Press, 1973.

Tietjens, Eunice. *The World at My Shoulder*. New York: Macmillan, 1938.

Trachtenberg, Alan, ed. *Memoirs of Waldo Frank*. Amherst: University of Massachusetts Press, 1973.

Trimberger, Ellen Kay, ed. *Neith Boyce and Hutchins Hapgood, Intimate Warriors: Portrait of a Modern Marriage*. New York: Feminist Press at the City University of New York, 1991.

Turkel, Pauline H., ed. *In Memory of Fitzi*. New York: Pauline H. Turkel, 1955.

Untermeyer, Louis. *From Another World: The Autobiography of Louis Untermeyer*. New York: Harcourt Brace, 1939.

Van Vechten, Carl. *Peter Whiffle*. New York: Knopf, 1929.

Vorse, Mary Heaton. *Time and the Town: A Provincetown Chronicle*. New York: Dial Press, 1942.

Wexler, Alice. *Emma Goldman: An Intimate Life*. London: Virago, 1984.

White, Ray Lewis, ed. *Sherwood Anderson's Memoirs*. 1942. Reprint, Chapel Hill: University of North Carolina Press, 1969.

Williams, William Carlos. *The Autobiography of William Carlos Williams*. New York: Random House, 1951.

Wilson, Edmund. *Shores of Light: A Literary Chronicle of the Twenties and Thirties*. New York: Farrar, Straus and Giroux, 1952.

——. *The Thirties: From Notebooks and Diaries of the Period*. New York: Farrar, Straus and Giroux, 1980.

——. *The Twenties*. New York: Farrar, Straus and Giroux, 1975.

Zorach, William. *The Autobiography of William Zorach*. New York: World, 1967.

Works on the Provincetown Players and Their Plays

For a full listing of the Provincetown plays and where they may be found, see Robert Károly Sarlós, *Jig Cook and the Provincetown Players: Theatre in Ferment* (Amherst: University of Massachusetts Press, 1982).

Bogard, Travis, and Jackson R. Bryer, eds. *Selected Letters of Eugene O'Neill*. New Haven: Yale University Press, 1988.

Bryer, Jackson R., ed. *"The Theatre We Worked For": The Letters of Eugene O'Neill to Kenneth Macgowan*. New Haven: Yale University Press, 1982.

Cook, George Cram, and Frank Shay. *The Provincetown Plays*. Cincinnati: Stewart Kidd, 1921.

Deutsch, Helen, and Stella Hanau. *The Provincetown: A Story of the Theatre*. 1931. Reprint, New York: Russell and Russell, 1972.

Estrin, Mark W., ed. *Conversations with Eugene O'Neill*. Jackson: University Press of Mississippi, 1990.

Goldman, Arnold. "The Culture of the Provincetown Players." *American Studies* 12, no. 3 (Autumn 1978): 291–310.

Grumbackh, Jane. "The Provincetown Playhouse: Its History and Its Influence." *New York State Community Theatre Journal* 9, no. 2 (April–July 1969): 12–22.

Hartley, Marsden. "Farewell Charles." In *The New Caravan*, edited by Alfred Kreymborg, Lewis Mumford, and Paul Rosenfeld, 552–62. New York: Norton, 1936.

Kemp, Harry. "A Few Words Beforehand." In *Bocaccio's Untold Tales*, 1–10. New York: Brentano's, 1924.

———. "George Cram Cook (In Memory of George Cram Cook Who Revolutionized American Playwriting)." *The Quill* 14, no. 2 (February 1924): 12–13.

———. "O'Neill of Provincetown." *Brentano's Book Chat* 2 (May–June 1929): 45–47.

———. "Stray Cats, Purple Cabbages, and a Shaky Throne: It Is the Unforeseen and Unrehearsed Incidents in a Play That Make It or Break It." *Theatre Magazine* 48 (May 1927): 32.

Kenton, Edna. "Provincetown and Macdougal Street." In *Greek Coins*, by George Cram Cook, 17–30. New York: George H. Doran, 1925.

———. "The Provincetown Players and the Playwrights' Theater." *Billboard*, 5 August 1922, 6.

———. "The Provincetown Players and the Playwrights' Theatre, 1915–1922." *Eugene O'Neill Review* 21 (Spring–Fall 1997).

McDermott, Dana Sue. "The Apprenticeship of Robert Edmond Jones." *Theatre Survey* 29, no. 3 (November 1988): 193–212.

O'Neill, Eugene. *The Collected Plays of Eugene O'Neill*. Edited by John Lahr. London: Jonathan Cape, 1988.

Ozieblo, Barbara, ed. *The Provincetown Players: A Choice of the Shorter Works*. Sheffield, Eng.: Sheffield Academic Press, 1994.

Pfister, Joel. *Staging Depth: Eugene O'Neill and the Politics of Psychological Discourse*. Chapel Hill: University of North Carolina Press, 1995.

Roberts, Nancy L., and Arthur W. Roberts. *"As Ever, Gene": The Letters of Eugene O'Neill to George Jean Nathan*. London: Associated University Presses, 1987.

Sarlós, Robert Károly. *Jig Cook and the Provincetown Players: Theatre in Ferment*. Amherst: University of Massachusetts Press, 1982.

———. "Producing Principles and Practices of the Provincetown Players." *Theatre Research / Récherches Théâtrales* 10, no. 2 (1962): 89–102.

———. "The Provincetown Players' Genesis or Non-Commercial Theatre on Commercial Streets." *Journal of American Culture* 7, no. 1 (Fall 1984): 65–70.

———. "Wharf and Dome: Materials for the History of the Provincetown Players." *Theatre Research / Récherches Théâtrales* 10, no. 3 (1970): 163–78.

———. " 'Write a Dance': *Lazarus Laughed* as O'Neill's Dithyramb of the Western Hemisphere." *Theatre Survey* 29, no. 1 (May 1988): 37–49.

Sayler, Oliver M. "From Play at Provincetown to Work in New York and All for Native Drama." *Boston Evening Transcript*, 28 May 1921, 6.

Shay, Frank, ed. *The Provincetown Plays: Second Series*. 1916. Reprint, Great Neck, N.Y.: Core Collection Books, 1976.

———. *The Provincetown Plays: Third Series*. New York: Frank Shay, 1916.

Williams, Gary Jay. "Turned Down in Provincetown: O'Neill's Début Re-Examined." *Eugene O'Neill Newsletter* 12, no. 1 (1988): 17–31.

Works of General Interest

Aaron, Daniel. *Writers on the Left: Episodes in American Literary Communism*. 1961. Reprint, New York: Octagon Books, 1979.

Aarons, Victoria. "A Community of Women: Surviving Marriage in the Wilderness." *Rendezvous: Journal of Arts and Letters* 22, no. 2 (Spring 1988): 3–11.

Abrahams, Edward. "Randolph Bourne on Feminism and Feminists." *Historian* 63, no. 3 (May 1981): 365–77.

Agate, James. *The Contemporary Theatre*. London: Chapman and Hall, 1926.

Ahlstrom, Sydney E. *A Religious History of the American People*. New Haven: Yale University Press, 1972.

Allen, Frederick Lewis. *Only Yesterday: An Informal History of the Nineteen-Twenties*. New York: Blue Ribbon Books, 1931.

Andrews, Clarence A. *A Literary History of Iowa*. Iowa City: University of Iowa Press, 1972.

Archer, Williams. "Great Contributions of 'Little Theatres' to Our Drama's Future." *New York Post*, 24 February 1921.

Arens, Egmont. *The Little Book of Greenwich Village: A Handbook of Information concerning New York's Bohemia*. New York: Washington Square Bookshop, 1919.

Austin, Gayle. *Feminist Theories for Dramatic Criticism*. Ann Arbor: University of Michigan Press, 1990.

Avrich, Paul. *The Modern School Movement: Anarchism and Education in the United States*. Princeton, N.J.: Princeton University Press, 1980.

———. *Sacco and Vanzetti: The Anarchist Background*. Princeton, N.J.: Princeton University Press, 1991.

Bablet, Denis. *The Theatre of Gordon Craig*. Translated by Daphne Woodward. London: Eyre Methuen, 1981.

Baigell, Matthew. *An History of American Painting*. London: Thames and Hudson, 1971.

Baker, George Pierce. *Dramatic Technique*. Boston: Houghton Mifflin, 1919.

Banner, Lois W. *Women in Modern America: A Brief History*. New York: Harcourt Brace Jovanovich, 1974.

Baritz, Loren, ed. *The Culture of the Twenties*. New York: Bobbs-Merrill, 1970.

Basso, Hamilton. "Profiles: The Tragic Sense." *New Yorker*, 28 February 1948, 40.

Baur, John I. H. *Revolution and Tradition in Modern American Art*. Cambridge: Harvard University Press, 1954.

Beard, Rick, and Leslie Cohen Berlowitz, eds. *Greenwich Village: Culture and Counterculture*. New Brunswick, N.J.: Museum of the City of New York/Rutgers University Press, 1993.

Bentley, Eric. *The Theory of the Modern Stage: An Introduction to Modern Theatre and Drama*. 1968. Reprint, Harmondsworth, Eng.: Penguin, 1989.

Bigsby, C. W. E. *A Critical Introduction to Twentieth Century Drama*. Vol. 1. Cambridge: Cambridge University Press, 1982.

Biographical History and Portrait Gallery of Scott County, Iowa. Chicago: American Biographical Publishing Company, 1895.

Blanchard, Charles. *Building for the Centuries: A Memorial of the Founders and Builders, Semicentennial, 1881–1931.* Des Moines, Iowa: Drake University, 1931.

Borus, Daniel. *These United States: Portraits of Americans from the 1920s.* Ithaca: Cornell University Press, 1992.

Bourke, Paul E. "The Social Critics and the End of American Innocence, 1907–1921." *Journal of American Studies* 3 (July 1969): 57–72.

Brater, Enoch, ed. *Feminine Focus: The New Women Playwrights.* New York: Oxford University Press, 1989.

Bray, Elizabeth McCullough. "Panorama of Cultural Development Here in Last Half a Century." *Davenport Democrat*, 31 March 1929, 4.

Brewster, Edwin Tenney. "Dreams and Forgetting: New Discoveries in Dream Psychology." *McClure's Magazine* 29 (October 1912): 714–19.

Brigham, Johnson, ed. *A Book of Iowa Authors by Iowa Authors.* Des Moines: Iowa State Teachers Association, 1930.

Brookeman, Christopher. *American Culture and Society since the 1930s.* London: Macmillan, 1984.

Brown, Dorothy. *Setting a Course: American Women in the 1920s.* Boston: G. K. Hall, 1987.

Buhle, Mary Jo, Paul Buhle, and Dan Georgakas, eds. *Encyclopedia of the American Left.* New York: Garland, 1990.

Burnham, John Chynoweth. "Psychiatry, Psychology, and the Progressive Movement." *American Quarterly* 12 (Winter 1960): 459–61, 65.

Burns, Mantle. *Contemporary American Playwrights.* 1938. Reprint, New York: Dodd, Mead, 1940.

Carson, Mina. *Settlement Folk: Social Thought and the American Settlement Movement, 1885–1930.* Chicago: University of Chicago Press, 1990.

Carter, John F. " 'These Wild People' by One of Them." *Atlantic Monthly* 126 (1920): 302.

Case, Sue-Ellen. *Feminism and the Theatre.* New York: Macmillan, 1988.

Chapin, Anna Alice. *Greenwich Village.* New York: Dodd, Mead, 1917.

Cheney, Sheldon. *The New Movement in the Theatre.* 1914. Reprint, Westport, Conn.: Greenwood Press, 1971.

———. "New York's Best Season." *Theatre Arts Magazine* 1, no. 2 (February 1917): 66–70.

Chinoy, Helen Kirch, and Linda Walsh Jenkins. *Women in American Theatre.* New York: Crown, 1981.

Churchill, Allen. *The Improper Bohemians: A Re-creation of Greenwich Village in Its Heyday.* 1959. Reprint, London: Cassell, 1961.

Clark, Barrett H. *An Hour of American Drama.* Philadelphia: Lippincott, 1930.

Clark, Barrett H., and Kenyon Nicholson, eds. *The American Scene.* New York: Appleton, 1930.

Cleaton, Irene, and Allen Cleaton. *Books and Battles: American Literature, 1920–1930.* 1937. Reprint, New York: Cooper Square, 1970.

Clogg, Richard. *A Short History of Modern Greece.* Cambridge: Cambridge University Press, 1986.

Cohn, Ruby. "Twentieth Century Drama." In *Columbia Literary History of the United States*, edited by Emory Elliott, 1101–25. New York: Columbia University Press, 1988.

Crunden, Robert M. *American Salons: Encounter with European Modernism, 1885–1917.* New York: Oxford University Press, 1993.

Davis, Mary Caroline. "Drama, Women, and the American Theatre." *The Nation*, 1 June 1918, 665.

Dell, Floyd. *Love in the Machine Age: A Psychological Study of the Transition from Patriarchal Society*. New York: Farrar, 1930.

———. "Rents Were Low in Greenwich Village." *American Mercury* 65 (December 1947): 662–68.

———. *Women as World Builders: Studies in Modern Feminism*. Chicago: Forbes, 1913.

Dickinson, Thomas H. *The Insurgent Theatre*. New York: B. W. Huebsch, 1917.

———. *Playwrights of the New American Theatres*. New York: Macmillan, 1925.

Downer, Alan S., ed. *American Drama and Its Critics: A Collection of Critical Essays*. Chicago: University of Chicago Press, 1965.

Duffey, Bernard. *The Chicago Renaissance in American Letters: A Critical History*. 1954. Reprint, Westport, Conn.: Greenwood Press, 1977.

Edwards, Robert. "The Story of Greenwich Village," part 11. *The Quill* 13, no. 6 (December 1923): 16–21.

Fieve, Ronald. *Mood Swing*. New York: Morrow, 1975.

Fishbein, Leslie. "Freud and the Radicals: The Sexual Revolution Comes to Greenwich Village." *Canadian Review of American Studies* 12, no. 2 (Fall 1981): 173–89.

———. *Rebels in Bohemia: The Radicals of "The Masses," 1911–1917*. Chapel Hill: University of North Carolina Press, 1982.

Flannery, James W. *W. B. Yeats and the Idea of a Theatre: The Early Abbey Theatre in Theory and Practice*. Toronto: Macmillan, 1976.

Flexner, Eleanor. *American Playwrights, 1918–1938: The Theatre Retreats from Reality*. New York: Simon and Schuster, 1938.

Forrey, Carolyn. "The New Woman Revisited." *Women's Studies* 2 (1974): 37–56.

Fredericksen, Mary K. "The State of the State: Iowa in 1885." *Palimpsest* 65 (January–February 1984): 3–8.

Garrison, Winfred Ernest. *An American Religious Movement: A Brief History of the Disciples of Christ*. 1945. Reprint, St. Louis, Mo.: Bethany, 1960.

Goldberg, Isaac. *The Drama of Transition: Native and Exotic Playcraft*. Cincinnati: Stewart Kidd, 1922.

Goldman, Emma. *The Significance of the Modern Drama*. Boston: Richard G. Badger, 1914.

Gordon, Lynn D. "The Gibson Girl Goes to College: Popular Culture and Women's Higher Education in the Progressive Era, 1890–1920." *American Quarterly* 39 (Summer 1987): 212–30.

Grace, Sherrill E. *Regression and Apocalypse: Studies in North American Literary Expressionism*. Toronto: University of Toronto Press, 1989.

Hale, Nathan G., Jr. *Freud and the Americans: The Beginnings of Psychoanalysis in the United States, 1876–1917*. New York: Oxford University Press, 1971.

Hansen, Harry. "A Davenport Boyhood." *Palimpsest* 37, no. 4 (April 1956): 161–224.

Harrop, John. "'A Constructive Promise': Jacques Copeau in New York, 1917–1919." *Theatre Survey* 12, no. 2 (November 1971): 104–18.

Heller, Adele, and Lois Rudnick. *1915, The Cultural Moment: The New Politics, the New Woman, the New Psychology, and the New Theatre in America*. New Brunswick, N.J.: Rutgers University Press, 1991.

Hoffman, Frederick J. *Freudianism and the Literary Mind*. 1945. Reprint, Baton Rouge: Louisiana State University Press, 1967.

Homberger, Eric. *American Writers and Radical Politics, 1900–1939: Equivocal Commitments*. London: Macmillan, 1986.

Humphrey, Robert E. *Children of Fantasy: The First Rebels of Greenwich Village*. New York: John Wiley and Sons, 1978.

Jones, Robert Edmond. *The Dramatic Imagination: Reflections and Speculations on the Art of the Theatre*. New York: Theatre Arts Books, 1941.

Katz, Albert M. "Jacques Copeau: The American Reaction." *Players Magazine* 45 (February 1970): 133–42.

Kaufman, Rhoda H. "The Yiddish Theatre in New York, 1888–1920: A Secular Ritual." *Theatre Studies* 30 (1983–84): 57–61.

Kazacoff, George. *Dangerous Theatre: The Federal Theatre Project as a Forum for New Plays*. New York: Peter Lang, 1989.

Kenton, Edna. "The Militant Women—and Woman." *The Century* 87, no. 1 (November 1918): 13–20.

Key, Ellen. *The Woman Movement*. New York: G. P. Putnam's Sons, 1912.

Kimmel, Michael S., and Thomas E. Mosmiller, eds. *Against the Tide: Pro-Feminist Men in the United States, 1776–1990—A Documentary History*. Boston: Beacon, 1992.

Kinne, Wisner Payne. *George Pierce Baker and the American Theatre*. New York: Greenwood Press, 1968.

Kiper, Florence. "Some American Plays from the Feminist Viewpoint." *Forum* 51 (June 1914): 921–31.

Kramer, Dale. *Chicago Renaissance: The Literary Life in the Midwest, 1900–1930*. New York: Appleton Century, 1966.

Krutch, Joseph Wood. *The American Drama since 1918*. 1939. Reprint, New York: George Brazilier, 1957.

Laing, R. D. *The Divided Self: An Existential Study in Sanity and Madness*. 1859. Reprint, Harmondsworth, Eng.: Penguin, 1976.

Larsen, Lawrence H. "Urban Iowa One Hundred Years Ago." *Annals of Iowa* 49, no. 6 (Fall 1988): 445–61.

Lasch, Christopher. *The New Radicalism in America, 1889–1963: The Intellectual as a Social Type*. New York: Knopf, 1965.

Lock, Charles. "Maurice Browne and the Chicago Little Theatre." *Modern Drama* 31, no. 1 (March 1988): 106–16.

Macgowan, Kenneth. *Footlights across America: Toward a National Theater*. New York: Harcourt Brace, 1929.

———. *The Theatre of Tomorrow*. London: T. Fisher Unwin, 1923.

Macgowan, Kenneth, and Robert Edmond Jones. *Continental Stagecraft*. New York: Harcourt Brace, 1922.

Mackay, Constance d'Arcy. *The Little Theatre in the United States*. New York: Henry Holt, 1917.

Marriner, Gerald L. "A Victorian in the Modern World: The 'Liberated' Male's Adjustment to the New Woman and the New Morality." *South Atlantic Quarterly* 76 (Spring 1977): 190–218.

Mathews, Jane de Hart. *The Federal Theatre, 1935–1939: Plays, Relief, and Politics*. Princeton, N.J.: Princeton University Press, 1967.

Matthews, F. H. "The Americanization of Sigmund Freud: Adaptation of Psychoanalysis before 1917." *Journal of American Studies* 1, no. 1 (April 1967): 39–62.

Mennell, S. J. "Prohibition: A Sociological View." *Journal of American Studies* 3, no. 2 (December 1969): 159–75.

Munsterberg, Hugo. "The Third Degree." *McClure's Magazine* 24 (October 1907): 614–22.

Murphy, Brenda. *American Realism and American Drama, 1880–1940*. Cambridge: Cambridge University Press, 1987.

Narodny, Ivan. *American Artists*. 1930. Reprint, Freeport, N.Y.: Books for Libraries Press, 1969.

O'Connor, John, and Lorraine Brown. *The Federal Theatre Project: "Free, Adult, Uncensored."* London: Eyre Methuen, 1980.

Parry, Alfred. *Garrets and Pretenders: A History of Bohemianism in America*. 1933. Reprint, New York: Dover, 1960.

Paul, Norman H. "Jacques Copeau Looks at the American Stage, 1917–1919." *Educational Theatre Journal* 29 (March 1977): 67–68.

Pinkowicz, Christine A. "The Bramhall Playhouse: New York's Oldest Off-Broadway Theatre." *Theatre History Studies* 13 (1993): 95–113.

Quinn, Arthur Hobson. *American Fiction: An Historical and Critical Survey*. New York: Appleton Century Crofts, 1936.

——. *A History of the American Drama from the Civil War to the Present Day*. New York: Harper and Brothers, 1923.

Repplier, Agnes. "The Repeal of Reticence." *Atlantic Monthly* 113 (March 1914): 297–98.

Robinson, Alice M. *Notable Women in the American Theatre*. Westport, Conn.: Greenwood Press, 1989.

Sayler, Oliver. *Our American Theatre*. New York: Brentano's, 1923.

Schwarz, Judith. *Radical Feminists of the Heterodoxy: Greenwich Village, 1912–1940*. Norwich, Vt.: New Victoria Publishers, 1986.

Shay, Frank. *The Practical Theatre*. New York: Appleton, 1926.

Sievers, W. David. *Freud on Broadway: A History of Psychoanalysis and the American Drama*. New York: Hermitage House, 1955.

Skinner, Richard D. *Our Changing Theatre*. New York: Dial Press, 1931.

Snell, George. *The Shapers of American Fiction*. New York: Dutton, 1947.

Sochen, June. *The New Woman: Feminism in Greenwich Village, 1910–1920*. New York: Quadrangle Books, 1972.

Steffens, Lincoln. *The Shame of the Cities*. New York: McLure, Phillips, 1904.

Stratton, Clarence. *Producing in Little Theatres*. New York: Henry Holt, 1921.

Tookey, John L. *A History of the Pulitzer Prize Plays*. New York: Citadel Press, 1967.

Trimberger, Ellen K. "Feminism, Men, and Modern Love: Greenwich Village, 1900–1925." In *Powers of Desire: The Politics of Sexuality*, edited by Ann Snitow, Christine Stansell, and Sharon Thompson, 131–52. New York: Monthly Review Press, 1983.

Valgemae, Mardi. *Accelerated Grimace: Expressionism in the American Drama of the 1920s*. Carbondale: Southern Illinois University Press, 1972.

Ware, Caroline F. *Greenwich Village, 1920–1930*. 1935. Reprint, New York: Octagon Books, 1977.

Watson, Steven. *Strange Bedfellows: The First American Avant-Garde*. New York: Abbeville Press, 1991.

Zurier, Rebecca. *Art for the Masses: A Radical Magazine and Its Graphics, 1911–1917*. Philadelphia: Temple University Press, 1988.

Index

Browne, Maurice, 64, 80
Bryant, Louise, 89, 96, 112, 127, 134, 295 (n. 56)
Burt, Frederick L., 86, 90, 152

Cambridge Festival Theatre (Cambridge, England), 2, 243
Cannell, Kathleen (Rihani), 104
Cape Cod School of Art, 76
Carb, David, 90, 92
Carbon, 182
Carlin, Terry, 84, 85, 86, 87
Carnegie, Andrew, 19, 129
Carthaios, C., 225
Castellun, Maida (critic), 165
Cedar Rapids Republican, 26
Chicago Evening News, 50, 60, 63
Chicago Little Theatre, 64, 80, 171
Christian Church, 7, 8, 9, 11, 14, 22, 38
Civic Repertory Theatre (New York), 180, 238, 240, 313 (n. 52)
Clark, Barrett, 239–40, 252, 256
Commonweal, The, 242
Comstock Law, 159
Cook, Ellen Dodge (Ma-Mie; Cook's mother), 35, 112, 209; regards Cook as genius, 36; and beauty, 48; in Provincetown, 56–57, 70, 73, 93, 152, 192; as model for Glaspell, 58, 113, 136; death of, 128
Cook, George Cram (Jig): death of, 1, 2, 15, 16, 53, 114, 150, 223, 266; family of, 35; youth of, 36; and mother, 36, 48, 128, 136; nervous instability of, 36, 57, 59, 109, 135, 173, 176, 197, 208, 213; and Monist Society, 37; character of, 37, 117, 136, 152; and socialism, 39, 50; as mystic, 39, 67, 74, 88, 132, 173, 178, 193, 204, 207, 220; and Mollie Price, 39–54 passim; on sex, 40–41, 49, 214; courts Glaspell, 40–50; on *The Glory of the Conquered*, 44–46; on women, 48, 117–19, 135, 141, 144, 173, 175; jealous of Glaspell's success, 48, 181–82, 203; divorces Mollie Price, 54; marries Glaspell, 54; and drinking, 58, 101, 127, 129,

151, 154, 192, 199, 203, 216, 224, 232; mystical experience of, 67, 99; and music and dance, 104; and World War I, 116, 124, 127; on theater, 116, 133, 135; and Ida Rauh, 119, 134, 152, 154; dependence on Glaspell, 128, 197, 208; fear of aging, 136, 152, 167, 214; identification with Nietzsche, 173; eccentric behavior of, 192, 198, 220, 222; decision to go to Greece, 195, 197, 209; as poet, 197, 209; plans for theater in Greece, 208, 222; health of, 212, 213, 214, 221, 222, 223; on death, 214, 223; acquires Greek outfit, 216; burial of, 223; Dr. Marden's diagnosis of illness of, 223, 224, 225, 309 (n. 107)
—and Provincetown Players: as actor, 64, 65, 74, 109, 179; desire to create an American drama, 65, 70, 79–80, 81, 86, 88, 108, 121, 134–36, 229, 232, 266; as founder of Players, 70, 78, 88; and beloved community, 74, 88–89, 97, 99, 101, 109, 126, 132–43, 149, 170, 172, 193, 194; and dream theater, 79, 80, 120, 132, 168, 181, 193, 233; and O'Neill, 89, 137, 191, 194; elected president of Players, 90; as director, 142, 170, 179, 194; and *The Emperor Jones*, 168, 170; and dome, 169–70, 174, 191, 195, 253; and younger Players, 181, 192, 195; and *The Hairy Ape*, 193–94; and putative successor, 194; and failure of Players, 214; plaque dedicated to, 269, 310 (n. 3)
—works, 286 (n. 5)
Athenian Women, The, 116–20, 124, 132, 147, 208, 225
Change Your Style, 77, 92
Chasm, The, 39, 47
Evolution, 39, 286 (n. 16)
Greek Coins, 230
In Hampton Roads, 39
Roderick Taliaferro, 36
Some Modest Remarks on Socialism, 39, 287 (n. 19)

Loy, Mina, 103
Lysistrata, 116–18

McClure's Magazine, 69
MacDougal, Duncan, 108
Macdougal Street, 2, 80, 96, 109, 134,
    149, 154, 162, 169, 200, 227; no.
    139, 93, 95, 120; no. 133, 121, 128,
    131, 194
Macgowan, Kenneth, 170, 171, 172,
    176, 188, 201, 227, 228, 229, 232;
    on use of Provincetown Players
    name, 233
MacNichol, Kenneth, 109
Maeterlinck, Maurice, 64
Ma-Mie. See Cook, Ellen Dodge
Mantle, Burns (critic), 165
Masses, The, 57, 60, 66, 68, 79, 110, 111,
    125, 130, 137, 177, 195
Masters, Edgar Lee, 256, 257
Matson, Anna Walling, 245
Matson, Norman, 1, 4, 15, 56, 159,
    230–57 passim, 263, 266, 267, 277;
    and feminism, 247
Meyer, Josephine A., 64
Middleton, George, 61
Millay, Edna St. Vincent, 104, 105–7,
    108, 137, 187
Millay, Norma, 137
Miller, Arthur, 257
Modern Art School (Provincetown),
    152
Moeller, Philip, 64
Moffet, Langston, 250, 251
Moise, Nina, 109, 110, 142
Monist Society, 33, 37, 38
Morosco Theatre (New York), 158,
    249, 312 (n. 37)
Munsey's, 14, 30
Munsterberg, Hugo, 69

Nathan, George Jean, 69, 172, 193, 303
    (n. 10)
Native Americans, 8, 71, 77, 132, 167,
    172, 173, 177, 251, 256, 303 (n. 10)
Neighborhood Playhouse (New York),
    63, 132
New Republic, 189, 281
New Woman, 72, 75, 119, 140, 240
New York Call, 165
New Yorker, 170

New York Evening Globe, 116, 166
New York Evening Post, 174, 311 (n. 20),
    312 (n. 26)
New York Evening Sun, 206
New York Herald, 100, 142, 147, 165,
    188, 235, 265, 281
New York Morning Telegraph, 138
New York Sun, 120, 243
New York Times, 110, 113, 122, 313
    (n. 53)
New York Times Book Review, 313
    (n. 56)
New York Tribune, 121, 137, 193, 312
    (n. 37)
Nezer, 152, 153, 167, 182
Nietzsche, Friedrich, 4, 38, 39, 47, 57,
    126, 132, 146, 173, 186, 188, 192,
    194, 223, 266, 281
Nordfeldt, Bror, 77, 95, 134
Nordfeldt, Margaret, 90, 99

O'Brien, Joe, 74, 78, 89, 236; death of,
    79
O'Neill, Eugene, 94, 96, 116, 121, 134,
    137, 143, 151, 176, 187; discovered
    by Glaspell, 1, 2, 3, 84–87, 262;
    Cook's influence on, 89, 132–33,
    136, 168, 170, 171, 191, 193, 195,
    196–97; Glaspell's influence on,
    89, 150–51, 171, 186; experimen-
    tation of, 101–2, 145, 149–50; and
    lifesaving station, 114, 152; and
    Boulton, 123, 152, 154–55, 247;
    and Glaspell, 125–27, 147, 155–57,
    177, 179, 180, 188, 228–29, 238,
    256, 257, 278; and Broadway, 126,
    149, 152; on Cook, 126, 167, 170,
    171, 175, 228; and list of sub-
    scribers, 158; and Macgowan,
    172–73, 228; and Triumvirate,
    229, 232; Pulitzer Prizes for Anna
    Christie and Beyond the Horizon,
    238
—works
    Ah, Wilderness!, 102
    All God's Chillun Got Wings, 310
        (n. 8)
    Anna Christie, 238
    Before Breakfast, 101
    Beyond the Horizon, 102, 126, 147,
        152, 155, 158, 168, 171, 238

311 (n. 26), 312 (n. 28); disband-
ing of, 233
—plays performed
Angel Intrudes, The, 105
Aria da Capo, 105, 106, 107, 108
Baby Carriage, The, 133
Bound East for Cardiff, 86–87
Constancy, 73, 74, 75, 88, 98, 100
Contemporaries, 77, 78
Emperor Jones, The. See O'Neill,
Eugene: *Emperor Jones, The*
Enemies, 99, 100
Eternal Quadrangle, The, 73
Freedom, 81, 99, 100
Game, The, 96, 104
Gee-Rusalem, 133, 142
Hairy Ape, The. See O'Neill, Eugene:
Hairy Ape, The
King Arthur's Socks, 96
Lima Beans, 103, 111
Long Time Ago, A, 108
Moon of the Caribbees, The. See
O'Neill, Eugene: *Moon of the*
Caribbees, The
Night, 81, 102, 106
Peace That Passeth Understanding, The,
142
Pie, 32
Princess Marries the Page, The, 106
Rescue, The, 137
Two Slatterns and a King, 104, 105
Two Sons, The, 98, 101, 102
Provincetown Players Inc., 195, 196,
228
Provincetown Playhouse, 175, 228, 232,
233, 303 (n. 20)
Psychoanalysis, 65, 66, 67, 68, 69, 70,
75, 99; and repression, 65, 69, 70,
188; and suppression, 69, 99, 188
Pulitzer Prize, 2, 158, 181, 238, 241,
243, 254, 257, 313 (nn. 53, 54)
Pyne, Mary, 101, 102, 179, 299 (n. 71)

Rapp, William J., 53, 212, 213, 222, 310
(n. 12)
Rauh, Ida, 53, 98, 134, 169, 194, 251;
as actress, 61, 64, 77, 100, 119,
137, 147; as feminist, 75, 158–59;
as defense lawyer, 95, 251; as
Glaspell's rival, 99, 119, 135, 151,
152, 154, 155, 166

Reed, John (Jack), 53, 93, 111, 134,
142, 159; and *The Masses,* 57, 130;
and Mabel Dodge, 60, 71; plays
of, 73, 81, 99, 100, 142; and Provincetown Players, 79, 85, 89, 97,
131; resolutions of, 90, 95, 98, 103
Regent Theatre (London), 2
Reinhardt, Max, 74, 168, 171
Reitman, Benjamin Lewis, 129
Reviews of Glaspell's works, 46,
137, 165–66, 179, 182, 186, 189,
236–37, 242–43, 296 (n. 70), 313
(n. 56); in England, 2, 112, 177,
180, 244, 305 (n. 72)
Ritual, 54, 63, 132, 133, 170–73 passim,
177, 200, 211, 221, 247, 253
Ritz Theatre (New York), 239
Roberts, Ellis (critic), 2
Rohe, Alice, 138
Rostetter, Alice L., 133

Sabbatical of Glaspell and Cook, 105,
151, 156, 166, 172, 173, 181
Sac tribe, 173. *See also* Sauk tribe
Sanger, Margaret, 159
Sarton, May, 232
Sauk tribe, 8, 176. *See also* Sac tribe
Scarmouche, Elias, 197, 215, 220, 221
Schnitzler, Arthur, 73
Sedition Act (1918), 13, 106, 125, 177,
178
Shay, Frank, 95
Sheffield, Justus, 100
Sikelianós, Angelos, 205, 207, 223
Sikelianós, Eva, 205, 207, 208, 210, 225,
309 (n. 110)
Simonson, Lee, 157
Sinclair, Upton, 39, 232, 288 (n. 77),
309 (n. 109)
Sloan, John, 111
Solow, Eugene (critic), 150
Speaker, The, 30
Stage Society (New York), 97, 100, 294
(n. 15)
Stanton, Elizabeth Cady, 21, 138
Steele, Margaret, 75
Steele, Wilbur Daniel, 75, 77, 78, 134
Sterne, Maurice, 71, 75
Stevens, Wallace, 105, 138
Stokes (Glaspell's publisher), 47, 236,
265, 269, 312 (n. 37)

Strindberg, August, 111, 149
Suffrage, 21, 27, 57, 60, 61, 84, 138
Summer School of Painting (Province-town), 76
Swain, Sara (Cook's first wife), 36, 39
Synge, J. M., 86

Taggard, Genevieve, 239, 241, 313
    (n. 58), 314 (n. 66)
Tannenbaum, Frank, 77
Tchakalós, Athanasius, 202, 212, 213,
    216, 220, 221, 223, 308 (n. 65)
Thanet, Octave. *See* French, Alice
Theatre Arts, 171, 189
Theatre Guild, 157, 238, 240, 272
Théâtre Libre (Paris), 89
Thorndike, Sybil, 2, 184, 190; on *The
    Verge*, 184
Throckmorton, Cleon, 162, 174, 188,
    195, 201, 202, 249, 305 (n. 66)
Times, The (London), 180, 245, 305,
    (n. 72)
Times Literary Supplement, 311 (n. 20)
To-Puppy, 212, 222, 223
Triumvirate, 229, 232
Tucker, 249, 250, 270
Tuesday Club (Davenport, Iowa), 22,
    37, 46, 112
Tyler, George C., 155, 156, 160

University of Chicago, 29

Vechten, Carl Van, 71
Victorian attitudes, 5, 18, 40, 72, 140,
    142, 146, 198, 242
Vorse, Mary Heaton, 53, 77, 87, 88, 98,
    123, 134, 172, 230; and Glaspell,
    60, 234, 241, 247, 249; and
    O'Brien, 74, 79; and wharf fish-
    house, 75–76, 80

Walling, Anna Strunsky, 53, 159, 245,
    246, 247
Walling, William English, 53
Washington Square Players, 65, 100,

103, 110, 121, 131, 149, 158, 238;
    and Glaspell, 2, 96, 149, 238; and
    Provincetown Players, 4, 85, 121,
    158; manifesto of, 64; founding
    of, 64–65; reject *Suppressed Desires*,
    67, 70
Webster, Ambrose, 76
Weekly Outlook (Davenport, Iowa), 20,
    22, 26
Weinberger, Harry, 130, 175, 195
Wellman, Rita, 108
Westley, Helen, 61, 64
Westminster Weekly (London), 244
Weyrich, Joseph Lewis, 95
Wharf Theatre, 2, 75, 76, 77, 78, 80, 81,
    84, 87, 89, 90, 92, 100, 270
White, Francelina, 274, 276, 277
Whitman, Walt, 40, 111, 132, 270, 273,
    286 (n. 5)
Williams, John D., 155, 157, 158
Williams, William Carlos, 51, 103, 126,
    155, 157, 158, 188
Wilson, Edmund, 105, 244, 249, 251,
    270, 272; on Glaspell, 250, 265
Wilson, Woodrow, 108, 138
Works Progress Administration, 252,
    254, 258, 260, 261, 263
World War I, 12, 13, 19, 56, 57, 65, 74,
    75, 108, 116, 122, 124, 125, 128,
    138, 206
World War II, 252, 266, 269, 272
Wycherley, Margaret, 189

Xylocastro, Greece, 210, 211

Yeats, W. B., 132, 207
Young, Stark, 189, 228
Young Men's Christian Association,
    206, 213
Youth's Companion, 14, 15, 30, 285
    (n. 86)

Zits Weekly Magazine, 179
Zorach, Marguerite and William, 95,
    104, 105, 134

Parts of this book were published previously in slightly different form in the following works, which are used by permission:

"Discovering and Reading the American Woman," *Revista Alicantina de Estudios Ingleses* 2 (1989).

"The First Lady of American Drama: Susan Glaspell," *Barcelona English Language and Literature Studies* 1 (1989).

"Love-Ordained Woman's Sphere: Susan Glaspell and the Relations of Men and Women," in *Estudios de Filologia Inglesa, Anejos de Analecta Malacitana*, volume 6, edited by Blanca Krauel (Málaga, Spain: Servicio de Publicaciones de la Universidad de Málaga, 1989).

"Rebellion and Rejection: The Plays of Susan Glaspell," in *Modern American Drama: The Female Canon*, edited by June Schlueter (London: Associated University Presses, 1990).

"A Struggle Shared: Susan Glaspell and Eugene O'Neill," in *Studies in American Literature: An Homage to Enrique Garcia Diez*, edited by Antonia Sánchez Macarro (Valencia, Spain: Universitat de Valencia, Facultat de Filologia, 1991).

"Suppressed Desires: Freud and American Misunderstanding," in *XIV Congreso de AEDEAN*, edited by Federico Equiluz, José María Santamaría, Inés Uribe-Echeverría, and Raquel Merino (Bilbao, Spain: Servicio Editorial de la Universidad del País, 1992).

Introduction to *The Provincetown Players: A Choice of the Shorter Works* (Sheffield, England: Sheffield Academic Press, 1994).

"Love and Envy in Provincetown: Susan Glaspell, George Cram Cook, and Eugene O'Neill," in *Amor, Odio y Violencia en la Literatura Norteamericana*, edited by José Antonio Gurpegui (Alcalá de Henares, Madrid: Servicio de Publicaciones de la Universidad de Alcalá de Henares, 1994).

"Suppression and Society in Susan Glaspell's Theater," in *Susan Glaspell: Essays on Her Theater and Fiction*, edited by Linda Ben-Zvi (Ann Arbor: University of Michigan Press, 1995). © 1995 The University of Michigan Press.

"Susan Glaspell," in *American Drama*, edited by Clive Bloom (London: Macmillan, 1995).

"American Lovers of Greece: George Cram Cook and Susan Glaspell," in *Nationalism and Sexuality: Crises of Identity*, edited by Yiorgos Kalogeras and Domna Pastourmatzi (Thessaloníki, Greece: Aristotle University, 1996).